The Skilled Consultant

A Systematic Approach to the Theory and Practice of Consultation

Richard D. Parsons
West Chester University

Allyn & Bacon
Boston • London • Toronto • Sydney • Tokyo • Singapore

98.00

To Karen, Kristian, Drew and Jon . . .
the loves, joys and meaning in my life.

Series Editor: Ray Short
Editorial Assistant: Christine M. Shaw
Marketing Manager: Kathy Hunter
Editorial-Production Administrator: Joe Sweeney
Editorial-Production Service: Walsh Associates
Composition Buyer: Linda Cox
Manufacturing Buyer: Aloka Rathnam
Cover Administrator: Suzanne Harbison

Copyright © 1996 by Allyn & Bacon
A Simon & Schuster Company
Needham Heights, MA 02194

Library of Congress Cataloging-in Publication Data

Parsons, Richard D.
    The skilled consultant : a systematic approach to the theory and
practice of consultation / Richard D. Parsons.
        p.   cm.
    Includes bibliographical references and index.
    ISBN 0-205-16119-7
    1. Mental health consultation.   I. Title.
RA790.95.P37   1995
362.2'0425—dc20   95-20870
                                                    CIP

Printed in the United States of America

10 9 8 7 6 5 4 3 2   00

WITHDRAWN

Contents

Preface

While certainly atypical of a book's preface, it may be useful to begin this text with a **reader's warning:**

The Skilled Consultant is NOT a traditional text on consultation that might open with "... too much is demanded of too few..." and then proceed to allow the reader to passively review empirical data or theoretical positions extolling the virtues and value of mental health consultation. This text is not a traditional text. It is an invitation—no, not just an invitation—rather it is a challenge to the reader to become an active participant in a *revolution.* The text will question many of the reader's professional assumptions and challenge the reader to embrace a new paradigm of professional service. Such a shift of paradigm is neither easy nor painless!

Consultation as presented within this text and in previous works (e.g., Meyers, Parsons, & Martin, 1979; Parsons & Meyers, 1984; Parsons & Wicks, 1994) is not viewed as simply an add-on task for mental health workers, or an additional tool in their arsenal of helping strategies. Consultation as discussed within the chapters to follow is truly a revolutionary model or paradigm for service delivery.

As with any new model or paradigm, consultation will require a shift in the practitioner's fundamental view of his or her role and function, the roles of those with whom he or she works, the focus of his or her diagnostic and intervention efforts, and the nature and definition of successful outcomes.

Changing Needs Need Changing Approaches

Cliche or not, the harsh reality is that too much is needed from too few. There is abundant evidence, both anecdotal and empirical, that suggests our society is in crisis. Statistics on divorce rates, poverty, sexism, racism, violence within and outside of our families and institutions, drug and alcohol abuse, sexual abuse, joblessness, and homelessness all give evidence of a people under stress and a society in crisis. However, even with this increasing need for supportive services, the current fiscal crisis in mental health services and the reduction in financial support for mental health programming has drastically reduced the availability of and access to *direct* mental health services for many of those individuals most in need of such services.

In addition to the increased number of individuals seeking mental health services, the nature and complexity of the problems they bring to the counselor's office has drastically changed to the point where they often stretch the competency and professional adequacy of any one service provider. It is less likely that it is sufficient for a mental health provider to simply provide support to an individual with grief or bereavement issues. It is more likely that the grief expressed is compounded and exacerbated by many other crises in the person's life (e.g., lack of insurance, history of alcoholism, or current experience of elder abuse). Counselors in our schools have also experienced the increasing complexity and multiplication of problems. For example, it is all too easy to find a school child who is not only failing fifth grade, but is also the primary caretaker of his four siblings in an abusive house where a mother shoots up cocaine and her transient boyfriend physically and sexually abuses the children in the house.

It is too much (both in number and complexity) for anyone to adequately handle, so we are becoming increasingly aware of the necessity of working together. Mental health professionals are being called to share expertise and resources with one another and to employ approaches and techniques that share the responsibility for problem solving and may even provide opportunities for prevention along with intervention. Mental health consultation is just this type of an approach.

Consultation—Both a Technique and a Frame of Reference

The idea of coordinating services and sharing expertise and consulting is far from a new or novel idea (see Chapter 1). Clinicians working in industries and hospitals have long valued and employed consultation as a mode of service delivery. However, it is also a mode of professional functioning that is increasingly being valued and employed by mental health counselors, especially those serving school, college, and community populations (Scott, 1990; Wilgus & Shelley, 1988). Consultation, with its emphasis on indirect services, operates as a vehicle within which any number of target problems can be addressed (Bundy & Poppen, 1986; Dustin & Ehly, 1992). Results of research on consultation in school settings, for example, have been generally encouraging (Polsgrove & McNeil, 1989). Efficacy reviews of outcome research (e.g., Mannino & Shore, 1975; Medway, 1982; West & Idol,1987) and meta-analyses of consultation studies (Medway & Updyke, 1985; Sibley, 1986) have revealed positive effects of consultation on attitudes and behaviors of consultants, consultees, and clients.

Consultation as a mode of service delivery is a vehicle that will not only allow the consultant to efficiently and effectively intervene in problem situations (see Bundy & Poppen, 1986), but do so in a way that impacts the milieu, or matrix, in which the problem is presented and thus increase the counselor's effectiveness by adding a preventive element to that service. Applied researchers (e.g., Graden, Casey, & Bonstrom, 1985; Ritter, 1978) have suggested that a well designed consultation program may significantly reduce the number of subsequent referrals and the long-term need for consultative services (Phillips & McCullough, 1990).

While both the interest in and utilization of consultation has clearly increased, it appears that what is often presented and practiced may be best described as "consultation-as-technique," rather than "consultation-as-paradigm." For example, the counselor working with a runaway child may consult with school personnel as part of his or her direct service intervention plan, attempting to identify curriculum options with which he or she and the client could work. Or perhaps the mental health counselor working with a depressed individual may consult with the human resource person at the client's place of employment in order to better understand the client's job stressors. While each of these interactions provides useful information and may loosely be defined as consultation, each fails to tap the rich value of consultation as an *indirect mode of service delivery.*

In order to reap the full benefits of a consultation mode of service delivery, the practitioner will be required to make a paradigm shift. The revolution of consultation is that it invites those in the mental health arena to reconfigure frames of reference, professional orientations, and approaches to service delivery. This does not require us to abandon our models of direct service, but rather to employ consultation as the umbrella beneath which to modify and deliver numerous forms of intervention and prevention services, including some of those that had previously been defined exclusively as direct service.

Special Orientation, Special Skills

Clearly, being a consultant demands much more than simply giving advice or conversing with another. Because of its uniqueness as a paradigm of service conceptualization and delivery, it will require a modification of our professional attitudes and orientation and the development of additional professional skills.

A review of the research would suggest that various counselor training programs, as well as the professional associations, are recognizing the importance of consultation as a mode of service delivery and are requiring that increased levels of formal training occur. For example, as of the early 1980s only 33 percent of counselors reported having a full developed consultation course (Splete & Bernstein, 1981), whereas by 1988, Curtis and Zins (1988) found that 41 percent of the counselor training programs had fully developed consultation courses. The trend for including consultation courses within the curriculum continues to be supported by professional organizations (e.g., ASCA, 1990) and clinicians in the field. Yet the depth of the training still appears less than sufficient (Brown, Spano, & Schulte, 1988; Campbell, 1992).

The primary purpose of this text is to provide a practical means for assisting counselors, both within training programs and those in professional work, to address this limitation of training and to begin to make the paradigm shift and develop the professional skills necessary for effective consultation.

Not Just Another Text

This is really neither a "how-to" book nor an esoteric exercise in model building or theory explication. Since consultation is a complex mode of service delivery that must be founded on a sound base of knowledge and the application of specific attitudes and skills, it calls for a text which blends theory and practice.

While understanding the theoretical underpinnings of a particular skill or approach is of value, the theory must be integrated with the reality of one's professional experience if it is to truly be assimilated and employed. Thus, this text will integrate the "hands-on" of case illustration and practice exercise, with the "heads-on" of theory and research review.

The current text is unique in that it

1. Presents an integrated model of collaborative consultation, which provides an umbrella for direct and indirect service to the client, direct service to the consultee, and direct service to the system.
2. Articulates a step-by-step decision tree that will assist the consultant in knowing how and when to employ specific consultation approaches.
3. Employs a skills training approach (with case illustrations and guided training exercises) to the development of the essential knowledge and skills required of an effective consultant. This approach emphasizes theory and research in service of specific attitudinal and behavioral competencies essential for effective consultation.

Each chapter will follow the same general format. The focus of each chapter will be on teaching through case illustration. Further, in the spirit of having theory and technique *come alive* and be readily understood and translatable to the reader's own experience, each chapter will

- Provide the theoretical/didactic presentation of the topic being illustrated—including extensive reviews of current research.
- Provide a case presentation to highlight the point(s) discussed.
- Provide skill-focused exercises to be used as application exercises by the reader.

An Overview

In the first chapter, the reader is given a view of the history of mental health consultation. This chapter will help the reader place consultation within the larger context of mental health service and see consultation as not simply an add-on technique but rather as a revolutionary frame of reference for counselor service delivery. The next chapter (Chapter 2) describes the various roles (provisional, prescriptive, mediational, collaborative), major theories (behavioral, organizational development, mental health), different skills (expert, process), and foci (crisis, developmental) that have been used to differentiate the various types of consultation. Further, Chapter 2 provides a *multidimensional model* for conceptualizing and employing all these varied approaches in an *integrated,* theoretically sound, and empirically supported model.

The next two chapters (Chapters 3 and 4) will emphasize the need for consultants to serve as agents of change. In addition to providing a model for directing the consultant's efforts in order to maximize his or her impact, the chapters will also discuss ways to reduce the individual and systems-based resistance experienced by consultants in their efforts to promote change. Chapter 5 and 6 look at the unique relationship and communication skills required for effective consulting and Chapters 7, 8, and 9 begin to address the specific diagnostic and intervention skills needed for successful consultation.

Chapter 10 approaches the unique ethical and professional concerns confronting the consultant. While the importance of being sensitive to the consultee's personal and organizational culture has been emphasized throughout the chapters, special attention will be given to the ethical issues involved with working with culturally diverse populations. The final chapter will provide the reader with a flow chart that can be used to navigate through the process of consultation from the point of entry through the final evaluation. This chapter also provides an extended case illustration and case exercise that will help to bring the previous information and skills together in one final capping experience.

While the text is intended to meet the needs (both conceptual and skill-based) of those employing consultation, it is only a start. Ongoing training and supervision are essential if one wishes to be an effective, ethical consultant. It this author's hope that the current text will serve as foundation for such ongoing professional development.

Acknowledgments

While many researchers and theorists provided the foundation for the material presented, the real substance of the text comes from case illustrations and examples. For these experiences I must thank the many forward-looking consultees who have invited me to share in their growth. Also, with much appreciation I recognize the many hours of library research and xeroxing performed by my junior researcher, Drew Parsons, and graduate assistant, Helen Buchanan. Further to all those sometimes anxious, always challenging, and ever giving graduate students who have endured this author's ramblings for more years than I care to remember and have provided me with much insight and growth, I say thank you.

Finally, while it may appear almost obligatory when writing a book to thank previous professors for their insight and guidance, thanking Joel Meyers as a mentor, a colleague, and a friend is a privilege not an obligation. Without Joel's introduction to Gerald Caplan, small-N research, and the subtleties of individual and institutional resistance, I could not have written this text.

Chapter *1*

The (R)evolution of Consultation

The mental health profession is in the midst of significant change. The number and variety of professionals (e.g., counselor, psychologist, psychiatrist, drug/alcohol preventionist, social worker, pastoral counselor, crisis interventionist, etc.) providing mental health service are rapidly expanding. New approaches and new techniques are employed by a wide variety of mental health providers, in many diverse settings. But perhaps the most significant change that is occurring is that providers have begun to embrace a new perspective, a new paradigm, or frame of reference from which to utilize the specific techniques and tools of their practices. It is this new perspective, consultation, that is the focus of this text, and its definition and evolution are the focus of this chapter.

This chapter will provide a brief overview of the origin and historical context of this evolution and detail the significant implications for the role and practice of the counselor in the field. Specifically, you will learn

- To define consultation as a mode of service delivery
- To view consultation as a significant shift in paradigm, and not simply an added technique used to complement direct service

The Evolutionary Context of Consultation

Why Look Back?

To be honest, reflecting on history has never been a point of interest or value to me. Many texts provide a historical overview to the development of a theory or concept as a foundation for the research and findings to be discussed. While I understand and appreciate the intellectual integrity of such an approach, I have always been too concrete in my thinking and too action-driven in my learning style to truly savor the value of such a chapter. Given my own limitations and style, you might wonder why I would author a "skills" based text that would open with a chapter on the history and evolution of consultation.

Consultation is presented within this text as a *revolutionary* movement in mental health delivery. While consultative techniques have been used as adjunctive to direct service, the real import and value of consultation becomes evident when it is employed as a frame of reference from which to meaningfully interpret the reality of mental health problems and services. Employing a consultation frame of reference from which to define one's helping role and function is revolutionary and reflects a significant paradigmatic shift in mental health services.

The revolutionary nature of consultation as a paradigm for service delivery becomes apparent when viewed within the context of the evolution of the field of mental health services. However, prior to briefly reviewing the three major movements in mental health services that served as predecessors to consultation, it may be useful for you to reflect on your own model or approach to mental health services. Exercise 1-1 will assist you in this process.

First, a brief note about the learning exercises found within this text. Throughout the text you will be invited to participate in a variety of learning exercises. The purposes of these exercises are twofold. First, they will help to clarify the points under discussion. Second, and perhaps more important, they will help you to personalize the material presented and assist you in assimilating the material into your own consulting. To facilitate this personalization process, you may find it helpful to keep a personal journal to identify your insights, reactions, and general experience as you perform the exercises. Further, you may find it useful to review your journal from previous exercises to see if, with additional information presented, you gain further personal insight into your role and style as a consultant.

Another point for consideration is that the exercises have been found to be more effective if done with a colleague, mentor, or supervisor, or in a small group. The dialogue and sharing of common and diverse perspectives has been found to be quite growth producing by those who have used these exercises in just such a fashion. Regardless of the approach you employ, the benefit accrued is to a large extent a result of the energy placed into the process.

The First Shift in Paradigm: Humanizing the Mentally Ill

If you shared your responses to Exercise 1-1 with several colleagues or classmates, you most likely experienced both a degree of uniqueness and variation in the ways the problem was approached, as well as much in common. As members of the field of mental health service providers we share many common biases. Some of these shared biases are obvious, others more subtle.

In reviewing the responses to Exercise 1-1, it would most likely be safe to assume that no one suggested that Felicia should undergo exorcism, hypothesizing that her "symptoms" were a direct result of demonic possession. What might appear to be a somewhat offbeat, if not ludicrous, perspective to a mental health service provider in the twentieth century, the use of exorcism was not such an alien approach to "health care" providers in the early 1700s. Seeing emotional disturbance as evidence of supernatural possession (i.e., demonology) was the rule of the day, prior to the first revolution in the mental health movement.

EXERCISE 1-1   The Case of Felicia

Directions: Review the following brief case information. After reviewing the brief description of the client and client problem, answer the questions provided for your consideration. You will be invited to reconsider your responses at a later point in this chapter.

Referral

Felicia, age 15, came to your office. Felicia was referred by her English teacher. The note Felicia presented read: "There appears to be something VERY SERIOUSLY wrong with Felicia. Since the beginning of this new marking period, she has been TOTALLY nonattentive and nonresponsive in class." The teacher continued, "I have taught British literature for now over twenty-six years and I know when a student is heading for trouble. Trust me. This young lady is on the road to ruin! I hope you can help her!"

Felicia appeared tearful, physically agitated (unable to sit still, pacing back and forth) and disheveled in her appearance (clothes and hair unkempt). Felicia explained that for the last two days she has been sleeping in a car. She has not returned home since Saturday (two days ago) and will "never go back until her mother gets rid of the creep she is living with" (referring to her mother's boyfriend). Felicia complained that "everything is going wrong," " (her) grades stink," "(her) boyfriend is angry with (her)," and "now this creep (her mother's boyfriend) is butting in!" Felicia stated that she was very embarrassed because of the way she looked and she even thought of trying to call somebody at school to find out about coming in early to use the showers, but she just did not know who to talk to.

Professional Reflections

1. In a sentence or two, describe your initial impressions regarding the nature of this problem. _____
   _____
   _____

2. What type of additional information would you like to know? _____
   _____
   _____

3. Even with the limited information provided, what do you think needs to be done? ___
   _____
   _____

4. What would be the next two things you would want to achieve in upcoming sessions?
   _____
   _____
   _____

Analysis

After responding to the above questions, share your responses with a colleague, a fellow student, or a mentor. How did your responses differ? How were they the same? Keep your responses available for further reflection and analysis.

The first revolution in mental health services moved us from such a dehumanized view of the mentally ill to a "natural scientific" paradigm for viewing and treating such difficulties. Dr. Philippe Pinel (1745–1826) freed the enslaved inmates of La Bicetre where inmates were tortured and persecuted as "agents of Satan" (Deutsch, 1946). Dr. Pinel's action not only freed the inmates, but freed those interested in working with the mentally ill, who could now employ the same scientific approach to the diagnosis and treatment of this class of "illness" as was then practiced with other conditions of illness. Shifting perspective from one of supernatural demonic possession to one of natural illness, from needing chains to needing hospitals, dramatically shifted the paradigm or frame of reference from which mental health problems were defined and services provided.

This shift in paradigm that is now taken for granted remains evidenced in our language of *mental illness, mental hospital, patient,* and *syndrome.* The natural scientific approach to conditions of dysfunctionality is encouraged through academic training and professional modeling with such pervasiveness that most of us have a difficult time attempting to see it from another (e.g., demonic) frame of reference.

Our own responses to the case of Felicia most likely reflected the revolutionary work of Philippe Pinel. We too most likely approached the case with a mindset or orientation that immediately assumed the problem fell within the realm of the natural, the understandable, and the treatable. However, unlike many of our historic colleagues and contemporaries of Dr. Pinel, we may not have restricted our hypothesizing to only the somatic, or biological, base for Felicia's action, but expanded our hypothesizing to include the psychic realm. Our inclusion of problems of psychogenic origin reflects the impact of the second revolution in mental health services—a revolution most poignantly characterized by the work of Sigmund Freud.

The Second Shift in Paradigm: The Realm of the Psyche

While Pinel's efforts humanized our approach to the mentally ill, the work of Sigmund Freud (1856–1939) expanded our perspective, our frame of reference, to include not only the biological, organic base of mental illness but also the psychological.

Freud's extensive work on the nature and working of the human psyche had an enormous impact on the way human behavior was viewed and emotional problems addressed. Those in the "human services" began to emphasize the symbolic value of client's symptoms, the role of intrapsychic conflict, and the importance of early childhood experiences in their diagnoses and treatment of those with emotional difficulties. Further, the clinical approach that continued to develop after Freud's initial work promoted the idea and therapeutic value of one-to-one, intense, direct service.

The cumulative impact of the early work in this clinical, intrapsychic conflict model of mental health services is most likely evidenced in our own ways of conceptualizing and approaching emotional and/or behavioral problems. Exercise 1-2 will ask you to consider your response to the case of Felicia in light of the influence of this second revolution.

In reflecting upon and discussing your responses to the questions in Exercise 1-2, you may discover the subtle or not so subtle influence this second revolution may have had on your own orientation to mental health and mental health services. For example, your responses may have clearly reflected the influence of those models or theories promoting a clinical, intrapsychic approach. Perhaps you questioned the psychosexual issues being

---

EXERCISE 1-2   A Second Look at Felicia

Directions: Review your initial responses to the questions found in Exercise 1-1. With a colleague, mentor, or peer reconsider your responses in the light of the direct or subtle influence the second revolution may have had on your conceptualization and approach to providing human services. Specifically consider each of the following.

1. Do you feel that there was "more" to the story than simply Felicia's anger at her mother's boyfriend? What perhaps? _____

2. Do you feel the need to know more about her relationship with her mother? Her biological father?_____

3. Do you want to know more about her past and her experiences in her family?_____

4. Felicia is exhibiting a number of behaviors, such as being furious with her mother's boyfriend, coming to school disheveled, and her recent problem with her own boyfriend. Do you find these suggestive or symbolic of some deeper, underlying problem?_____

5. Was most of your focus and "hypothesizing" targeted to Felicia and what may be going on *within* her? _____

---

manifested in Felicia's acting out, or the possibility that the intense disdain for her mother's boyfriend may be a reflection of reaction formation, or that her attitude toward her teacher may be displaced anger belonging to her mother. You may have even questioned the intrapsychic impact of being abandoned by her biological father, her boyfriend, and now her mother.

Whether you adhere to a psychoanalytic model of helping or some other classical school of counseling, your perspective—your orientation—probably reflects the subtle influence of the clinical model of Freud's early investigations. As a clinical model of providing human services, this second revolution invites us to not only value the one-to-one relationship between the client and the helpgiver as the essential medium of therapeutic change, but also subscribes to the position that it is the client or patient who was "abnormal," thus needing to adjust to what was also assumed to be a "normal" environment.

Perhaps many of us perceived Felicia's problem as having a point of origin within her own psychic or emotional structure. Thus, we may have begun to conceptualize our interventions from a one-to-one, direct service frame of reference. If so, the influence of this second shift in paradigm is present.

The Third Shift in Paradigm: A Comprehensive Community Model

The clinical model, or client-targeted approach to helping, that was promoted by the second shift in paradigm often operated as if unaware of the role played by significant others or conditions in the client's life. While emphasizing the historical role of significant people, the clinical perspective oftentimes failed to appreciate the role and value of our environment and the interrelated and interdependent relationships we have with one another and with our environment.

Criticism of this orientation proliferated (e.g., Albee, 1967; Aubrey, 1969; Eckerson, 1971, Palmo & Kuznian, 1972). The third (r)evolution in the development of mental health services emerged in response to some of that criticism, with emphasis on the value of psychoecology.

Much of the initial criticism surrounding the clinical model focused on the questionable efficacy of traditional evocative psychotherapy in both terms of the length of time required and the limitations to successful outcomes it produced (e.g., Eysenck, 1952; Levitt, 1963). But beyond the questions of treatment efficiency and effectiveness, basic research and clinical practice of the late 1950s and early 1960s began to question the very cause and effect aspect of this intrapsychic conflict model.

For example, some of the early research provided conceptual models based on learning theory for understanding the cause and treatment of emotional problems (Krasner & Ullman, 1965; Wolpe, 1958). With this shift in emphasis to learning theory came a shift in focus and emphasis to environmental factors that may lend to both the creation and amelioration of psycho-social-emotional problems. And even more than simply shifting the focus of cause and treatment to extrapersonal variables, this new movement challenged the very nature of the crisis-oriented remediative and therapeutic approach that typified most mental health service.

No longer were our approaches to the treatment of emotional and behavioral problems restricted to the medical or the clinical and to those uniquely trained (e.g., psychiatrists, analysts, etc.). Therapy and therapeutic intervention would now be found in many educational and social activities and programs. Further, many individuals previously viewed as outside the boundaries of mental health services were now included as rich, potential resources for providing therapeutic input (e.g., ministers, counselors, social workers, teachers, parents).

Thus, this comprehensive community model served as the third (r)evolution in mental health services by shifting our frame of reference to include:

1. Emphasis on the environmental stresses that cause mental health problems;
2. A community rather than clinical orientation;
3. A readiness to experiment with innovative, short-term remedial strategies;
4. Uses of new resources (e.g., paraprofessionals); and perhaps most significantly,
5. A shift to prevention rather than intervention (therapy).

(Bloom, 1973)

Again, the subtle or not-so-subtle influence of this paradigmatic shift may be evident in your own approach to mental health services. Consider Exercise 1-3, where further questioning reflects the impact of this third revolution in mental health services.

The Fourth Shift in Paradigm: Consultation—Moving from Technique to Paradigm

The philosophical foundation established by the comprehensive community mental health movement oriented healthcare providers to offer services that would impact all members of the community (i.e., preventive educational and social programs). Further, the community health movement encouraged mental health providers to focus on indirect service delivery (e.g., educational services, environmental interventions, etc.). As such the comprehensive community mental health movement also provided a rich base for nurturing the practice of consultation.

Consultation Roots

While the value of consultation within the comprehensive community mental health movement is obvious, the history of the practice of consultation extends beyond that movement,

---

EXERCISE 1-3   A Broader Based View of Felicia

Directions: Again, review and discuss your initial responses to the case of Felicia (Exercise 1-1) in light of the following.

1. In addition to focusing on Felicia, did we or our colleagues shift focus to the family system and its impact and Felicia?_____

_____

_____

2. Did anyone initially consider the existence of community services available to support Felicia (and others in her state of homelessness)? Did we question community awareness or ease of access to such facilities, should they exist? _____

_____

_____

3. Did we begin to identify other professionals and nonprofessionals with whom we could team in service of Felicia? (e.g., community social worker, job corps, home visitor, tutor, teen shelter, etc.) _____

_____

_____

4. As we considered our plans to intervene and to help Felicia, were we also considering additional preventive steps that we could begin to implement?_____

_____

_____

and could most likely be traced to the earliest forms of helping existing in primitive societies. A more systematic look at the history of consultation would reveal that it had been a common medical practice involving the comparing of diagnosis and treatment plans as early as the thirteenth century (Kutzik, 1977). But perhaps the real impetus for the current emphasis on consultation as a mode of human service delivery has as its roots the development of organizational development theory and practice (Bennis, 1969; Lippitt, Watson, & Westley, 1958; Schein, 1969; Schmuck & Miles, 1971) and the early writing and practice of mental health consultation by Gerald Caplan (1951, 1955, 1964, 1970).

Roots in Organizational Theory: The introduction of "expert as consultant" within industry is evident in the time and motion research of the early 1900s (Taylor, 1911). These early forays into consulting depicted the consultant's role as one of external expert. From such an expert model, the consultation relationship was defined as hierarchical, with the consultant empowered to impart expertise on the consultee and the consultee's organization (Pryzwansky, 1974).

Such an expert model appeared to work well, especially in those situations in which the focus was on technical efficiency. And while initially focusing efforts on increasing technical efficiency by designing more efficient tools and structuring workplaces for increased productivity, these "consultants" soon turned their attention to the human side of enterprise.

The importance of the worker's social and psychological needs, as precursors to effective and efficient performance, took center stage with the research on worker motivation (McGregor, 1960; Roethlisberger & Dickson, 1939), leadership style (White & Lippitt, 1960), and the role of social dynamics (Homans, 1950; Lewin, 1951; Miller & Rice, 1967) and social setting (Argyris, 1970; Bennis, 1969; Moos, 1973). These new approaches and the bodies of knowledge provided uncovered a new arena for consultants—the social and psychological processes of organization (Gallessich, 1982).

Roots in Mental Health Service: In contrast, to the expert prescriptive model most often found in business, the consultation model that seemed to surface in mental health services was characterized as both expert and collegial in nature (Caplan, 1964).

In the collegial relationship, peers who share some basic body of knowledge joined in exchanging specific ideas and experiences to solve problems encountered in areas of mutual understanding and interest. Collegial consultation apparently developed out of the need to pool and effectively multiply professional expertise in application to particularly difficult, unusual, and intractable problems. It could be suggested that the early work and writing of Gerald Caplan served as a primary impetus to the current interest in mental health consultation and consultation with a collegial, collaborative focus.

Caplan's early experiences were as a direct service provider in Israel in the late 1940s. The overwhelming number of referrals, when matched to the very small number of personnel available to provide service, made the typical diagnostic-prescription-remediation paradigm of the clinical, direct service model simply unfeasible. Caplan began to experiment with a shift in focus to a more indirect, preventive approach. Rather than working directly with the new immigrant children, Caplan would work with the various caretakers of the children to see if the problems could be addressed through them.

From these early experiences, Caplan continued to research and write about the theory and practice of mental health consultation (Caplan, 1964, 1970). A keystone to both his writing and his practice was his depiction of consultation as a nonhierarchical, or coordinate, relationship (Caplan, 1970). Thus, while allowing for differential expertise, the model assumed equal importance of contribution and thus reduced the power differential between the consultant and the consultee. Not only did this perspective help to reduce the oftentimes experienced resistance on the part of the consultee to being "told what to do" but it also began to expand the types of "experts" who now felt comfortable serving as consultants and/ or seeking consultation assistance.

In addition to emphasizing the collaborative or coordinate form of consultation, Caplan's writings began to expand the targets for mental health consultation in order to promote prevention as well as intervention. In addition to supporting consultation that targeted the client, Caplan also suggested that consultation could focus on specific programs, the consultee, or the entire system. This conceptualization will be discussed in greater detail in Chapter 2.

Roots in Contemporary Practice: A consistent press that continues to move the helping professions toward the utilization of consultation is the ever-increasing specialization and professionalization of those in human services. The information era has completely precluded the possibility of any one service provider being a true master of all that is known about human service or all that can be done for a client.

Consider the various dimensions and possibilities involved in working with a young "accident prone" machinist. Perhaps, our own training in a direct service, clinical paradigm forms our conceptualization of the problem around questions of client motivation (e.g., desire for self-destruction?) or secondary gain (e.g., the benefits of workers compensation, sympathy, and time off from work?). While such questions and conceptualization can be useful, it also can be limiting and professionally myopic. Moving from the client-centered type of questions most often asked by mental health practitioners, one may begin to question the possible influence of the physical environment (e.g., design and distractions within the workplace), the social environment (e.g., sociometries), physiology and neurology (e.g., the possibility of an attention deficit disorder or allergies), and even organizational analyses (e.g., management style, selection procedures, training, etc.) as being pertinent to the understanding of the current problem. Clearly it is hard for any one individual to be completely versed within his or her own discipline, much less versed across disciplines, even though such cross-disciplined information may prove essential. Therefore, the increased specialization of knowledge and the increased compartmentalization of both knowledge and service require that "consulting," "teaming," or "coordinating" among specialists becomes the operative mode of service delivery.

From Specialty or Strategy to Paradigm
What is obvious in the very brief history of consultation is that often consultation is or was practiced as a specialty within a broader field of mental health services. Further, quite often consultation was offered as a technique, a strategy, to be employed in direct service diagnosis, remediation, or as a replacement to such direct service.

However, consultation is much more than a technique or subspecialty. Consultation, as presented within this text, is a shift in perspective. Consultation marks a new frame of reference, a new paradigm from which to conceptualize mental health issues and services. Embracing consultation as a new paradigm, as a fourth major movement in mental health services, is far from easy. As was the case for all those who previously made transitions from one paradigm (e.g., demonological or clinical) to the next (e.g., naturalistic or community), shifting perspective and frame of reference is difficult because it often appears that one need surrender previous useful and comfortable beliefs. This need not be the case.

Resistance: As with any shift of paradigm, the challenge is to embrace the new orientation so that it can incorporate all that preceded. If an evolutionary or developmental view is taken, one can see that each new paradigm is not only stimulated by the limitations of the one that preceded it, but also reflects the wisdom of all previous paradigms. Thus, the task is not to surrender our old models and orientations, but rather to allow the new paradigm to act as a more efficient and encompassing structure from within which to perform new (and old) services.

However, often when a new orientation is developed, it is not initially seen as enveloping, but rather excluding. As such, new perspectives, new paradigms, are not readily embraced but rather coexist with the older approaches. Such coexistence is currently apparent in the tendency to compartmentalize practitioners into those who employ the new paradigm (e.g., indirect, preventive service as suggested by the inclusion of job definitions for "preventionist") and those who continue to provide services from the previous orientation (e.g., direct service counselors).

As long as the new orientation can be compartmentalized, it will remain either the domain of only a special subset of the helping profession and practiced by only a few who are specifically trained (i.e., consultants) or who will be relegated to the role of an "add on" strategy or technique to be employed as supplemental to direct service. The true revolution in consultation occurs when it moves from simply being a technique to becoming a new frame of reference, a new paradigm for mental health services. Such a movement is currently underway!

Blending Direct and Indirect Service: As this fourth revolution continues to move consultation from the status of supplementary technique to position of paradigm, practitioners will come to conceptualize the two (direct and consultative services) not as polarized, but rather as services along a common dimension, a continuum (Meyers, Parsons, & Martin, 1979; Parsons & Meyers, 1984). Consultation, as a continuum of service conceptualization, moves from a more or less remedial, client-focused orientation to a more or less preventive, system-based focus. Figure 1-1 provides an conceptual view of this continuum.

The position taken here and elsewhere (see Meyers, Parsons, & Martin, 1979; Parsons & Meyers, 1984) is that direct services, such as counseling, need not be counteropposed to consultation as if the two were mutually exclusive. Nor, as apparently has become the practice, do direct service and consultation need to be compartmentalized as if separate forms of service delivery. Rather, what is proposed throughout this text is that all service, including those forms that involve direct diagnostic and intervention interaction with the client, can be conceptualized and practiced as a form of consultation, and as such provide expanded, preventive service as well as the more traditional intervention services. This point will be addressed in detail in Chapter 7.

FIGURE 1-1: Continuum of Consultative Service

	Direct ←——————————→ Indirect	
Primary Role:	Remedial	Preventive
Target:	Client	System
Focus:	Intrapersonal	Extrapersonal

Such a shift in perspective—in paradigm—may at first feel somewhat uncomfortable. However, such a shift in the way we conceptualize client problems, the role we play in light of other significant caretakers in the clients environment, and the possibility of melding intervention and prevention elements into *all* of the services we provide will afford us the opportunity to expand and increase the impact of our services.

Consultation: An Operational Definition

The forms of service and interaction that have been grouped under the rubric of consultation are many and quite varied. From the informal discussion between friends regarding an issue of importance, or a husband and wife consulting their calendars to plan a dinner party, to sharing of advice and service by an expert or one with specialized training, consultation has come to generally imply the provision of advice and/or services. However, such a colloquial definition fails to encompass the value, the uniqueness, and the complexity of consultation.

A variety of professions have employed the term consultation to refer to a myriad of roles, activities, and relationships (Kurpius & Robinson, 1978). And more formally, numerous definitions of consultation have been offered in the professional literature (e.g., Conoley & Conoley, 1982; Brown, Pryzwansky, & Schulte, 1987; Friend & Cook, 1992; Gallessich, 1982; Meyers, Parsons, & Martin, 1979; Rosenfield, 1987).

However, attempts to identify one single, operational definition of consultation applicable across the spectrum of human services has been less than successful (e.g., Brown, Wyne, Blackburn, & Powell, 1979, Gallessich, 1982). Much of the difficulty in establishing a common definition rests in the variations of elements that practitioners and theorists choose to emphasize.

Consultation has been defined as based on the focal point of the interaction (i.e., content or process), the nature of the interaction (i.e., crisis or developmental), or the role to be played by the consultant (i.e., provisional, prescriptive, mediational, or collaborative). Further lack of clarity or consensus around the issue of a definition may be attributed to the specific theoretical model (e.g., behavioral, mental health, or organizational development) employed as the base from which to define consultation. But even with the variations of focus and the subtleties of differences in definitions, a number of core characteristics can be articulated and at a minimum serve as the components to this text's operational definition.

Consultation can be characterized as a helping, *problem-solving* process involving a helpgiver (the consultant), a helpseeker (the consultee), and another (the client). This

EXERCISE 1-4   Consultation—A Triadic Relationship

Directions: For each of the following scenarios label the consultant (C), the consultee (C), and the client (CL). Remember, the client is the person exhibiting a problem for which the consultee, the party responsible or accountable for the client's performance, is seeking help. Finally, the consultant is the individual who, while not directly responsible for the client's performance, is serving as a helpgiver to the consultee.

Example: Sheila, the night foreman, complained that no matter what she tries, she cannot get Joel, her primary driver, to call in after each of his stops. She has gone to talk to Tom, the day manager, knowing that he has successfully resolved similar things in his twenty years with this company.

Consultant: Tom
Consultee: Sheila
Client: Joel

Scenario 1: Tom, the general foreman for T. R. products, contacts Earl, the human resource director, to discuss the rules and regulations applicable for a worker, Al, who may be drinking on the job.

Consultant:
Consultee:
Client:

Scenario 2: Dr. Peterson, a private clinical psychologist, asks to talk with Mr. and Mrs. Ablin in order to coordinate efforts to assist with their 12-year-old son Alfonso's weight reduction.

Consultant:
Consultee:
Client:

Scenario 3: Mr. Elberson, the seventh grade mathematics teacher, came to Ms. O'Neill, the guidance counselor, upset and concerned over the disruptive and disrespectful behavior exhibited by Claire.

Consultant:
Consultee:
Client:

Scenario 4: Louis, the principal of P.S. #142, contacts the local community mental health center to request assistance with providing some AIDS awareness programming for his senior high students.

Consultant:
Consultee:
Client:

voluntary, triadic relationship involves *mutual* involvement on the part of both the consultant and consultee in an attempt solve *the current work-related problem* in a way that it not only stays solved, but that future problems may be avoided and or more efficiently handled (*prevention*).

Because of the importance of each of these salient characteristics to the nature of the dynamic and the role and function of the consultant, each is described in a bit more detail. As you read more about the characteristics of consultation, you will begin to understand how this is not just simply another technique, but rather an orientation, a paradigm, a way of framing problems and their resolution. It is a new orientation that will require both new knowledge and new skill.

Triadic Relationship: As noted, consultation is by definition a process involving a help-giver, a helpseeker, and the person for whom the consultee is directly responsible, that is, the client. The triadic nature of this helping relationship immediately distinguishes it from direct service counseling.

The consultee can be a parent, a teacher, a supervisor, a manager, or a fellow human service provider. The consultee is the party generally (although not always) initiating services. The consultee has responsibility for the client and is experiencing some concern or difficulty in relationship to that client or that client's performance. The consultant is a person in a position to have some influence over an individual, a group, or an organization, but who has no direct power to make changes or implement programs (Block, 1981). Exercise 1-4 is provided in order to help further clarify the triadic nature of the consultation.

Unlike direct service models, such as counseling, that have linear relationships where the service provider is working directly with the client (Figure 1-2), consultation as an indirect form of service means that the work to be accomplished will at some level involve the consultee in both the diagnostic and intervention planning and implementation.

Thus, rather than having a one-on-one linear relationship with the client, the consultant is now involved in a nonlinear way to both the consultee and the client. For example, the consultant may work with the consultee gathering information about the client and in turn provide recommendations to the consultee for implementation (Figure 1-3, prescriptive

FIGURE 1-2:   Triadic Nature of Consultation

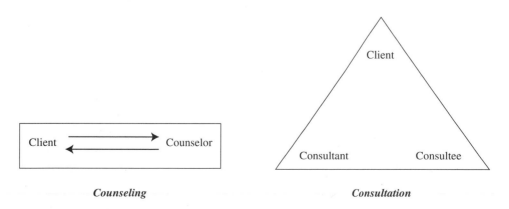

Counseling   *Consultation*

FIGURE 1-3:   Prescriptive Form of Consulting

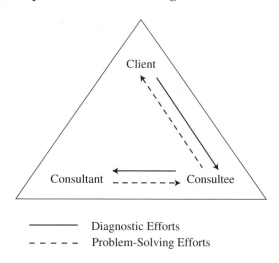

Diagnostic Efforts
Problem-Solving Efforts

model). Or the consultee may gather information from the client and then provide intervention programming (Figure 1-4, a provisional model).

For further clarification, consider one of the examples provided in Exercise 1-3. The consultant, Tom, may find himself working with Joel directly trying to diagnose the situation and encourage (intervene) Joel to call in. Or, Tom may suggest a number of strategies to Sheila for implementation and continue to work with Sheila fine tuning the plan, having only indirect contact with Joel. Or, Tom may simply work with Sheila developing her own self-confidence or managerial skills and competence, thus focusing on Sheila directly and ignoring Joel.

FIGURE 1-4:   Provisional Consulting

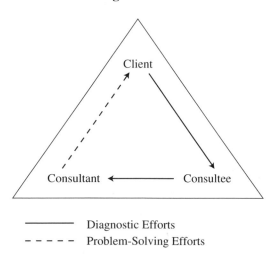

Diagnostic Efforts
Problem-Solving Efforts

The types and number of focal points for the helping relationship are clearly multiplied once the service moves from dyadic, as in counseling, to triadic, as in consultation. Further, the inclusion of this third party as coparticipant in the problem-solving venture, while providing additional resources and perspective, also demands a new shift in focus, and a new set of skills previously unused in a direct service model. Understanding and coordinating multiple perspectives, varied terminology, turf concerns, and power issues are but a few of the additional variables included in these dynamics.

Problem Solving: Consultation is most often characterized as a problem-solving process in which the target of such problem solving is the work-related role and function of the client. While most definitions suggest that consultation is a problem-solving process targeting work-related issues, work is broadly defined to include any and all mission-driven needs for the institution, agency, and/or consultee.

The intent of focusing consultation on work-related issues is to highlight the fact that the consultant is NOT providing the consultee with mental health counseling or psychotherapy, but rather the service to the consultee is always performed with an eye to impacting the performance of the client.

This is not to suggest that the consultee may not also grow in personal insight, or emotional well being, or that the focus of the interaction cannot be centered on the skills, knowledge, or objectivity of the consultee. What is being highlighted is that consultation, even when taking such a consultee-centered focus (see Chapter 8), emphasizes problem solving around issues of the client's performance, in direct contrast to therapeutic personal insight and growth for the consultee.

This definitional element requires that the consultant employ helping interaction while at the same time avoiding developing a therapeutic contract with the consultee. And while perhaps appearing relatively simplistic and clear, it is not always easy to walk the fine line between consultative help and personal therapy. Consider the case of Allen T.

Allen was a high school history teacher with forty-two years of teaching experience. Allen requested the consultative services of the school psychologist because he was very worried about a boy in his class. Allen described Dennis as "a good boy, who last year was quite prompt in completing assignments. This year, however, Dennis has been frequently late with assignments and (I) must always give him extra time." Allen continued, "I think he's going through some very painful times, since his dad died only six months ago."

As the consultant worked with Allen, two things became quite clear. First, the student, Dennis, was grieving the death of his father; his grief reaction appeared appropriate in both intensity and duration. Also, Dennis was involved in supportive counseling with his family, which seemed to be very effective. The second and perhaps more essential issue identified by the consultant, was that Allen's objectivity and professional approach to Dennis had been compromised. Allen, by his own admission, was overly solicitous of Dennis and provided him more slack in meeting deadlines than he normally would allow. It became apparent that Dennis was responding to the extra time given him by making the most of it. It was also apparent that Allen's own personal issues surrounding the delayed grieving of his own parents' death and the anticipatory grief connected to his upcoming retirement were interfering with his own professional objectivity and ability to hold Dennis responsible for deadlines.

While the consultant needed to help Allen see the connection between his overreaction to Dennis and Dennis' lack of performance in class, it was imperative that he avoid focusing his energies and interventions on Allen and Allen's own delayed grief. This is not to suggest that recommendations to Allen to consider some individual work would be inappropriate. What is being presented is that the contracted nature of the consultation should remain on resolving the work-related problem of the client and not the therapeutic needs of the consultee. Knowing how to walk the fine line between work-related problem solving and personal therapy is essential for the mental health practitioner operating from a consultative frame of reference.

Mutual and Voluntary: While consultation has most often been presented as an expert relationship (Friend & Cook, 1992), most definitions acknowledge the need for the participants to share in the process. The value of a collaborative model in which both the consultant and consultee approach the consultation as co-equals, sharing in the ownership and responsibility for the consultation interaction and outcome, has been emphasized by many (e.g., Block, 1981; Brown, Kurpius, & Morris, 1988; Caplan, 1970; Parsons & Meyers, 1984). But even when less than collaborative approaches have been discussed or employed, the value of consultee involvement and ownership has been highlighted.

Moving the relationship to one with mutual responsibility and shared ownership for the process and ultimate content, while valuing the individual differences in perspective and expertise, requires that the human service provider develop additional interpersonal skills aimed at reducing consultee resistance and equalizing psychosocial power differentials.

Dual Focus: Consultation has as its focus the alleviation of a work problem. However, more than simply intervening in order to resolve a current work problem (remedial/intervention focus), consultation as presented here attempts to resolve the current dilemma in such a way that it not only "stays fixed" (Block, 1981), but in a way that the consultee is left better prepared to avoid similar problems in the future or handle future problems with increased skillfulness and efficiency (prevention focus).

When operating from a consultation paradigm, one needs to expand the perception of the problem as well as the work that needs to be accomplished in order to include growth and development (i.e., prevention) goals (Kurpius & Fuqua, 1993). The preventive focus of consultation requires that strategies be conceptualized and enacted that will facilitate the spread of effect, or generalization of impact, to other non-referred clients. Strategies that promote the emotional well being of all members of a particular situation and not just the identified client are clearly serving this preventive purpose. However, such primary prevention is not always possible. But even when requested to assist *after* a problem has emerged, a consultant with a grasp of prevention can intervene in ways that shorten the duration, impact, or negative effect of the problem and thus prevent (secondary prevention) the typical cycle for this type of problem. Or, even after the problem is fully manifested, preventive elements can be included in the consultant's interventions by assisting the client and the consultee to develop more adaptive styles of coping (i.e., tertiary prevention).

For many mental health practitioners, trained to work with pathology, the invitation to work in a preventive mode can be both challenging and somewhat unsettling. Shifting focus from one of remediation to one of prevention requires practitioners to expand their focus to include not only the client but also ecology, environment, and extrapersonal factors affecting the client. It will also require the human service provider to see him- or herself as an agent of change, proactive in conditions that may prove detrimental to the well being or continued functioning of those involved. This position will also require the human service provider to shift his or her orientation from one of being reactive and responsive in time of need, to being proactive and preventive (educative) prior to needs emerging.

Consultation as a new paradigm for mental health service conceptualization and delivery may challenge you. It may confront your paradigm of service. As such, consultation may be experienced as a revolution both for the profession and for the practitioner.

Trying It!

Prior to beginning our discussion of the specific knowledge and skill required for effective consulting, it is useful to attempt to slip into the orientation in order to see the value of this way of making meaning of our professional data. Exercise 1-5 will provide you an opportunity to try on a consultation perspective.

Summary

Consultation as presented within this chapter is much more than a new technique or a new strategy to be employed by direct service providers. In reviewing the historical evolution of mental health services, this chapter attempted to demonstrate how paradigms have shifted from supernatural to natural, biological to psychological, and from intrapsychic to extrapersonal. Through each of these evolutionary changes, professionals were challenged to adopt a new perspective, a new frame of reference, a new paradigm—an invitation that was often resisted.

While consultation as a specific strategy has been used as a supplement to direct service, it is now emerging as a perspective, a paradigm from which to conceptualize problems and employ a variety of more or less indirect forms of intervention. This shifting of consultation from the status of strategy to the level of paradigm marks a new level of evolution in mental health services.

The chapter demonstrated that as a new frame of reference or paradigm that mental health professionals use to make sense of their professional reality, consultation

1. Invites providers to modify their view of service, from one of intervention to one of prevention.
2. Facilitates their development of an expanded view of the target for service to include focal points beyond the client, such as the consultee, programs, and systems.
3. Demands that providers develop additional knowledge and skills, culled from extensive work in the disciplines of mental health and organizational development.
4. Requires that providers understand the unique dynamics that result when operating from a triadic, mutual, dual-focused, problem-solving process, and employ the skills needed to successfully navigate through such a process for the benefit of the client.

EXERCISE 1-5   Revisiting, Re-visioning Felicia

Directions: Below you will find the original referral information regarding the case of Felicia. Use the referral information in order to respond to each of the following questions. In responding to the questions, you will begin to see both the value and challenges of employing a consultation paradigm of practice.

Referral

Felicia, age 15, came to your office having been referred by her English teacher. The note Felicia presented read: "There appears to be something VERY SERIOUSLY wrong with Felicia. Since the beginning of this new marking period, she has been TOTALLY nonattentive and nonresponsive in class." The teacher continued, "I have taught British literature for now over twenty-six years and I know when a student is heading for trouble. Trust me. This young lady is on the road to ruin! I hope you can help her!"

Felicia appeared tearful, physically agitated (unable to sit still, pacing back and forth) and disheveled in her appearance (clothes and hair unkempt). Felicia explained that for the last two days she has been sleeping in a car. She has not returned home since Saturday (two days ago) and will "never go back until her mother gets rid of the creep she is living with" (referring to her mother's boyfriend). Felicia complained that "everything is going wrong," "(her) grades stink," "(her) boyfriend is angry with (her)," and "now this creep (her mother's boyfriend) is butting in!" Felicia stated that she was very embarrassed because of the way she looked and she even thought of trying to call somebody at school to find out about coming in early to use the showers and things, but she just didn't know who to talk to.

Analysis

1. Generate two hypotheses about the role the teacher may play in the creation or maintenance of the problem (extrapersonal focus). _____
   _____
   _____

2. Generate two hypotheses about the role the teacher may play in the creation or implementation of the intervention (triadic focus). _____
   _____
   _____

3. Identify two points of resistance or problems you may encounter attempting to work with the teacher (relationship as mutual and voluntary). _____
   _____
   _____

4. Identify a prevention goal (either primary, secondary, or tertiary) that may result from this consult (dual goals). _____
   _____
   _____

It is hoped that the reader will begin to understand that the redefinition of roles and function invited by a consultation approach truly reflects not just the evolution of service, but a revolution of orientation, a shift in paradigm. As presented within this chapter, consultation as an approach to helping will challenge and confront the reader's previous view of helping. Rather than focusing on the intrapsychic exclusively and/or primarily, it invites us to focus on the extrapersonal. Rather than encouraging an individualistic view, which suggests that the problem and the solution rest within the client, consultation suggests an interactive view of systems-client-consultee. Rather than presenting the helping process as a direct, dyadic encounter, consultation offers an indirect triadic model. Finally, rather than seeking reconciliation, remediation, or intervention alone, consultation incorporates prevention as a needed and desired outcome.

C h a p t e r 2

Integrating the Various
Consultant Roles and
Functions

A wide variety of activities and services have been clustered under the rubric of consultation. This diversity, this variation, is evident in the many ways that the role of the consultant and the process of consulting have been described.

The consultant has been depicted as either an individual who provides technical expertise to another in need or one who facilitates the consultee's use of his or her own expertise. The process of consulting has been presented as both a prescriptive venture between an expert and one needing assistance, and as a collaborative enterprise between two individuals sharing expertise. Further, consultation has been portrayed as a tool for crisis intervention, and as an opportunity and means for providing preventive services. Clearly, the term consultation has been applied to a wide variety of activities and practices that significantly differ in terms of goals, focus points, and roles to be played by the consultant and consultee.

This vast diversity of emphasis can prove quite confusing for the consultant in the field. Not knowing which role to employ, which target to focus upon, or even which goals appear appropriate for a particular consult can induce frustration in the consultant and lack of confidence in the consultee. The current chapter will provide a model for integrating this diversity of role, function, and focus. More specifically, the chapter will:

1. Highlight the differentiating characteristics or dimensions of the various activities and services deemed to be consultation
2. Demonstrate how each specific form or type of consulting would approach a single problem
3. Provide a multidimensional model for consultation that allows for the integration of the variety of approaches, goals, and services

4. Offer a set of guidelines or decision criteria to guide the practicing consultant in the selection of the most appropriate form of consultation for a given situation

The Many Faces of Consulting

A review of the consultation literature will highlight both the vast degree to which consultation is practiced and the vast diversity that exists among those who practice consultation. While there may be a number of taxonomies that could be employed to classify consultation activities, the current discussion will employ the following dimensions as a means of differentiating the unique forms of consultant function and consultation focus:

Dimension I: Nature of the Consult (Crisis or Developmental)

Dimension II: Problem and Goal Definitions (Depth and Breadth)

Dimension III: Theory and Assumptions (Mental Health, Behavioral, Organizational Development)

Dimension IV: Consultant Skills (Content or Process Expert)

Dimension V: Modes of Consultation/Consultant Role (Provisional, Prescriptive, Collaborative, Mediational)

Each of these dimensions will be discussed in some detail. This investigation will assist the reader to more fully appreciate the complexities and subtleties of consultation. However, it is in the integration of these various dimensions into a flexible, multidimensional approach to consultation that the consultant's value will be maximized. Therefore, following the presentation of the separate dimensions, the chapter will outline an integrated multidimensional model of consultation.

However, before discussing the various forms and foci of consultation, it would be helpful to review the case of Tommie S. (Case Illustration 2-1). This case will be used as a reference point from which to discern the subtle variations among consultation formats and approaches.

Dimension I: The Nature of the Consult— Crisis or Developmental

Consultation has been differentially defined and discussed as either a mode of remedial/crisis service or as a method for providing developmental (primary prevention) services.

Crisis Consulting

Consults of a crisis nature are those in which the individual consultee or consultee system experiences pain or dysfunction and requests the consultant's assistance. The consultant's form of response and the degree to which he or she can take time to fully develop the nature of the problem and the various options for intervention depend to some extent on the inten-

CASE ILLUSTRATION 2-1   The Case of Tommie S.

Referral

Tommie S. was referred to your office by his teacher Ms. Casey. Tommie is in fifth grade. He lives at home with his mother (a corporate lawyer) and his father (a psychiatrist). Tommie has an older sister (Julie) who is a senior in high school and an older brother (Alex) who is attending Columbia University Law School.

Ms. Casey sent Tommie with a note that read: "Tommie needs your help! He is a disturbed child. I found Tommie dropping his pencil in class in order to look up the dress of the girl who sits behind him. I also found some drawings that I would be embarrassed to show you. Tommie is inattentive. He is always fidgeting in his seat, looking around in class and doing things (like dropping his pencil) to get people's attention.

I have tried talking to Tommie, I have kept him after school, I have talked to his parents and NOTHING works. It seems I spend more time calling out Tommie's name than teaching. Please help him get it together!"

Observations

When you meet Tommie, you note that he is a very neat, mannerly, and articulate youth. Tommie "admits" that he was looking up the girl's dress, but stated that "it's just a game, other guys do it too!" Tommie complained that Ms. Casey is always "on his case," and that she is really "boring."

When describing his home life, Tommie noted that he really misses his older brother (who had been at home up until this past month). He explained that he has a small job (taking care of his neighbor's dogs) after school. This keeps him busy from the time he gets home (3:00) until the time his mom comes home from work (4:15). Tommie discussed the many hobbies and sports activities he enjoys and noted that his Dad has been the coach for both his soccer and baseball teams.

Tommie has been described by other teachers as a "good kid" who is somewhat of an "itch."

About the Consultee

Ms. Casey has been a teacher for the past 27 years, and has taught grades K through 2 for most of her career. This is the first year she has ever taught fifth grade. Ms. Casey stated that she "loves teaching and wouldn't know what to do if (she) couldn't have her classroom."

She expressed concerns over the real possibility of being forced to retire, so she wants to "demonstrate to the administration that (I) can be in complete control of (my) classroom." She noted that other children in her class have "discipline problems" and appear a bit "itchy." She noted, however, that she is concerned about referring these children for counseling, since "a good teacher should be able to handle her own problems within the classroom!"

About the School

The school contains grades K through 5, with a student population of 520 students. The school has 18 classroom teachers, 3 supplementary teachers, a school psychologist, a learning specialist, and 2 school counselors. Within the last five years the community has grown significantly in size, educational background, and financial status. Most of the children come from homes in which both parents work in professional capacities, and the family expectations are that education will be valued and achieved.

The goals of the school are to "foster academic development, inspire pride in self and country and to promote the development of self-control and responsible decision making." Informally, the school seems to value calmness, order, and neatness.

The school employs a self-contained mode of classroom education; teachers are responsible for all subject curricula (with the exception of physical education).

sity and duration of the crisis along with the consultee's and consultee's system resources. When a consultee experiences serious dysfunction and is in need of immediate assistance, the consultant responds to this crisis with a focus on remediation.

It is with the specific issue or source of that crisis that the consultee seeks assistance. Economy and efficiency of service is typically what is desired.

The benefit of crisis consulting is that with the consultee and/or the consultee's system experiencing pain or dysfunction, the services provided by the consultant are often readily accepted and resistance is minimized (Meyers, Parsons, & Martin, 1979). Consultee and system resistance will be discussed in detail in Chapters 3 and 4.

Developmental Consultation

Much of what is described in the literature as consultation could be defined as providing developmental or preventive service. Consultation services that focus on human potential by promoting self-enhancement, self-awareness, and actualization are clearly developmental in nature. Similarly, consultation activities that focus on increasing human adjustment by improving interpersonal skills, problem-solving abilities, and stress management skills are also considered developmental and preventive in nature. Finally, consultative activities that alter potentially inhibiting or detrimental elements in a person's physical-social-psychological environment (e.g., Moos, 1974) also reflect a developmental/preventive focus.

Unlike the crisis-oriented consultation, developmental consultation is quite often initiated by the consultant (as opposed to the consultee). Further, developmental consultation may be introduced at a time when the consultee and/or consultee's system appear to be operating and functioning appropriately. As a developmental activity, the focus for this form of consulting is on growth and prevention rather than pain reduction and remediation.

The absence of crises allows the consultant and the consultee the luxury of time to plan and implement the most growth-filled form of service. However, the same absence of pain and crisis often reduces the felt need for such service, and developmental consultation may be met with resistance. Overcoming this "if it ain't broke, don't fix it" mentality requires additional interpersonal marketing skills on the part of the consultant to enlist the consultee's cooperation and ownership of this developmental process.

As suggested in Case Illustration 2-2, any one consult may have both a crisis element and a developmental opportunity. And as will be discussed later within this chapter, it may be more effective and efficient to approach each consult with an integrated perspective that allows the consultant to remediate the immediate pain (crisis) while attending to developmental/preventive goals. Exercise 2-1 is provided to further demonstrate this point.

Dimension II: Problem and Goal Definition Varying in Depth and Breadth

A second way of differentiating consultation is based on the way the problem, and thus the specific goal, is defined. A number of dimensions have been identified that differentiate such problem conceptualization and goal definition (e.g., Gallessich, 1982).

**CASE ILLUSTRATION 2-2   Case Application—Tommie: Crisis and/or
Developmental Focus**

We can begin to see more clearly how consultants operating from either a crisis or developmental focal point would approach a consult by reviewing the case of Tommie S.

A consultant operating from a crisis frame of reference would have a number of points of
contact in the case of Tommie. Clearly, Ms. Casey is in need of assistance (in crisis). Providing
remediation for Ms. Casey's limited understanding of typical 5th grade behavior or ineffectual
classroom management skills would seem appropriate. Similarly, intervening with Tommie,
who is also in crisis, "bored," and in trouble with Ms. Casey, would appear appropriate. Working with Tommie and Ms. Casey to develop a behavioral contract aimed at increasing his time
on task and positive classroom behavior, for example, would appear to be a potential useful
plan for crisis consultation.

Even though the referral was made in a crisis, a consultant with a developmental orientation
may see other potential problems that need addressing. A consultant approaching this situation
from a more developmental perspective may target each of the following as points for preventive programming:

- Teacher inservice and preparation, especially in light of new grade-level assignments
- Retirement planning and transitional support
- Afterschool programming for latchkey children
- Sex education curriculum development

Problems can be conceptualized as varying in breadth and depth. The breadth of a
problem can be as restricted as a single individual, or more broadly identified as involving
a group or department or even an entire organization. A problem can be defined as varying
in depth, from a single issue to multiple issues, from a surface problem to a more hidden,
implied, or convoluted issue. Further, the problem can be defined as either one of a technical nature or one involving a human systems or process glitch.

Just as the problem definition can vary along breadth and depth dimensions so can the
goal statement and focus. Goals can be operationally defined to involve changes in a person
(client, consultee, etc.), a policy, or a system structure or process. The size of the goal can
vary from micro to macro or anywhere in between (Gallessich, 1982). The specific goal(s)
will be determined by the unique characteristics and needs of the consultee. But even considering all this, it could be assumed that a generic goal for all consultation would be the
improvement of client, consultee, and system functioning.

Exercise 2-2 is provided to further clarify this dimension of consultation.

Dimension III: Theory and Assumptions—
Mental Health, Behavioral, Organizational Consultation

Like other forms of helping, the consulting process and focus will be guided and shaped by
the consultant's operating set of assumptions or theory of helping. The role the consultant

---

**EXERCISE 2-1   Identifying the Crisis or Developmental Nature
of Consultation**

Directions: Below you will find a series of brief referrals. While each originates in response to a felt need, and as such qualifies as crisis consultation, each suggests or articulates a target for preventive service as well. With a colleague, classmate, or supervisor discuss the crisis and developmental nature of each.

Situation I: Mr. Thompson, the night shift manager, has requested your services. It appears that Jimmy (a new employee) and Malcom (a line worker for the past 28 years) have gotten into a number of verbal arguments about the music Jimmy plays during work. According to Malcolm, "Me and the boys don't like these young guys comin' in here and taking over."

Situation II: Maria is a psychiatric nurse at a local outpatient clinic. She has requested your assistance in regard to one of her patients, Mr. L. It appears that Mr. L has "sexually threatened" one of the night attendants. Maria stated that Ellen, a recent college graduate, works the 1 A.M. to 9 A.M. shift. It is an easy shift, according to Maria. All Ellen has to do is check in on the patients as they sleep. If there is a problem, she is to alert the doctor on call. It appears that when Ellen checked on Mr. L., he sat up in bed and made very sexual comments. Ellen is very frightened and refuses to check on him.

Situation III: Alfred is a 9th grader who was sent to your office by the dean of students. It appears that Alfred has been coming to class late, especially 5th period Algebra, and seems, according to the dean, "afraid of his own shadow!" Alfred admits to being late, saying that it is hard for him to get to the 3rd floor classroom because he has 4th period lunch in the basement. Alfred complained that this school is too big, and "is not like middle school." He further stated he feels he is "getting better and more familiar with the layout." "After all," he continued, "school just started last week and I've only been here for 6 days!"

**CASE ILLUSTRATION 2-3   Case Application—Tommie: Many Targets,
Many Goals**

A review of the case of Tommie (Case Illustration 2-1) might clarify how a consult could be differently defined and approached along this dimension of problem and goal conceptualization.

It may appear obvious that the breadth of the focus of the referral could be narrowed and restricted to working directly with Tommie, or defined more broadly to include working with Ms. Casey's entire 5th grade. Further, goals may be established and intervention procedures employed that attempt to produce changes in various targets. The breadth of the intervention and goal may be limited to an individual, for example, modifying Tommie's inattentive behavior or increasing Ms. Casey's classroom management skills. Goals and interventions could also be expanded to include changes within a group—for example, educating the students in Ms. Casey's class about the issues of preadolescent development. Or even more broadly defined goals could include the development of institutional policies and procedures that would protect against inappropriate teacher-grade assignments, or provide a system of supports for preretirement planning.

EXERCISE 2-2   Various Problems, Various Goals

Directions: Below you will find three consultation scenarios. For each scenario, identify a specific or restricted problem and corresponding goal. Next, review the same scenarios, redefining the problem more broadly, making the goal more encompassing. Share your perspective with a colleague, classmate, or supervisor to see additional perspectives.

Scenario I: As a sports psychologist, you have been called in to a local college to teach team members stress-reduction techniques. As you discuss the proposed program with the athletic director, you are informed that the point of this program is to give the team that little edge over the competition. You are also told that this is a highly competitive institution, and winning isn't everything—it "is the only thing." The coaches need every advantage to keep the alumni off their backs.

Scenario II: You are contracted to work with a local police force. It appears that two of the street teams working the night shift have been a bit "on edge." The captain stated, "These four fellows have been pretty argumentative and I won't have that among my team members!" He continued, "These guys are going to be working that shift for another 3 months (it is a 6-month rotation of duty), and they'd better start pulling together!" Your task is to get these four officers to work out their problems with each other.

Scenario III: The Ajax company is about to be bought out by a multinational corporation. According to the manager, some workers seem to be more interested in chatting about rumors than in doing their jobs. He wants you to help him get them "back in line—doing their job more and gabbing less!" The manager is of the opinion that what happens at the top is none of their business. He will "tell them what they need to know, when they need to know it . . . otherwise they are to do their jobs!"

---

employs, the outcomes expected, and the strategies chosen are usually derived from the consultant's assumptions about how change can best be effected (Chin & Benne, 1969). While many of these assumptions are unique to the individual consultant, others reflect theoretical orientations adopted as part of professional training and development.

Three major models of consultation—mental health consultation, behavioral consultation, and organizational consultation—have been presented quite extensively in the literature (see Gallessich, 1982; West & Idol, 1987). Each of these models is presented below as representing a third dimension defining the form and focus of consultation.

Mental Health Consultation

This model, with roots in the clinical practice of one physician (the consultee) seeking assistance from a more knowledgeable and specialized physician (the consultant), was adopted by psychiatry (Mendel & Solomon, 1968) and popularized by Gerald Caplan (Caplan, 1970). The mental health model of consultation is practiced in community agencies (Altrocchi, 1972; Crego & Crego, 1983; Rogawski, 1979), school settings (e.g., Conoley, 1981; Curtis & Zins, 1981; Meyers, Parsons, & Martin, 1979), and even business or industrial settings (Gallessich, 1985).

The triadic relationship identified as a core characteristic of consultation is evident in the mental health model of consultation. For example, Caplan worked as consultant to a small staff of psychologists and social workers responsible for the mental health needs of immigrant children in Israel. His efforts were initially aimed at simply providing the staff (i.e., the consultees) with new techniques for coping with the problems they had identified with the children (i.e., the clients). Unlike a number of the earlier "expert" models in which the consultant would diagnose the problem and provide authoritative, expert prescription, the keystone to Caplan's approach was the nonhierarchical or coordinate relationship that existed between the consultant and the consultee. Caplan conceptualized the relationship between the consultee and the consultant as one of equals, where the consultant had no direct-line authority over the consultee. However, Caplan saw consultation as different from collaboration in that in consultation the consultee retained full responsibility for the outcome of the case, even though he or she promoted coequal, mutual, coordinate involvement in the consulting process (Altrocchi, 1972; Caplan, 1970; Caplan & Caplan 1993; Gallessich, 1982).

The mental health consultation model, focusing on the client's (i.e., individual, group, or organization) functioning, emphasized the role of the consultee's knowledge, skill, and objectivity as related to both the remediation and prevention of the problem at hand. The basic premise was that increasing the knowledge, skills, or professional objectivity of the consultee would not only result in the amelioration of presenting concern, but also serve a preventive function, thus reducing the need for future consultation on similar types of issues.

The mental health model views consultation as a pyramid in which the mental health professional (at the apex) consults with and educates the consultees (in the middle of the pyramid) who in turn work in the agencies that provide the direct service to the client. The consultant gains an extended impact in that the consultee is now better prepared to cope with other clients in that environment. Gallessich (1982) noted that this "spread of effect" concept is central to the mental health approach to consultation. From this orientation, the consultant is not only a service delivery expert but an educator and facilitator.

The mental health model of consultation presented in Caplan's work, while revolutionary in terms of delivery and framework, took a somewhat traditional, dynamically oriented approach to problem conceptualization. Caplan (1970) emphasized the role of the consultee's personal themes (i.e., emotionally toned cognitive constellations relating to unresolved personal conflicts) in his or her inability to resolve the current client-related problem.

While Caplan highlighted the need to change the consultee's attitudes (e.g., theme interference reduction techniques), he also cautioned that such confrontation was not designed to threaten the defenses of the consultee, as might be expected in traditional analytically oriented psychotherapy. Rather, he suggested that it was both inappropriate and counterproductive for the consultant to confront these themes or conflicts directly. The consultant's emphasis should be on the client and only indirectly on the consultee's themes as they may come to bear on the current work-related client situation.

Behavioral Consultation

A contrasting set of assumptions about the targets for both problem identification and resolution can be found within the behavioral model of consultation (Bergan, 1977; Bergan & Tombari, 1976; Kuehnel & Kuehnel, 1983; Russell, 1978). Unlike the mental health model, behavioral consultation was founded on social learning theory and focused on the overt behaviors of the consultee and the client.

Behavioral consultation emphasizes learning principles and the effect of environment on current functioning. Further, most consultants operating from a behavioral model employ intervention strategies drawn from behavioral and social learning theory (e.g., contingency management, shaping, or social modeling).

Even though behavioral consultation lacks a central theory (Gallessich, 1985), it has provided a number of major elements that have expanded the consultant's range of options. Gallessich (1982, p. 34) noted that this model contributed: "1) [the concept of] learning theory as a means of understanding the behavior of individuals, groups, and organizations; 2) a source of techniques to change behaviors of both consultees and their clients; and 3) an intervention model with a built-in paradigm for evaluation and change."

The behavioral consultant often assumes a directive role—monitoring the consultee's implementation of a prescription. The consultant may be directly active in observing client behavior or client-consultee interaction and gathering descriptive data about the conditions and frequency of the particular problematic behavior. If not directly collecting the needed information, the consultant will be actively involved in directing the consultee to collect similar observational information as methods for diagnosis, intervention planning, and intervention monitoring.

Organizational Consultation

Organizational consulting (Argyris, 1970; Beckhard, 1969; Bennis, 1969; Schein, 1969) has in fact two significant paths of service. One path is the "expert" who is able to provide technical specialization and support to an agency. In this situation, the consultee or the consultee's system called on the consultant to work in a variety of roles including technical advisor, applicator, trainer, or mentor. In this form, the organizational consultant may be involved in designing and defining work tasks, overseeing employee selection and training, and implementing skill development training. In either case, the consultant tended to be expert in focus and directive (i.e., provisional, prescriptive) in mode of delivery.

As more attention was given to the human side of the business enterprise, consultants shifted focus from tools, technical skills, or structures to the social dynamics and processes involved in the work setting. The second path organizational consulting has taken is one involving combined knowledge of social-psychological, cognitive-behavioral, and ecological-systems theories and principles. The target for this approach is to improve the socioemotional dynamics of the workplace.

Research on the importance of quality of work life, leadership style, group dynamics, and morale to productivity encouraged organizations to review and monitor their systems and processes. One consultant, Edgar Schein (1969), championed the value of process consultation, in which members of an organization would become more aware of the events and processes in their work environments and the impact of these processes on their performance. The process consultant is an organizational consultant interested in improving the interpersonal skills, interpersonal climate, and social dynamic existing within the work setting.

From this orientation, the organizational consultant was not only the prescriber or provider of expert knowledge, but a facilitator of effective interpersonal behavior. The roles played by such a process consultant included systems analyst, administrative coach, action researcher, and educator/trainer.

CASE ILLUSTRATION 2-4   Case Application—Tommie: A View from Three Perspectives

Returning to our sample case, Tommie S., we can readily begin to appreciate how the theoretical model, or set of operative assumptions, focuses the consultant and the consultation dynamic. One disclaimer should be noted. For purposes of this discussion, a rather simplistic and single-minded sample of consultant focus and style is being presented for each theory.

Mental Health Consultation: The consultant employing this particular orientation with Ms. Casey may be most interested in and focused upon:

1. Increasing Ms. Casey's understanding of preadolescent males and their sexual play behavior, and
2. Increasing her awareness of her own concerns about sexual themes, respect and authority themes, and any emotional issues tied to the process of retirement that may be interfering with her ability to effectively work with Tommie.

Behavioral Consultation: The behavioral consultant may assist Ms. Casey in taking baseline data regarding the specific problematic behavior exhibited by Tommie. A system will be developed for defining the specific behavior, describing the conditions that seem to precede the occurrences (antecedent conditions), as well as those that follow Tommie's behavior (consequences). Further, a count of the frequency of occurrence will be taken as a baseline from which to assess progress. These data will then be employed to identify the specific conditions supporting this behavior, as well as to formulate the types of conditions that need to be introduced to modify it.

Organizational Consultation: The organizational process consultant may be less directly interested in Tommie S.'s behavior or Ms. Casey's lack of professional objectivity and more interested in the nature of the organizational structures and processes that may be supporting such behavioral and emotional reactions. The process consultant may look at:

1. The process for assigning teachers to grade levels and the consideration given to previous experience with a particular grade level;
2. The institutional support provided teachers in terms of inservicing on topics such as classroom management and developmental issues, and
3. The process involved in preparing teachers for retirement. Specifically, the communication of policies regarding retirement, the provision for emotional support, and a mechanism to facilitate teacher pre- and post-retirement planning.

Dimension IV: Consultant Skills—Content or Process Expertise

In the previous discussion of organizational models, it was noted that some organizational consultants employ a technical focus, providing content, or technical expertise, whereas others focused more on the organizational structures and process. While it is obvious that consultation always involves some level of expertise, the focus or emphasis of the expertise may vary from content/technical expertise to process expertise.

This distinction of consultant skills as either "content expert" or "process expert" provides a fourth way to categorize the form and function of consultation.

Content Expert

The consultant who is operating as a content expert will most often directly provide intervention or problem solving (Kurpius, 1978). The content/technological expert consultant's goal is to provide the needed information, material, principles, or programs aimed at resolving the problem. The operative assumption underlying the role of content expert is that the current concern can be resolved by the direct application of specific knowledge or techniques. It is assumed that the consultant possesses the needed knowledge and techniques that the consultee lacks.

Most often, the technological/content nature of this consultation results in the consultant's embracing full responsibility for the design, implementation, and therefore ultimate success or failure of the intervention program. Decisions on how and when to proceed are made by the content specialist consultant and the consultee often is directed to the passive role of observer. Further, most often all technical control rests with the consultant and communication is typically one way—consultant to consultee. The goal of such content expert consultation is for the consultant to solve the immediate problem and the consultee to judge and evaluate it after the fact (Block, 1981; Kurpius, 1978).

While such an approach may be needed and useful in highly specialized and technical situations, it may be somewhat less useful with situations of a "people problem" nature. Under conditions in which the operational relationships, communication, or decision making patterns are the major source of the problem, a process approach to consultation may be more desirable.

Process Expert

Process consultation, as briefly presented in this discussion of organizational consulting, has been cogently described by Edgar Schein (1978, 1991) as involving work with a consultee to actively implement a planned change process.

The process consultant operates from the assumption that those within the system are unaware of the recurrent processes that have been or could be significantly impacting their performance and may be the source of their current difficulties. The process consultant will attempt to increase the consultee's awareness and understanding of the nature and impact of his or her system's patterns or processes. The process consultant may attend staff meetings, pointing out significant patterns of interaction, communication, or decision making; or with the consultee review formal communication processes, or lines of authority and de-

---

CASE ILLUSTRATION 2-5   Case Application—Tommie: A Technical or Process Approach

A consultant approaching the case of Tommie clearly has a number of targets that he or she could address (Tommie, Ms. Casey, the classroom, etc.) and from a number of theoretical perspectives. But regardless of the target or the theoretical model, the consultant could emphasize either content/technical expertise or process expertise.

The content expert may:

1. Provide Ms. Casey with a specific set of behavior modification recommendations;
2. Offer a "packaged" inservice program for teachers regarding classroom management, preadolescent sexuality, or retirement planning; or even
3. Suggest to the school board or building principal the inclusion of a sex-education component to the curriculum, or the development of a afterschool latchkey program.

Regardless of the target or the model, the content expert consultant brings to the situation a formulated set of principles, techniques, strategies, or programs that he or she believes have value to the current difficulty.

The process consultant, while certainly attempting to bring expertise to the resolution of the problem at hand, will approach it with a different focus. As such he or she may:

1. Assist Ms. Casey to review her current classroom management decisions and procedures in an attempt to increase her awareness of how these processes may be impacting the current difficulty;
2. Identify a faculty ad hoc group that will begin to discuss common professional concerns and generate possible actions to be taken (which may include the development of inservice training); or finally
3. Review with the relevant administrators operating procedures for teacher-grade level placement, teacher evaluation processes, or retirement programming as they may come to bear on this one specific work-related difficulty.

---

cision making; or even employ actual critical incident situations so that the consultee can review the dynamics of an event to better understand the processes operating and the impact of those processes. The focus of the process consultation is on those individual roles and functions, intergroup and intragroup dynamics, communication patterns, leadership styles, or decision-making mechanisms that appear problematic. The operational assumption is that through such increased awareness, the consultee will be able to adjust or in some way change the problematic process and thus increase the effectiveness or productivity of the system. Because the shift of emphasis is on the increased awareness and effectiveness of the consultee, the process consultant will typically employ a less directive role in which there is more shared responsibility (ownership) and focus on education and prevention. The process consultant operates more as a facilitator than director; more as a coordinator and less as the expert problem solver.

Exercise 2-3 is provided to help sharpen the distinction between a content consultant and process consultant.

Dimension V: Modes of Consultation—
Provisional, Prescriptive, Collaborative, Mediational

A fifth way to differentiate the various examples of consultation is to contrast consultation as a function of the particular role played by the consultant. Kurpius (1978) describes four modes of consultant behavior that could be used to differentiate consultation: the provisional mode, the prescriptive mode, the collaborative mode, and the mediational mode. Each mode and its application to the case of Tommie is presented below.

Provisional Mode

In the provisional mode, or what has been termed a "pair-of-hands" role (Block, 1981), the consultee retains full control of the focus of the consultation, and the consultant is expected

---

EXERCISE 2-3   Content or Process Consultation?

Directions: Below you will find a brief description of a consultation scenario. As presented, the case could benefit from either content or process consultation. Answer the questions found after the scenario and discuss your responses with a classmate, colleague, or supervisor.

Scenario: Mr. L. P. Good, president of a mid-sized importing business, called, very concerned about two of his employees. Mr. and Mrs. L both work for Mr. Good and are responsible for the management of two separate yet interdependent departments in the company. The work flow between the departments has not gone smoothly of late and each party blames the other for "poor communication." Mr. Good revealed that Mr. and Mrs. L are also having marital problems and he "wondered" if these were spilling over into the workplace.

Mr. Good stated that he has spoken to both Mr. and Mrs. L. in an attempt to "find out what is wrong—since we are all one big family here, and as Dad to my employees, I should be able to smooth things out, but you know...it's getting worse!"

1. As a content expert, what could you bring to this situation? _____
    _____
    _____

2. As a process expert, what part of the organization's structure and/or operational processes would you attempt to bring to Mr. Good's awareness? _____
    _____
    _____

3. If you could only function as one or the other (i.e., content or process) consultant, which would you choose? Why? _____
    _____
    _____

to apply specialized knowledge to implement action plans toward the achievement of goals defined by the consultee. It is as if the consultant, while possessing specialized knowledge or skill, functions as an extension of the consultee, employing his or her specialization in the manner designed by the consultee.

Even though the consultant is providing specialized service, the consultant does so at the specific request and direction of the consultee. As such, the consultant plays a some-what passive role, with decisions on how to proceed made by the consultee. The consultee selects methods for data collection and analysis as well as specifies procedures to be imple-mented. The consultee judges and evaluates the process and outcomes, while the consultant attempts to make the system more effective by the application of specialized knowledge. The consultant is most often operating as a technical/ content expert, providing a direct, yet reactive (i.e., crisis-oriented) service.

In this role, two-way communication is limited (consultee initiates, consultant re-sponds) and control rests with the consultee. Clearly the effectiveness of the consultant's intervention is strongly affected by the accuracy of the consultee's diagnosis and selection of the consultant's services.

Prescriptive Mode

The prescriptive mode is also somewhat of a reactive (i.e., crisis-related) form of consulta-tion in that the consult is typically initiated by the consultee, out of a sense of need.

While the service provided may tap the consultant's content or process expertise, the focus of the role is for the consultant to serve as a diagnostician and a provider of prescrip-tions for intervention. The application of the intervention is the responsibility of the con-sultee, who may be directed and guided in this application by the consultant.

The prescriptive mode operates from an implicit assumption that the consultee lacks the knowledge and/or skills needed for diagnosis and resolution of the problem at hand. The consultant provides that expertise.

Collaborative Mode

In the collaborative role, the consultant assumes that joining his or her specialized knowl-edge and skill with that of the consultee will increase accuracy of problem identification and maximize intervention resources and approaches. It is assumed that through such an expansion of resources and perspective the probability of effectiveness will be increased. In the collaborative mode, both the consultee and consultant play an active role. Responsi-bility for data gathering, analysis, goal setting, and intervention planning are shared. The responsibility for success and failure of the consult is also shared and communication is two way.

As with the preceding modes, the collaborative mode is viewed as reactive, with the consultant being invited into the referral, typically because of the consultee's concern. Be-cause of the interactive, mutual nature of the collaborative consultation, it allows for target-ing the dual goals of intervention and prevention. It is hoped that by working together—sharing expertise and perspective—not only will the current problem be resolved, but the consultee will be better able to resolve or prevent similar problems in the future.

CASE ILLUSTRATION 2-6   Case Application—Four Modes for Tommie

In order to more fully appreciate the role differentiation suggested by the modes of consultation, consider how a consultant from a provisional, prescriptive, collaborative, or mediational mode would assist Ms. Casey.

Provisional: As an added pair of hands, the consultant might take Ms. Casey's request to "... please help him to get it together" literally. The provisional consultant may meet with Ms. Casey to more concretely identify what she sees as the problem and what she wants the consultant to do with Tommie. Perhaps Ms. Casey wants Tommie removed from her class, since he is such a disruption. She may also want the consultant to see that his parents get Tommie professional help. If the consultant modifies Tommie's schedule to place him in another class and speak to the parents about professional counseling for Tommie, he or she would be operating from a provisional mode.

Prescriptive: Since Ms. Casey is in crisis, the consultant may respond to her need by providing suggestions on what to do with Tommie and/or for herself. Perhaps after getting a better understanding of the nature of the problem, the prescriptive consultant might suggest any one of the following:

1. Ms. Casey should talk to the principal about moving Tommie to the other 5th grade.
2. Ms. Casey should use the filmstrip and programmed unit on respecting each other (provided by the consultant) as a way of helping the class modify such behavior (looking up skirts).
3. Ms. Casey should be instructed to review material (provided by the consultant) on the behavior modification principles of extinction, shaping, and reinforcement so that she would be more competent to apply these principles to shape Tommie's behavior.

Collaborative: While each of the recommendations either enacted by the consultant in the provisional mode or provided to Ms. Casey in the prescriptive mode may have value, they were generated from only one source (either the consultee or the consultant). As a result of this unidirectional action, understanding and complete ownership for the interventions may not be shared, and a second potential resource would have gone untapped. The collaborative consultant will attempt to work with Ms. Casey in order to come to common agreement regarding the nature of the problem. As a result of their discussions, Ms. Casey and the consultant may agree that while Tommie is most likely neither an evil child nor a child with a sexual problem, his behavior in class is somewhat disruptive and should be modified. Further, from a sharing of ideas about what could be done (from the consultant) and the identification of the natural conditions of the classroom environment and the procedures that have already been applied (from the consultee), a new situationally specific application of the behavioral principles may emerge to which both the consultant and consultee had input and ownership.

Mediational: Even though the consultant has been asked to intervene in the case of Tommie, and thus is reacting to a crisis, the conditions of the referral also provide a number of targets for mediational consultation. While Ms. Casey's immediate concern is Tommie, it is clear that the process of teacher evaluation and the eventuality of her retirement also loom as future stressors that may negatively impact her professional performance and her students' performance. The mediational consultant will attempt to elevate Ms. Casey's awareness of the potentially detrimental effects of these possible stressors and help her begin to plan methods for reducing the negative stress of these events and/or increasing her ability to cope and adjust to such stress.

While this is certainly a proposed benefit of this model, there are also potential costs. One of the potential costs of a collaborative model is that it clearly involves much more energy and attention on the part of the consultant. Not only must the consultant employ creative problem-solving energy to address the presenting concern, but the consultant also needs to employ energy and skill to develop and maintain a relationship conducive to collaboration. Keeping the relationship open, mutual, and coequal is an intervention in and of itself, above and beyond the specific focus of the presenting problem. Quite often the consultee who initiates or invites the consult expects a more provisional or prescriptive role from the consultant and thus may resist the invitation to be coequally involved and responsible for the outcome. One author (Block, 1981) suggests that the consultee who prefers (or expects) the consultant to be the "expert" and operate from a prescriptive mode may see attempts at collaboration as reflecting the consultant's indifference or foot dragging. Similarly, a consultee who anticipates that the consultant will serve as an "extra pair of hands" (provisional mode), directly providing the intervention, may see attempts at enlisting mutual involvement between the consultant and the consultee as insubordination (Block, 1981).

Because of the unique nature of the collaborative relationship and the potential value of such an approach, the skills required to manage this dynamic will be highlighted throughout the later chapters of this text.

Mediational Mode

The consultant who is operating from a mediational role or mode will take a much more proactive stance than in any of the previously discussed modes. Unlike the previous modalities where the consultant responds to the request for service by the consultee, the consultant in the mediational mode will initiate the contact with the consultee, having recognized a recurrent problem prior to the consultee's recognition or experience of need. In this mode, the consultant will gather, analyze, and synthesize existing information as a way of defining the problem, and develop an intervention plan for implementation.

When operating from a mediational mode, the consultant not only has to address the problem at hand, but "sell" the need for intervention to the consultee. The consultant will have to demonstrate to the consultee the wisdom and value of consultation, since up to this point the consultee has been operating without crisis or need. It is as if the consultant is trying to demonstrate the value of fixing something, when the consultee feels that very something "ain't broke."

The developmental/preventive orientation of this form of consultation clearly distinguishes it from the previous reactive or crisis forms of consultation.

Exercise 2-4 will allow you to apply your knowledge of the various modes of consulting to another case.

Artificial Dichotomization

The categorization of consultation as either crisis or developmentally oriented, content or process focused, and provisional, prescriptive, collaborative, or mediational in mode, not

---

EXERCISE 2-4   Multimodes of Consultation

Directions: With a colleague, classmate, or supervisor, discuss how a consultant operating from each of the previously described modalities might approach the case. Discuss which mode you feel would be most effective.

Scenario: As a director of pupil services at a local college, you are asked for assistance by a residence assistant at one of the college's dorms. Carlos (the R.A.) explained that this was his first year as an R.A. and even though he has a handbook of rules and procedures to follow, he is having a lot of trouble controlling curfew violations on one particular floor.

Carlos explains, "The girls on 3-B just don't seem to care about the weekday curfew. They are up late, talking and laughing. And when I go over to tell them it is past curfew, they just tease me, saying things like 'Oh, you just wanted to peek,' or 'he's so cute . . . how can anyone take him seriously?' I just don't know what to do."

Provisional mode: _____

_____

Prescriptive mode: _____

_____

Collaborative mode: _____

_____

Mediational mode: _____

_____

Your choice? (why?)_____

_____

---

only limits the nature of the consultative interaction, but promotes an artificial dichotomization of the nature, the skills, and the roles of consultants. For example, returning to our case of Tommie, it is clear that a consultant entering the relationship from an technical/content expert frame of reference, while most likely operating from a prescriptive or provisional mode, could, if trained, augment this approach with attempts to facilitate the consultee's active participation in both the analysis of and intervention in the problem. With such consultee inclusion, what started as a content-focused, prescriptive or provisional mode of consultation now includes a process focus and a collaborative style. An either/or conceptualization of the nature and form of consultation is neither warranted nor desirable.

While each of the previous descriptive classifications has value in highlighting a particular aspect or characteristic of a consult, such classification can be misleading if it is interpreted as reflective of real distinctions. In practice, consultations rarely fit into one or another of the previous classifications. More often a consultation involves a mix of these dimensions. Further, it is not unusual for the nature, focus, and target of the consultation to change as it develops over time. Therefore, it is much more functional and supportable to view the nature and form of consultation as a multidimensional, integrated activity that takes shape and distinctiveness by moving along continuums reflecting consultee-felt need, consultant expertise, and degrees of collaborative involvement.

A Continuum of Felt Need

Rather than seeing consultation as either crisis or developmental in nature, it is much more effective to view each consultation as existing on a continuum of crisis or felt need (Figure 2-1).

From this perspective, each consult is viewed as involving both a degree of felt need, either immediate or remote, and the potential to address possible future difficulties (i.e., developmental/preventive opportunity).

Consider the case of Tommie S. Clearly, while Ms. Casey was experiencing an immediate need for intervention, conceptualizing the consult from only a crisis orientation would have blinded the consultant to the preventive potential of the consultation. The consultant who viewed this interaction as one starting at the extreme left side of the felt need continuum will perceive the value of moving along the continuum toward the prevention end as the immediacy and severity of the need subsides. Thus, in addition to assuring Ms. Casey that something can be done to reduce the disruption in her classroom, this consultant will also have an eye to prevention, looking forward to ways to assist Ms. Casey to better cope with the demands of a new type of student population (i.e., 5th grade) and the press of her upcoming retirement.

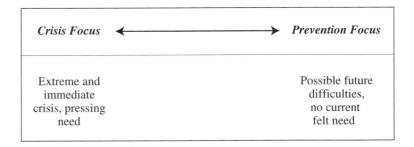

FIGURE 2-1:   A Continuum of Felt Need

A Continuum of Content-Process Expertise

Just as it was suggested that placing crisis consultation and developmental consultation on a single, felt-need continuum is more effective than dichotomizing these two forms of consultation, the same can be said for the content-process dimension of consultation. The position taken here is that it is more effective to conceptualize consultation as moving along a content-process expert continuum as opposed to being either a content/technical focus or a process focus (Figure 2-2).

The position taken here is that any one particular consult can be characterized as requiring both some level of unique technical specialization or content expertise as well as process expertise. A number of conditions (e.g., consultee need, original consultation contract, or consultee expectations) will help to define which end of the expertise continuum the consultant will initially emphasize. However, the point for consideration is that regardless of the level of emphasis, both technical and process expertise are important.

FIGURE 2-2:   A Continuum of Expertise

The unique technical expertise offered by the consultant provides a new resource, a new perspective, that is clearly needed to resolve the immediate problem. However, prescribing an intervention plan, in the absence of the input and concerns of the consultee or without fully appreciating the existing organizational dynamics or processes that contributed to the creation and maintenance of the current problem, will most likely result in an ineffective intervention. Without the consultee's understanding and ownership of the problem and the value of the intervention, the consultant's intervention program may at best be simply placed on the shelf with other "good" ideas, or even actively undermined by the consultee, should he or she feel detached and defensive. Further, without fostering the consultee's understanding and awareness of the process by that the problem emerged, or the processes that are available to the consultee for reducing the likelihood of this problem's recurring, hopes of prevention may be blocked. Rather than viewing a consultant as either a content or process specialist, it is more useful to see each consultant as varying along a continuum of expertise where the focus is more or less technical and content oriented in nature, or process focused.

Again considering the case of Tommie S., one could propose that the technical consultant simply observe the classroom and develop an appropriate system of behavior modification. A consultant skilled in behavioral techniques could certainly provide a specific remedial program for Tommie to be applied by either Ms. Casey as part of her classroom management, by the consultant, or by both.

From a process consulting orientation, the consultant would attempt to facilitate Ms. Casey's own analysis of the situation, along with her own identification of the specific factors characterizing her classroom process that may contribute to the current problem. In addition to more fully understanding the role that existing classroom structures and processes have played in the creation and maintenance of the current problem, Ms. Casey, through the support of the process consultant, may begin to identify those process elements that can be employed to remediate the current difficulty and prevent future similar problems from emerging.

Given the high level of experienced stress, the history of her own unsuccessful interventions, and the expectation that the consultant will "... help him (Tommie) get it together," the consultant may start by providing a number of specific technical steps to be taken. For example, the consultant could remove Tommie from the classroom and begin a behavioral contract system with Tommie that focuses upon his attending behavior. In addition to such technical intervention, the consultant will want to help Ms. Casey identify elements in her own style and classroom process and the impact these may have on the behavior of her students, including Tommie. Further, the consultant, acting as a process expert, may facilitate her understanding of this impact and the possible modification of her style to augment the work the consultant is doing with Tommie. In this way a consultant is employing both content/technical expertise and process expertise in the delivery of the service.

A Continuum of Collaboration

Finally, rather than artificially distinguishing the various modes of consultation as if they were exclusive and distinctive, it is more effective to view the role of consultant along a continuum of collaboration (Figure 2-3).

The approach suggested here is that consultation be viewed as taking shape along a collaborative continuum. The least collaborative mode of consulting would be that in which the consultant provides specialized services. The most collaborative form of consultation would be one in which the consultant and consultee engage in a coordinate relationship, mutually sharing diagnostic observation and coequally owning and developing intervention strategies. These two positions are identified as idealized poles at the extreme of the collaborative continuum, with the reality falling somewhere in between.

Regardless of position of a relationship on the continuum, collaboration as a process is valued. Thus, even while serving in a provisional role, the consultant values the need for the consultee's input into the specifics of service provision, as well as the need to provide educative and preventive feedback to the consultee. Similarly, the consultant operating from a prescriptive stance values and employs collaborative skills, to ensure not only consultee understanding of the prescription but consultee ownership of the intervention plan.

The model presented here clearly values and emphasizes the coordinate relationship, since this level of collaboration maximizes ownership and prevention potential of a consult. This is not to suggest that prescriptive and/or provisional modes should not be employed. It is recognized that for a consultant, serving in a provisional, prescriptive, or even mediational mode may be a useful tool for entry into a consultation relationship. These modes of operating can actually be tools that act as the first step toward establishing a collaborative consulting relationship. Kurpius and Fuqua (1993), for example, suggest that the consulting role be approached developmentally, in that during the early stages of a consulting relationship the consultant may have to function as expert and later move toward a more process/ collaborative stance.

While agreeing with the Kurpius and Fuqua (1993) conceptualization, the position presented here emphasizes that even when operating from one of these less than coordinate modes (i.e., provisional or prescriptive), the effective consultant attempts to maximize the mutuality of input and ownership and therefore includes elements of collaboration in the consult.

This would appear to be true in the case of Tommie S. The consultant would want to enter the relationship with Ms. Casey at the level of provision or prescriptive servicing, but

FIGURE 2-3:   Collaborative Continuum

attempt to maximize the active involvement of Ms. Casey along the entire process. Such involvement would not only increase the probability of developing a successful intervention plan for Tommie, but would provide the avenue through which preventive programming could be initiated.

Integrating Perspectives: A Multidimensional Approach to Consultation

The operational model to be employed here encourages the consultant to be flexible in the form and focus of consultation, allowing for technical and process expertise, crisis and developmental focus, and varying modes of collaboration. Like other attempts to differentiate types of consultation, the model presented here is also somewhat artificial. While detailing three discrete forms of consultation—client-focused, consultee-focused, and systems-focused—the reality is that these too are arbitrary points along a continuum of service, and the consultant will find him- or herself overlapping levels and/or moving between levels as he or she goes about the consultation.

This model represents an evolution from models initially presented by Gerald Caplan (1970) and Joel Meyers, Rick Parsons, and Roy Martin (1979). The model, as previously noted, places the varying levels of consultation along a continuum from direct service to indirect service (Meyers, Parsons, & Martin, 1979; Parsons & Meyers, 1984; Parsons & Wicks, 1994). While it is more typical to consider direct service and consultation as mutually exclusive, such need not be the case.

For direct service to be considered consultive, evidence of a triadic element is needed, showing the consultant interacting with the consultee. Further, such contact should be characterized by an exchange, both diagnostic and remedial, between the consultant and consultee with an eye toward servicing the client. Viewed from such a perspective, this continuum of more or less direct service consultation focuses on crisis intervention with a client focus at one end and a systems-oriented, preventive focus at the opposite end (Figure 2-4). The reality experienced by most consultants, however, its that consultation

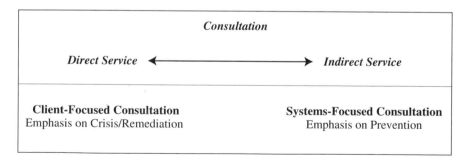

FIGURE 2-4:   Consultation: A Continuum of Felt Need

occurs somewhere in the middle, with the two ends merely representing conceptual reference points (Meyers, Parsons, & Martin, 1979).

As suggested in Figure 2-4, client-focused consultation (Chapter 7) allows for direct assessment of the client by the consultant and thus is the most direct form of consultation. Consultation focusing on the system (Chapter 9) uses techniques that may completely remove the consultant from direct contact with either the client or the consultee, thus proving to be the least direct form of service delivery. Each of these levels requires specific diagnostic and intervention skills and will be discussed in greater detail in later chapters (see Chapters 7, 8, and 9). However, a brief overview of each is provided below.

Level I: Client-Focused Consultation

The consultant seeking to modify the behavior, attitudes, and feelings of a particular client or clients may gather diagnostic data either directly (e.g., interviewing, individual testing, or observation) or more indirectly through the consultee. In either case, the focus of both the diagnosis and intervention is on the client.

The important defining characteristic of this mode of service, which distinguishes it as consultation, is that in both situations (i.e., consultant direct or indirect involvement with the client), the data collected and the intervention employed have involved the consultee. This point will be elaborated upon in Chapter 7.

Because the model presented employs an multidimensional, integrated perspective, the consultant in this interaction can work provisionally, by coordinating his or her diagnostic efforts and intervention plans with those of the consultee, or prescriptively, as would be the case when the consultant can employ his or her expertise to direct the consultee on how to better assist the client. Further, just as it might typically be the case that such a consultation occurs in the event of a crisis (i.e., the consultee experiencing difficulty with a client) where the goal may be to assist the consultee out of crisis, a second goal can also be of a preventive nature. The consultant can assist the consultee to use his or her experience with this case to improve his or her abilities to cope or even reduce the possibility of similar situations in the future.

Level II: Consultee-Focused Consultation

An approach derived from Caplan's (1970) consultee-centered case consultation, consultee-focused consultation still attempts to impact the client, but does so somewhat more indirectly by focusing intervention on changing the behavior, attitudes, or feelings of the consultee.

As noted previously (e.g., Caplan and Caplan, 1993; Parsons & Meyers, 1984), the consultee's difficulty with the case may be a result of his or her

1. lack of knowledge about this type of situation;
2. lack of skill in implementing that knowledge into skills of client management;
3. lack of self-confidence so that his or her use of this knowledge and skill may be forestalled;
4. lack of professional objectivity, which interferes with professional functioning.

It is reasoned that by increasing the consultee's knowledge, skill level, confidence, or professional objectivity, benefits will be accrued by the client. Thus, when compared to client-focused consultation, this form of consultation is more indirect in form.

In addition to impacting the client, a primary goal for this type of consultation is to serve as a educative mechanism for the consultee. The consultant, while working collaboratively, emphasizes a more prescriptive or mediational approach. The emphasis is on the consultee's level of need (crisis) and prescription of appropriate interventions, while at the same time keeping an eye to the preventive value (mediational) of this interaction. The consultant working at this level will employ expertise that is a blending of the consultant's technical content knowledge with the ability to facilitate the consultee's self-awareness and self-development (i.e., process consultation).

Level III: System-Focused Consultation

Since a system consists of a number interdependent elements, it could be argued that a consultant's efforts to influence the client and/or the consultee is in fact employing a system intervention. There are times, however, when the specific client need is best met by a modification of the processes or structures of the system within which the client operates. It is under these conditions that system-focused consultation is performed.

The goal of a system-focused consultation is to improve organizational functioning of the system. It is assumed that optimizing the processes, structures, and functioning of the system will indirectly increase the mental health and general functioning of the client and consultee within that system. Even though the specific focus of the consultation may be on improving communications within the system or modifying managerial or leadership styles, the impact will be on the overall functioning of the organization's members. The form of system intervention will not only remediate the initial presenting problem with the client but will also provide preventive services to others working within that organization.

Clearly, operating at the systems level is the least direct of all of the forms of consultation. It also could be argued that as the least direct form of consultation, system-focused consultation provides the greatest opportunity for impacting the largest number of potential clients and consultees with the highest degree of primary prevention (Parsons & Meyers, 1984).

Integrating Nature, Focus, and Modes

As with any categorization and compartmentalization of consultation, the model presented here is artificial, and if employed as a lock-step view of consulting can interfere with the flexibility needed for effective consulting. It is hoped, however, that this conceptualization of consultation along a continuum of direct-indirect foci will provide the reader with a cognitive map to employ in the process of diagnosing and intervening in any one consultation contract. It is has been this author's experience that this formulation of the levels of consultation, when placed within the backdrop of consultation as service along multidimensional continuum, offer a more flexible schema from which to integrate the various forms and foci of consultation.

For example, in a client-focused consultation that may have originated with a client problem (crisis) and a consultee who is seeking direct services (provisional) or recommendations (prescriptive), the consultant employing a multidimensional, integrated model of consulting can identify opportunities for preventive programming by targeting the consultee and/or the system at large.

Similarly, multidimensional opportunities could be experienced in a case of a system-focused consultation where contact was initiated because of a noticeable drop in worker morale (a crisis) by a consultee seeking prescription. In this situation the consultant operating from a multidimensional, integrated perspective may utilize the crisis as a point of entry and in addition to providing intervention strategies for the identified problem (i.e., low morale), employ the crisis as an opportunity to introduce preventive, process-oriented programs. Consider, for example, the consultant who is requested to provide a special program in communication and team-building skills to the middle line managers of a particular company. As the consultant responds to this request for technical expertise and provisional service, he or she may suggest that a more effective use of consultant time and energy would be to meet with representatives of both the managers and line workers in order to more clearly identify their concerns and develop a program tailored to meet their needs. Such a change in approach moves the consultee from a crisis/provisional orientation to a more collaborative, process view. The consultant now has the opportunity to "model" the value of teamwork and to utilize the organizational members as system resources for problem definition and remediation (i.e., collaborative process consultation). If, as a result of these meetings, the organization continues the work of the collaborative groups as a mechanism for ongoing planning and problem solving, then what may have originated as a content-specific, remedial concern has resulted in a process change with preventive impact.

Guiding the Consultant's Decisions Regarding Form and Focus of Consultation

A consultant truly needs to be a "jack of all trades" and master of some. In assuming an integrated multidimensional approach, the consultant enters a consultation relationship without a predetermined plan of operation. The consultant will be flexible and responsive to both the demands and opportunities of the situation, shifting the consult in terms of its nature, focus, content, and mode.

With so many modes of operation and points of focus possible, the role of consultant may soon become overwhelming. To be effective, the consultant needs to be able to select the level of service (e.g., client-focused, consultee-focused, system-focused) and the form of consulting (i.e., degree of collaboration) that will provide the greatest degree of immediate remediation and provide the highest level of prevention potential.

While there are no hard and fast rules to direct a consultant's decisions, there are a number of considerations that could be used as guidelines when selecting the form and level of a consultation. The process of selecting a form and focus for a particular consult will be influenced by the nature of the consultation contract, the nature of the problem and goal, the consultant orientation, and the consultee style. Each of these inputs (i.e., the consultation contract, the nature of problem and goal, consultant orientation, and consultee style) must be brought into the decision process as a guideline for the consultant's choice of mode, style, and focus. Each of these inputs will be briefly described below and expanded upon in later chapters.

The Contract as a Defining Element

It may seem obvious, but the consultant's form of operation will be at least initially defined by the nature and limits of the consulting contract. A consultant needs to understand and respect that, regardless of whether a written formal contract was developed or merely an implicit agreement with the consultee or representative of the system with whom he or she is consulting, a contract establishes a number of conditions that must guide the consultant's choices.

The contract marks the initial stage of any consult and involves achieving a level of acceptance and empowerment to perform the role of consultant. This initial stage has been identified as the entry stage (see Meyers, Parsons, & Martin, 1979; Parsons & Meyers, 1984). It is during this stage of the consultation process that the consultant needs to dissect what is expected by the consultee from what is required. Further, the consultant needs to begin to identify system and consultee openness to consultation as a way of discerning what is optimal from what is possible. How the consultant is accepted and empowered to work (i.e., entry) will influence the way a problem can be conceptualized and the level (i.e., client-focused, consultee-focused, system-focused) on which it can be approached. However, as will become evident throughout the remaining chapters, the process of consulting is fluid, and the effective consultant will continue to look for opportunities to re-enter, and even renegotiate, the consultative contract at levels that allow for more preventive and systemic impacts.

In the process of gaining entry and developing the working contract, the consultant should identify the nature and limits to the consultant's role, the objectives of the consult, the expectations and roles of others (e.g., consultee and client) in the consult, as well as other specific details of time schedule and manner of feedback or evaluation. It is important that the consultant be clear about the expectations of the contract, both in terms of what the consultant can and will do, as well as what the consultant will not do.

With this in mind, it is suggested that consultants approach contract formulation as an opportunity for intervention and education. It is important to establish, where possible, a broad-based contract that includes direct (client and consultee) contact along with indirect (systems) services. Further, it is important to contract to provide services of both a crisis and preventive nature. Finally, it is extremely important to emphasize the value of a collaborative mode of consulting along with defining the specific expectations of collaborative relationships (i.e., involving shared responsibility and effort on parts of the consultant and consultee). Clearly, establishing such a broad base will allow for more flexibility in decision making on the part of the consultant.

The Nature of the Problem and Goal

In the ideal world, the mode of consultation, the form of intervention, and the style of consultation employed should all be responsive to the specific nature of the problem presented, along with the nature and conditions of the goal(s) desired. However, there are many ways to conceptualize a presenting complaint. A single concern could be defined as a client-focused, consultee-focused, or even systems-focused issue.

Thus, while the consultant could possibly define both the problem and the goal at a number of levels, with each level helping to determine the nature and direction of the consultation, the consultant needs to adjust this conceptualization in order to make it coordinate with the conceptualization of the consultee. While there may be an optimal way of defining this or that problem and the subsequent goals, it is more important to present the problems and goals in ways that the consultee can embrace. The importance of consultant and consultee agreement regarding problem and goal definition has been supported by a number of researchers (Bergan & Tombari, 1976; Fuqua & Gibson, 1980; Kratochwill & Bergan, 1990). Decisions on how to proceed need to be influenced by the manner in which the problem and the subsequent goals are conceptualized. Such conceptualization must be tempered by the ability of the consultee and the consultant to find agreement.

Consultant Orientation

Gallessich (1982) argued that the factor most influencing a consultant's choice of approach is the "set" produced by his or her professional training and experiences. Because a consultant's personal and professional paradigm can be so influencing, it is important for the consultant to be on guard that his or her diagnosis and intervention planning reflects the problem at hand and not a biased approach. The consultant needs to be aware of his or her orientation, and sensitive to the possibility that this professional orientation or set can shape the way the problem becomes defined. The consultant also needs to be cautious that the strategies employed reflect the needs as presented and not simply the comfort level of the consultant with some strategies as opposed to others.

While being clear to operate in ways consistent with one's level of training, experience, and supervision, it is also incumbent upon the consultant operating from a flexible, integrated, multidimensional perspective to continue his or her professional development through ongoing training and supervision (a point to be discussed in Chapter 11). It is important that a consultant becomes increasingly aware of the variety of approaches available and begins to discern those methods and choices that are most functional and applicable to each situation. Such breadth of understanding and flexibility will require constant updating of professional skills and knowledge, as well as ongoing supervision and self-monitoring.

Consultee Experience, Expectations, and Style

When considering the manner in which one may consult, a consultant needs to understand the previous experience (both positive and negative) of the consultee and others within the system with consultation. It is important to identify how this previous experience and knowledge of consultation may impact the current expectations.

In selecting an approach or focus for consultation, the power of expectations needs to be taken seriously. Approaching the consultee with a style or focus that is so completely dissonant with his or her expectations may result in consultee resistance or defensive posturing.

While it is possible to continually shape (or reshape) the consultee's expectations, this may have to occur in small steps. It is important for the effective consultant to keep in mind that congruence between consultee expectations and experience with this or that consultant is a requisite to success.

In addition to considering consultee expectations and experiences when selecting a consultation approach, it is also important to attempt to blend the consultation with the unique style of the consultee (Pelsma, 1987).

One model for identifying personal styles was offered by Moore and Richter, and employed a two-dimensional representation. According to Moore and Richter, individual styles can be described along the dimensions of process/product and stability/change.

Process-oriented individuals tend to prefer to create ideas and enjoy the interaction with people, whereas those more product oriented focus on outcomes and achievement as satisfiers. The second dimension involves the individual's preference regarding the type of environment in which he or she seeks to function. Some individuals seek environments that are highly stimulating and changing, while other individuals prefer a more stable environment in which structures and supports exist and change is minimized.

To reduce the resistance to consultation and to increase the possibility of successful outcomes, the consultant should select an approach, target, and mode of operation with the consultee's personal style in mind. Clearly, a collaborative approach might be more congruent with the style of a process-oriented consultee in that it promotes dialogue and mutual influence. On the other hand, a consultee whose style approaches the product end of the continuum might feel more comfortable with a provisional or prescriptive mode of consultation. This is not to suggest a clear either-or approach but rather a point of emphasis.

Similarly, the consultant attempting to employ systems-focused consultation, focusing on modification of environmental structures or processes, may find it more acceptable to the change-oriented consultee than to one who is more oriented toward the stability end of the continuum. The personal style of the consultee who prefers stability would necessitate that the consultant introduces change slowly and in small, relatively nondisruptive steps. For this stability-oriented consultee, working at the client-focused level may be the easy point of entry into the relationship.

As with the previous guidelines, it is important to understand that these proposals are not hard and fast rules of consultation. Rather, what is suggested is simply that consultants consider the goodness of fit between the consultant's mode and level of operation and the consultee's personal style.

Summary

The current chapter provided a look at the wide variety of activities and practices that have been clustered under the rubric of consultation. The chapter highlighted the ways these various activities and practices differed in terms of goals, focus points, and roles to be played by the consultant and consultee. For this discussion, consultation activities were differentiated along five separate dimensions:

Dimension I: Nature of the Consult (Crisis or Developmental)

Dimension II: Problem and Goal Definitions (Depth and Breadth)

Dimension III: Theory and Assumptions (Mental Health, Behavioral, Organizational Development)

Dimension IV: Consultant Skills (Content or Process Expert)

Dimension V: Modes of Consultation/Consultant Role (Provisional, Prescriptive, Collaborative, Mediational)

However, the position presented within this chapter and carried throughout the text is that such categorization of consultation as either crisis or developmentally oriented, content or process focused, and provisional, prescriptive, collaborative, or mediational in mode, not only limits the nature of the consultative interaction, but promotes an artificial dichotomization of the nature, skills, and roles to be played by consultants.

While detailing the various dimensions (e.g., nature, focus, and consultant skill) along which consultation can be categorized, the focus for the chapter was on providing a model for integrating this diversity of role, function, and focus. The operational model employed encourages the consultant to be flexible in the form and focus of consultation, allowing for technical and process expertise, crisis and developmental focus, and varying modes of collaboration.

The model presented reflected an evolution from models initially offered by Gerald Caplan (1970) and Joel Meyers, Rick Parsons, and Roy Martin (1979), which categorized consultation along a continuum of more or less direct service, ranging from client-focused consultation, the most direct form of consultation, through consultee-focused consultation and finally systems-focused consultation (the most indirect form).

The wide range of potential forms, foci, and modes of consulting available to the consultant could prove overwhelming. The chapter closed with a set of considerations or guidelines to be used when selecting the form and level of consultation to be implemented. It was suggested that the process of selecting a form and focus for a particular consult should be influenced by the nature of the consultation contract, the nature of the problem and goal, consultant orientation, and consultee style.

$$Chapter\ 3$$

The Consultant as Agent for Change

The process of consultation is one of change and innovation. This really should not come as a surprise. Counselors are in the business of change. The client who is in pain and seeks assistance from a counselor clearly expects that things will be different (better) as a result of the client-counselor interaction.

The same is true for the counselor-as-consultant. The consultee enters a consultative relationship expecting that the consultant will provide, promote, or facilitate some form of change (improvement) in the conditions that led to his or her invitation into the consult. Thus, the counselor-as-consultant will function as an agent for change.

There is some potentially significant difference, however, between the counselor as agent of change for the client, and consultant as agent of change. These differences may at first be uncomfortable for the counselor new to consulting, and will often be unsettling to the system in which the counselor is consulting.

The current chapter will provide a look at the dynamics involved in the process of instituting innovation and change within an organization, highlighting the role of the consultant as one of change agent and innovator. Further, the chapter will discuss the basis of resistance often encountered by agents of change and provide a model for initiating change in the face of such potential resistance.

Specifically, the chapter will

1. demonstrate the role of consultant as inevitably one of change and innovation;
2. demonstrate that consultation is advocacy for system and client;
3. discuss the basis for system resistance to change; and
4. provide a Diffusion of Innovation model for reducing resistance and facilitating change.

Consultation—Inevitably Impacting the System

Organizational theory and research (e.g., French & Bell, 1990; Hackman & Oldham, 1980; Peters & Waterman, 1982) demonstrates that the behavior of the individual is greatly influenced by the climate, the structure, and the process of the organizational system within which he or she is functioning. Thus, organizational development and the creation of the optimum structure and processes for supporting individual performance could be a viable target for consultant innovation. In fact, Organizational Development (OD), as a target and form of consultation, is a field unto itself.

In Chapter 9, a number of diagnostic and intervention techniques and approaches targeted specifically on the structure, process, and environment of a client's system or organization will be discussed at length. Further, within that same chapter, procedures for deciding when organizational change is needed, the specific target for such change, and the model or theoretical approach to be employed will also be discussed.

But, organizational development consultation is not the only time the consultant acts to produce change or innovation within a system. Innovation and change within an organization happen any time a consultant impacts any one of the elements of that organization. Since the members of a system, along with the processes, structures, procedures, and products found within that system, are by definition interdependent, efforts taken to effect change in the client, the consultee, or any one of these process or structure elements, effects change within the system. For example, consider the situation of a client participating in an assertiveness training program. Not only will the client's attitude and behavior be modified, but that change may cause disruption in the interactional patterns he or she had established with significant others in his or her own life. Or, consider the case of the manager who, after attending a workshop on leadership and team development, comes back to her work environment and modifies the structures or procedures employed for work allocation. Impacting any one element in the system will cause a change in the system itself.

Thus, even without intending to impact the system, the consultant will inevitably function as an agent of system change. This becomes even more a point of consideration when viewed from the model of consultation that is to be presented within this text. Consultation as presented within this text is considered to be a process that is not only triadic, but is also one that emphasizes extrapersonal factors as contributors to a client's current problem. The model assumes that clients do not live and function within a vacuum or exist immune from the influences of those around them. It is assumed that the client's behavior occurs within the context of his or her psycho-social-physical environment. To be effective, the counselor-consultant needs to focus not just on the client's psychosocial dynamics but on the extrapersonal factors (e.g., role of the consultee, the tasks assigned, and the environment) contributing to the existence and maintenance of the current problem. In fact, if the intent of the consultant is to have long-lasting impact, then the consultant's efforts must be targeted to impact not only the client but also the extrapersonal variables in the client's environment (Kurpius, 1985).

In addition to seeking longstanding intervention, the position taken here is that a consultant is concerned with the broader issue of prevention. Consultants will need to consider the way extrapersonal variables may be changed in order both to maintain client intervention and to insure prevention. Consultants must help consultees recognize the level of interdependence that exists between the problem diagnosis, the intervention, and the contextual influence of the system in which they work (Fuqua & Gibson, 1980; Kurpius, 1985).

This emphasis on extrapersonal factors and prevention necessitates that in addition to effecting change within the client, the counselor-as-consultant will also, by design and intent, effect change within the system (Friend & Bauwens, 1988; Parsons & Meyers, 1984; Piersal & Gutkin,1983).

Status Quo, Change, and Issues of Advocacy

Historically, the political values and orientation of consultants have been presented as being either as an agent of change or an agent for the status quo. Rather than viewing the role of consultant as an "either/or" political position, it is more useful to perceive the consultant's orientation along a philosophical values continuum ranging from more or less status-quo-oriented to innovation-oriented (Crowfoot & Chesler, 1974; Pearl, 1974; Rappaport & Rappaport, 1981). This perspective more clearly reflects the reality that all consultation will manifest elements of innovation, while at the same time protecting the status quo of some of the components of the system.

One such model was presented by Pearl (1974), who described four positions along a consultative ideological continuum (Figure 3-1). According to Pearl, consultants at one end of the continuum function primarily to maintain the current conditions of a particular organization or system. Such consultants place their focus on increasing work efficiency and modifying workers behaviors to "fit in" the current work conditions. At the other end of the continuum is the consultant who identifies the existing system as dysfunctional and one requiring maximal change and revamping. This consultant operates as advocate for change. In between these two poles are consultants who attempt either to assist organizations to revisit and revise ineffective processes or who attempt to organize the "powerless" as a way of involving more within the system.

| Perpetuate status quo | Process consultant | Empowerment of powerless | Revamp system |

FIGURE 3-1:   Consultative Ideological Continuum

Even when presented as an agent for status quo, the reality is that the consultant is introducing change at some particular level. So the issue of change or no change is really moot—it is only a question of the level of change intended that needs to be considered, along with the possibility that such change may benefit some within the system while acting as a detriment to others.

Consultant as Advocate for Client and System

Implicit in many of the models presented regarding the role of the consultant is the opposition of client and system and the need for the consultant to advocate for one at the expense of the other. The consultant's role, especially when involving innovation of systemic change, is often confused with the role of advocate, even though their goals and boundaries are different.

Innovation as used here implies both the adoption and implementation of an idea or technique new to a particular organization (Brown et al., 1979; Mohrman, 1969; Zaltman, 1973). Innovation is called for whenever the current form of operations (techniques, processes, etc.) are ineffective in moving the system toward its stated goals and objectives. This is not innovation for innovation's sake, or to simply make something different! It is not innovation for the advantage of selected subgroup, but rather innovation to allow the system to reach its goals more effectively.

The traditional view of advocacy is conflictive. That is, there are a number of partisan groups within a system, and organizational procedures (e.g., tracking, curriculum development, promotion procedures, and supervisory models) work to the advantage of some and to the disadvantage of others. The advocate in this orientation attempts to gain advantage for his or her constituency at the expense of some others.

In consultation, the adversarial role is eliminated or at least minimized. This is contrasted with the traditional role of advocate, who, while seeking to support his or her client, most often does so by implementing adversarial actions on the client's behalf. Unlike the advocate who might impose or force him- or herself on a system, the consultant has been invited into a system and as such operates within the agency's values. The goal is to facilitate the system's achievement of its mission and publicly stated goals. This does not mean the consultant blindly supports policies or procedures when these policies and procedures are counterproductive or ineffective. However, it does suggest that change occurs not from a whim or the sole desire for change's sake, but rather that the change innovated by the consultant is in service of the agency's goals and mission, and thus in the direction and speed most facilitative of that system.

The consultant functioning as agent of change is truly operating as an advocate for the system. However, the model of consultation presented here does not counteroppose the client with others in the system. The client is an interdependent part of the system, just as the consultee is a part of the system. Change in the client, change in the consultee, or change in the process and structure of the system are all innovations within the system. Each is intended to service the system better, as well as all of those involved as they attempt to fulfill the mission of that system. Consultation as presented here is advocacy for both client and system.

When Goals Conflict

It is assumed that the goals of the system and those of the individual are not antagonistic. Therefore, in facilitating the development and healthy functioning of the individual within the system, one is also increasing the health of the system. Further, by improving the organizational structure and processes so that they are more mission driven, it is assumed that the goals of the individual will find a context that is more supportive and facilitative.

While it is desirable for a consultant to work with systems with which she or he feels congruent in both mission and goals, sometimes this is either not possible or not readily apparent. For example, when the consultee or system's members are actively engaged in unethical or illegal behaviors, then clearly the consultant must confront these behaviors and terminate contracts when they are not ceased. Because of the nature of the issues involved in such a conflict and the possibility of ethical compromise, this issue will be more fully discussed in Chapter 10.

While very few consultants will experience situations in which there is gross violation of ethical or legal principles, many may encounter systems in which the goals and processes, while not so radically incongruent with their own, do create conflict between the organization and the individuals within. Such conflict interferes with the system's goal attainment. Change in the individual, the system, or both is needed, and change that results in reduced conflict and increased harmony is the type of goal-directed change suggested here.

Being a consultant does not mean that one cannot advocate system change. While supporting the agency's mission and goals, the consultant can still advocate change in the practice and service of the system. When the organizational functioning, decision making, and other operations are incongruent with its own mission and goals, the consultant as change agent will address this incongruency. The realignment of the system functioning with stated goals and mission will have a positive impact on all of those within the system (consultees and clients). Similarly, when the operation and procedures of the system are detrimental to the members, the consultant's task may be to assist the system to redefine the responsibilities or re-envision its modus operandi in light of the original mission and purpose.

In those situations where a system is attempting to block, destroy, or inhibit the client's functional behavior and personal/professional development, the consultant needs to share his or her concerns and reluctance to support the system with the consultee so that decisions regarding the impact and continued usefulness of the consultant can be made collaboratively.

Reaction and Resistance

Systems are notorious for resisting any significant change in their current condition or manner of functioning (Argyris, 1970; Bennis, 1973; Blake & Mouton, 1976). The strength of this resistance is often difficult to penetrate and may even require a major social-political or economic force to open a system to change and innovation.

Consider the American educational system, for example. The 1958 National Defense Education Act following the launching of the Russian Sputnik clearly forced the American educational system to reconsider its current curriculum. Change was quick to follow. Similarly, the passage of the Education for All Handicapped Children Act (PL 94-142) in 1975 and the extension of that law's requirement of free and appropriate education to all handicapped children (PL 99-457) have caused significant adjustments in teacher preparation, school curriculum, and even physical organization of the plant. And just as these major social-political forces have forced change on the educational system, the passage of the Individuals with Disabilities Act has had a resounding impact on most public businesses and services. This act has forced such systems to reconsider their hiring practices, their programs for training, and their structures and processes of operation.

Radical and rapid system change typically requires such major social-political and economic forces. But radical and immediate change is not the only way to proceed, and clearly not typically within the realm of the consultant's resources. To initiate and maintain system innovation and change under less dramatic conditions it is necessary to understand the basis of system resistance and to be skilled in the employment of a model of system innovation.

Resistance as Self-Preservation

Initially, systems start out as open and responsive to the changing needs of the people they serve. As an example of an open system, consider the frontier clothier who responded to the changing interests, needs, and resources of the local townspeople, adapting inventory as a result of the townfolks' direct input. Other examples of an open system could be the one-room schoolhouse that adapted resources and curriculum as a function of the changing size and needs of its student population, or even a small contemporary business which, when starting out, has flexible worker rules and procedures, testing what works best at any given time.

Systems—be they textile firms, educational systems, or small businesses—develop structures, processes, and procedures, both formal and informal, aimed at channeling resources and energy toward goal attainment. Over time, these systems, which started out as flexible and responsive, begin to stabilize and concretize their structures and processes. These systems evolve into a state of stability, homeostasis, and potentially stagnation and death. What initially was developed as *a* way to achieve the system's goal, evolves into *the only* way to achieve that goal. Thus, processes and structures that started as informal and fluid, and as such much more adaptable to the changing needs and resources of the system, become rigid and static.

With this transition to a more stable formal structure comes a diversion of energy and resources. Now the system employs its resources for two ends. Energy and resources are deployed to continue its mission-driven activities, but part of these resources are also redirected to maintain the system's own structure and function. With the goal of self-maintenance, or system preservation, in mind, systems create organizational structures, role definitions, formal lines of communication, and a variety of procedures and policies aimed at keeping the style of operation and current character in its present form and configuration. Thus, where once change and adaptation were the rule of the day, innovation, experimentation, and change are now not only ignored, but actively resisted as threats not just to organization's stability but to its very existence. Any force, person, or idea that would indicate that the existing system be changed, be it as minute as expanding or modifying a job definition or as complicated as decentralizing the form of management, will run contrary to this self-maintenance goal and evoke system self-preservatory resistance (Napierkowski & Parsons, 1995).

Specific Conditions Stimulating Resistance

While any change may evoke a self-preservation response and thus system resistance, four specific conditions appear to actively evoke system resistance. These conditions involve change that threatens the balance of power, suggests the risk sunken costs, creates miscommunications, and/or challenges group norms (Kast & Rosenzweig, 1974). Understanding and ameliorating these conditions are essential if the consultant is to reduce system resistance to change.

Threats to Balance of Power

A primary source of resistance is the fear that innovation will upset the balance of power between the various subgroups existing within the system. Consider the case in which the consultant attempts to promote a change in the form of management and decision making employed in a particular system. If the innovation involves shifting from top down authority to a model of participative management, those who were previously empowered may feel threatened by the innovation. Similarly, the consultant who attempts to use nonprofessional staff in an educational setting in an attempt to expand counseling services (e.g., peer counselors, paraprofessionals, or regular classroom teachers as members on the child study team) may evoke some resistance from the professional counselors who feel they are losing some professional distinction and power.

Clearly, innovations that appear to be to the benefit of all members of the system or innovations that require the least amount of loss of power to any one group will be those that meet the least resistance. Consultants seeking to reduce resistance need to be sensitive to the different constituencies within the system and the perceived impact such innovation may have on their particular roles, functions, and power.

Sunk Costs

Concerns over utilization of available resources (i.e., time, energy, and money) needed to implement the change and the impact such resource reallocation may have on the system's stability serves as another source of resistance. The costs referred to include the psychic cost (e.g., stress, frustration, planning, and conceptualizing) involved with change, as well as the actual expenditure of physical resources. Without a clear sign of the return on the investment in this innovation, these costs are viewed as sunken, or empty, without return and naturally cause resistance.

It is important for the consultant to keep costs (both tangible and psychological) to a minimal, while at the same time demonstrating real, concrete and immediate payoffs or returns on the innovation.

Miscommunication

Quite often the individuals who are aware of the need (and potential benefit of change) fail to communicate the need and nature of the change in ways that can be understood and accepted by others within the system. Rumors, miscommunication, and conflicting data elevate system anxiety and confusion and with it increased resistance.

The very presence of the consultant within the system may be the occasion for the creation of wild rumors and miscommunications. Concerns over layoffs, realignment of jobs, new and threatening models of employee evaluations, and so on could all be generated in reaction to the lack of information or accurate communication and serve as sources of resistance.

It is important for the consultant to be sure to communicate to all involved the purpose and process of the consultation. Further, it is of great value to provide objective, clear, and consistent data as a base from which to derive consensual agreement on the nature of the problem and the possible strategies and avenues to pursue. The clarity and consistency of the data to be reported will highly affect the degree of resistance or acceptance experienced.

Group Norms—A Valuing of Tradition

A fourth major source of resistance in many systems is the rule of behavior (i.e., norm) that suggests that "we do it as we always have done it." Tradition is a powerful form of resistance. Change is a risk, especially if the traditional way of doing things has worked pretty well. But, when change is viewed as a challenge to a procedure that has become normative, almost sacred, resistance will be maximized.

Quite often the original reason for a particular process or procedure may have long passed and in fact those involved with the original decision to employ such a process or procedure may no longer be around, yet tradition can dictate that it be continued. It is not so much that the process is viewed as having much value, just that it has become such a part of the system's identity that tampering with it is mistakenly interpreted as tampering with the system's identity.

Consider, for example, the situation with Company L. This small plastics manufacturing company had shifted from a hourly wage system to a contract system for all employees. This contract system had been in effect for the past four years, yet the company still employed a punch clock. Not only were the workers finding the need to punch in and punch out an insult to their professionalism, but the payroll department was becoming overwhelmed with meaningless records and data. Even so, when it was suggested that this practice be terminated, a number of the older managers protested. Under these conditions the goal is not to compete with tradition or any way attempt to demean the status quo, but rather attempt to offer change as an alternative or a minor adjustment that can be used to affirm the value of the traditional way (Brown et al., 1979). In the case of Company L, the first step toward innovation was to simply require the workers to punch in (not out at breaks, lunch, or the end of the day), as a way of keeping a record of sick leave. This minor change was tolerable to the older managers, demonstrated that punch clock recordkeeping had value, and provided the first step to removing the system completely.

Addressing and where possible avoiding these and other points of resistance is essential for the consultant working as an agent of change.

Promoting Innovation: A Model of Diffusion

The consultant working as an agent of change operates within two different systems. The first system is the one to which the consultant had been invited to consult—a system of status quo. Through the processes of diagnosis and intervention the consultant begins planning a second system—a system of innovation and change. This second system has produced a set of knowledge and/or procedures innovative to the first system. It now seeks to create change by disseminating this knowledge, these procedures, to the first system whose function can be enhanced by using them (Meyers, Parsons, & Martin, 1979). In order to prove effective the consultant must act as a bridge between the system in pain and the system of innovation. That is, the consultant will in some way bring these two systems in line so that the information from the one can be disseminated and accepted by the other.

While there are variety of models of planned change (Argyris, 1970; Bartunek & Louis, 1988; Bennis, 1969; Drucker, 1985; French & Bell, 1990; Lewin, 1951; Mohrman, Mohrman, Ledford, Cummings, Lawler, & Associates, 1989; Schmuck & Runkel, 1985), the model to be discussed here is based on the Diffusion of Innovation model discussed by Rogers and Shoemaker (1971). This model has been adapted by this author and others (Meyers, Parsons, & Martin, 1979; Napierkowski & Parsons, 1995; Parsons & Meyers, 1984) and will be described in some detail below.

Diffusion of innovation is the term applied to the process by which new ideas are spread to members of a social system (Rogers & Shoemaker, 1971). Research that has investigated the process of diffusion of innovation (e.g., Havelock, 1973; Rogers & Shoemaker, 1971) has identified a number of factors that influence the degree to which innovation and change are embraced or resisted by a system. This same research would support a number of general principles that could be used to guide effective diffusion of innovation.

Five principles follow that have been culled from the social psychology literature on diffusion of innovation. These principles appear to have special utility to the consultant working as an agent of change (Meyers, Parsons, & Martin, 1979; Napierkowski & Parsons, 1995). The principles to be discussed are:

1. Keep innovation culturally compatible
2. Introduce change in small steps
3. Align change with opinion leaders
4. Increase consultant power and value
5. Move in a crisis

Principle 1: Keep Innovation Culturally Compatible

Acting as a bridge between the old system of status quo and that of innovation, the consultant as innovator will have to gain acceptance by members of the system where she or he wishes to introduce change. As such the consultant will have to understand and "speak" the language, values, and norms of that system. Similarly, the innovation that the consultant seeks to have accepted needs to be compatible with the cultural values and beliefs of the system.

This process of creating innovation in a form compatible to the culture of the parent system will require that the consultant consider

1. The mission and purpose of the system
2. The operating values and norms
3. The unique internal and/or external forces or presses impacting the system
4. Any unique history or tradition that may be affected by the change

For example, consider the following case of Sean, the Attention Seeker (Case Illustration 3-1).

In order to understand what happened in this particular situation, it is necessary to learn about the basic profile of the system in which the innovation was introduced.

CASE ILLUSTRATION 3-1:   Sean, the Attention Seeker

A consult with the counselor was requested by the fifth grade teacher. It appeared that over the course of the last five weeks, Sean, a fifth grade student, had been calling out in class and making inappropriate "animal noises." The teacher reported employing a number of techniques to stop Sean but all have proven unsuccessful. She noted that she has (1) verbally chastised Sean when he called out; (2) kept him in at recess; (3) made him take his seat out in the hallway, and (4) even threatened to send him to the principal.

In observing the class, the consultant noted that Sean was isolated from the rest of the class. The other class members worked in groups on learning projects, whereas Sean sat in his desk working on individual worksheets. The teacher reported that this was a result of Sean's disruptive behavior in the learning groups.

The consultant also observed that the teacher, who was in her first year of teaching, exhibited a lot of energy and enthusiasm going from table to table to work with the different groups of students. However, it was only when Sean called out or made an "animal noise" that she would attend to him.

Following upon her observations, the consultant suggested to the teacher that Sean was simply seeking attention and that her chastising and negative attending were actually reinforcing Sean's inappropriate behavior. The consultant suggested that the teacher begin to ignore Sean's inappropriate behavior (as a process of extinction) and begin to praise Sean when he was working on his worksheets (as an attempt to shape appropriate behavior). The teacher understood the concepts of shaping, extinction, and reinforcement and said she would try.

The recommendation failed. Sean's behavior grew more disruptive and the teacher lost confidence in the consultant. When the consultant followed up on the recommendation she found that the teacher failed to stick with the agreed upon plan. The consultant's innovation was not accepted.

Ms. L's fifth grade class was in a private elementary school. Among the many things the school valued and attempted to promote were respect, self-control, obedience to authority, order, and compliance. Further, a norm operating within the system was that every teacher was responsible for his or her own classroom and its management, and that a good classroom (and thus a good teacher) was one in which the children were quietly working on tasks and the teacher was in control.

The innovation recommended by the consultant, while theoretically sound, has a number of unique dimensions that seem incompatible with the culture of this school and therefore unacceptable to this consultee (i.e., the teacher). Behavior that was intermittently reinforced and now undergoing an extinction process at first tends to increase in frequency and/or intensity. Thus, the recommendation made by the consultant to ignore Sean's inappropriate behavior led to an increase in the disruptive behavior. This increase in Sean's calling out was in direct violation of the norm of working quietly. Further, the fact that compliance, obedience, and authority are valued, and the teacher is expected to be in control appeared to run contrary to the consultant's request for the teacher to ignore (or as she explained, "do nothing") when Sean acted out. Because of the felt incompatibility of the innovation with the norms and values of her own system's culture, the teacher simply failed to follow through.

Exercise 3-1 will help to highlight the importance of this particular principle of cultural compatibility.

EXERCISE 3-1   Innovation as Culturally Compatible

Directions: Below you will find a brief case presentation. After analyzing the presenting concerns and the description of a number of specific system characteristics, review each of the intervention plans suggested. With a colleague, classmate, or supervisor discuss the degree to which each intervention is compatible or incompatible with the current system profile. Which of the interventions provided would be most compatible? Could you create a fourth intervention that would be even more compatible and thus more likely to be accepted?

Problem: In general, the workers' morale seems to be low, and productivity has declined.

Situation: The company is an industrial manufacturing plant producing special tool dies for the manufacture of fiber optic material. The work is primarily line piecework, although each worker is required to produce a minimal daily quota. The employees have all worked for the company more than five years with the average worker being employed for eight years. The workers have a strong union that has fought for good per piece pay and good health and welfare benefits. While there is a working relationship between employees and management, tension is evident. Managers seem to use threats of punishment (deducting pay, restricting workers from overtime work, and formally writing the workers up as a step in eventual removal) if quotas are not met or workers appear to be working slowly.

Recommendations:
1. Develop a system or program of reinforcement for productivity above the quota. This system would include competition among the workers. For example, employee of the month would be the individual with the most productivity for the month. In addition to his or her pay, the employee could be awarded by having first choice on overtime, getting a dinner at a local restaurant, or movie tickets for self and family members.
2. Initiate a number of nonwork contacts between employees and managers. For example, develop a break room with coffee and snacks where managers and employees may mingle. Develop afterwork recreational activities—for example, volleyball, cards, aerobics, or others.
3. Empower the managers to be more strict. Encourage them to identify an employee who is not performing up to standard and attempt to make an object lesson of that employee. The managers should get tough on the employee, and dismiss him or her if necessary.
4. Begin to develop work teams in which small groups of managers, upper line administrators, and employees meet regularly to discuss concerns, productivity issues, and ways of improving work conditions. The decisions would be viewed as nonbinding and only implemented when consensus was established by all people involved.
5. (Write your recommendation): _____
   _____
   _____
   _____

Principle 2: Shaping—Introducing Change in Small Steps

While attempting to present innovation as culturally compatible, the reality is that innovation—change—will at some level alter the organization's manner of functioning and thus can never be completely compatible with the existing culture. Thus, in addition to introducing change that is compatible, innovation must be presented in ways that are perceived as tolerable and only minimally disruptive to the status quo.

Radical adjustments or changes are more likely to be met with resistance than those requiring small steps (Weick, 1984). Systems, like individuals, can be shaped toward change. Introducing the elements of innovation as small approximations of the desired goal may help to reduce the resistance to the innovation. Weick (1984), for example, found that a sequence of small wins (i.e., measurable outcomes of moderate importance) set up a pattern that can "attract allies, deter opponents and lower resistance . . ."(p. 43).

Innovations proving most acceptable will be those that (1) require the least amount of change, (2) require the least amount of resource expenditure, (3) require the least amount of adaption of roles or development of skills and knowledge, and (4) prove least disruptive to the organization's schema or frame of reference (Pettigrew, 1979; Torbert, 1985; Watzlawick, Weakland, & Fisch, 1974).

This last point regarding the possible negative effects of disrupting an organization's frame of reference is important and needs to be considered a bit more fully.

Bartunek and Moch (1987) discussed the concept of incorporating analysis of an organization's schema—that is, the way the organization interprets or gives meaning to its world—when developing intervention strategies. These authors suggest three different levels or order of change that go from the least amount of reframing of an organization's schema, to the most. And while these authors do not specifically refer to the process of shaping, it would appear that innovations requiring first-order change may be met with the least amount of resistance and thus prove to be a useful starting point from which to shape acceptance of the innovation.

First-Order Change

First-order change leaves the overall frame of reference intact while adjusting conditions within the system. Thus, while a number of processes may have changed, the members of the system perceive it as it was before. Consider the situation in which a small business adjusts its accounting and payroll process, shifting to the use of an external subcontractor. The shift may provide recordkeeping and tax benefits and may require an additional step (for example, faxing data to the company and having checks mailed back). It may even require an adjustment in the pay dates in order to allow for transferring of data. The overall frame of reference, however, for how the company and its employees function remains intact.

Change and improvement has occurred, and although the effects may be felt, the change has minimal or almost imperceptible impact on the overall frame of reference.

Second-Order Change

Second-order change requires some direct modification of the way the members of the system perceive it. This typically occurs when the innovation is such that it significantly impacts the form and function of the system. For example, in the rapidly changing economic environment of the 1990s, many large companies were forced to lay off, early retire, or even fire significant numbers of their workers as a means of cost reduction. Such change is often perceived as a sign of a failing corporation. However, for many of the more successful companies such size reduction was reframed (Bandler & Grinder, 1982; Kurpius, Brack, Brack, & Dunn, 1993). Rather than being presented as "downsizing" the cost reductions were defined as "right sizing." Rather than being perceived as a sign of weakness, the reframe was one of a company's becoming "lean and mean." Rather than portraying a loss of strength, a company was reframed to be perceived as sizing for speed and responsiveness to market opportunities.

The process of reframing is one in which the organization's perceptions of a situation are modified so that the situation can be viewed in a manner that facilitates the organization's ability to adapt and cope. It is truly helping the organization to view the change in a positive light, rather than focusing on the cost or disruption that it may entail.

Third-Order Changes

Third-order changes bring the full nature and implications of the changes to the consultees' consciousness. At this level the consultant will assist the members of the organization to recognize their schema, identify alternatives, and implement the steps necessary to modify their frames of references.

For example, a consultant was invited to work with a community of religious sisters who were experiencing conflict among their members. The presenting complaints included a loss of a sense of communality, the existence of cliques and small groups split along age lines, and a general level of tension and frustration that appeared disruptive to their mission.

After extensive data collection, the following became clear:

1. The community was aging and the reality was that new members were no longer joining. The community was in fact dying.
2. The community's mission was to educate. It enacted this mission by staffing fifteen elementary and two secondary schools. The reality was that the sisters were too few in number and too old to continue staffing all of the positions.
3. The residence, which originally housed 150 women, now housed only thirty-two, and the physical layout (e.g., long halls and numerous stairs) was not accessible for the aging sisters.

In this situation, the members had to recognize the incongruency between the way they saw the community (as it used to be) from the way it was and was going to be. Further, given this reality, the community then needed to identify alternative ways to continue its mission and purpose given the changing nature of their resources.

When proceeding to the higher levels of perceptual change, an increase in the general anxiety level of the system is experienced. Further, with higher levels of change, investment of increased resources will be required to complete the change in perception. Thus, a consultant attempting to promote change may experience more resistance when that change requires a complete shift or reframing of the organization's schema. Again, embracing such a significant change is facilitated by the process of shaping. Moving the consultee through the previous orders of change will help to make this very significant change more palatable.

Exercise 3-2 will help the reader employ the concepts of shaping and system's schemas in the development of an intervention plan.

EXERCISE 3-2   Change in Small Steps

You have been invited to consult with a family-run business that over the course of the last six years has tripled in number of employees. The owner and founder, Mr. G, reports that the workers (numbering thirty-five) don't seem to be as committed or invested as they used to be "back when we started." Mr. G complained that he has to tell them everything to do, just "like they were little kids!"

Mr. G stated proudly that he created this company. He noted, "Look, this is MY company and if they don't like it they can take a walk!" He defines the consultant's job to be to "shape them up, and get them in line." He noted that he was "not interested in any psychological stuff—just get them to do their jobs."

The data you collected revealed:

1. The company has been in existence for 22 years.
2. Of the thirty-five employees, four have been with the company 22 years, nine for more than 15 years, eleven for over 10 years, and the remainder at least 3 years.
3. The employees all reported an interest and commitment to the company; they also reported some concern over the fact that the company has grown and it no longer felt like family. They expressed feelings that they no longer had any say in the business, like they once did, and that Mr. G didn't seem to want to give them any power or authority to do their jobs.
4. The employees reported feeling like they were more invested in the company than Mr. G was in them!

Your data suggests that the workers would benefit from a more participative leadership style on the part of Mr. G. Many of the workers are truly committed and capable. They have exhibited an interest in the health of the company and have a number of good ideas regarding operations. You feel that a restructuring of the organization to allow the workers to take more ownership for the decisions and the direction and the quality of the work would be beneficial to all involved. But you also know that Mr. G will be resistant to any suggestions that seem to suggest that he is losing control and his workers are taking over his creation.

Using the principle of shaping and the concept of modification of system schemas, develop an intervention that may meet with limited resistance. Discuss this intervention with a colleague, classmate, or supervisor, attempting to identify points that may stimulate system resistance to its adoption.

Intervention: _____
_____
_____
_____
_____

Principle 3: Align Innovation with Opinion Leaders

Diffusion research (see Meyers, Parsons, & Martin, 1979) has indicated that to enhance the possibilities of adoption of the innovation, the change agent must concentrate his or her energies on the opinion leaders in the social system.

Social psychology research (e.g., Hollander, 1960; Napier & Gershenfeld, 1985) suggests that if members are respected and valued, they are given more leeway in adhering to group norms. Prestigious members who are innovative may be responded to in a number of ways. Other members may simply misinterpret the innovation so that it "fits" into the existing norms, or they may attempt to excuse it as idiosyncratic. But it is also possible that this nonconforming behavior or attitude, this innovation, may now be approved and become embraced by the other members (Napier & Gershenfeld, 1985). Thus, change and innovation, which is by definition outside the client-system's norms, may be more acceptable if associated with the opinion leaders.

Identifying the opinion leaders is not always an easy task. Opinion leaders are not always those individuals who occupy the formal positions of power, such as a manager, chairperson, or CEO. The consultant needs to be alert to identify those who appear most influential within the system, regardless of their formal roles or titles. While there are no hard and fast criteria with which to identify an opinion leader, any evidence that a person exerts influence over the functioning of the group's attitudes and behavior would be indicative of an opinion leader. These formal or informal leaders are the ones with whom an alliance needs to be forged and with whom innovation needs to be associated.

Identification and alignment with such opinion leaders often happens by engaging in the informal mechanisms and rituals in a system. Quite often taking a coffee break at the same time as those who appear to be the opinion leaders, or by engaging in committee work, and formal social activities and informal gatherings (after-work volleyball, or end of the week "happy hour," etc.) can provide the mechanism by which the consultant can come to know and be known by the opinion leader(s).

Exercise 3-3 will assist the reader in employing the concept of opinion leader in his or her own setting.

Principle 4: Increasing Value and Power as Consultant

Change agents are more successful when they are viewed as being of value to the system. When consultants have demonstrated a value to those of the client-system, they are more likely to have the power to effect system change, and to have innovation embraced. Value can be enhanced by (1) doing something, (2) increasing one's power, and (3) developing a collaborative relationship. While the issue of collaborative relationship will be discussed in some detail, the importance of "doing something" and "increasing one's power" is presented below.

Do Something

The consultant seeking to increase his or her value and power within the system needs to demonstrate value to the members of the system as rapidly as possible. This may be particularly difficult for a consultant who is new to the system because he or she has no history of effectiveness from which to draw value. Under these conditions the consultant needs to

EXERCISE 3-3   Opinion Leaders

Directions: Identify a work or social group with which you are familiar. Identify by name and, where appropriate, formal title or role four individuals who are active in that group. Place a check mark under the name of the individual who most exemplifies the indicators listed. Next, share your observation with another member of that same group. Covalidation may be indicative of the identification of the group's opinion leader.

Name of Group:_____

Names/Roles

1_____   2_____   3_____   4_____

Indicators

1. Keeps the group on task

2. Sets direction for group

3. Most directly influences mood or tone of group

4. Tends to be most listened to

5. Most often sought out for advice

6. Individual with whom others wish most to relate

7. Perceived as most important to the group

8. Most often sought out at breaks in the group's meetings

9. Individual whose absence would be most felt

10. Seen as the prime resource for the group

identify any role or function that may be of value to the members of the system and attempt to implement that role or function.

The concept of doing something is not restricted to the realm of the esoteric or the strictly professional. Quite often a consultant can begin to be perceived as valuable after serving a very practical function. Consider the following case illustration.

> *Dr. R was a school psychologist assigned to work in a particular inner-city elementary school. The school had had a series of very negative experiences with previous school psychologists and as a result were somewhat nonresponsive to Dr. R's attempts to work with the teachers and staff. Dr. R attempted a number of different approaches, such as sharing interesting articles that he had read and going to faculty meetings and contributing to discussions, but nothing seemed to break through the resistance. In spite of all his professional competence and sophistication, the event that resulted in his breaking through the resistance involved his driving ability.*
>
> *The school had scheduled a day at the zoo for the lower grades (1–3) as a reward for children's participation in a "Read-a-thon." As might be anticipated, the children were extremely excited about the day, and teachers, while somewhat apprehensive about monitoring the children, all felt that it would be a wonderful experience. Because of a mix-up with insurance paperwork, the bus company contracted to transport the children the one-half mile to the zoo canceled on the morning of the planned trip. As fate(?) might have it, Dr. R was licensed to drive a school bus and he volunteered to transport the children (a total of five trips both ways). Further, he suggested calling the central office to see if a small bus could be made available to the school. Not only was his suggestion successful, but his willingness to roll up his sleeves to help with this problem, along with the rapport he demonstrated with the children as he transported them to the zoo, impressed the teachers and parents involved and resulted in a lowering of their resistance to working with him.*

Thus, while a consultant wants to demonstrate that his or her interventions are useful and of value and thus increase his or her own perceived value within the organization, oftentimes perceived value can be enhanced by meeting any of the system's felt needs—even when those needs require practical, rather than professional, knowledge and skill.

Increase Value by Increasing Power

The ability to influence another person to modify behavior or attitudes is increased by the position of social psychological power. Counselors may resist the idea of employing power to influence another. This may be due to the fact that too often power is narrowly equated with coercion or authoritarianism (Lambert, 1973; Reger, 1964; Martin, 1978). There are a number of forms of social power besides that of coercive power or authoritarianism. And while the use of coercion or authoritarianism may be inappropriate for use in collaborative consultation, other forms of power are more or less available and appear appropriate in consultation (French & Raven, 1959; Martin, 1978; Meyers, Parsons, & Martin, 1979; Napierkowski & Parsons, 1995; Raven, 1965; Strong, 1978). One classification of social power was put forth by French and Raven (1959) and included:

1. Coercive power or the ability to reward and or punish another.
2. Legitimate or traditional power, that is, the power that stems from society's sanctioning of a person's role and authority to control the attitudes and behavior of another, as may be the case with a parent or public official.
3. Informational power is that power accrued because the information provided by one person is viewed as highly relevant and useful by the second.
4. Expert power, or the power that we associate to a person who is perceived as having special knowledge and skill that is valued or necessary by another. This is similar to informational power except that the focus is on the person (in expert power), whereas in informational power it is on what the person says.
5. Referent or identification power is the power to influence that accrues to a person because he or she is attractive, a person with whom another wants to like and be liked by—in short, a role model. Most often in referent power a party is viewed as having characteristics similar to the second person or desired by the second person so that the second party identifies with the first. It is this process of identification that serves as the source of influence.

Of these forms of power it would appear that two, expert and referent power, are appropriate avenues for a consultant to demonstrate value within the system.

Expert Power.   The very nature of asking the consultant for assistance would suggest that the consultant is perceived as having some form of expertise, and thus expert power. When the particular knowledge or skill proves useful to those within the client-system (e.g., the consultee), then the consultant's value and resultant power are increased. And as might be assumed, as the consultant's value and power increase, resistance to the consultant's innovations should decrease.

Research suggests that the perception of expertise and the resulting assignment of expert power to another can be enhanced by indications of advanced education, relevant experience, and higher social status—for example: awards, citations, or affiliations with prestigious institutions (e.g., McGuire, 1969; Martin, 1978). Therefore, consultants attempting to increase their expert power should find ways to communicate their experience and education and highlight factors that could increase their perceived social status (e.g., articles written, testimonials from other consultees, special awards, or recognitions received.)

In addition to these general indicators of expertise, a consultant seeking to effect change should develop a small number of content areas of real expertise over and above his or her general knowledge and competency. And, as suggested by Martin (1978), the consultant should be more careful to limit consultation to these areas of real expertise.

While an important ingredient in effecting change, expert power alone is not enough. Consultation as presented here is a relational process. The consultee needs to feel as if he or she can approach the consultant and work openly with him or her. Thus, in addition to having specialized knowledge and skill, the consultant must also exhibit conditions that facilitate rapport and connectedness with the consultee (Caplan, 1970; Dinkmeyer & Carlson, 1973; Parsons & Meyers, 1984). In fact, relying solely on expert power may be detrimental to the effectiveness of the consultant in that it places the consultant in a one-up position, inviting the consultee to anticipate prescription or provision from the "expert" consultant. Bennis, Benne, and Chin (1969) noted: "The extent to which a change agent is successful (that is, influential) is dependent on the degree to which he is perceived as susceptible to influence by the client" (p. 148). Thus, one could argue that the more a consultant is perceived as the "expert," the less he or she is perceived as open to influence by the consultee. Therefore, while exhibiting some expert power, it is important to develop the collegial relationship, one in which the consultant is perceived as coequal, approachable and susceptible to consultee influence. Under these conditions, a second form of power, referent power, seems to hold special value.

Referent Power.   When the consultee perceives the consultant as manifesting feelings, attitudes, interests, and behaviors similar to those of the consultee or to those that the consultee would like to possess, the consultant has referent power. Thus, the consultant's effectiveness will be enhanced when the consultant shares certain values, personal characteristics, behaviors, background experiences, knowledge, and interest with the consultee. Being able to relate to the local sports teams or political scene, sharing a common cultural background, or simply enjoying the same type of food, music, or entertainment increase one's referent power. Clearly the directive is for the consultant to empathically and in a nonjudgmental manner get to know the consultee while at the same time providing appropriate and parallel self-disclosures. This is often best achieved in informal settings such as the lunchroom, afterwork social settings, break rooms, or even at the water cooler.

Blending and Balancing Power.   The use of expert and referent power might at first appear somewhat incompatible, since it is difficult to highlight one's unique expertise while at the same time emphasizing one's similarity. In fact, Aronson, Willerman, and Floyd (1966) demonstrated that with increased expert power comes a reduction in attraction value and overall influence. It could also be argued that if one is perceived too similarly then little or no expertise will be assigned and thus the person will not be sought out for assistance.

A proper blending of expertise and referent power seems desirable (Cienki, 1982; Martin, 1978; Parsons & Meyers, 1984). The consultant who has accrued a good deal of referent power will benefit from emphasizing his or her expertise. Similarly, the consultant who is perceived as "expert" will do well to balance this perception by highlighting points of commonality between him- or herself and his or her consultee. This becomes a particularly important point for consultants working from within the system, versus those who are called in from without.

In most situations consultants who are internal to a system have had the opportunity to disclose and to be known. These consultants may be viewed as part of the culture—that is, similar in goals, interests, and style with the others—and thus have accrued referent power. Under these conditions it may be important for the consultant to publicize recent professional involvement or scholarship, communicate (even using professional jargon) knowledge of relevant information, and demonstrate (perhaps by providing in-service training) competency in specific areas of expertise. Similarly, for the external consultant, energy should be given to making the personal connections with the consultee. While the external consultant's advanced marketing package most likely highlighted his or her degrees, experience, and previous successes (testimonials), the person of the consultant is still an unknown. Thus, the external consultant would do well to spend time in the informal settings getting known and getting to know the consultee.

Demonstrating practical and immediate usefulness (i.e., doing something) along with developing expert and referent power are useful tools for the consultant seeking to decrease resistance and diffuse innovation. Exercise 3-4 will help the reader more fully understand the concepts described and begin to concretely apply these concepts to his or her current professional experience.

Principle 5: Move in a Crisis

The old adage "if it ain't broke, don't fix it" bodes poorly for those of us with prevention focus. When systems are at points of equilibrium and stability and are not experiencing "pain," resistance to change will be at its maximum. Thus, a final principal of diffusion of innovation would be to be alert to signs of instability and disequilibrium as opportunities for diffusing innovation. The directive for the consultant is to move in a crisis.

When experiencing a crisis, individuals and systems are placed into a disequilibrium; what results are feelings of imbalance and urgency. For example, legislation regarding sexual harassment has placed the practice and procedures of many organizations into disequilibrium. Similarly, legislation supporting open access to the workplace has forced many organizations to reconfigure the workplace and reconsider hiring and training procedures.

When a system's stability has been disturbed by forces outside—such as legislation or forces internal to the system, such as loss of market share, unionization of workers, and the like—change is more possible. When a system is in pain, it is more receptive to possible solutions that will help lead it back to a point of stabilization. The consultant seeking to act as an agent of change needs to be sensitive to points of disequilibrium and to be able to respond at moments of crisis.

However, waiting for the disruption to the stability of the organization before having innovations embraced may not be desirable. A consultant most often hopes to gain entry and diffuse innovation prior to the experience of such disruption. Consultants may need to use data feedback in order to emphasize discrepancies and problems in an attempt to create or highlight a sense of urgency and crisis, thereby producing that disequilibrium that can allow innovation. For example, providing a principal with demographic data and projections on the declining tax base for the school district may serve as the stimulus for consideration of innovation. Or, consider the consultant who was seeking to innovate the nature of the workplace. The consultant was able to point out to the employer the statistics on her changing workforce, which demonstrated an increasing number of single-parent workers. Even though the company had not experienced any crisis, the data was used to facilitate the acceptance of changes in company health policies, space utilization (e.g., on-site daycare), and even social events (parties for employees and friends, and not just employees and spouses). Under these conditions the consultant is using data to reframe current conditions and to assist the consultee to accept the eventual pain. But it is not in embracing the eventuality of pain that change is accepted. It is in the focusing on steps to be taken—the intervention or more accurately the prevention—which provides the motivation for change. It is this sense that one's pain is reducible (or avoidable) that motivates change (Kurpius, Fuqua, & Rozecki, 1993).

Exercise 3-5 will help clarify this point of moving in a crisis.

EXERCISE 3-4   Increasing Power and Value

Part I Directions: Below is a description of a presenting complaint, along with the character-istics of the consultee and the system involved in this consult. After reading the descriptions, answer the questions that follow. It would also be beneficial for you to share your response with a colleague, classmate, or supervisor since each consultant differs in both areas of exper-tise and referent abilities and thus will most likely respond differently to the opportunities pre-sented.

Presenting Complaint

The consultee (Dr. Seronita Torres) came to you with a problem she is having with one of her clients. The client is Regina, age 14. Regina is an IV drug user (heroin) who was court assigned to the drug and rehab center where Dr. Torres is currently employed. In addition to her drug involvement, Regina has been living on the streets for the past three months and only recently has met a man (age 31) whom she feels she loves. Regina told Dr. Torres that she was consid-ering secretly trapping her boyfriend into marriage by becoming pregnant. Dr. Torres has at-tempted to use a number of therapeutic interventions to get Regina to see the potential danger involved with her decisions, but all of these have proven unsuccessful. Dr. Torres admitted that she does not know what to do with Regina and would really like your assistance.

Consultee and Consultee Setting

Dr. Torres is a 57-year-old counselor with her doctorate from the University of Mexico. She has been in this country eighteen months and has been working at her current position for only three weeks. She states that she feels somewhat "out of her element" working in her current setting.

The center in which she is working services an inner-city, poor population of hardcore drug users. Most of the clients are either Hispanic Americans or African Americans. Dr. Torres re-vealed that she has limited knowledge and experience working with this population and that she took this position as a temporary post while she completed her requirements for licensing for private practice. Dr. Torres noted that she was able to get the job because of her political connections.

Dr. Torres comes from a very affluent and influential family in Mexico City. She expressed her difficulty with truly understanding the experience of the people with whom she works giv-en her background, which included private schooling, extensive family affiliations, and "strict Catholic values." Dr. Torres also expressed her interest in and concern about the role and future of females within the Hispanic culture and she is very politically active on women's rights.

You are the first external consultant to be used by the staff at the Center. Dr. Torres stated that there have always been resources available for utilization of external consultants, but the other staff members "have generally felt that unless a person lives this existence (i.e., working with this population) there is no way he or she could help." While Dr. Torres wants some as-sistance, she is also very concerned about how her peers and supervisors may perceive her if they know she sought outside consultation.

Questions

Consider each of the following and discuss in as concrete terms as possible.

1. Expert Power: What specific area of expertise do you bring to this situation? How might you convey this expertise to Dr. Torres and to the other staff, as a way of diffusing the potential resistance to your presence?
2. Referent Power: Identify at least two areas of dissimilarity and two areas of similarity between yourself and Dr. Torres. What elements could you highlight as a way of elicit-ing referent power? How would you reduce the perception of difference?
3. Do Something: Given the concerns expressed by Dr. Torres, what one, immediate thing would you do in order to demonstrate your value?

EXERCISE 3-5   Highlighting and Moving in a Crisis

Part I Directions: For each of the following scenarios identify (a)the felt, or perceived area of crisis; and (b)how you as consultant could use that as a point of diffusing innovation and reaching the listed goal.

Scenario 1

Conditions: The consultee, Mr. LP, president of LP Widgets, invited you in as consultant. Mr. LP is very upset at the amount of money his company loses because of workers' taking off sick days, the high rate of turnover (workers quitting), and even on-the-job accidents. He wants you to come in to "train the managers to keep the worker to the grindstone!"

Problem: Decision making and communication is centralized, top-down, and authoritarian.

Goal: Move decision making to a decentralized, worker/team model. Empower workers to help define work conditions and processes. Institute a Total Quality Management approach.

Consultant Strategy: _____

_____

Scenario 2

Conditions: The consultee is a high school principal. Her school has recently experienced an increase in student population and faculty as a result of absorbing the students and faculty from a neighboring school that was forced to close. Recent student conflict (gang fights) has stimulated the principal to call you in to provide "assertive discipline training" for the teachers, "so that they can learn to intervene before problems emerge."

Problem: In addition to the student problem with assimilating, the faculty from both schools were exhibiting symptoms of burnout. Faculty from the school that had closed had not adequately grieved the loss of their school and its tradition. The host faculty felt resentment toward the crowding and were somewhat jealous of the attention the new faculty were receiving. Both faculties reported feeling disempowered, having not been consulted or really even advised about the move until the very last moment.

Goal: To reduce the faculties' feelings of disenfranchisement, and facilitate faculty ownership and decision making around the steps to be taken to develop a blended identity of the two schools.

Consultant Strategy: _____

_____

Scenario 3: Local Children and Youth Services Agency

While there are no immediate problems that the workers or supervisors report, you observe that the amount of work as well as the complexity and severity of the cases managed has clearly increased over the course of the last year.

Problem (identify potential problem area):

_____

_____

Goal (identify change in the current operation that may prevent the problem from developing):

_____

_____

Strategy (identify how consultant could reframe the lack of pain to encourage change):

_____

_____

Summary

The role of the consultant is clearly one of change. A consultant not only intervenes with the client, but does so in ways that impact the extrapersonal variables effecting the client. Even when the specific focus of the consultation IS NOT on organizational change, the preventive extrapersonal focus of consultation will result in system change. Thus, the counselor-consultant is truly an agent of change, working to bring the system's goals and individual's goals into harmony in order to reflect the mission for which they have come together. Attempting to serve as advocate for the client and advocate for the system is possible but not without points of tension and conflict.

Systems have developed a number of mechanisms through which they attempt to maintain the status quo and thus by definition resist any form of change that may be perceived as threatening to the balance of power, the utilization of resources, or simply the existing state of functioning. Consultants need to be able to recognize these points of system resistance and navigate through them using a model of planned change.

The chapter presented an adaptation of one model of change, the diffusion of innovation model (Rogers & Shoemaker, 1971; Meyers, Parsons, & Martin, 1979; Napierkowski & Parsons, 1995). This model suggests that innovation is most readily embraced when a number of principles are taken into consideration. The principles discussed were (1) keeping innovation culturally compatible, (2) introducing innovation in small steps (shaping), (3) aligning innovation with system opinion leaders, (4) increasing a consultant's value and power within the system, and (5) introducing change at times of system crisis.

Resistance to innovation is not limited to the system level. Resistance is also experienced at the interpersonal level of the consultant and consultee. The next chapter will begin to look at the nature of the consultation relationship, conditions that evoke interpersonal resistance, and strategies for reducing or overcoming that resistance.

Chapter 4

Working through Consultee Resistance

Just as systems often respond to consultation in a self-protective, somewhat closed and defensive manner, so to may a consultee. A consultee's resistance to consultation may be a direct reflection of his or her own issues and concerns, the style and the characteristics of the consultant, or the unique nature of the consultation relationship.

It is sometimes hard for a consultant to recognize that while his or her intentions may be pure, ideas reasonable, and communication clear, resistance may still be encountered! In fact, it may be reasonable to assume that resistance is a probable (albeit not inevitable) accompaniment to any consultation.

Consultants who are ill-prepared to work with resistance, when encountered, will often attempt to push through it or overcome it. Such consultants may get louder, more forcible, and more directive in their attempt to overcome resistance. This approach is not only ineffective but is actually counterproductive.

Peter Block (1981) suggests that while many people use the phrase "overcoming resistance" to describe what a consultant needs to learn, the reality is that resistance need not be defeated. This author would agree with Block (1981) and suggest that resistance need not be an adversary, nor something to be subdued. Rather, resistance is an important element to the consultation dynamic and needs to be understood and embraced. Accepting and working with resistance can lead a consultant to better understand the consultee. Working with the consultee's resistance can result in the development of a more productive collaborative relationship.

Therefore, to be effective, a consultant needs to maintain emotional objectivity when confronted with resistance. The effective consultant needs to understand the nature of resistance and employ skills to *work with,* rather than push through, consultee resistance. Because the knowledge and skill required to work with consultee resistance is so essential to effective consulting, they will be the foci of the current chapter. The information and exercises provided in this chapter will assist the reader to develop the understanding and consultative skills needed for effectively working with consultee resistance. More specifically, the chapter will facilitate the development of the reader's ability to

1. Diagnose the existence and source(s) of resistance, including those originating with the consultee, the consultant, or the consulting relationship
2. Embrace resistance as part of the growth and change process (rather than as a personal attack)
3. See the process of the consulting relationship as an invaluable resource to the consultation and as such accept the resistance as an opportunity for increased clarity and direction in the relationship
4. Employ strategies to work with resistance, including assisting the consultee in identifying his or her emotional concerns or uncertainties that may serve as the foundation for this resistance
5. Develop preventive strategies aimed at reducing the risk of resistance

Resistance in the consultative relationship has received a great deal of attention in the literature (e.g., Abidin, 1975; Dorr, 1977; Grieger, 1972; Gutkin & Hickman, 1990; Hughes, 1988; Kratochwill & van Someren, 1985; Piersel & Gutkin, 1983; Tingstrom, Little & Stewart, 1990; Witt, 1986), and it is this and other research that serves as the basis for the ideas and recommendations that follow.

Diagnosing Resistance: The First Step in Working through Resistance

Resistance may be defined as any behavior that thwarts the probability of a successful process or outcome (Cormier & Cormier, 1991). In consultation this is often manifested as a consultee's failure to actively engage in the problem-solving process (Piersel & Gutkin, 1983).

While potentially quite frustrating for the party whose efforts are being thwarted, resistance is not by definition undesirable, nor always irrational, and rarely is it not understandable. Understanding the basis for consultee resistance—be it reasonable or not—is an important first step to the process of working with that resistance.

Resistance—A Reasonable Response

A consultee may exhibit resistance as an attempt at self-preservation. Consultee resistance can be a protective response instituted when an individual feels that the perceived change is too risky and too dangerous. Resistance may in fact be an appropriate response at those times when the interventions, the activities and the recommendations suggested by the consultant are in fact too threatening to the consultee's sense of safety. Consider the situation where a consultee is directed to confront and "stand up to" the aggressive gang leader who is disrupting her class. The consultee may find such a suggestion threatening to her well-being and safety and thus resist the consultant's recommendation. Under conditions where the health and well-being of the consultee or the consultee's system are threatened, resistance may be a reasonable response.

Resistance—A Response to Consultant Insensitivity

Since resistance can be a reasonable response, the consultant must not ignore it or attempt to overcome or push through it. Rather, a consultant needs to respect the fact that this resistance is evidence that the consultee is feeling uncomfortable. Often this discomfort can be a direct result of the consultant's insensitivity. Consider my own introduction to the reality of consultee resistance, an introduction that came at the direction of a very competent and devoted 26-year-old first grade teacher.

At the time of our encounter, I was quite a novice in the profession. While being aware and knowledgeable of the theory and research on consultation, I was equally unaware of the realities of the practice.

Ms. L asked if I could assist her with Timothy, one of her "troublesome" first graders. She noted that over the course of the last five weeks Timothy's behavior had become increasingly disruptive to the class. According to Ms. L, Timothy began by calling out in class (without raising his hand and waiting to be recognized), but has since escalated his disruptive behavior to the point where he now "throws books up to the front of the room!" After listening to Ms. L's brief description, I thanked her for her confidence in me as a consultant, and I asked if I could visit the classroom to observe Timothy in action.

The next day I stopped in to observe Ms. L's class. What I noticed was that Ms. L was a very creative, animated, and apparently interested teacher. Her room was brightly decorated and the children were working at one of five learning stations located around the classroom. The children appeared very involved and attentive to the particular tasks they found at each learning station. Ms. L was enthusiastically moving from station to station, both lending support and providing extensive verbal reinforcement.

In this environment of active, cooperative learning sat Timothy. He was isolated from the other children and the learning stations and was sitting at his own desk working on individual worksheets. Ms. L stated that Timothy tended to be too disruptive in the small groups and thus was given individual seat work during these periods of cooperative learning.

As I sat and observed, I noted that Timothy would wait until Ms. L was engrossed in discussion or demonstration at one of the learning stations and then he would reach under his desk and select a book, which he would promptly throw up to the front of the room. Needless to say, the loud sudden noise startled every one in the room and resulted in Ms. L's coming over to Timothy and reprimanding him for his behavior. I observed this scene played out four more times in the span of twenty minutes. I felt my observations confirmed by initial hypotheses about what needed to be done, so I excused myself and informed Ms. L that I would provide her feedback at her lunch period (which was in about 30 minutes).

During the interim I went to my office where I promptly *typed* a proposal for extinguishing this attention-seeking behavior, along with a detailed instruction on how to employ teacher attention to shape Timothy's positive behavior. The proposal was detailed, providing step-by-step instruction on the shaping process, along with a number of supportive references and recommended readings on extinction and shaping. It was truly a paper worthy of any graduate student.

I handed Ms. L the paper and suggested that after she read it she could contact me if she had any questions. Otherwise, I was sure that things would work out fine as long as she followed my recommendations. Fine! The end result of this insensitive display of pomposity was that the recommended program failed miserably. Timothy became more disruptive in his attention-seeking behavior. Ms. L became more frustrated with Timothy, stopped the implementation of the plan and reported to her fellow teachers that "(the psychologist's) plan made things worse!" Further, she swore to her colleagues that she would NEVER consult with "that guy" again.

A plan that made things worse? It made no immediate sense to me. The plan was detailed. The plan was founded on good solid research and well articulated theory. And yet the plan failed.

As you most likely recognize, the problem was not in the plan, but in the planner; not in the product, but the process. And what resulted was a consultee who felt insulted, unheard, humiliated, and angry. What was experienced by the consultant was the reality of resistance—a resistance—which in this case, he (I) truly deserved.

As is evident in my own experience, resistance is often an indirect way for the consultee to express discomfort with the consultant or the consultation process. Being sensitive to this indirect expression of discomfort and being able to discern the basis (rational or ill-founded) upon which the discomfort rests is an essential diagnostic first step to successfully working with this dynamic of consultation. The effective consultant will need to recognize resistance in its many forms and identify the possible cause(s) for this resistance if she or he is to work effectively.

Recognizing the Many Forms of Resistance

The ways a consultee can manifest discomfort and resistance are many and have been conceptualized in a variety of ways (e.g., Block, 1981; Friend & Bauwens, 1988; Karp, 1984). Regardless of the system employed or the label applied, consultee resistance involves an action on the part of the consultee that in effect thwarts the process of consultation. Some of the forms are quite obvious, as in the situation where the consultee directly, explicitly, and perhaps even quite dramatically says NO to the process. But most often resistance is less obvious, less direct, and therefore less easy to assess. Below are nine ways resistance may take shape or be presented within the consulting relationship.

1. Ultimate Resistance . . . just NO!
2. The Push Away
3. Yes, But. . . .
4. (Silence) I'm Listening
5. The Inquisition
6. Passive Aggression
7. Requesting Counseling
8. Quick Sell/Quick Buy
9. Suddenly Healthy

This listing of forms of consultee resistance is not intended to be all-inclusive nor necessarily exclusive of one another. Rather, it is simply a sampling of the various forms resistance may take—ranging from the more direct and obvious to those forms that can be quite subtle. The intent is simply to provide a "feel" for the many faces of resistance in hopes of increasing the reader's ability to recognize the presence of resistance in his or her own consulting.

Ultimate Resistance—Just NO!

Quite often the consultee will simply and directly refuse to participate in the consultation or follow the consultant's prescription. While such resistance may involve strong negative emotions, as would be the case when the consultee angrily rejects the consultant's suggestion, this expression of negative feelings need not be present for the block to be experienced. Consider the response of the following consultee to the invitation to engage in collaborative consultation.

> **Consultant:** *I understand from Mr. Johnson that you are having some difficulty with the security guard on third shift, Mark L. Perhaps we could talk about your experience with Mark and together we might come up with some ideas on how best to proceed.*

> **Consultee:** *Thanks for your interest and concern, but I am going to pass on your invitation. I feel confident that Mark and I can work out the problem without your assistance, but thanks anyway.*

While the consultee is apparently calm and without expression of negative feelings, the assertion of not wishing to engage in consultation is quite strong. The obvious and direct nature of this resistance allows for immediate recognition and thus facilitates the consultant's efforts to address the resistance.

As will be discussed later within this chapter, this direct resistance, as with all of the forms of resistance, needs to be identified and presented to the consultee for consideration. The consultant will need to clarify the nature and source of the resistance. Questions that the consultant needs to address in confronting consultee resistance are: What is the consultee attempting to achieve by refusing to participate in a working relationship with the consultant? What might the consultee achieve by working with the consultant?

By addressing these and similar questions, the consultant can begin to re-establish goals and approaches that will now be aimed at highlighting the possible benefits of working together, while at the same time empowering the consultee to freely and coequally engage in the consultation (Johnson & Johnson, 1987; Schmuck & Runkel, 1985). In the previous scenario, the consultant may recognize the consultee's lack of interest, but respond by pointing out the apparent interest and concern that Mr. Johnson (the consultee's boss) has regarding the "value" and need for this consult. Further, the consultant may respect the consultee's need to be self-sufficient and simply ask for the consultee to define the role he would like the consultant to play so as to make his (the consultee's) job easier, while at the same time satisfying Mr. Johnson's need for this consultation to occur.

The Push Away

Often this refusal is less direct and thus less obvious. The consultee may initially approach the consultation as if willing and interested, only to find reasons within the dynamics of the relationship to push the consultant away and terminate the relationship.

The consultee resisting by pushing the consultant away will find an opportunity to become angry at the consultant. The consultee may blame the consultant for having imposed an overwhelming amount of work on the consultee. The consultee may complain that doing what the consultant requests is disrupting the normal flow of his or her work. Whatever the form of blaming, accusing, and fault finding, these are manifestations of the consultee's desire to resist consultation by pushing the consultant away.

Consider the following dialogue.

> **Consultee:** *I know I told you I was willing to work with you, but I didn't realize you were going to come into my classroom and disrupt the class.*

> **Consultant:** *Disrupt the class? I am a bit confused. I thought we agreed that observing Karen was a good way to begin to gather some information.*

> **Consultee:** *It may have been a good idea for you, but it was clearly disruptive for me! You saw how excited the children became. They were almost unmanageable. They kept looking back at you and not paying attention to the story being read. I mean, Karen even asked if you were my boyfriend. That's all I need. This is making things worse, not better!*

The consultee's attempt to push the consultant away by being annoyed, irritated, or stimulating a sense of guilt or responsibility onto the consultant can prove very effective should the consultant take it personally and counterattack or respond in a defensive mode. The consultant needs to be careful not to be seduced into the anger or accept the guilt. The consultant should avoid getting into a competition about what "we" agreed upon. Rather, the consultant will prove more effective if she or he increases empathic listening skills, attempts to label the feelings being experienced by the consultee, and invites the consultee to work with the concern at hand.

For example, continuing with the above scenario, the consultant may suggest the following:

> **Consultant:** *I can see how upset you are about the classroom visit. And even though I didn't experience the same degree of disruption in the class as you did, I respect how it may have impacted upon you. It certainly was not what I intended, nor what you or I anticipated when we discussed it yesterday. While this is certainly something we didn't anticipate, it is something with which we can still work. Let's think of ways that we can gather the information we were seeking while being sure not to disrupt the class.*

Yes, But...

A more subtle form of resistance, and one that can prove extremely frustrating for a consultant, is that which comes in the form of "agreement...but." The consultee employing a "yes, but..." form of resistance will demonstrate a willingness and even an enthusiasm for the process or direction of the consultation. However, this enthusiasm, this willingness is quickly followed by a point of objection and concern that undermines the previous work.

For example, the consultee might suggest that other competing demands make the consultant's suggestion impossible.

Consultee: I think this is a great idea, but you know with all the things I have to do, it is simply going to be impractical.

Or, the consultee may attempt to deflect the consultant by suggesting that a newer crisis is making it difficult (if not impossible) to continue with the consult.

Consultee: I know you want me to gather baseline on Kathy, but we were just informed that we are beginning Middle States Accreditation visits and I am on the Governance Committee. So we'll have to get back to this at a later time. I really want to follow through on Kathy, because we had some really good ideas, but you know how it is!

The consultee may even attempt to displace the responsibility for the resistance on to others in the environment.

Consultee: I really like the idea, it is very creative, but you know the others in the work group are not going to go for this. I know it's frustrating. But it's not me, I simply don't have the authority or power to influence the rest of the managers.

In the situations where the consultee is exhibiting resistance through a "yes, but..." response, the consultant may be seduced into believing the consultee is cooperative and thus feel maximum frustration when the blockage occurs. When the consultant encounters repetitions of the "yes, but..." consultee response, the consultant should summarize the pattern and invite the consultee to discuss his or her own discomfort with the process or direction of the consultation.

Consultant: Tom, I really appreciate your enthusiasm and energy during this brainstorming session. We have come up with six pretty good ideas for working with Louise. However, I have noted that each time we get an idea that at first seems good, you identify some reason that it won't work. It is possible that you may be feeling some apprehension or concerns that we could talk about?

Again, as with all interventions with resistance, this form of confrontation will require all the helping attitudes and skills the consultant can muster. This point, along with other guidelines for intervention, will be discussed later within this chapter.

(Silence) I'm Listening

A much more seductive form of resistance and one that may go unnoticed, especially in the early phases of consultation, is when the consultee takes the role of passive partner. In this role, the consultee appear to be intensely listening and may even employ minimal encouragers, such as "uh, huh," "OK," or "go on" in order to demonstrate his or her attending.

While listening is certainly desirable, it is only part of an active collaborative process. By maintaining silence and taking up the role of listener (or even observer), the consultee not only forces the consultant to provide the entire impetus and direction for the consultation but also fails to provide the consultant with feedback that is needed to tailor the consultant's ideas to the specifics of this situation.

In this form of resistance, the consultee appears present and willing. However, after a number of exchanges the consultant may begin to feel as if he or she is interacting in a vacuum or consulting in a void. The consultee may suggest involvement through his or her intense listening, the reality is that the consultee is engaged in avoidance. The consultee, while listening, is most likely neither hearing nor embracing the consultant's message. This becomes obvious when at subsequent meetings the consultant is forced to reiterate points previously explained, or revisit plans that appeared to have been crystal clear.

Consider the following brief exchange and imagine how you would feel as the consultant in this interaction, especially as it continues throughout a number of consulting sessions.

> **Consultant:** *I think that if we pull our experience and our ideas we will be able to generate some useful approaches.*
>
> **Consultee:** *Oh?*
>
> **Consultant:** *Well, perhaps we could begin by sharing some of the thoughts we had about the situation.*
>
> **Consultee:** *OK.*
>
> **Consultant:** *Now, you are the one most immediately impacted by the policies, so could you give me an idea about how this has impacted you?*
>
> **Consultee:** *Oh, sure . . . but maybe you could help me understand what you think may be going on. I'm getting some different ideas and perspective just by listening to your point of view.*

The seductive hook for the consultant may be that she or he will feel needed and in the role of expert. The downside is that this becomes a one-sided operation, rather than collaborative exchange, and the possibility of consultee ownership is diminished.

The Inquisition

While the "listener" may appeal to the consultant's need to assume the expert role, the Inquisitor and the Inquisition may appeal to the consultant's need to educate.

A consultee may actively engage with the consultant around the definition and description of the problem and the suggested intervention plan. On first blush having the consultee seek clarity and greater understanding would appear to be desirable. However, closer inspection will reveal that the nature of the communication is very much unidirectional and it is not understanding that the consultee seeks, but rather avoidance.

The consultee actively engaged in the Inquisition will eagerly and enthusiastically pursue the consultant's presentation, asking for more detail, more explanation, elaborations, and examples. This can suggest the consultee's heightened interest and personal involvement in the process of consultation. However, if it is not balanced by the consultee's equally enthusiastic contributions and suggestions, then it is most likely the consultee's tool for maintaining noninvolvement. As long as the consultee can direct the consultant to expand, elaborate, enumerate, and in some way continue to provide the information that serves as the substance of the exchange, the consultee can remain detached, uninvolved, and removed. Consider the following exchange.

Consultee: Now, I know from your background that you must have encountered situations like this before?

Consultant: Actually, this is not too unlike a consult I recently completed.

Consultee: Could we use some of the ideas and suggestions you developed there for this situation?

Consultant: Perhaps.

Consultee: Like what, for example?

Consultant: Well, one of the things we attempted (and which seemed somewhat successful) was to develop a brief survey to administer to the staff in order to begin to assess their perception of the climate of the workplace.

Consultee: The climate of the workplace?

Consultant: Oh, things like the degree to which the environment is personal, or the communication is open, or whether or not the staff felt personally valued by the administration.

Consultee: That's interesting. Could you tell me more about it, and how it was received, and then what do you do with the data?

While the consultee gives the appearance of being interested and engaged, the energy contributed is of the sort that truly disengages the consultee from active participation and ownership in the process—a dynamic that will eventually prove resistant to the conjoint work of consultation.

Passive Aggression

Passive aggressiveness has been presented both as a personality disorder (see *The Diagnostic and Statistical Manual of Mental Disorder,* III-R, 1987) and as an organizational profile (Parsons & Wicks, 1983). Used here, passive aggression refers to an indirect form of resistance expressed through such maneuvers as forgetfulness, procrastination, repetitive mistakes, and inefficiencies.

Consider the resistance exhibited by the consultee in the illustrations below. The consultee had met with the consultant previously and was scheduled for a followup meeting, at which time they would discuss the data the consultee was to have collected. Rather than outright refusal, the passive-aggressive consultee will feign eagerness to perform only to have been blocked by events beyond his or her control. As you read the following consultee responses consider how you might feel as the consultant.

Consultee A: I'm sorry about missing our meeting—I know, third time (is it a charm?), but I simply have so much on my mind that I forgot. Oh, I know I was supposed to do something, or prepare something for today, but it really slipped my mind. I simply have to start writing things down.

Consultee B: Hi, how goes it? Before you begin, I know I promised to gather that baseline data, and actually I started, but there has been so much other stuff going on I just didn't get a chance to do it this week. I promise you, I'll complete it next time! So, anything else I can do?

Consultee C: I gathered the data you asked for, but I can't seem to find the file. It's here somewhere! I think I can remember what I wrote, because it was only five items, you know I counted how many times he was late following morning break. Oh, I'm sorry. I was supposed to record how many times he was late following both morning and afternoon breaks?

While it is not suggested that this response style is reflective of a personality disorder, it is clear that such an indirect expression of resistance not only actively blocks progress but can act as a major source of frustration and irritation to the consultant. The danger is that the consultant may in fact be seduced into venting his or her own frustration and anger, giving the consultee justification for terminating the specific process, if not the entire relationship.

Requesting Counseling

An interesting form of resistance identified by Caplan (1970) was that involving the consultee's request for personal counseling. It is interesting in that as a mental health consultant one might be easily seduced into believing this is a profitable direction for the consultation to go. But the fact is that engaging in counseling is effectively terminating the consultation.

A request for counseling actually directs the focus away from the consultation. Such a request attempts to change the nature of the relationship. No longer is the focus on the client, but now on the consultee; no longer is the target a work-related issue, but now on the consultee's personal problem and no longer is the relationship one of coequal problem solving but of a helper-helpee encounter.

While the consultee may ask the consultant for counseling directly, often the consultant is seduced into this role shift by the consultee's expression of negative effect around his or her work performance (Randolph & Graun, 1988). For example:

Consultee: You've been a godsend. If it hadn't been for you, I would have quit long ago. I just can't take it. I can't do it anymore (starting to tear up). Look around—we don't have needed supplies. The VP could care less that we are breaking our backs. And everybody is trying to stab you in the back in order to make it up the corporate ladder. You know, it just isn't worth it. I can't cut it anymore. I really don't know what I'm going to do (crying).

In these situations the consultant must remember that consultation IS NOT counseling. What is needed in situations like this is for the consultant to provide the consultee with "supportive refocus" (Randolph, 1985). The consultant, while showing a level of empathic support, needs to draw the consultee and the relationship back to focus on the client, or the consultee's skills, knowledge, and objectivity with working with the client.

> ***Consultant:*** *Tom, I can tell you really feel like it is a lot to handle. Today is obviously not a good day for you and you sound like you really feel overwhelmed and perhaps a bit unappreciated. But you and I had begun to develop some really interesting and useful ideas about getting Kevin and the rest of that night shift back on track. So why don't we go grab a cup of coffee and I'll show you that information on safety programs that I was supposed to get. We could check it out together and see how it applies to Kevin and the other guys.*

Quick Sell/Quick Buy

In discussing the process of entering a consultative contract Meyers, Parsons, and Martin (1979) warned that "even when no reservations or concerns are raised, the consultant should raise typical concerns to be sure there are no problems" (p 66).

These authors' experience negotiating contracts for consultation with a system has application when "negotiating" the more informal contracts with the consultee. While it can be quite gratifying for the consultant to have the consultee immediately embrace his or her orientation and consultation delivery model, the reality is that often too rapid agreement and blind acceptance of the consultant's recommendation may be one way the consultee can avoid involvement in the process.

The consultee who actively nods agreement and provides verbal affirmation for the suggestions ("Oh, yes"..."absolutely"... etc.) may be dismissing the consultant and the consultation process. Quite often the rapid, "that's great, you bet, no problem" response reflects either a lack of understanding or an intentional decision not to follow through, even though providing wholehearted verbal support.

Consultation involves change and resistance is to be expected. The consultee who expresses concerns, wants to problem solve together, and manifests some degree of anxiety about the process is most often actively engaged in the process and aware of the work it entails. The consultee who exhibits blind, rapid acquiescence may later demonstrate through his or her lack of follow through or inappropriate application of the steps discussed that he or she was not truly aware or involved in the consulting dynamic.

If the consultation is to be one of collaborative effort, one is to expect differing opinions and compromise. Blind total acceptance of the consultant's direction or recommendation is contraindicative of this type of collaboration. The consultant confronting such a situation would be wise to encourage discussion of reservations, objections, or concerns experienced by the consultee. The consultant, while not attempting to create problems, should be willing to raise typical concerns that could be discussed when the consultee fails to identify his or her own concerns. For example:

> ***Consultant:*** *I feel really good about our meeting today, and your willingness to work with me on this situation. I know that you initially expected me to work with Linda directly.*

Consultee: No problem. I really hadn't considered the fact that I could be of assistance to you or that somehow we could combine our efforts with Linda. I am really looking forward to it.

Consultant: I would imagine that this idea of collaborating with me in the development and implementation of a behavioral modification plan for Linda is adding to your workload. Do you see any problems this may cause for you?

Consultee: No, I don't think it will be a big deal.

Consultant: Great, I just know that oftentimes learning a new technique or applying some new methods takes time and energy.

Consultee: Nope! Sounds great!

Consultant: Do you have concerns about our meeting regularly? I know for some it could be seen as an added burden in terms of time and energy.

Consultee: Well, obviously it would be nice if things were simply OK and I could use this time for preparation, but actually I am excited about some of the new techniques and feel that they will help me in the future.

Consultant: Super. I'm looking forward to it as well. You know, it may even be a good idea for us to periodically review both how well we are doing with Linda and how well we are doing with this consulting process. That way if there are any issues or concerns that come up we will be sure to address them.

Suddenly Healthy

One of the most subtle forms of resistance occurs when somewhere within the process of consulting, the consultee no longer appears to have the problem that brought him or her to consultation.

Block (1981) noted that this is similar to the situation often experienced in marriage counseling in which the symptoms that stimulated the call for assistance often disappear as the therapy session approaches. Such symptom reduction may be real, but it is often quite temporary. However, for the troubled couple, the symptom reduction and the accompanying experience of relief will provide a way, a reason, to step out of what might become an emotionally involving experience—therapy.

The same experience of rapid cure, or flight into health, can be evidenced in consultation. Clearly, the added attention to the problem along with the sense of support received from the consultant may help the consultee to either increase his or her tolerance for the situation and thus reduce the felt need for assistance or in fact begin to reduce the manifestations of the problem (i.e., symptom reduction). While the possibility of being seen as such a rapid savior and problem resolver can be absolutely seductive for the consultant, she or he must resist the temptation to assume that all is truly right with the world. The consultant needs to be sure that the consultee is not simply smoothing over the issue, or settling for symptom relief, as a way of resisting the hard work involved in changing the core of the problem.

Flight into health is not only subtle but potentially quite seductive. The consultant hoping to demonstrate his or her value may only too quickly embrace the rapid solution, as evidence of the consultant's expertise. As consultants we must try to remember that it most cases the problem has taken time to develop and has been around for some time. It typically does not disappear after one or several consultative sessions. While symptoms may be reduced, the problem may still remain.

Understanding the Possible Sources of Resistance

A number of authors have conceptualized and described the many causes for resistance (e.g., Friend & Cook, 1992; Margolis & McGettigan, 1988; Piersel & Gutkin, 1983; Powell & Posner, 1978; Waugh & Punch, 1987). While the specifics of these various categorizations may vary, they all seem to suggest that resistance is an emotional response to a perceived or real threat. The source of that threat can lie within 1) the consultee's own issues and concerns, 2) the consultant's style, or 3) the nature of the consulting relationship. It is important for the consultant to discern the source of this threat so that it can be best addressed.

Resistance—A Reaction to Consultee Issues and Concerns

As noted above, resistance is at one level an emotional response to a perceived or real threat. Often the source of the threat, while initially placed on the consultant, the consultation relationship, or the specific recommendations or processes encountered, actually stems from the consultee's personal issues. Five such issues or concerns—1) stereotyping and theme interference, 2) negative or conflicting expectations, 3) concerns regarding control, 4) feelings of vulnerability, and 5) anxiety around problem finding and/or problem solving—are discussed in some detail.

Stereotyping/Theme Interference
It is possible for the consultee to transfer feelings from past relationships onto the client or consultant. Whether this is termed stereotyping (Beisser & Green, 1972), theme interference (Caplan, 1970), or transference (Racker, 1968), the loss of objectivity experienced can serve as a source for resistance.

Transference of feelings is not restricted to those consultees who are emotionally unhealthy. This form of resistance "... also occurs among the fairly healthy" (Caplan & Caplan, 1993, p. 115). Consider Case Illustration 4-1 involving a pediatric nurse, Nurse J, and the transference of her feelings onto her clients.

Resistance can also be a direct result of negative stereotyped attitudes about consultants and/or the nature consultation. Consider Exercise 4-1. It will help to highlight the variations with which resistance may be presented, while at the same time highlighting how stereotyped attitudes may be displaced onto the consultant and serve as a source of resistance.

The steps needed for working effectively with consultee resistance will be discussed later within this chapter. But it should be pointed out the process involves elevating the con-

---

CASE ILLUSTRATION 4-1   Resistance due to Transference of Feelings

Ms. J worked in a children's orthopedic rehabilitation unit. She came to the consultant's attention because it was noted that many of the children with whom she worked were atypically slow in developing independence.

At first Ms. J attempted to refuse the consultation assistance (Just NO) by stating that she was "completely aware of what needed to be done and fully able to achieve it." When her supervisor made it clear that working with the consultant was expected, Ms. J quickly shifted to a yes, but . . . form of resistance and ultimately to a passive aggressive approach, forgetting to record the needed data, misplacing information provided, and so on..

Noting the lack of progress and the apparent resistance, the consultant attempted to back off the task at hand and turn her attention to developing a more personal (referent) relationship with the consultee. Through a number of informal, nonbusiness luncheon meetings, the consultant discovered that Ms. J had been married for 34 years and she and her husband had always wanted a large family. Ms. J had had difficulty in carrying a child and had miscarried on three separate occasions. It became apparent that Ms. J's intense desire to have children appeared to cloud her own objectivity when working with the rehabilitated children. She would foster overly dependent relationships, encouraging the children to ask for her help (rather than attempting things on their own). This dependency seemed to satisfy her own need to nurture. As a result, the clients' rehabilitation was delayed and any and all consultant suggestions that would ameliorate this dependency (and thus reduce the consultee's opportunity to infantilize and nurture the clients) were resisted.

---

sultee's awareness and acceptance of the resistance and is therefore somewhat confrontational. In working with consultees exhibiting such emotional blockage, a consultant needs to be able to confront the consultee in ways that are truly inviting and not threatening. Caplan (1970) suggested a number of indirect confrontational strategies for addressing such blocking, such as the use of parable and modeling. Each of the these techniques will be fully explored in Chapter 8.

Negative and Conflicting Expectations

In addition to these less conscious sources of resistance, a consultee may exhibit resistance as a direct result of his or her conscious negative expectations about the need, or potential costs of this consultation encounter.

The consultee may exhibit resistance because of differing perceptions and expectations. The consultee may not agree with the consultant that a problem exists or that one exists at a level of severity necessitating this consultation (Piersel & Gutkin, 1983). Or, in those situations where there is agreement on the existence and nature of the problem, differing expectations regarding the strategies or even the goals to be achieved may serve as the source of resistance. Certainly, the more the consultant's expectations regarding the nature of the problem, the goal to be achieved, and the specific recommendations are compatible with that of the consultee, the less resistance is encountered (Elliot, 1988a, b; Kazdin, 1981; Witt & Elliot, 1985).

EXERCISE 4-1   Stereotyping a Source of Consultee Resistance

Directions: As you read the following case presentation,

1. Using the previously described six forms of resistance, identify the forms of resistance demonstrated.
2. Place yourself in the role of the consultant and attempt to become aware of the point in the interaction where you may have sensed the presence of resistance.
3. With a supervisor, instructor, or colleague, discuss what you feel is the source or base for Mr. Robinson's resistance, the underlying concern or theme; and,
4. Discuss the personal impact you may have experienced if you were the consultant in this situation. Identify your own reactions that may prove valuable in diagnosing future experiences with consultee resistance.

Background: Mr. Robinson is a fifth-grade teacher who requested a consult with the school psychologist regarding the recent decline in performance of one of his students, Kristian.

Mr. Robinson is a first-year teacher and, while very enthusiastic about his profession, he is also somewhat anxious about his ability to perform his job and the impression he will make on the children, the parents, and most of all, his supervisors. While not having previously worked with the consultant, Mr. Robinson had an experience with a school psychologist when he was a student in high school. Mr. Robinson (Bill) went to his own school psychologist when he was in eleventh grade and expressed his concern that he may be gay. The school psychologist informed his parents who immediately "forced" Bill into therapy. This was a very traumatizing experience for Bill and one that left him wary of school psychologists.

Meeting 1:

Consultant: Well, Bill, I know I have been doing most of the talking, but I feel like we are getting some good ideas about what to do with Kristian. How do you feel?
Consultee: Great! I like your ideas. I think you are going to help a lot, but I am concerned that focusing so much time on Kristian may interfere with my attention to the other children.
Consultant: Well, perhaps that is one of the things we have to investigate. So let's start. I know you are going to check your lesson plan and let me know which day is the best to come into your class to observe.
Consultee: Oh, right...I almost forgot. Now what is it you're going to be looking for?

Meeting 2:

Consultee (comes 15 minutes late): I'm sorry I'm so late, but I got involved making Thanksgiving decorations and I almost forgot about the meeting.
Consultant: It's OK. Since we were unable to connect during to week to set a date for the observation time, I was hoping that you remembered to bring your plan and your calendar today.
Consultee: Yikes, in my hurry...I forgot! But I have to tell you—since our meeting last week, Kristian and I talked and he explained that he had been upset (something to do with his dog dying). But anyway, he has gotten back on track. So I don't think you need to observe me! See, just coming to you works like a miracle...thanks!

Even with such agreement of need, goals, and strategies, the consultee may exhibit resistance as a simple result of his or her negative expectations regarding time, resources, and energy cost that may be incurred as a result of engaging in consultation (Parsons & Meyers, 1984; Randolph & Graun, 1988). This seems especially true for individuals who are overwhelmed or experiencing burnout. These individuals may simply not have the energy to participate in the change that is anticipated will result from consultation. They may see the consultation as one added burden to an already overburdened agenda (Friend & Bauwens, 1988).

In attempting to address this last point, regarding potential costs, the consultant needs to keep in mind that the less change indicated and the more culturally (and personally) compatible the change, the less costly such change will be and thus the less resistance one should encounter. Further, the more rapidly the consultant can identify the consultee's motivations and needs and enter the relationship at a level that will satisfy at least one of these motivational states, the more payoff will be experienced by the consultee, and thus the less resistance encountered (Parsons & Meyers, 1984). For example, when working with a consultee who is experiencing burnout and/or crisis around a particular client, a consultant can reduce or even prevent resistance by providing immediate relief (even if it is short term). Stepping in with hands-on assistance, such as removing an extremely disruptive client, may prove more useful in reducing resistance than would be engaging the client in a lengthy data-gathering process. Requiring the overburdened consultee to collect data, learn new observation or intervention techniques, or such activities would increase the consultee's expectations that such a relationship will be too costly and thus should be resisted.

The consultant experiencing consultee resistance as a result of negative expectations regarding need-goal-strategies and/or value (i.e., cost-payoff benefit) will need to clarify and (re)establish specific elements of a collaborative consultation contract. Specifically, the consultant would need to

1. Provide or review for the consultee the rationale and potential benefits of using consultation, highlighting the preventive value.
2. Re-emphasize the confidential nature of the relationship.
3. Reiterate the consultee's right and responsibility to accept, modify, or reject the recommendations and the freedom to renegotiate and/or terminate the contract at any time.
4. Clarify the goal and direction that is mutually acceptable.

Exercise 4-2 is provided to assist the reader in identifying the existence of negative or conflicting expectations and developing strategies aimed at reducing the resistance experienced.

Concerns regarding Control
Resistance often reflects the consultee's concern about losing control, or being perceived as without control. Block (1981) noted that control not only reflects on the person's level of competence and professional maturity but is often the mark of success within the organization. The more control, responsibility, and authority an individual is able to obtain, the more she or he is perceived as successful (Block, 1981).

From this perspective, enlisting the assistance of a consultant may be perceived (by self or others) as an act of surrendering control and thus personal and organizational failure. As a result, a consultee may feel that maintaining the semblance of control is more important than increasing his or her own professional effectiveness. Therefore, the consultee may be willing to resist consultation and maintain control even if it results in poorer performance (Block, 1981).

Consider the case with which the chapter was opened. By inappropriately employing the consultant's recommendations for extinction and behavioral shaping, the consultee not only was able to find "justification" for her own inability to rapidly resolve the problem, since the consultant also unable to resolve the problem, but she was also able to dismiss the consultant, take back control of her class, and suggest to the world, "...I'll simply have to do it myself!"

EXERCISE 4-2   Recognizing and Working through Negative and Conflicting Expectations

Directions: Since there may be multiple approaches to working with resistance, it would be beneficial to work this exercise with a colleague, supervisor, or mentor. For each of the following scenarios you are to

1. Identify a possible negative and/or conflicting expectation that may serve as a source of consultee resistance; and,
2. Suggest the specific strategy you may employ to reduce or prevent this potential source of resistance.

Sample: The consultant, Ms. Eberly, is a human resource director for a small insurance company. Ms. Eberly receives a call from Gail, the claims department supervisor.

Gail: (voice is cracking, shaking) "I would like to talk with you. I could...(starts to cry)...could really use your advise. I (long pause)...really have a situation with Helen, one of my claims people. I am really worried (crying). I think I blew it!" (in the background the consultant hears Helen, yelling about taking Gail to the union representative).

Recognizing the consultee was in crisis, the possibility that the consultee was feeling vulnerable and out of control, and the real press of Helen's threatening the consultee, the consultant:

1. Decides to go to Gail's office, rather than having Gail come to her office (reduce cost) and reduces her feeling of vulnerability by not exposing her to others she may encounter coming to his office.
2. Entering Gail's office, decides to ask Helen to sit in an outer office rather than attempting to mediate in the situation (hands on, meeting needs to reduce attack, serves as payoff).
3. Begins to speak to Gail, rather than asking Gail what happened (reduced costs of possible vulnerability and provides emotional support and consultation refocus that serve as need satisfier).

   "Gail, I can see you are very upset. And Helen sounded angry. Helen is in the outer office, she's calming down. I let her know I will talk with her and that we can probably

Continued

EXERCISE 4-2   *Continued*

resolve whatever it is. She seems to be okay with that. I know you are concerned that you blew it, but it may not be that bad. Together I am sure we can work something out. Look, let's get this coffee and we can begin to talk about it."

4. Having reduced the immediate crisis (separating Helen and calming Gail), the consultant begins the problem identifying and resolving processes.

Consultant: "Perhaps you could tell me a little about the problem and what you would like to see happen. I feel that if we work together on this we probably can figure out what to do."

Scenario 1: The principal asks that you "consult" with Ms. Hopkins, the tenth-grade English teacher. Ms. Hopkins is in her last year of teaching and is scheduled to retire at the end of this year.

The principal has had a number of parent complaints about her inability to manage her classroom. He is concerned that perhaps she is simply too old and may need to be removed. But he is hoping that you can assist her to develop some new classroom management techniques.

Prior to your contacting Ms. Hopkins, she approaches you and asks that you work with Drew, a "real problem child." From Ms. Hopkins' perspective, Drew is the source of all the problems in her class.

Scenario 2: Helen B is a bright, attractive, 33-year-old manager of a mechanical engineering unit of a waste management company. After working for the company only three years, she was appointed to the managerial post. She is the first woman to have achieved this position in this company and has been in this position for only three months. You are the Human Relations Director for the company and she requests a meeting with you.

At the meeting Helen appears upset, but with great effort, controls her emotions and explains that "the men in my department are less than professional. They show little respect for me, make inappropriate comments, often quite sexually suggestive. They also seem to be teaming up to make me look bad. I want you to speak with them. Find some excuse to provide us a workshop on the changing laws regarding harassment, diversity, and so on. They'll get the message. But you can't let on that I requested it!"

The more the consultant can enlist consultee participation and thus ownership, the more control the consultee will feel. With this increased sense of control, resistance will be reduced. The challenge for the consultant is to allow the consultee to feel in control.

The effective consultant, while being interested in demonstrating his or her own value and effectiveness, will not compete for control over the recognition for the operation and success of the consult. Rather, it is important to allow the consultee to feel actively contributing, and directing the process and outcome, while at the same time feeling as if he or she can share the work, the burden, and the responsibility for possible failure.

Feeling Vulnerable

Engaging in consultation, like any helping encounter, requires the consultee to disclose—to share—to reveal his or her professional (and perhaps personal) experiences. In the process of such sharing the consultee exposes his or her competencies and incompetencies, strengths and weaknesses. Sharing with the consultant about professional practices that have proven unsuccessful increases the consultee's vulnerability, to recognition of imperfection and failures. This sense of vulnerability can often be compounded by the very fact that consultation often involves learning new behaviors. As a natural outcome of the learning process, the consultee will experience an increase in incompetency during the early stages of learning these new behaviors. This possible demonstration of reduced competence may increase the consultee's sense of vulnerability, especially if the consultee is unclear about the nature of the consultation or the role and function of the consultant and anticipates that the consultant may evaluate him or her personally or professionally (Parsons & Meyers, 1984).

In addition to the possibility of experiencing personal vulnerability as a result of disclosing and demonstrating one's level of incompetence, many consultees experience vulnerability within the organization should they enlist the support of a consultant. The climates of many organizations are not conducive to asking for help. Organizations tend to be quite competitive; asking for help can be viewed as a sign of weakness, and may even be used by others as a way of advancing over the individual seeking help. In these environments, engaging in consultation can at some level place the consultee at risk and vulnerable to others who seek to get ahead (Block, 1981).

The strength of such a feeling of vulnerability was highlighted by one request for consultative support that came from a Director of Personnel for mid-size utilities company.

Ms. Wilson called the consultant's office in order to contract for consultative services. The consultant was not in at the time and Ms. Wilson left the following message:

> *My name is Anita Wilson, I would like to discuss the possibility of contracting your services for managerial training. I am the Director of Personnel at the Ajax Utility company and I am responsible for offering management training programs around issues of cultural diversity, sexual harassment, and racial tension. I would like to discuss with you the ways you may be of assistance to me. My phone number is 555–5555. If I am not in my office, PLEASE introduce yourself to my secretary as a friend—and not as a Psychologist/Consultant. I will explain why this is important when we speak. Thank you.*

The simple possibility that her attempt to contact an external consultant may be discovered appeared quite threatening to Ms. Wilson. Her vulnerability may be based in some political or organizational reality or may be truly a personal self-induced vulnerability. Regardless, the consultant who ignores such signs of vulnerability may also proceed in insensitive ways that increase that sense of vulnerability and the resistance that will follow.

While it would be most ideal to change the norms and values of both the consultee and the system in which the consultee works so that consultation was be viewed as a desirable and professionally competent activity, until such value shift can occur, it is important for the consultant to remain sensitive to the consultee's experience of personal and organizational vulnerability. The consultant needs to remain descriptive and nonjudgmental in his or her communications with the consultee, demonstrate respect for the consultee, exhibit a belief in the value of discussing success and failures as a way of growing, and highlight the confidential nature of the relationship. These and other skills and attitudes needed to maintain a helping, collaborative consultative relationship will be discussed in Chapter 5.

Anxiety about Problem Finding/Problem Solving

Meyers, Friedman, Gaughan, and Pitt (1978) noted that consultee anxiety and hostility increased with consultant entry. Most likely this is not a direct result of the particular characteristics of the consultant, but more likely a defense against the anxiety one feels around the possibility of uncovering problems (Piersel & Gutkin, 1983).

Block (1981) noted that as consultants we are forcing the consultee to face difficult realities. These difficult realities are reflected in the existence of the problem to be discussed or in the requirements involved in implementation of the solution. The consultee's discomfort and resistance may therefore be a defense against the reality that they will have to make difficult choices, confront their reality, and change (Block, 1981). Identifying, embracing, and working with our problems can be painful and thus may be a process that is resisted.

A very subtle twist on this source of resistance comes in the form of the consultee who is eager to identify problems, but may be less than eager, and thus resistant, to finding solutions. Often the change signified by the process of consultation also suggests the potential of loss of some vested interest or aspect of value to the consultee. While experiencing the difficult realities of a problem, the consultee may also be experiencing some personal gain or need satisfaction by the existence of that problem and as such may feel anxious that such a problem will be resolved.

For example, there may be contingencies operating within the system that maintain the old approach while resisting the new (Piersel & Gutkin, 1983). Consider the situation in which a company "rewards" an efficient, effective manager by reducing the amount of support staff provided ("since she is able to do it on her own") or even by increasing the amount of work assigned ("since she is so capable"). In this setting, having a problem that interferes with one's efficiency may result in increased support and reduced adjunctive work. Thus, finding a solution to the "problem" could prove costly to this manager.

Most often, however, it is some personal, idiosyncratic need that is being met by maintaining the problem. For example, change may be perceived as reducing the security, status, privacy, or autonomy of the consultee. Consider Case Illustration 4-2 involving a change in leadership style.

In the same sense, yet somewhat less obvious, is the consultee who may resist coming to a successful resolution of the presenting complaint, simply because he or she experiences additional need satisfaction by the very nature of needing consultation. For example, by continuing the process of consultation, the consultee may experience added attention, the permission to complain, or even receive feedback from others that implies the consultee is pitied as a victim.

When the consultee experiences need satisfaction by delaying or avoiding problem resolution, such forms of secondary gain need to be removed. The consultant needs to help the consultee identify his or her needs and find other more beneficial ways to satisfy these needs.

CASE ILLUSTRATION 4-2   Resisting Solutions

The consultee was a 55-year-old senior engineer in a large multinational engineering firm. The company had moved to increased decentralization of decision making and was encouraging all levels of management to develop collaborative work teams. The consultee was seeking consultant support because the team that he managed seemed, in his perspective, "to be resisting this decentralized approach."

The consultant met with the consultee on two occasions and sat in on a strategic planning session led by the consultee. After observing the consultee's group leadership style and reviewing the nature and the tone of the directives he gave in his many and frequent work memos, it became clear that while he was talking about developing collaborative work teams and decentralizing his decision making, his actions were maintaining his own autonomous decision-making control.

The consultee would resist the consultant's recommendation for improving team decision making and empowering team members since such empowerment would undermine his own current level of power and control—a level in which he found much personal satisfaction.

Resistance—A Reaction to Consultant Style

An interesting position presented by Lazarus and Fay (1982) in their discussion of client resistance in therapy was that resistance "is probably the most elaborate rationalization that therapists employ to explain their treatment failures" (p. 115). These authors assert that what appears to be client resistance often has its source within the therapist's approach.

The position taken here is that a similar explanation may be applicable to certain types of resistance found within consultation. Certain consultant thoughts, feelings, and actions can contribute to resistance or blockage experienced in consultation. Specifically, consultants who restrict consultee freedom, exhibit abrasive characteristics, and lose professional objectivity may stimulate consultee resistance.

Restricting Consultee Freedom

According to the theory of psychological reactance (J. W. Brehm, 1966; S. S. Brehm, 1976) individuals are more likely to resist attempts by another to change them whenever they perceive their freedom to be reduced or eliminated. Thus the consultant who attempts to impose control over the consultee or employ power to coerce the consultee to embrace the recommendations may threaten consultee freedom and thus elicit resistance.

One simple directive aimed at reducing consultee resistance would be to always *ask* consultees to do something, rather than *tell* or *direct* them to do something. In addition to this simple step, a consultant can increase the consultee's perception of freedom and control by developing a *collaborative relationship* that: 1) emphasizes the consultee's freedom to accept or reject consultant recommendations, 2) encourages consultee participation, and 3) de-emphasizes consultant contribution (see Chapter 5).

Abrasive Personal Characteristics

We may all like to perceive ourself as likable, approachable, and credible. The truth of the matter may be that this is not how we are always perceived by our consultees. The consultant's personal characteristics can impact the degree of consultant persuasiveness (Kenton, 1989) and thus influence the degree to which resistance will be experienced within the consultee-consultant relationship.

The consultant's manner of self-presentation, manifestation of helping attitudes and skills, and (mis)use of power can either increase or decrease the level of resistance encountered. Thus a consultant who is perceived by the consultee as inappropriately dressed, using unprofessional or inappropriate language, or manifesting distracting and distasteful personal habits will elevate the possibility of resistance. Consultants who are perceived as lacking dynamism, energy, and confidence, or having limited verbal skills and lacking the ability to be flexible and adaptive are perceived as less credible (Kenton, 1989) and thus may experience more resistance.

Further, consultants who fail to exhibit essential helping attitudes and skills and thus appear nonauthentic, uncaring, or lacking effective communication skills will also experience increased consultee resistance. But perhaps it is the consultant's use and or misuse of power within the consultation relationship that may contribute the most to the resistance encountered.

As noted in the previous chapter, the consultant who can find the appropriate balance between expert and referent power may be able to reduce the amount of system resistance encountered; the same is true for the relationship with the consultee. Establishing oneself as an expert by way of demonstrating professional preparedness, experience, competence, and intelligence is important for the persuasive consultant (Kenton, 1989). Thus, consultants who fail to be perceived as possessing specialized knowledge or ability may have greater chance of experiencing consultee resistance. In addition to possessing and appropriately employing expert power, consultants need to be perceived as able to relate to the other and concerned for helping the consultee (and the client), rather than simply furthering their own personal goals (Tingstom, Little, & Stewart, 1990). Consultants who are unapproachable, who remain detached and/or aloof, even while possessing great expertise, may experience consultee resistance.

It would appear that by properly blending expert and referent power (French & Raven, 1959; Martin, 1978; Meyers, Parsons, & Martin, 1979; Parsons & Meyers, 1984) the consultant will elicit both perceptions of competence and willingness to help (Cienki, 1982), and thus reduced resistance.

Failure to Maintain Objectivity

If a consultant is to be effective, she or he must remain objective when working with a consultee. Should the consultant personalize consultee resistance or feel like the consultee's resistant behavior is aimed solely at him or her, the consultant may begin to respond defensively. In situations like this, the consultant may fail to encourage participation, may attempt to push through the resistance using coercive power, or may simply terminate the consult.

While it may be difficult, the consultant needs to remember that the consultee's reaction is more likely a response to "needing help" than it is resistance to the consultant or consultant's style. The resistance encountered is most often aimed at the prospect of having to engage in difficult decisions and change. It may even help to consider resistance as a healthy indicator that the consultee is comprehending and becoming involved in what the consultant may be proposing (Friend & Cook, 1992).

With this orientation and objectivity, a consultant may be in a better position to respond to consultee resistance by increasing his or her collaborative empathic mode of consultation, which, according to conflict theory and research (Deutsch, 1973; Meyers, 1978), should reduce the resistance. That is, rather than responding to resistance (a force) with increased force, the effective, objective consultant will increase efforts to understand what the consultee is experiencing and is attempting to convey through the resistant behavior (Meyers, 1978).

Maintaining objectivity may allow the consultant to emphasize mutual interests and coordinated efforts through open, honest, and empathic communication, which in turn should reduce the resistance and move the interaction toward one of collaboration and cooperation (Deutsch, 1973; Parsons & Meyers, 1984).

Resistance—A Reaction to a Dysfunctional Consulting Relationship

Consultation as viewed from a social psychological perspective is first and foremost a social interaction, a relationship (Parsons & Meyers, 1984). As a social interaction, success and failure can depend in large part on the dynamics of the social encounter (Tingstrom, Little, & Stewart, 1990). Consultee resistance is often an indication of dysfunction within the consulting relationship (Parsons & Meyers, 1984).

Specifically, consultee resistance may indicate that the consultation process is experienced as aversive, or as incongruent to expectations.

Consultation as an Aversive Process

Abidin (1975) suggested that resistance was a reaction to the fact that the procedures and process required in consultation were experienced by the consultee as aversive (Abidin, 1975). In a similar line of reasoning, Piersel and Gutkin (1983) suggested that consultation may be resisted if engaging in consultation may be met with punishing contingencies initiated at the systems level. Clearly if the consultation process is aversive, then it will be resisted.

In their very functionalist approach to studying relationships, Thibaut and Kelley (1959) proposed that relationships are based on the satisfaction of the participants' needs. These authors further contended that a person's willingness to engage in a particular relationship or in particular behaviors within a relationship is a function of the perceived rewards or payoffs that will be accrued versus the perceived costs that may occur. It is this author's position that the concept of reward/payoff to cost ratio has special significance to understanding resistance of consultation as an aversive process. It would appear that any time engaging in consultation is more costly—physically, socially or psychologically—then it is rewarding, the consultee will find the interaction aversive and tend to resist it. This is somewhat indirectly supported by the findings of Tingstrom, Little, and Stewart (1990), who noted after reviewing the literature that reduced resistance was found (1) the more severe the problem, and (2) the less time and fewer resources required to implement the treatment. Thus it would appear that when the payoff is greater due to the severity of the problem, or the cost is reduced, as in the case of less time and fewer resources required, resistance is decreased.

With this in mind, the effective consultant will attempt to maximize payoffs within the consultation relationship and as a result of engaging in consultation, while at the same time reduce the costs associated with and experienced in consultation. Rewards include any aspect of the relationship that is enjoyable or satisfying. These payoffs may be those gratifying experiences that come as a direct result of the interchange between the consultant and consultee (i.e., endogenous rewards) or those that result as a byproduct of the interaction (i.e., exogenous rewards). Clearly, reducing the presenting complaint would be an example of the exogenous payoff, whereas "feeling heard and supported" by the consultant could be an endogenous payoff. Costs can also be exogenous (e.g., any requirements on the consultee to modify his or her style or to collect data) and endogenous (e.g., the anxiety felt disclosing one's inadequacies as the consultant and consultee analyze the problem at hand). While there will always be costs in a relationship, be it as simple as the amount of energy one has to employ to meet and exchange with another, the important point is that the payoffs or rewards need to outweigh these costs in order for the relationship to be maintained, rather than resisted. Exercise 4-3 should help to clarify this point.

Consultation as Incongruent to Expectations

The discomfort and dissonance experienced when the consultee and consultant have incongruent expectations about the nature of consultation and the roles to be played may serve as a primary source of resistance (Piersel & Gutkin, 1983). For example, a consultee expecting that the consultant will take a provisional or prescriptive role may resist the active, contributory role of consultee required by a collaborative approach. The consultee and consultant may also be in conflict over the focus of the problem. This may be a problem in situations where the consultee targeted the source of the problem as resting with the client, whereas the consultant has identified the source as within the consultee or the system at large. Finally, resistance may occur when the consultee and consultant disagree in terms of the intervention to employ (e.g., removal of the client versus modification of consultee style).

In order to avoid or reduce incongruent expectations, the consultant needs to be clear in defining the nature of the contract, the process to be employed, and the roles to be played by both the consultant and consultee (Caplan, 1970; Parsons & Meyers, 1984; Sandoval, Lambert, & Davis, 1977). This clarification and definition needs to occur early in the relationship and may need to be reiterated throughout the consultation contract. In addition to defining the role and parameters of the consult, the consultant needs to help the consultee to achieve clear agreement on both the problem to be addressed and the strategies to be employed. This agreement on to the problem to be addressed has been identified as the most critical step in the problem solving process of consultation (Nezu & D'Zurilla, 1981).

Working with Resistance

As noted in the introduction of this chapter, consultee resistance need not be an adversary, nor something to be subdued. The position here is that the effective consultant who under-

---

EXERCISE 4-3   Reducing the Aversive Nature of Consultation

Directions: This exercise is best accomplished by working in a small group or a dyad (with a supervisor, mentor, or colleague) in order to allow for brainstorming. You are presented a brief description of characteristics surrounding a consultation. After reading the description:
1. Identify three possible costs that could occur within the relationship (endogenous), three costs that may be incurred as a result of the encounter (exogenous). Similarly, identify three exogenous and three endogenous rewards.
2. Be specific and concrete and generate strategies aimed at reducing each of the identified costs.
3. Generate strategies for adding as many additional payoffs as you (or the group) can generate.

Scenario 1: Because of recent school redistricting, Mr. Adams, a teacher with 33 years experience at the junior high level, has been assigned to teach third-grade social studies. Mr. Adams is one year away from retirement age, even though he hopes to continue teaching for at least five years past this point. Mr. Adams has been experiencing a lot of frustration and stress because of the "immaturity of his class." He approaches you informally at lunch one day and states: "Boy, kids are really different today. I don't know where they get the energy. Sometimes an old guy like me can feel pretty worn out at the end of the day. You have any magic tricks you could share with me?"

Scenario 2: Hector Gomez is a recent appointee to the post of branch manager at a local bank. Hector contacts your office and asks you, as Director of Personnel for the bank chain, if you could reassign two women from his branch.
   Hector, the first Hispanic American to serve as branch manager, complained that the women are prejudiced and he is afraid that he will "lose his cool, and tell them where to go." Hector made it very clear to you that he has a very hot temper and he wants these women out. Further, Hector suggests that he is aware that there are people within the organization that would like to see him fail, and that he "hopes that you are not one of them."

---

stands consultee resistance can utilize that understanding to develop an effective, productive, collaborative relationship with the consultee. In order to effectively work with resistance a consultant needs to develop skills of recognition, identification, invitation, and reframing.

Recognition

The first step in working with resistance is *recognition.* That is, the consultant must increase his or her awareness of resistance when it is present. Too often, consultants get lost in the task of problem solving and fail to register or record the interpersonal cues conveyed by the consultee that suggest that the consultee is not totally embracing this process. Unlike this author's experience with the first-grade teacher presented in the introduction of this chapter, a consultant needs to remain sensitive not only to the progress of the problem solving but also to the health and well being of the relationship. It is important for the consultant to be aware of the verbal and nonverbal cues that provide evidence of the consultee's experience in the consultation. The consultant must learn to not only recognize repetitive behaviors or verbalizations that are blocking the process, but also needs to be sensitive to the level of participation demonstrated by the consultee. Considering each of the following will help to maintain that sensitivity: Is the consultee attentive? Is the consultee enthusiastic and participative? Is the consultee demonstrating a sense of ownership or is he or she exhibiting signs of resistance?

In addition to looking for subtle signs of potential discomfort or resistance, the consultant would be wise to ask directly about the consultee's level of comfort or feelings of apprehension or concern. This inquiry into the consultee's experience with the consultative process is not only a useful form of evaluation but is also a valuable means of involving and empowering the consultee throughout the consultation.

Finally, while being sensitive and alert to the presence of resistance, the consultant would be wise to keep in mind the story of Sigmund Freud who when asked whether the cigar he was smoking was also a phallic symbol, was reported to say: "Sometimes a cigar is just a cigar." Often, the objections from a consultee are simply that—objections— and not forms of resistance (Block, 1981). In the collaborative model the consultee has the right to reject, even when such rejection is aimed at the entire consulting contract. Deciding to end the consult, or not follow through on a plan of action, or simply quitting is clearly the right of the consultee. The consultant, while considering the possibility that such a reaction may be a response to emotional vulnerability, needs to accept that the reality may simply be that the consultee has changed his or her mind, and a "No thanks" is simply a "No thanks."

Identification

Once it is clear that resistance is present, the consultant needs to determine if resistance is appropriate. It is possible that the goals and/or methods to be employed, along with the consultant's approach to the problem, may simply be inappropriate and the consultee's resistance serves as a directive that an adjustment is needed. This would be the case when the consultant recommends interventions that are immoral, unethical, illegal, or simply beyond the values and culture of the consultee and his or her organization; or when the goal to which the consultant is working is antithetical to the original reason for the consultee's seeking consultation. Under these situations resistance is appropriate and it is the consultant, rather than the consultee, who needs to adjust.

Assuming that no such adjustment is warranted, the consultant needs to elevate the consultee's awareness of his or her resistance by *identifying* or naming the resistance. In order to assist the consultee to become more aware and more responsible for the dynamics of the consultation, the consultant needs to describe his or her own experience in the consulting process up to that moment. This is not a point of evaluation or personal judgment. It is a simple description of the apparent repetitiveness, difficulty, or blockage being experienced.

The consultant needs to employ appropriate helping skills and attitudes and present his or her experience in genuine, nonjudgmental, nonaggressive, and empathic language. It is also important to focus on the current, here-and-now experience, rather than reporting or describing something that has passed and for which our memories may be clouded. For example, consider the following responses to these typical forms of resistance.

Situation 1: *The consultee employing the (Silence) I'm Listening form of resistance:*

Consultant: *You appear to be listening. But I don't know how to read your silence. Could you share your ideas and your feelings about what I have been saying?*

Situation 2: *The Yes . . . But form of resistance:*

Consultant: *I am a bit confused. For the last 10 minutes I have been making suggestions and you seem to initially to agree and support the suggestion. You have been nodding and saying "Yes, that's a good idea." However, each time we can begin discussing how to implement the idea you seem to offer a "but" as to why it won't work.*

Situation 3: *Passive Aggressive, forgetting:*

Consultant: *I know you said that you were sorry that you forgot about the assignment and even apologized for the fact that this was the third time in a row that you forgot to do it, but you don't sound sorry, rather you sound and look to be angry or annoyed at something.*

Invitation

The *invitation* stage is intricately tied to the identification state in that the consultant is inviting the consultee to take ownership for the resistance described. Block (1981) suggests that a consultant take on somewhat Zen quality to working with resistance. Rather than intensifying and buffering one's argument with more data and research, only to find the consultee more entrenched in his or her defense, it would be more useful to sit quietly following the identification step in order to allow the consultee to reflect and take ownership. This period of silence is not employed as a technique or tool to make the consultee uncomfortable or defensive, rather it is used as time to reflect, consider, and embrace what is being said.

Should the consultee fail to respond to the period of silence, the consultant may directly encourage the consultee to fully express his or her concerns, reminding the consultee about the collaborative contract and the consultee's right to reject any suggestion. The consultant needs to invite the consultee to share his or her experience with both the progress and direction of the problem solving and the process of the consultation and the relationship with the consultant.

The goal of this step is to move the consultee from indirect expression of concerns (i.e., resistance) to direct expression of concerns, which now can be addressed.

Reframing

Resistance can often be minimized by affecting the consultee's perceptions of the consultant and the consulting process (Dougherty, Dougherty, & Purcell, 1991). Therefore, once the consultee has taken ownership over his or her concerns and the expression of resistance, the consultant needs to assist the consultee to accept these concerns as valid and to *reframe* these apprehensions and concerns so that they are viewed as important data to the process of the consultation. Rather than attempting to suppress these concerns or express them indirectly, the consultee needs to be encouraged to work with the consultant around these concerns as if they were prerequisite conditions to successful consulting.

As the consultant elicits and works with the consultee's concerns, the goal is to reframe the consultee's experience in consultation in a more positive and hopeful light, thus reducing the need for resistance. The persuasive element of the reframing must exceed the consultee's perceived threat to his or her freedom to engage in a particular behavior or to hold a particular attitude (Brehm, 1976).

A number of factors in the consultant's style and way of presenting recommendations and suggestions can increase the consultant's ability to persuade the consultee to reframe the experience in a more positive light. First, the consultant's persuasive ability is increased by exhibiting qualities of goodwill, expertise, prestige, and self-presentation (Kenton, 1989). It is important for the consultant to present ideas in ways that demonstrate concern for the consultee (i.e., goodwill) and exhibit professionalism and competence (i.e., expertise) with confidence, energy, and flexibility (self-presentation). Secondly, a consultant is more successful in reframing if that consultant presents ideas in a way that suggests that the consultee needs be reduced, not increased. It is important to reframe suggestions or interventions in ways that demonstrate immediate utility to the consultee (Elliot, 1988a; Reimers, Wacker, & Koeppl, 1987). Along this same line, it is suggested that highlighting the positive outcomes associated with the process of consulting and the specific recommendations made will increase the consultant's reframing abilities (Miller, 1980). Finally, connecting the proposed change to the consultee's current knowledge, experience, and even perceptual frame of reference will help the consultee reframe the experience in a more positive light (Sherif & Hovland, 1961).

Exercise 4-4 is provided to demonstrate the four steps of working with resistance and to facilitate the development of the reader's skills to employ these steps.

Reducing the Risk of Resistance

Developing the knowledge and skill needed to recognize and identify consultee resistance and to successfully invite the consultee into a reframing of his or her concerns in light of a positive view of consultation is essential to effective consulting. However, establishing conditions that reduce the risk of resistance may prove even more beneficial to successful consultation.

Social psychologist Jack Brehm (1966, 1972) proposed that when a person feels that his or her freedom has been threatened or abridged, he or she will engage in actions that help him or her regain control and personal freedom. The specific state of motivation that energizes their attempts to regain control he termed reactance. Consultee resistance has been viewed and interpreted within the context of reactance (Hughes & Falk, 1981). Thus, from this perspective, a consultant who can develop a consultation relationship and dynam-

---

EXERCISE 4-4   Working with Resistance

Directions: Because resistance is experienced at different levels of awareness by different consultants, and because the manner in which a consultant identifies, invites, and reframes varies from consultant to consultant, completing Exercise 4-4 is best performed with another or in a small group. Additional cues will be identified and alternative ways of inviting and reframing can be experienced by working within a group.

The task involves reading the consultative interaction to follow and responding to each of the following:

1. While it is hard not to recognize this as an example of resistance, since it is an exercise on resistance, your task will be to identify the specific point in the exchange that you became aware of the resistance. Identify what it was that specifically cued you to the resistance. Identify how you would feel as the consultant, up to that point. Your awareness of your reaction may be a useful diagnostic cue.
2. After recognizing the presence of resistance, write out the specific response that you would employ to "identify" and "invite" the consultee to embrace this resistance. Be sure to employ nonjudgmental, descriptive, empathic, and here-and-now response.
3. After reading the entire exchange, identify how you would respond to the consultee's implicit concerns in order to reframe the consultation experience in a more positive and hopeful light.

Consultant: Hi, Marie, it is very nice to meet you. I understand through Dr. Kahn (the principal) that you wished to speak with me regarding your third-grade student, Jonathan.

Consultee: Yes. I am really grateful you had time to see me. Jonathan has been a real problem. I was hoping you would talk with him.

Consultant: Well, that certainly could be a possibility, but I generally find that it is much more effective if I work along with the teacher to develop some problem-solving ideas. After all, you really are the expert when it comes to Jonathan and the work that he is failing to produce. So perhaps you could help me know what it is that Jonathan is doing (or not doing) that concerns you, as well as some of the things you have tried up to this point.

Consultee: Oh, I thought you were going to simply take him out of my class and do counseling with him.

Consultant: Again, Marie, if after discussing the situation we feel that is the best strategy, it certainly will be considered. So why don't you tell me what is up with Jonathan, and what kinds of things you have tried.

Consultee: Ok, but I only have a 30-minute free period now so we may have to do this another time?

Consultant: No, really, I'm OK with at least starting on this if you are, and 30 minutes is really quite a bit of time.

Consultee: Well, what is it exactly I should tell you?

Consultant: Marie, there really isn't anything in particular that you should tell me, but anything that could help me get a feel for what it is about Jonathan that is concerning you would be useful. Further, it might help both of us to understand the kinds of things you have found that work and those that haven't been as successful.

Consultee: Did Dr. Kahn seem to be concerned that I needed help?

Consultant: No, Dr. Kahn actually appeared impressed with your concern for Jonathan and your willingness to seek assistance.

Continued

EXERCISE 4-4   *Continued*

Consultee: Assistance! That's putting it mildly. You know maybe I ought to be talking with you about me—I think I'm losing it.

Consultant: I know it can feel overwhelming at times, but I feel confident that if you could help me understand a little about the situation with Jonathan, you and I could begin to work out some things that could help.

Consultee: You know, I guess you are right, maybe working together will help, but right now I really have to prepare for class. I'll give you a call and set up an appointment so we can meet again.

ic that maximizes consultee control and personal freedom should reduce reactance and thus reduce the risk of resistance.

The best means of preventing, or at least reducing, the risk of resistance would be to create a consultation relationship that is a truly collaborative working relationship (Caplan & Caplan, 1993; Friend & Cook, 1992; Parsons & Meyers, 1984). The unique characteristics of a collaborative consulting relationship that stimulate a sense of freedom and control and thus reduce the need for reactance and resistance are

- an interchange between colleagues
- confidentiality
- voluntary nature
- providing the consultee freedom to accept or reject all ideas
- needing/desiring active consultee contribution and shared responsibility
- coequal and mutual relationship with a balance of power and ownership for decision making
- mutual understanding and agreement on need, goal, and approach

The nature and value of a collaborative relationship, along with the uniqueness of its characteristics and ways to develop such collaboration, will be the focus of Chapter 5.

Summary

Resistance is the emotional and behavioral reaction to the experience of something unwanted. While often irrational, resistance may also be a rational reaction to a proposed change that in fact threatens the security or safety of the other.

Consultee resistance can be stimulated as a direct result of a consultant's abrasive style or as a result of the aversive and incongruent nature of the consulting relationship. However, consultee resistance is most often a reaction to the consultee's sense of vulnerability, loss of control, feelings of disequilibrium, or anxiety surrounding the nature of the problem or the consulting relationship.

When resistance is presented in its most direct form, such as when the consultee simply refuses to follow a suggestion or participate in the consultation exchange, the consultant is more apt to recognize its presence and be in a position to work with it. Often, however, resistance takes a more indirect form such as: silence, the consultee as listener; the yes . . . but consultee; or even flights into health. These less direct forms of resistance need to be recognized and identified if the consultant and consultee are to successfully work with the resistance in order to address the consultee's underlying concern.

Once resistance is recognized, the consultant needs to assist the consultee to take ownership for the resistance and be assisted in reframing his or her concerns so that the consultation and the consultant are viewed in a more positive light.

In addition to learning how to work with resistance, the effective consultant will learn how to increase the facilitative, collaborative nature of the consulting relationship as a way of reducing the risk of resistance. The position taken here and elsewhere (Parsons & Meyers, 1984) is that resistance is most likely indicative of a limitation to the facilitating nature of the consulting relationship. While this limitation may be a direct result of the concerns and anxieties of the consultee or the nature of the interpersonal process, the best way to manage and reduce resistance is to maintain a collaborative relationship with the consultee. This position will be elaborated upon in Chapter 5.

Chapter 5

Consultation: A Unique Form of Relationship

Being an expert in behavioral management, product control, systems applications, motivational theory, or any other area of professional expertise, while necessary to effective consultation, is far from sufficient. A brief review of the case that introduced Chapter 4, regarding the first-grade teacher with the attention-seeking student, will highlight the importance of the interpersonal process and climate of the consultation relationship to the eventual outcome.

Regardless of the area of expertise, the way the consultation process itself is managed will impact the consultee's utilization of even the most technical expertise. The success and failure of a consult, while not exclusively attributable to the nature of the relationship, depends in a large part on the dynamics of this social interaction (Tingstrom et al., 1990). It is in the context of relationship that consulting occurs. It is through the exchange of the consultant and the consultee that the problem is identified, the institutional context is described, and the possible role of the consultee in the intervention plan can be articulated. The quality and nature of the consultation relationship is clearly critical to the outcome of consultation (Bergan & Tombari, 1976; Schowengerdt, Fine, & Poggio, 1976).

As essential as the relationship is to the eventual outcome of a consultation, the development and maintenance of an effective, facilitative consulting relationship is not automatic. In fact, creating and maintaining an effective consultation relationship can be quite difficult. Therefore, to be an effective consultant, one needs to be proficient both in a specific content/technical area and in the art of developing and maintaining a productive consultative relationship (Block, 1981; Idol & West,1987; Parsons & Meyers, 1984; West & Cannon, 1988).

The purpose of this chapter is to assist the consultant in the development of the cognates and competencies required for fostering and maintaining an effective consultation relationship. Specifically, the chapter will assist the reader to

1. View consultation as fundamentally a dyadic relationship, affected by the same interpersonal processes and principles influencing all interpersonal relationships
2. Understand and employ the essential facilitative skills characteristic of all helping encounters and essential to consultation
3. Appreciate the value of the collaborative process and employ the skills essential to the development and maintenance of a collaborative relationship.

Consultation as an Interpersonal Process

Consultation has been discussed as a problem-solving process (e.g., Brown, Kurpius, & Morris, 1988; Caplan & Caplan, 1993; Parsons & Meyers, 1984). As will become evident, it may be more appropriate to suggest that consultation involves two problem-solving processes—one focusing on the needs of the consultee, and one focusing on the dynamic between the consultant and consultee (Parsons & Meyers, 1984). Brown, Kurpius, and Morris (1988), for example, noted that consultation was "two interlinked subprocesses occurring, one between the consultee and consultant and one between the consultee and client" (p. 4). Being knowledgeable and skilled at resolving the work-related problem between the consultee and the client is only part of the requirements for effective consulting. The effectiveness of the intervention is highly dependent upon the effectiveness of the subprocess or dynamic between the consultee and the consultant. The effective consultant, therefore, will be knowledgeable and skilled in the area of interpersonal dynamics.

As is true any time one engages in a relationship, the consulting dyad (i.e., consultant and consultee) will need to identify shared goals, articulate rules of interaction (i.e., norms), and define the roles to be played by either party. Whereas these processes may occur more subtly in some informal relationships (e.g., marriage), they will occur nonetheless. For formal encounters such as consultation, identifying goals, articulating rules of interaction, and defining roles must be addressed directly and as early in the relationship as possible in order to facilitate the interpersonal exchange.

Identifying Goals

In each consultation encounter it would appear that there are at least three types of goals that the consultant and consultee are attempting to accomplish. These goals (i.e., task resolution, personal need satisfaction, interpersonal need satisfaction) are discussed below.

Task Resolution
One goal for which the consultation relationship has been formed is to assist the consultee with his or her present work problem. Working on this specific goal is the task focus for the specific consultation encounter and the processes used to identify and achieve these specific goals will be outlined in Chapters 7, 8, and 9. However, beyond this task function of problem solving, the consultant must also attend to what is identified here as the maintenance focus. The consultant can attend to this maintenance focus by satisfying the needs of the participants (i.e., consultant and consultee). The effective consultant will learn to at-

tend to both the task demands and interpersonal maintenance needs of the consultation dyad. To accomplish this, the consultant must be sensitive to the unique needs of the consultee.

Personal Need Satisfaction

The consultee joins the consultation relationship expecting that some progress, if not resolution, of the presenting complaint will be achieved. Thus, relief from the presenting complaint is clearly one of the consultee's personal needs. Beyond this task-focused need, the consultee also brings other personal goals, needs, and agendas to which the consultant should be attentive.

The consultee may anticipate satisfying his or her need for affirmation, support, stimulation, professional gratification, increased status or esteem, or other such goals. Obviously, the more the consultee experiences need satisfaction within the consultation relationship, the more she or he will actively engage in the process.

In order to adequately provide for such individual need satisfaction, the consultant must get to know the consultee. Caplan and Caplan (1993) noted the importance of this process of getting to know the consultee and suggested that the consultant employ either "spontaneous proximity" and/or formal scheduled meetings as the medium through which this "getting to know" is accomplished. Employing spontaneous proximity requires the consultant to be alert to social opportunities and to be within talking distance of the consultee. Settings such as the employee's break room or lunch room, common meeting places (e.g., water cooler or coffee urn), or after work recreational activities (e.g., employee sports or exercise programs, student games, "happy hours," etc.) are all conducive to such spontaneous proximity, since they are settings where such exchanges are both expected and sanctioned. A primary objective for such meetings is not only to get to know the consultee but to begin to exhibit those characteristics of similarity that may increase the consultant's referent power and subsequently increase his or her ability to influence.

This concept of spontaneous proximity might at first appear quite simplistic and obvious. However, for the consultant who has become accustomed to working from behind a desk, spontaneous proximity may mean modification of his or her past practice and thus require some conscious effort.

Satisfying Interpersonal Needs

In addition to the unique personal needs that the consultee may bring to the relationship, the consultee will also bring certain interpersonal needs that he or she will attempt to satisfy in the process of the consultation exchange. As with the task needs and personal needs, the effective consultant will be sensitive in working with these consultee interpersonal needs so as to maximize the satisfaction experienced within the relationship.

One model for understanding these interpersonal needs was provided by William Schutz. Schutz (1967) posited that individuals interact with one another in an attempt to satisfy three basic interpersonal needs: the inclusion need (i.e., need to belong/need to associate), the control need (i.e., the desire to dominate others or give direction to the encounter), and the affection need (the desire the share close personal/emotional material with others). Schutz (1967) further suggested that each individual approached relationships with a fundamental style of satisfying these needs, a style he labeled a fundamental interpersonal relationship orientation (FIRO).

The consultee's inclusion component of his or her fundamental interpersonal relationship orientation will be reflected in the degree to which he or she desires to be included in the consultant's life as well as the degree to which the consultee wishes to include the consultant in his or her own life. The consultee's control need will be manifested in the degree to which she or he wishes to dominate and control the consultant within the context of the consultation relationships, or the degree to which she or he may wish to be dominated or controlled by the consultant. Finally, the degree to which the consultee wishes to express close personal and emotional feelings or wants to receive such expressions from the consultant would be reflective of his or her fundamental need for affection.

Schutz (1967) posited that when two individuals exhibit compatible FIRO patterns, their relationship will most likely be easy and productive. Thus it could be suggested that consultants who are aware of their own interpersonal orientation and are able to "read" the orientation of the consultee may be able to adjust their interpersonal behavior in order to make the interaction more compatible and thus more satisfying for the consultee.

Schutz (1989) has created a scale for assessing a person's fundamental interpersonal relationship orientation (FIRO-B). While the FIRO-B measure has numerous applications, in most cases requesting the consultee to take this measure would be not feasible. However, understanding the model and employing observational skills should assist the consultant in appraising the consultee's fundamental interpersonal style, in order to make the needed adjustments in his or her own consulting style.

Table 5-1 presents a number of consultee FIRO profiles and suggested consultant behaviors which may prove more compatible with that type of consultee. The suggested consultant behaviors are offered as samples of what might be useful. The suggestions found in Table 5-1 are not intended to be inclusive of all the compatible behaviors a consultant could demonstrate, nor is it meant to be an all-inclusive list of the various ways the consultee may exhibit his or her interpersonal needs. However, it is hoped that in reviewing Table 5-1, the reader will begin to appreciate the value of recognizing consultee interpersonal needs. It is also hoped that the reader will begin to appreciate the value of adjusting his or her own interpersonal consulting style to best meet the consultee's needs. Thus, a consultee who demonstrates a high need to control (and a subsequent low need to be controlled) will feel compatible with the consultant who empowers the consultee to set the agenda for the meetings or who allows the consultee to direct the time and place for the meeting. With a consultant who has a similar high need for control, the session should be structured to allow both the consultee and consultant to direct those areas of personal competence. Exercise 5-1 will help the reader to develop this awareness of his or her own interpersonal orientation as well as how that orientation may be adjusted given specific consultee needs.

Articulating the Rules of Interaction

In addition to identifying both formal and informal goals for the interaction and being sensitive to both task and maintenance needs, the consultant will need to help the consultee understand the rules or norms operating in this somewhat unique interpersonal encounter.

TABLE 5-1:   Consultant Behavior as Compatible with Consultee FIRO

Consultee FIRO	Behavior Manifestations	Consultant Interpersonal Behavior
CONTROL		
High expressed	Tries to take charge	1. Invites consultee to contribute to agenda 2. Encourages participation
	Directs consultant	3. Highlights contributions
		4. Asks for feedback and desired direction
High wanted	Appears easily led	1. Structures sessions 2. Contributes ideas first, requests consultee feedback
	Waits for direction	3. Provides reinforcement for consultee input
INCLUSION		
High expressed	Likes to talk about current activities	1. Allows for time to warm up, "chat," share. 2. Asks "How was your weekend?"
	Tries to include consultant in social activities	3. Is open to taking part in some social activities with consultee
High wanted	Hints at wanting to know more about consultant	1. Shares some personal information 2. Where appropriate invites consultee to share in social activity (e.g., coffee, lunch)
AFFECTION		
High expressed	Tries to get personal	1. Asks consultee about feelings
	Is emotive	2. Uses reflection of feeling along with reflection of content
	Is demonstrative	3. Mirrors expressive body language
High wanted	Asks consultant about his/her feelings	1. Expresses/discloses feelings 2. Closes interpersonal space 3. Increases demonstrated warmth
	Seeks more personal versus professional exchange	4. Discloses appropriate personal information

EXERCISE 5-1   Identifying and Working with One's Interpersonal Orientation

Introduction: In Part I of this exercise you will be asked to consider your typical style of approaching social interactions. In Part II you will be asked to pair with a colleague or classmate. One of you should assume the role of consultant, the other the role of consultee.

Part I: Reflecting on Personal Orientation

Directions: Assume that you are at a wedding reception where you know only the bride. On each of the continuum lines presented below, place an (X) in the approximate location that may describe your interpersonal style at that wedding. The descriptions are intended to present the extremes on each of the interpersonal need dimensions.

Inclusion:

Expressed (i.e., desire to include others)

|———————————————————————————————————|

1 (low)   10 (high)

Happy to stand at at the buffet table. Gives name, rank, and serial number when introduced to others. At the end of the party no one knows anything about him or her.	Says hello to everyone, willing to share story with anyone interested in listening. At the end of the party everybody knows, or at least met, him or her.

Wanted (i.e., desire to be included by others)

|———————————————————————————————————|

1 (low)   10 (high)

Not interested in being involved. Stands to the side, observing. Would prefer eating his or her meal as opposed to listening to others talk and share their stories.	Interrupts people in conversation to invite self into the interaction. Asks many personal questions. Doesn't miss a point of information about others.

Control:

Expressed (i.e., desire to direct and influence)

|———————————————————————————————————|

1 (low)   10 (high)

Happy to follow the program or do his or her own thing. Sits where told or directs self, but is not interested in directing others to their seats, food line, etc.	Organizes which tables go first in the food line. If any confusion about what's going, jumps in with ideas and attempts to organize others

Continued

EXERCISE 5-1   *Continued*

Wanted (i.e., seeks, wants direction from others)

|——|

1 (low)   10 (high)

Resists direction from others.   Actively seeks and asks for
Doesn't like the formality and   direction, from others. Wants
direction of being told where   to be told what to do. Where
to stand for the photos, whom   do I sit? When do we toast the
to sit with, or when to dance   bride and groom? What comes
with the bride, etc.   next? are questions she or he
                                                                        would express.

Affection:

Expressed (i.e., seeks opportunity for personal, emotional disclosure)

|——|

1 (low)   10 (high)

When talking of his or her own   Very emotionally discusses his
wedding is fact based versus   or her own wedding. Cries
feeling based. Discusses   (from happiness). Expresses
apparent expense of the wed-   "how pretty the bride is,"
ding.   "what a cute couple," "isn't
                                                                        love wonderful."

Wanted (i.e., desires others to express, discloses at the personal feeling level)

|——|

1 (low)   10 (high)

Becomes embarrassed or even   Inquires as to others feelings:
annoyed with another's   "How does it feel to be marry-
expressions of feelings: ing off your only daughter?"
"Would you knock it off with   "It's OK, come here cry on my
the tears?"   shoulder."

Part II:

Directions: Given your patterns of interpersonal orientation, as depicted through Part I of this
exercise, consider ways in which you could attempt to work with or modify your orientation
in order to maximize the interpersonal needs satisfaction of your consultee (the partner with
whom you are doing this exercise).

Arousal of Hope—the Greeting

Arousal of hope and positive expectations about the outcomes of this consultative encounter may be at the core of successful consultation, just as it is for other forms of helping (e.g.,
Frank, Hoehn-Saric, Imber, Liberman, & Stone, 1978). As suggested in Chapter 4, the consultee, while experiencing a need to be in consultation, may also feel anxious about "needing help" and perhaps somewhat hopeless about the possibility that help will be obtained.

Because of this, in addition to exhibiting normal greetings, ice-breaking, and warm hellos, the consultant should begin to convey the message that it is not only okay to be here, but that it is more than okay. The consultee needs to feel that the consultant values his or her professional concerns and feels hopeful about the positive outcomes of this interaction.

Establishing Norms

Once the initial social greetings and ice-breaking have been accomplished, the consultant needs to begin to define the nature of the consulting relationship and the rules that govern the interaction.

Regardless of the nature of the relationship or the particular people involved, all encounters, be they within a large bureaucracy or an intimate dyad (such as a husband and wife), have rules that guide the participants' interactions. In consultation it is important to clarify the rules of interaction. It is especially important that such a clarification occurs within the early stages of the relationship.

The consultee may enter the relationship with numerous questions regarding what is appropriate. What can she or he talk about? How personal does this have to be? What will she or he need to focus on (job, personal life, etc.)? How will the consultant act? Is this confidential? How often and how long will we meet? Who takes responsibility for the work? The interaction? These are questions, which even if unspoken, need to be clarified in order to begin to define the rules of the interaction.

One special point needs to be highlighted. People often bring rules or norms of previous encounters to new ones. While the use of such carry-over rules may prove effective in some circumstances, they may be counterproductive in other encounters. The consultee, for example, who because of previous experience with specialists or helpers anticipates that the consultant will tell him what to do, will act in ways that are quite appropriate for a prescriptive type of consultation. However, if the consultant approaches this consultee in a collaborative manner, the behavior that the consultee may carry over may result in the consultee responding rather than initiating, accepting rather than challenging, surrendering rather than collaborating. A consultee who is experienced with therapeutic encounters (i.e., counseling, psychotherapy) and who carries over the norms from those encounters to this consultation may expect the focus of the conversation to be on personal-emotional issues, rather than work-related concerns. The effective consultant will be sensitive to the possible carry-over norms of the consultee and be able to assist the consultee to redefine or re-norm the consultation interaction when necessary.

In attempting to avoid leaving to chance what one might be able to structure, the consultant should explicate the specific norms of the consultation each time a new consultee is encountered. By discussing the rules of the interaction early within the encounter, the consultant can reduce any contradictory expectations or misunderstandings and establish a smooth operational structure.

Defining the Roles

A role defines the limits, responsibilities, and expectations of a participant. A consultant is most likely both familiar and invested in the role and process of being a consultant in consultation. The consultee, however, is in a new role and may feel uncertain and uncomfortable in that role. The consultee may also have unrealistic expectations regarding the consultant's role, influence, and power. The roles of the consultee and the consultant need to be clearly defined if the consultation is to proceed smoothly.

The specific definitions and boundaries of the roles of consultant and consultee will be determined by a number of factors, such as: 1) the nature of the specific consult (i.e., provisional, prescriptive, collaborative, mediational), 2) the focus of the consultation, and 3) the unique needs and skills of the parties involved. However, even with such consult-specific definitions, a somewhat generic definition of the roles provides a useful starting point.

Consultant

The consultant is a specialized professional whose primary role and function is that of technological expert or adviser. In this capacity the consultant has been called upon to assist with a current work-related problem and will introduce new information, concepts, perspectives, and skills into the problem-solving equality. The consultant, while being in a position to influence others, has no direct power to make changes or implement programs. Further, the consultant accepts no direct responsibility for implementing programs aimed at impacting the client; rather, this responsibility remains with the consultee, as it had prior to the consultation relationship.

Consultee

The consultee is the party accountable for the performance of a third party (i.e., the client) and who in the process of carrying out his or her work-related performance has sought out the expertise of the consultant. The consultee has direct control over the implementation of intervention programs. The consultee is free to accept or reject all or part of the consultant's advise and assistance. Further, the consultant has no administrative power or responsibility for the consultee and thus is not in a position of supervisor, evaluator, or manager.

Since this text emphasizes the collaborative approach to consultation, additional characteristics will highlight the role of consultant and consultee, as well as the dynamic of the consultation process. These specific collaborative elements are discussed later within this chapter and should be discussed with the consultee at the time of the initial contract and highlighted throughout the consultative interaction.

Role Conflicts

In addition to outlining the roles and functions of the consultant and the consultee, the consultant should be sensitive to the possibility that the role of consultee may in some way conflict with other roles which the consultee serves. For example, as manager, or supervisor, or in some capacity as a "person in charge," the consultee may have the self-perception of being a help provider and now may feel conflict and dissonance over being in the role of "help seeker."

The consultant needs to recognize this possible interrole conflict and help the consultee to reframe or redefine the role of consultee as collaborative problem solver, rather than that of dependent help seeker.

Consultation as a Helping Relationship

While consultation is certainly a dyadic encounter, it is an encounter of a special sort. Consultation is a helping process. The effective consultant will not only be skilled and knowledgeable in basic interpersonal dynamics but will also be competent in the skills of helping. As noted by Brown, Kurpius, and Morris (1988), the skills required to initiate a consulting relationship are very similar to those needed in other helping situations. The effective consultant, therefore, will have those skills needed to establish a working alliance in which the consultee and consultant can explore the depth and breadth of the problem and initiate and maintain actions aimed at achieving their goal(s).

Establishing a Helping Alliance

Once the foundation has been laid and the basic nature of the encounter described and structured, the consultant can now provide the consultee with the sense that a meaningful, working, helping relationship is possible. The consultant can foster this expectation by exhibiting those interpersonal traits and characteristics that demonstrate that he or she is a warm, accepting, understanding individual who has both the desire and the competence to assist the consultee.

Rogers (1961) and others (e.g., Berenson & Carkhuff, 1967; Carkhuff & Berenson, 1977; Parsons, 1985; Truax & Carkhuff, 1965) posited that a successful helper must exhibit qualities of *acceptance, warmth,* and *genuineness.* While research would suggest that these conditions are not sufficient (Beutler, Crago, & Arezmendi, 1986; Gurman, 1977) for positive outcomes in every case, it does appear that these conditions are key to the development of the helping alliance and contribute in a facilitative way to the positive outcomes of helping.

Much of the research pointing to the value of these facilitative conditions focused on counseling or therapeutic relationships. Other research (e.g., Horton & Brown, 1990; Meyers, Friedman, & Gaughan, 1975; Schowengerdt, Fine, & Poggio, 1976; Weissenburger, Fine, & Poggio, 1982) has demonstrated the value of these same facilitative conditions to the process of consultation. These conditions will be discussed in some detail as necessary for effective consulting.

Acceptance

If consultation is to be effective, the consultant must demonstrate acceptance of the consultee. This means that the consultant does NOT try to control the consultee or demand that the consultee behave or think in any certain way. Rather than attempting to impose control on the consultee, the *accepting* consultant allows the consultee to be who he or she is.

To truly accept this other, this consultee, the consultant must put aside any formal status and informal social roles that may interfere with a mutual, open relationship. It does not matter that the consultant may have more degrees, more money, or more friends. All that matters is that this is an encounter between two, less than perfect human beings who are interested in facilitating the solution of a problem.

This is not always easy to achieve. It requires that the consultant interact with the consultee in a real "here and now" frame of reference and ignore roles such as male-female, young-old, black-white, rich-poor, expert-novice, or even consultant-consultee.

Acceptance of another does not mean absolute, wholesale approval of everything that person says or does. If one really cares for another, then he or she will extend him- or herself in hopes of educating, motivating, or encouraging the other to grow. However, even when the consultant has intentions of changing the consultee, true acceptance demands that the consultant allow the client freedom to choose NOT to change.

Feeling accepting of another is only part of the process. For it to truly affect the consultation relationship, the consultant's acceptance must be demonstrated and conveyed to the consultee. This is an important point to consider. It may be easy for one to *say,* "I accept you as you are," but that acceptance needs to be demonstrated and not just spoken. Exercise 5-2 encourages you to discover ways of *expressing* and *demonstrating* acceptance.

Nonpossessive Warmth and Respect

In addition to feeling accepted, the consultee needs to feel valued or prized by the consultant. Often coming for help is a blow to one's sense of maturity, independence, and personal

---

EXERCISE 5-2   Demonstrating Acceptance

You can demonstrate acceptance of the consultee by

1. Actively encouraging the consultee to express the ways in which he or she is different from you.
2. Showing care and concern for the consultee and the consultee's problem.
3. Allowing the consultee the freedom to choose NOT to change or follow your helping lead.

Directions: For the first two situations consider the effect of each consultant's response. Identify which response appears to be demonstrating acceptance. For the last situation, write a nonaccepting response and one that demonstrates acceptance. As with previous exercises, it is useful to discuss your response with your colleagues, classmates, or supervisor.

Situation 1:

Consultee: " I know I am taking up your time, but I am stuck and have absolutely no idea how to handle Charlie!"
Consultant A: "Hey... you can count on me!"
Consultant B: "Feeling like you're stuck can be very frustrating, but I'm certainly willing to share ideas with you regarding Charlie and how to best approach him."

Situation 2:

Consultee: "This idea you have is stupid!"
Consultant A: "As we discussed last time, I thought we both believed it was the best we could do. But if you have other ideas, or are willing to keep banging away at it, it is OK with me."
Consultant B: "I don't understand—you agreed to do it. After all, it is the best solution. So what's your problem with it?"

Situation 3:

Consultee: "I'm a mess... you gotta tell me what to do... should I fire him, or quit myself?"
Consultant A: (write a nonaccepting way of responding)
Consultant B: (write a response that demonstrates acceptance)

and professional competence. The consultee may question his or her own professional or even personal value. Thus it is important that the consultant demonstrate respect for the consultee by exhibiting an appreciation and valuing of the consultee and the consultee's involvement in the consultation.

This characteristic has been termed unconditional, nonpossessive regard (Rogers, 1957). This unconditional regard or warmth reflects the consultant's deep nonevaluative respect for the thoughts, feelings, wishes, and potential of the consultee. It is the ability to look beyond the conditions of others—for example, their appearance, their manner of presentation, their backgrounds, or even their beliefs and actions—in order to value the fundamental person behind these conditions. The consultant exhibiting nonpossessive warmth and respect communicates the message that the consultee is a worthwhile person, regardless of what he or she is experiencing.

The belief in and communication of such nonpossessive prizing is not easy, especially for those in the industrialized climate where status, power, and social prestige have been equated with human worth. Exercise 5-3 invites you to look at some of the conditions surrounding a human being that may bias your valuing or prizing that person.

As you reflect upon your responses to Exercise 5-3, as well as those of your colleagues and classmates, you may notice something of interest. While many of us may be positively biased toward individuals who are attractive, articulate, educated, achieving and successful—and conversely, negatively biased against those lacking these conditions—most of us will respond warmly and nonpossessively to a 2-day-old-infant. This perhaps is the model or prototype to approaching others that we need to highlight. Even though the newborn is often not attractive (using adult standards) or articulate, educated, achieving, or successful, we clearly value and prize him or her simply because he or she exists as a fellow human being. It is this nonpossessive warmth or unconditional regard that we want to feel and convey to the consultee.

As an effective, caring consultant, you need to monitor the degree to which you are communicating your respect and unconditional warmth for the consultee. This process of monitoring can take place by considering each of the following questions as you reflect on your approach with any one consultee (Parsons & Meyers, 1984):

1. Was I attending? Was I actively and accurately listening?
2. Did I actively encourage the consultee to contribute?
3. Did I demonstrate the belief that the consultee is competent and capable of caring for him/herself?
4. Did I enter the relationship assuming "good will"?
5. Did I demonstrate (appear?) appropriately warm, close, in the relationship?
6. Did I give evidence of spending time and energy truly understanding the consultee and his or her problem?
7. Was I judgmental or evaluative in my language?
8. Did the consultee show signs of feeling appreciated? Cared for?

Genuineness

The previous elements of acceptance and warmth will prove ineffective if they are performed or exhibited artificially. Being real, being genuine, is essential to effective

---

EXERCISE 5-3   Distracting from Nonpossessive Regard

Directions: Nonpossessive regard or unconditional prizing requires us to look beyond the trappings and conditions of another in order to value the person. However, these conditions and trappings are sometimes hard to ignore and bias (both positively and negatively) our valuing of another. For each of the conditions listed identify the degree (i.e., not at all, somewhat, strongly) and the direction (positive or negative) these descriptions would bias your evaluation of the person.

As you reflect on your immediate, honest reactions, ask yourself what can you do to assist yourself in looking beyond these biasing conditions in order to value and prize the person.

Description of Consultee	Direction of bias	Degree of bias
1. President of a Fortune 500 company		
2. A night manager of manufacturing plant with high school equivalency degree		
3. A very bright and attractive legal counsel for large engineering firm		
4. A near retirement age, British literature teacher in a private girls' preparatory school		
5. A person with very poor personal hygiene habits		
6. A very famous person in the field of medicine		
7. A renowned educator		
8. A 2-day-old infant		

---

consultation. Yet, as with the other characteristics, being genuine is not always easy to achieve.

In my own anxiety as a new consultant, I sometimes felt like I had to put on a "game face" every time I met a new consultee. In my eagerness to "do it correctly," I would sometimes try too hard and become somewhat artificial. Often our desire to do it correctly or to be liked by another forces us to play out a role. We may feel like we are bound to perform or enact certain types of behaviors such as those associated with the roles of a male or female, a parent, or even a consultant.

When we act out of a role, we may not be truly genuine. To be genuine requires us to be role-free. This does not mean to imply that we should reject or ignore normal conventions of appropriate professional behavior. What is suggested is that we assimilate these conventions into our own natural style, so that what is exhibited is us and not a formula for behaving. Further, being genuine does not suggest that we can say or do whatever we desire just because it is truly what we are feeling. Being genuine points more to the fact that the consultant is open to his or her own experience. The form and depth that the sharing of that awareness may take will be shaped by a sense of care for the consultee. It is important to remember that honest, open disclosure is appropriate only as it facilitates the consultative process.

There may be times when you are experiencing some negative feelings in response to the consultee. As an effective consultant you will need to consider whether you are to share these feelings. If the feelings can be expressed without being judgmental and with a proper sensitivity for how they will be received by the consultee, then expressing them may prove helpful.

In order to become more aware of threats to your own genuineness, consider Exercise 5-4.

Maintaining Genuineness

While we may understand how roles can interfere with our being genuine and authentic, it may be more useful to begin to understand what it is to be genuine and how best to maintain our genuineness, especially within consultation. Gibb (1978) identified characteristics of the genuine helper, which this author feels has application to consultation. A modification of Gibb's (1978) list is presented in Figure 5-1, to be used as a guideline for assessing the degree of genuineness exhibited within any one consultation. It may be useful to employ this list as a reference upon which to reflect and assess each of your consultation interac-

---

EXERCISE 5-4　Role-Bound or Role-Free?

Directions: In order to become more genuine in our consultation, we must become sensitive to the conditions and the experiences that inhibit our genuineness and encourage our role playing behaviors. Consider each of the following. What implications may your responses hold for you as a consultant? Discuss your responses with a colleague, classmate, or supervisor.

1. Have you ever responded to another's question of "How are you doing?" by saying "Fine!" even when you were not? Can you think of other examples where an "expected" response may interfere with your genuineness? What motivates such scripted responses? How might that motivation interfere with genuineness in consultation?

2. Can you think of roles that sometimes require those in them to be role-bound? What normal, appropriate, feelings, thoughts, or actions might be inhibited or prohibited by each of the following roles?
   - The role of teacher
   - The role of police officer
   - The role of clergy person
   - The role of counselor/therapist
   - The role of consultant

3. Think of the roles you enact (e.g., male/female, student, professional, etc.). Discuss with a colleague, mentor, or supervisor how they could interfere with your genuineness as a consultant.

tions. Considering whether you exhibited each of the following may prove useful in developing and maintaining genuineness within your consultation interactions.

As might be obvious from Gibb's (1978) description, a consultant who is genuine is one who is *open* as opposed to defensive, is *real* as opposed to phony; a consultant who is genuine is *congruent*. His or her words, actions, tone, thoughts, and feelings are all expressing the same message. The genuine consultant is able to express and admit discomfort or even disappointment when experienced rather than pretend that everything is fine. Clearly it will be hard to exhibit these characteristics if we are rigidly following a script that we feel accompanies the role we need to play.

Each situation, each encounter we find ourself in challenges our ability to remain genuine. Exercise 5-5 is presented to help you increase your awareness of what it is like when you are communicating genuinely.

The genuine consultant

- expresses directly to the consultee what he or she is experiencing.
- communicates without distorting his or her own messagees.
- listens without distorting the consultee's messages.
- learns to live and communicate about the here and now (rather than the there and then).
- is spontaneous and free in his or her communications rather than using planned strategies.
- reveal his or her true motivation in the process of communicating his or her messages.
- is concrete in his or her communications.
- is willing to commit him- or herself.

FIGURE 5-1:   A Checklist of Genuineness

Consultation: A Relationship Involving Collaboration

To this point consultation has been defined as a professional social encounter of a helping sort. But as evidenced by the discussion in the previous chapters, the unique concerns, problems, and points of resistance often experienced in consultation, along with the unique demands and opportunities made available by the conjoining of consultee and consultant resources, makes effective consultation different from other helping encounters. Effective consultation, even when taking a provisional or prescriptive focus, involves a degree of collaboration. Understanding the defining elements of collaboration and having the skills to foster the development of a collaborative relationship within consultation are essential for essential to effective consulting.

EXERCISE 5-5   Identifying Genuine Communication

Directions: This is a two-stage exercise that will require you to record a brief (10–15 minute) consultative interaction. If you are not currently in a consultative relationship, the exercise could be done with a partner with whom you are fairly unfamiliar.

Part 1: Record a conversation between yourself and your partner (consultee). The conversation should last a minimum of 10 minutes with the goal being simply to become better acquainted with one another and to begin to identify an area in which some "work-related" assistance could be provided by you, the consultant.

Part 2: Below you will find five characteristics of genuine communications. Review the tape recording of your conversation. As you listen ask yourself the following questions, noting places where you were clearly being genuine, as well as places where you were perhaps a little less than genuine. Increasing your awareness of these shifts is the first step in increasing your ability to become (remain) more genuine.

1. Role Freeness
   - Did I hide behind titles, labels, degrees?
   - Did I fall into a gender, age, race, or class role?

2. Spontaneity
   - While being sensitive to the strength of the other person, was I responsive to the moment rather than acting out of a preplanned and rigid script?
   - Although there are instances when it is appropriate not to express feelings or thoughts, did I make these decisions in light of an active awareness of these thoughts and feelings and with an eye for what is best for the other person?

3. Nondefensiveness
   - If questioned or criticized, was I able to listen and even demonstrate a willingness to understand the other's point of view?
   - Did I demonstrate defensive communications and even counterattack when challenged?

4. Congruency
   - Did my words, tones, and bodily actions seem to be expressing the same thing?
   - Did I appear consistent in expressing my thoughts, feelings, and behaviors?
   - Were there any discrepancies between what I was thinking, feeling, and doing?

5. Openness
   - Did I demonstrate a capability of self-disclosure and mutual sharing appropriate to the relationship?

Collaboration—a Definition

Caplan and Caplan (1993) see mental health collaboration as

> *. . . an interprofessional method in which a mental health specialist establishes a partnership with another professional worker, network, group, or team of profes-*

*sionals in a community field or a human service institution. The mental health spe-
cialist, by agreement with his colleagues, becomes an integrated part of their
evaluation and remedial operations and accepts responsibility for contributing his
specialized knowledge and for personally using his specialized diagnostic and remedial skills in dealing with their case (p. 295).*

Collaborative consultation has been described as "an interactive process that enables
teams of people with diverse expertise to generate creative solutions to mutually defined
problems" (West & Idol, 1987, p. 389). The outcome has been defined as "enhanced, altered, and different from the original solutions that any team member would produce independently" (Idol, Paolucci-Whitcomb, & Nevin, 1986, p. 1).

As used within this text and elsewhere (e.g., Friend & Cook, 1992; Parsons & Meyers,
1984), collaboration refers to a style or an approach to professional interaction. It defines
the *how* of the interaction and not necessarily the *what* of the consult. Consultation of various forms and foci (e.g., prescriptive, provisional, mediational, crisis, developmental, etc.)
can be approached by a consultant employing a collaborative style. Further, as a style, a
consultant may actually approach different stages or points within a single consult with a
more or less collaborative manner. And even when the nature of the consult requires more
directive, expert action on the part of the consultant—as may be the case in a crisis consultation—elements of collaboration could be and should be included.

The Value of Collaboration

Recognition of the potential value of collaboration is evident in education and industry. Numerous authors (e.g., Cook & Friend, 1991; Maeroff, 1988; Ross & Ross, 1982; Tjosvold,
1987) have noted the improvement in organizational effectiveness by involving employees
in the decision making. These authors noted increased productivity, satisfaction, and ownership when employees are involved in the decision making. It is this same sense of empowerment and participatory management that is created in a collaborative consultation
and the same benefits that are accrued (Curtis & Zins, 1981; Hinkle, Silverstein, & Walton,
1977; Wenger, 1979; Wilcox, 1977).

While not always possible to achieve, collaboration may always be a goal worth pursuing. In theory, collaboration offers a number of potential benefits to consultation. First,
it is a means of maximizing the use of resources, both those of the consultant and those of
the consultee. In the optimal, somewhat ideal collaborative consult, each side gives to and
takes from the other in synergistic ways that maximize problem-solving resources. Secondly, the investment in time and energy on the part of the consultee results in ownership
and increases the likelihood of implementation (Block, 1981). Finally, through collaboration, the exchanges become educational for both the consultant and the consultee. Both the
consultant and consultee increase their skills and knowledge as a result of working and
sharing together. This educational component increases the likelihood that the consultee
will be better able to cope with similar problems in the future, a preventive goal for
consultation.

The Salient Characteristics of Collaborative Consultation

A number of authors (e.g., Caplan, 1970; Caplan & Caplan, 1993; Curtis & Meyers, 1985; Friend & Cook, 1992; Parsons & Meyers, 1984;) have identified the salient characteristics of a collaborative relationship. These characteristics are

1. Nonhierarchical interchange between colleagues
2. Mutual, shared responsibilities
3. Freedom to accept/reject

Because of the importance of each of these characteristics and the possible difficulties encountered when attempting to maintain such characteristics within the consultation relationship, each will be discussed in some depth.

Nonhierarchical Interchange between Colleagues
As noted elsewhere (Parsons & Meyers, 1984), one important characteristic of collaboration is that it involves an interchange between professional colleagues.

The relationship is nonhierarchical. That is, as colleagues with coequal responsibility, the relationship is without differential status, with neither the consultant nor the consultee being identified as THE expert or THE superior to the other. Both the consultant and consultee are viewed as having valuable input and areas of expertise.

While this is the condition of collaboration, it is a condition or characteristic that is not always easy to achieve. Often consultees approach consultation having had authority and power over their own work-related decisions. Most likely consultees are experts in their own areas of professionalism and now must adjust to relying on, or at the minimum, working with another. Under these conditions it is important for the consultant not only to accept the consultee's areas of expertise, but to be able to demonstrate his or her own particular unique expertise. This is not to suggest that this is a competition, but rather a meeting of two individuals with separate and unique areas of competence and expertise that, when pulled as collaborative resources, can maximize the problem-solving potential of the consultation.

Another potential roadblock to the establishment of such a collegial exchange occurs when the level of competence and expertise is unequal. When the discrepancy in knowledge and skill obviously tips in favor of the consultant, attempts to create even the rudimentary beginning of a collaborative relationship could be threatened. Under these conditions, that consultant needs to remember and convey to the consultee that technical or content expertise is only part of the problem-solving equation. The unique experience and knowledge around the day-to-day workings of this setting are essential for problem solving, and the consultee is the expert in that area.

A similar roadblock to maintaining a nonhierarchical relationship occurs when the consultee, even when possessing expertise, approaches the consultation defeated and feeling in need. Under these conditions, the consultant will need to employ a number of communication skills (see Chapter 6) aimed at influencing the nature of the relationship. These communication skills will move the relationship from a position of status and power differential to one of mutuality and collegiality. In addition to the communication techniques presented in Chapter 6, it is useful for the consultant to directly encourage consultee participation while at the same time playing down his or her own participation.

In these situations the consultant should attempt to reduce the visibility of his or her own efforts by taking a low public profile. It is useful to use "our"-type language when referring to what was accomplished. It is also useful for the consultant, where possible and when appropriate, to encourage the consultee to take the lead in reporting the data or the results of the interaction to those who may need to know. These steps will help to reinforce the sense of collaboration while at the same time allowing the consultee to be viewed as operating in a lead position.

Mutuality and Degree of Interdependence

The collaborative relationship is one in which both the consultant and consultee share responsibility for action planning, implementation, and results. Both consultant and consultee agree on the need, the goal, and even the approach to be employed. The relationship is reciprocal in that all parties have equal access to information and the opportunity to participate in problem identification, discussion, decision making, and all outcomes. This is different than cooperation, in which one directs another who is willing to follow.

In collaboration communication is two way. Both the consultant and consultee take the initiative and set direction, depending on the issue under consideration and the unique skills and expertise of each member. Data collection and analysis are conjoint activities. The types of data to be studied as well as the method to be employed are conjointly agreed upon by the consultant and consultee.

The value of such consultee involvement is that it not only increases the consultee's sense of control and thus reduces resistance, but it also increases the quality of interventions produced. Further, as Kopel & Arkowitz (1975) noted, self-attributed change is more likely to be maintained than change attributed to someone else, and collaboratively produced interventions will more likely be maintained than those prescribed.

In collaboration, the mutuality referred to implies that both parties share direction and ownership for outcome. Decision making is shared and bilateral. Decisions reflect the mutual exchange and shared respect for the expertise and responsibilities of both the consultant and consultee. Mutuality as applied here does not mean that both parties need to be equally responsible and involved in completing activities or tasks. The consultant interested in collaboration need not be concerned with dividing up the tasks equally. Division of labor should follow practical lines.

Freedom to Accept or Reject

As suggested in the previous two characteristics, in a collaborative relationship both members are truly free to accept or reject any part or whole of the interaction. The consultee is not under obligation to follow the specific recommendations or suggestions of the consultant.

In order for this sense of freedom to be achieved, the consultation must be voluntary. The consultee's perception of freedom and control can be increased by communicating clearly to the consultee that consultation is a voluntary process and that all consultant recommendations are tentative. The collaborative consultant will provide the consultee with options whenever possible, even the option to reject the entire process.

In addition to experiencing the consultation as voluntary, the consultee needs to feel that the interaction is confidential. The consultee must feel as if she or he can react honestly to the consultant without fear of reprisal or any harmful repercussion (Parsons & Meyers, 1984). It is even useful to highlight the potential value of such rejection. Consultee rejection of suggestions can lead to further exchange and development of ideas, and often results in fuller understanding and agreement.

Summary

A level of technical expertise and/or proficiency can be assumed as fundamental for consultants. However, as suggested throughout this chapter, the effective consultant will need more than technical expertise.

The utilization of the consultant's technical skills and knowledge takes place within the matrix of a consultation relationship. As such, effective consultants will have the knowledge and skills necessary to navigate the dyadic, helping, and collaborative nature of the relationship found in consultation. The specific knowledge and skill needed are those necessary to

1. Establish a need-fulfilling relationship
2. Facilitate problem definition, resource identification, and remediation
3. Interact in a way that makes maximum use of the synergistic value of the interaction and promotes the mutual ownership of the decisions and outcomes

As reviewed in this chapter, consultation is first and foremost an interpersonal exchange and can be facilitated by providing structure, role definitions, and rules for behaviors. At a minimum, therefore, the effective consultant will

1. Introduce who he or she is and what his or her role and responsibilities will be
2. Detail expectations about role of consultee
3. Clarify conflicting expectations
4. Outline (thumbnail) the process (time, frequency, structure, etc.) of consulting and what he or she hopes to achieve (goals, subgoals)
5. Discuss limits of confidentiality and limits to consultant's role in regards to evaluation

Further, as noted in the chapter, effective collaboration is more than just a professional, social encounter, it is a helping encounter. And, as a helping encounter, the process of problem identification and remediation can be facilitated by the consultant who exhibits the characteristics of acceptance, warmth, and genuineness.

Finally, to be truly effective and to maximize the synergistic potential of the consultation interaction, it was suggested that the consultant strive to make the relationship collaborative—one in which the consultant and consultee interact in a nonhierarchical, mutually interdependent manner in which both parties retain the freedom to accept or reject not only the recommendations but the relationship itself.

If it is appropriate to suggest that the consultant's technical expertise takes shape within the context of a relationship, then it is also appropriate to suggest that the relationship is given context and shape by the forms of communication employed. The value and role of communication within consultation cannot be overemphasized and as such serves as the focus for the next chapter (Chapter 6).

Communication: A Tool for Effective Consultation

Perhaps it could be said that if the relationship is the context, or backdrop, of consultation, then communication is the medium that colors that context. As with other forms of helping, effective communication is the keystone to effective consulting.

Since consultation as presented within this text will involve transactional, or two-way, reciprocal interaction (Schmuck & Runkel, 1985), the effective consultant will need to be proficient in the communication skills of sending and receiving. Further, because of the value of establishing and maintain a collaborative relationship, the skilled consultant will be proficient in those communication processes that facilitate the development and maintenance of a collaborative interaction.

The current chapter highlights this *interactional process* of consultation. Specifically, the chapter will provide the information and guided practice needed to:

1. Develop skills of communication essential to all helping encounters, including consultation
2. Increase awareness of and the ability to employ those communication elements that facilitate the development and maintenance of a collaborative relationship

Knowledge and Communication Skills Essential to the Helping Nature of Consultation

As may be obvious, consultation, while being a unique form of helping, is nonetheless a helping process. As with all forms of helping, effective consultation requires that the helper, or in this case the consultant, understand and clarify the nature of the problem and focus the consultee on specific targets and steps to be taken. During the early stages of consultation, the primary goal for the consultant is simply to achieve and demonstrate understanding of the consultee situation. The consultant will employ a variety of communication skills aimed at facilitating the consultee's disclosure and increasing the consultant's accurate understanding of those disclosures. In addition to gathering a clear picture of the nature of the problem, the consultant also hopes to achieve an understanding of the resources available.

Understanding, therefore, and NOT problem resolution, is truly the first goal for the consultant. Yet as essential as it is, the task of understanding is far from an easy one. The process of accurately understanding another is far from a given—even for the professional consultant.

In order to accurately communicate that understanding to the consultee, an effective consultant will need to be proficient in the fundamental skills of helping. These skills are presented in detail below. The material is based on and adapted from a previous presentation by this author (Parsons, 1995).

It should be noted that while these are the same skills typically employed in other helping encounters, such as counseling or therapy, they are used to different ends in consultation. Unlike in counseling or therapy, the skills used by the consultant will address the work-related problems of the consultee's client and not for the personal therapeutic benefit of the consultee. Thus, while employing these communication skills of helping to build a working relationship with the consultee and to explore the depth and breadth of the problem and identify and employ strategies for resolution, the consultant must be sensitive to avoid allowing the consultation to slip into consultee therapy (Brown, Kurpius, & Morris,1988; Caplan, 1970; Caplan & Caplan, 1993; Parsons & Meyers, 1984).

Skills of Attending and Active Listening (Preconditions to Understanding)

In our typical day-to-day conversations, be they at the water cooler or at home over morning coffee, we may find ourself enacting a role of listener, which is characterized as being quiet, polite, and noninterruptive. While these are certainly nice and socially acceptable ways of behaving, they are also ways that may interfere with understanding of another person's message. Often in our polite quietness we may find ourself listening with half an ear and understanding with reduced accuracy. The same can be true in consultation. The consultant who engages in listening quietly and passively to the consultee may find that he or she is drifting off into a daydream (What a great day for golf!), focusing on a personal concern (Where do I have to be this afternoon?), or even jumping to conclusions about what is being said (. . . oh, I know where this is leading!").

If we are to be helpful in a consultation interaction, we must understand what the consultee is attempting to convey. Thus, these tendencies to jump to conclusions or become inattentive or self-absorbed must be avoided.

Given that humans are communicative animals, it may seem strange to suggest that we—especially as adults—need to learn to listen. However, the reality is that while hearing may be naturally perfect, listening is NOT perfect . . . naturally!

The fact is that some of the lessons of communications that we have been taught while growing up may actually interfere with effective listening. The instructions "be quiet and listen!" or "don't interrupt" or "let the other person finish!" are directives that can actually impede our listening for understanding. The sad truth is that while hearing may be a passive, quiet activity, effective listening is an active, engaging process requiring energy, motivation, skill, and patience! In fact, we may need to rewrite the rules you previously learned about being a good listener to now include:

- One must NOT be still and quiet . . . one must be ACTIVE!
- One must NOT passively await the reception of the consultee's messages, rather one must reach out and actively involve him- or herself in the gathering of the information provided.
- One must NOT listen with only his or her ears. A consultant must use all of his or her senses to listen effectively.

Prior to employing the skills of active listening, the effective consultant will need to learn to fully attend to the consultee and to demonstrate to the consultee that he or she is attending. There are many roadblocks to our ability to fully attend to another. In order to overcome these roadblocks, the effective consultant will become knowledgeable and skilled in the physical and psychological techniques that facilitate his or her ability to attend.

Attending as a Physical Response
Attending or "being with" another requires both a physical posture and a psychological orientation. Gerard Egan (1977), for example, pointed out the importance of one's body orientation in the accurate reception of information during a face-to-face encounter, such as found in consultation. He suggests that proper attending behavior may be characterized as being:

- **S**traight, face-to-face body orientation, with
- **O**penness in body posture and a slight, forward
- **L**ean, while maintaining
- **E**ye contact, all done in a
- **R**elaxed manner

The value of this **SOLER** posture (straight, open, lean, eye contact, relaxed) within typical helping encounters is supported by numerous authors and researchers (e.g., Asbury, 1984; Hermansson, Webster, & McFarland, 1988; Mehrabian, 1967). A survey of this research would suggest that the value of this body position for the consultant may be twofold.

First, the posture places the consultant in a body orientation that facilitates reception of the consultee's message. This SOLER position opens the consultant to a number of channels of information reception while at the same time narrows the band of potential interference. Just consider the increased number of competing stimuli you would be receiving if rather than facing the consultee and focusing on his or her eyes, you faced a window, back turned to the consultee.

The second value of the SOLER posture is that it conveys to the consultee (via body language) that the consultant is attending and truly open to receive his or her messages. In therapeutic encounters such as counseling, this body language message has been found to not only encourage disclosure but also increase the client's sense that the counselor is warm and caring (e.g., Argyle, 1967; Mehrabian, 1967). A similar impact should be anticipated when this posture is employed in consultation.

In addition to serving as a strategy for increasing and communicating the consultant's attention, understanding the elements of such attending behavior also provides the consultant with much needed diagnostic information. For example, the consultee who in the process of listening to the consultant's feedback begins to adjust his body position, moving away from straight, open, forward-leaning posture to the more closed and defensive posture (i.e., arms and legs crossed, leaning back in chair with body askew), is signaling to the consultant that "this message is NOT being openly received." Learning how to read a consultee's openness and attentiveness will prove invaluable as a guide to the timing and styling of the consultant's feedback.

Attending—a Psychological Response

In addition to taking an actively receptive physical stance, the consultant must also be *psychologically active* in the communication exchange. Too often in our communications we simply hear the words but fail to truly understand the message. For example, consider conversations you may have had with a friend or colleague in which you felt and perhaps stated that: "...(they) don't understand!" This sense of frustration, along with the reality that while words may be heard yet message misunderstood, is evidence in the following exchange between Jack, a project manager at a small engineering firm, and Nick, the external consultant.

> **Jack:** *Nick, could you look at my financial projections? I am really worried about the possibility of overrunning our budget on this project. This is first time I have been selected to manage a project, and I really want Dr. Carroll to be impressed.*
>
> **Nick:** *Hey kid... everybody goes over budget (looking at the printout). Yeah, you're over all right. No big deal. Just get out there and do a quality job!*

It is clear that Jack asked Nick to look. Nick "understood" the request and did look at Jack's budget. However, Nick looked with the eyes of an experienced engineer and project manager. He also looked at it through the eyes of an external consultant, secure in his own self-image and relationships with the boss (Dr. Carroll). He did not LOOK at the budget as Jack had requested, that is, with the eyes and experience of a young engineer with his first project to manage and who was desperately trying to impress the boss. While the words were heard, the message was missed! Jack really needed more affirmation than the simple "no big deal."

The recommendations suggested for improving counselors' ability to listen and understand (Carkhuff, 1987) have similar value for consultants. They are:

1. Remember our reason for listening. Our attention and our listening will increase if we remember that we are attempting to gather data, clues—from the consultee's words, tone, and manner—that will help us understand the nature of the problem or the goals presented.

2. Suspend our personal judgment. We need to remember to focus on what the consultee is actually saying and not our personal judgment or evaluation of the comments. Fixing on our own opinion, evaluation, or frame of reference could prevent us from understanding the consultee's (Friend & Cook, 1992). Clearly at some point in the relationship we may want to share our opinions or values, but for now it is important to "hear" the consultee's position, not ours!

3. Focus on the consultee. It may seem obvious, but the effective consultant will resist distractions and keep his or her focus on the consultee's explicit messages as well as the more subtle indications of the consultee's experience. This focusing on the consultee may be the most important thing the effective, active-listening consultant can do. Focusing on the consultee to the degree that we psychologically step into the consultee's frame of reference so that we can experience what he or she experiences, or see and hear as he or she sees and hears, will clearly increase the accuracy of our understanding. With such active, empathic listening we will hear the consultee's message as it was intended and experienced by the consultee.

We can begin to develop such active, empathic listening and accurate understanding by developing the skills of paraphrasing and reflection of feelings.

Paraphrasing Content.   *Paraphrasing* is the process by which the consultant takes the basic message provided by the consultee and in his or her own words "reflects" the content of that message to the consultee. This can be very helpful in letting the consultee expand or clarify issues as well as to invite him or her to correct any misunderstanding. Consider the following brief exchange:

> ***Consultee:*** *I've been a teacher for 34 years. I have never encountered a situation like the one I have with Jeremy. I want your help in developing some techniques, strategies . . . something, to help me manage him in class!*
>
> ***Consultant:*** *Jeremy's behavior appears to be something that you have never encountered in all of your 34 years of teaching and you're hoping that perhaps I could assist you with some approaches to managing Jeremy in class?*
>
> ***Consultee:*** *It is not just his behavior—I have had students who were itches like him—but . . . it is more his attitude. He really seems almost mean.*

The consultant reflected the consultee's content by correctly identifying the length of teaching experience and the purpose for the consultee's engaging with the consultant (i.e., to gain management strategies). However, the assumption that it was Jeremy's behavior that was causing the most problem for the teacher was corrected by the consultee and expanded to include, if not emphasize, Jeremy's attitude. Thus, the paraphrase demonstrated that the consultant was attending and had accurately received this initial information. Further, the paraphrase provided the consultee an opportunity to expand and clarify the information presented.

In responding to the content of the consultee's message, the effective consultant rephrases that content in his or her own words in order to demonstrate understanding. It is important that the consultant attempt to reflect the consultee's message but not simply "par-

EXERCISE 6-1:   Paraphrasing

Directions: For each of the following, read the paragraph and in:

Part 1 Identify the key experiences—who or what is involved along with the consultee's expressed feelings and actions.

Part 2 Write a response summarizing in your own words these explicit experiences, behaviors and feelings. Start your response with either "In other words...." or "I hear you saying...."

Part 3 Share your responses with a colleague or colearner and compare responses. Did you stay with the explicit message and NOT interpret? Did you simply parrot the consultee, or place the message in your own words?

Example:

Frustrated Teacher: These darn kids! I've had it! I am so frustrated, I could scream. I tried my best—spent hours—worked hard on developing an exciting lesson and today nothing. They don't care, they goofed off rather than pay attention. Why bother?

Part 1
Experiences: kids, teacher, and lesson
Behaviors: teacher prepared lesson; kids unresponsive, inattentive
Feelings: frustrated, had it, doubt.

*Part 2 -***Paraphrase:**
   I hear you saying how frustrated you feel and how you are even beginning to doubt the value of working so hard, because you worked hard on the lesson and the students didn't respond.

   1. **Consultee** (a drug and alcohol counselor): Susan is coming in for an appointment today. I'm stuck. I have tried to confront her about her drinking but she continues to deny that this is a problem for her, even though she has been arrested as DUI. I have no idea what else I can do.

      Part 1
      Experiences: _____
      Behaviors: _____
      Feelings: _____

      Part 2
      Consultant Paraphrase: _____
      _____
      _____

   2. **Consultee** (third-grade teacher): These kids are getting out of hand. They don't listen anymore, they do whatever they darn well please. It's like you have to yell or scream or threaten them before they listen. I don't want to be that kind of teacher. It is really upsetting.

      Part 1
      Experiences: _____
      Behaviors: _____
      Feelings: _____

      Part 2
      Consultant Paraphrase: _____
      _____
      _____

3. **Consultee** (college residence assistant): I am about to call it quits. I don't think I can take it anymore. No matter what I try I can't get the girls on 5B to adhere to the "quiet time" rules. Study time comes and I go ask them to turn down the music and return to their rooms and no sooner do I leave the floor that I get a call from somebody on 5A complaining about the noise. I have no idea what to do.

Part 1
Experiences: _____
Behaviors: _____
Feelings: _____

Part 2
Consultant Paraphrase: _____
_____
_____

rot" back the words, exactly as initially presented. This is not a test of memory, nor is it an exercise in mirroring the consultee. The goal is to share with the consultee our understanding of what it was that the consultee was attempting to explicitly convey to us. The consultant is also not attempting to interpret or guess at hidden meaning or even add new interpretations or points of view. Rather, the consultant is simply attempting to accurately understand the consultee's point of view. Exercise 6-1 will help you become familiar with the process of paraphrasing the content of the consultee's message.

Reflection of Feelings.   In addition to hearing the words of the consultee and accurately reflecting those words, the effective consultant must also begin to recognize the feelings—the emotions—underlying those words. It is very important to note, however, that in consultation, unlike therapy or counseling, the goal is not to direct the consultee to a discussion of these feelings. Generally, the consultant's interest in the consultee's feelings is simply to register the consultee's feelings as essential information that will color the way the content of the message needs to be interpreted. For example, perceiving the residence assistant cited in Exercise 6-1 as being extremely frustrated and perhaps anxious about the possibility of losing her much-needed job will help the consultant to appreciate the "crisis" nature of this problem. With this perspective, the consultant will approach the problem with the sensitivity it deserves as much more than simply a minor issue of conflict over power and authority. The one exception to this rule of NOT focusing upon the consultee's feelings is when the consultee's emotional reaction is the source of the client's problem (see Chapter 8). In this situation the consultant will focus on the consultee's feelings—not in and of themselves—but as they directly impact the current work related problem. This point will be elaborated upon in Chapter 8.

Like paraphrasing, reflection of feelings requires the consultant to provide a brief statement reflecting the essence of the message received. However, where paraphrasing generally reflects the facts of what was said, reflection of feelings reflects the emotions related to those facts. For example:

Consultee: I don't know what's wrong with our team (voice somewhat shaky, frown on brow). We use to be so close, real tight. We would approach every work issue with a single mind. Now nothing, a big void, nobody seems to care or feel connected (voice pitch trails off, looks down).

Consultant: You feel confused, saddened, and somewhat anxious about the transformation you perceive is happening with your team.

In order for a consultant to accurately reflect the consultee's feelings she or he must learn to listen with eyes as well as ears. How does the consultee look as he or she shares his or her story? What might the consultee be expressing by his or her posture, facial expressions, or gestures?

An additional technique for a consultant to consider is one suggested for use by counselors. Carkhuff (1987) suggests that in order to identify what the client may be experiencing that a counselor ask him or herself the *empathy question.* Following upon Carkhuff's suggestion for counselors, it would appear an effective consultant needs to ask him- or herself: "How would I feel if I were doing or experiencing these things?" It would be this information that we wish to reflect to the consultee as our *reflection of feelings,* and through which we wish to process the other content-type material. Exercise 6-2 will help you begin to develop the ability to reflect feelings accurately.

As the consultant begins to attend to both the content and the feeling expressed in the consultee's message, she or he may come to experience that at times the words of the consultee convey one thing and the expression or tone of voice suggests something else. One of the values of reflecting both content and feelings is that it may help expose and clarify these mixed messages. If the consultant discerns more than one message—for example, "No, I really like Tom" (said very curtly and with a frown)—the consultant needs to reflect both the content—"I like Tom"—along with the feelings suggested by the frown and curt style (annoyed?).

Under these conditions it is important not to evaluate the message, rather simply describe it and ask the consultee to confirm your accuracy of understanding. A response such as: "I hear you saying that you like Tom, but I detect in your tone and facial expression that there is something bothering you about him?" will invite the consultee to clarify the message.

Moving from the Explicit to the Implied.   Theodore Reik (1948), in describing the therapeutic encounter, described a process in which the therapist uses his or her own internal experiencing to "hear" meanings that go beyond the words the client uses. The concept is that when we are truly present to another, when we are fully attentive to another's messages, we will begin to record not just the words but the tone, not just the verbal message but the feelings beneath the message, and not just the intended message but often the issues well beneath the intended. And while it must be emphasized that consultation is NOT therapy, the effective consultant who employs intense listening and attending behaviors may discover that he or she hears the meanings beyond the message.

For example, consider the following:

Karen (smiling, somewhat nervously): "What a week. First, our supplier calls and tells us there will be a delay in shipping, then our biggest account wants us to re-

bid our job, and finally, the snow closed the plant for three days. I guess it is nice to take a couple days off?"

At one level the consultant could respond: "It seems that you have had three things happen to your company" (paraphrase). The consultant may even reflect the feelings expressed and respond, "Your tone of voice and smile suggests to me that you feel nervous." However, looking at the person's expression, listening to the tone and nervous laugh, and truly putting him- or herself in the consultee's shoes, the consultant may find that he or she hears something a little differently and responds: "You're really upset and concerned— seems like nothing is going right. I guess you're really wondering if trying to keep this busi-

---

EXERCISE 6-2 Reflection of Feelings

Directions: After reading each of the following statements and attending to the behavioral expressions, ask yourself: "How would I feel saying these things?" and "How do I usually feel when I act or sound that way?" Then write a response using the formula "It seems that you are feeling. . . ." or "You're feeling. . . ."

It is helpful to share and compare your responses with those of a colleague or colearner. Did you agree on the feelings expressed? If not, which cues were you using? Did you agree with the level of intensity? If not, again what cues were you each picking up and responding to?

Example:

Consultee: (sighing) I just don't know what to do (looks down to the ground with a frown in her brow and sighs a second time).
Consultant: It seems that you are feeling confused and somewhat hopeless about what to do.

1. **Consultee:** (sitting up on the edge of the seat—turning red in the face, and raising his voice) If you only knew what I got to put up attempting to run this damn department! (smacks his hands down on the chair).
   Consultant: You seem to be feeling_____
   _____
   _____

2. **Consultee:** But you have got to help. . . . (voice is high pitched, face appears to be pleading, actually reaches toward you). Our certification is almost up and our certifying team is due on campus next month!
   Consultant: You're feeling _____
   _____
   _____

3. **Consultee:** Oh, you've got to hear this! (sitting up, gesturing with hands, and smiling as she speaks) That technique we talked about? Well, you are not going to believe what happened.
   Consultant: You feel _____
   _____
   _____

ness afloat is possible or even worth it?" If that reflection is greeted by "Oh, yes . . . that's it . . ." from the consultee, it can be assumed that both the implied message as well as that explicitly stated were heard.

As Reik suggested, it is like listening with the *third ear.* It is that "ear" that leads you to draw conclusions or inferences that accurately reflect another level of the consultee's words.

Listening to hear and understand a consultee's hidden feelings and meaning is neither an automatic response nor an easy process to develop. The skills needed take time and experience to develop, but they can be developed. Understanding what is implied in another's message requires that we listen intently to experience the entire story as if we were experiencing it, and then put our understanding into words that the consultee can affirm or correct.

It must be noted that this is NOT an open invitation to guess and interpret underlying issues. Such "mind reading" and "playing psychologist" can end open communications. Premature interpreting may cause the consultee to feel extremely vulnerable, and as a result move to close down and protect him- or herself, rather than to continue with the open self-disclosure. What is suggested is that as you develop your attending skills—learning to hear the explicit messages, both content and feeling—you will find yourself moving to reflect that which is implied. You need to let it flow from the deep and accurate understanding of the relationship and not try to force it like a technique!

The Skills of Exploration

This process of exploration entails a real reconnaissance or exploration of the consultee's total experience so that all of the relevant data can be gathered and processed. As will become more obvious after reading the next chapters, the quantity and diversity of the information a consultee gathers during this exploration stage can become overwhelming. The consultant will attempt to gather data, not just on the client, but also relevant information about the consultee and the consultee's system. The specific types of information to be gathered will be discussed in the upcoming chapters. The focus here is on the "how" of exploration with specific emphasis given to the art of questioning.

Exploring through the Art of Questioning
In addition to gathering data by way of observation, the effective consultant also wants to engage the consultee and invite him or her to share his or her perspective and expertise around the issue at hand. Facilitating such disclosure and gathering the data needed to be of assistance is greatly aided by the artful use of questioning.

The art of questioning is a keystone to the exploration process. The consultant who has mastered the use of questions can elicit very helpful information from the consultee and do so in a way that is nonthreatening and even comforting to the consultee.

One of the primary values of questioning to the consultant in the exploration stage is that it serves as a vehicle from which to *probe* more deeply into the issue. For example:

Consultee: *I just don't understand—I invite the others to provide input and take part in decision making, but they still seem reluctant to do so.*

Consultant: Take part in the decision making? What is it that you are hoping they will do?

In addition to having value as a probe, questions can also be used to *highlight* a certain piece of information for *clarification*. Often such highlighting or emphasizing will help the consultee become a bit more specific, or will invite the consultee to focus more intensely on one specific aspect of his or her experience. For example:

Consultee: OK, so I tend to be a little gruff with the employees. I know I snap at Ellen (my secretary) and tend to get emotional with Frank (the foreman) and Barbara (the night manager), but gads, is it really that bad? So I am a little rough around the edges.

Consultant: You say you are a little rough around the edges, but it seems that a number of people, in more than one role and at more than one time, have expressed real concerns around your style of interaction. Can you help me understand why so many people may be concerned about what you call a little rough?"

Guidelines for Effective Questioning

Questioning can be a very useful tool for a consultant to use in order to begin to gain a real understanding of the issues confronting the consultee. However, questioning, if done inappropriately, can do much to block a helping, facilitative consultation relationship. The effective use of questioning will be guided by the following principles: (1) be purposeful; (2) be clear, concrete, and simple; and (3) ask as few questions as possible. Each of these guidelines is discussed in more detail.

Be Purposeful: It may be said that one of the most basic rules governing the use of questioning is that questioning and data collection should be purposeful. We can ask questions for a variety of reasons. We could use questions as a form of "small talk," or use questions as a way of backing another into a corner, almost as a prosecuting attorney may use questions.

We must remember that unlike other times in which we are engaged in social interchanges, as consultants, we are there to assist or to help the consultee. We are not simply asking questions for our own benefit or as a way of "peeping" into another person's life. We are attending and questioning because we wish to understand the nature of the problem at hand, as well as the possible avenues for intervention that may be available. The asking of questions within consultation is purposeful. When we keep our purpose in mind, our questions will reflect that intent. When we keep our purpose in mind, when our questions are aimed at helping us clarify the nature of the problem, identify available resources, and select the most appropriate strategies, then the questions we ask will be helpful.

Be Clear, Concrete, and Simple: A second guideline for asking questions in the context of consultation is to keep our questions clear and simple. Questions should be asked in a manner and with a language that the consultee can understand. Asking compound questions or using slang or jargon will not only be confusing to the consultee but may make the consultee increasingly nervous and thus block communications.

For example, consider the following scenario:

> ***Consultee:*** *"Gads, I'm nervous. I don't know why...just kind of seems strange having to talk to a consultant—I'm so use to handling my own problems."*

> ***Consultant:*** *"Is it strange that you have to talk with someone, or are you saying it is strange for you to be talking with someone—you know, is it a commentary on your social style, or the fact that your ego defenses block you from seeing yourself as a person who would need help...any thoughts?"*

With a consultee who has already expressed some anxiety and nervousness about talking to a consultant, it is clear that the multiple questions and the introduction of terms like "social style" and "ego defenses" may be somewhat unnerving and actually block the exploration of the issue.

Be Conservative—Ask as Few Questions as Possible: The third guideline is to use as few questions as needed to gather all the relevant data required to help another. The consultee comes to the interaction with an agenda, a desire to receive some assistance with a work-related problem. Our first goal as consultants is to interact in such a way as to facilitate this expression and clarification of that concern. Thus, while we need to gather information, we need to be careful not to turn our questioning into a extensive barrage of rapid fire interrogations which may prove anxiety-provoking to the consultee.

> ***Consultee:*** *I don't know where to begin...*

> ***Consultant:*** *Tell me about your problem.*

> ***Consultee:*** *OK, I'm the supervisor on the pediatrics ward, third shift. I am having...*

> ***Consultant:*** *Which hospital are we talking about?*

> ***Consultee:*** *St. Lukes.*

> ***Consultant:*** *What is the third shift?*

> ***Consultee:*** *It is the shift that goes from 11 PM until 7 AM.*

> ***Consultant:*** *So you have a problem at work. What is it? Who is it with? What are you hoping I can do?*

> ***Consultee:*** *Well, as I started to say, I am the supervisor for the third shift, and I am having problems with one of the nurses, Ellen.*

> ***Consultant:*** *What is your role in relationship to Ellen? Are you responsible for her job? Her schedule? Does she report to you?*

Asking a set of rapid-fire, interrogating questions does little to place the consultee at ease and may in fact force the consultee into a shut down, protective mode. Questions that can be answered with a simple yes or no response, or that can be answered with a few words, multiple choice style, are generally considered *closed questions*. These types of closed questions not only set the stage for the consultee's feeling as if he or she is on the witness stand, but they will create a pattern of communication that places all of the responsibility for its structure and direction on the consultant, as opposed to allowing the consultee to give the needed direction. Thus if the consultant is attempting to create an atmosphere of mutuality and collaboration, closed questions, presented in such an interrogating style may prove very counterproductive.

In contrast to this style of closed questioning, the effective consultant will develop the ability to employ questions that invite the client to expand, elaborate and expound on a point, rather than simply answer yes or no. Questions that invite the consultee to expand on their point and elaborate as they wish are considered *open questions*. While many authors, especially in counseling and psychotherapy literature, will emphasize open questions—almost to the exclusion or even prohibition of using closed questions—such restriction is not suggested here. Open questions are valuable as invitations for the consultee to speak, but in effective consultation, systematic inquiry will include the use of both open and closed questions. During the early stage of the consultation, when a consultant is attempting to explore the depth and breadth of the consultee's problem, open questions appear to be most useful. But in the later stages of the interaction, when problem identification and specific intervention strategies are being developed, closed-ended, focused questions may prove to be more useful. Exercise 6-3 provides an illustration of the differential effect of closed- and open-ended questions.

While closed questions may be useful in narrowing down the information or focus of the conversation and can even be used to obtain clearly defined factual input, they often restrict the consultee's opportunity to reveal feelings, unique style or approach to the job, or other data that may prove useful in developing the intervention plan. Under these conditions, open questions appear much more useful. Further, the encouragement of the consultee to disclose and exchange rather than simply react and respond, as would be the case with a barrage of closed questions, fosters the feeling of control and mutual involvement, both of which are essential to the creation of a collaborative relationship.

As previously suggested, open questions are particularly useful in the early stages of the helping process, in that they invite the consultee to structure the direction of the interaction. They act as invitations for the consultee to tell his or her story. The use of open questions provides the consultant with the most "cost-effective" means of gathering data, thus adhering to the Be Conservative guideline for questioning.

The open questions can be framed in ways that express interest ("Could you tell me more?"), or the desire for clarification ("What did you do when she responded with anger?"), or even direction ("Would you give me an example of how that might look?"). Thus, while allowing the consultant to retain some control over the direction of the helping process, open questions do not restrict the types of information provided by the consultee as might be found in a very structured, question/answer format of closed questioning. This freedom to respond as needed will foster a sense of mutuality and participation on the part of the consultee.

Open questions often begin with words such as *who, what, when, where, how* and *why*. For example:

EXERCISE 6-3   Styles of Questioning

Directions: Review the following two dialogues between a consultant and a consultee. In both situations the consultant is attempting to *explore* the nature of the problem. The first consultant employs a number of closed-ended questions, whereas the second consultant relies on a open questioning style. Answer and discuss the questions following each of the dialogues.

Scenario I: **Closed Questioning**

Consultee: Boy, am I having a problem with Alfred!

Consultant: Is he refusing to do his work?

Consultee: No, not exactly.

Consultant: Oh, is he disrespectful?

Consultee: Well . . . it's a bit more than that!

Consultant: So he's really acting out, causing a disruption in class? Maybe even undermining your authority?

Consultee: Yeah, I guess you could say it like that.

For consideration and discussion:
1. How do you think the consultee feels at this moment?
2. What is the consultee expecting from this relationship?
3. What has the consultant learned about the consultee?
4. What has the consultant learned about the nature of the problem?

Scenario II: **Open Questioning**

Consultee: Boy, am I having a problem—Alfred!

Consultant: When you say "problem," what is it you mean?

Consultee: Well, Alfred is one of the brighter boys in my fifth period World History course. For the first two months of class he was polite, attentive, and very productive. Lately, he has been late with assignments, doing poorly on quizzes, and appears to have some very strong negative feelings toward me.

Consultant: Strong negative feelings toward you? Could you tell me more about that?

Consultee: Well, I tried to talk to him about his poor performance one day after class. He was standing with a group of his friends, and I walked over and simply said that I need to talk to him about his class production. Well, he gave me this look like he wanted me to drop dead. And then when he did walk over to me he said that he doesn't understand why I am picking on him. Picking on him! I really like this kid, I am just trying to help.

For consideration and discussion:
1. How do you think the consultee feels about the interaction up to this point?
2. What is the consultee expecting from this helping relationship?
3. What have you learned about the consultee?
4. What have you learned about the nature of the problem?
5. Contrast the data you received using open questions as opposed to that in Scenario I. What type of information was attained, and what about amount of return on consultant energy was received from both approaches?

Who is involved with this project?
What are the factors that need to be considered?
Where do these types of interactions typically occur?
When do you typically intervene?
How long have you been experiencing this situation?
Why do you think she (the client) reacts that way?

Even though a "why" question invites the consultee to talk, it may also make some consultees feel defensive, as if they need to justify what happened, or know all the answers. It is usually more effective to ask what and how questions to get at the same information. For example, rather than ask a consultee "Why do you feel she reacts that way?" it may be less threatening to ask "What happens to make her react that way?" or "When does she most often react that way?"

The Skills of Focusing

Following the initial exploration and facilitation of the consultee's ventilation, the consultant needs to assist the consultee to begin to identify and define, in clear, specific, concrete terms, the nature of his or her concern and the nature of the problem. This process of focusing is facilitated through the proper use of *clarification* and *summarization*.

Clarification

As a consultee shares his or her story and explores its various dimensions, he or she may employ inclusive terms (e.g., they and them), ambiguous phrases (e.g., you know), and words with a double meaning (e.g., stoned, trip). Such inclusive, ambiguous, mixed presentations of the consultee's concerns are nearly impossible to resolve. When the consultee presents such vague, generalized, or ambiguous descriptions, the consultant, through the use of clarification, will invite him or her to elaborate or expand on the topic. A clarification not only assists the consultant in developing a fuller understanding of the issue under discussion, but serves as a tool to assist in focusing the conversation.

Typically, the consultant's request for clarification is posed as an open question and simply asks the consultee to elaborate on something that is vague or ambiguous to the consultant.

For example, assume that a consultee stated the following:

Consultee: *It makes me bonkers when Conrad pulls that nonsense!*

Obviously, it will be hard to assist the consultee in this situation unless the consultant clearly understands what is meant by terms such as "bonkers" and "nonsense." Through the use of a clarifying question, the consultant will attempt to gain a better understanding (i.e., clarification) of what the consultee is intending. For example,

Consultant: *What exactly do you mean when you say "that nonsense"?*

or

Consultant: *Perhaps you could give me an example of what it is that you call "nonsense"?*

A request for clarification from the consultant will not only provide a more accurate picture of what it is the consultee is experiencing, but depending on what it is the consultant selects to have clarified, may actually act to focus the discussion. In the above example, the consultant asked for clarification on the term "nonsense" as opposed to asking for clarification on the term "bonkers." This selection will focus the consultee away from a discussion of personal feelings and concerns and will invite her to speak more about what is happening in a work-related situation.

Clarification may also prove to be the help that the consultee is actually seeking. Mehrabian (1970), in discussing counseling, suggested that clarification is actually one of the major steps to problem resolution. It is the position here that the same is true in consultation, in that it is often the consultee's initial lack of clarity about the nature of the problem that leads to feelings of helplessness and blocks his or her own appropriate problem solving. As the consultee gains increased clarity about the specific behaviors, attitudes, and factors involved in his or her problem, the feelings of confusion and helplessness diminish and direction for resolution may become more apparent.

The use of clarification is thus a key element in the process of consultation, as it is with other forms of helping. To be an effective consultant, one needs to resist assuming understanding when the consultee employs generalized, vague, or ambiguous terms. The effective consultant develops skills in focusing discussion with a goal of clarification. Exercise 6-4 provides an opportunity to identify vague, generalized, and ambiguous terms and to develop a request for clarification.

Summarization

A second communication skill that allows the consultant to both explore with the consultee and assist the consultee to focus is the use of summarization. In summarizing, the consultant pulls together several ideas or feelings provided by the consultee into a succinct, concrete statement, which is then reflected to the consultee. Such a summarizing process has been found useful in bringing a discussion around a particular theme to a close or even exploring a particular theme more thoroughly (Brammer, 1988). This is a point to remember.

Often, with very enthusiastic and verbal consultees, a consultant may feel as if the consultation is out of control. For the consultant who feels as if he or she has lost control of the interaction, summarization provides a tool to bring a given conversation to closure. The appropriate use of summarization, followed by the intentional employment of questions, can provide the consultant with the tools needed to regain control and direction for the interaction.

For example, consider the following example of a consultant attempting to respond to a consultee who has a tendency to ramble off in many directions:

Consultee: Wow, what a week. You gotta hear this and then I'll tell you what happened with my confrontation with Alice. You know the thing we decided on telling her. Well, anyway it's Monday and I'm going in to schedule her feedback session, just like we planned. But you're not going to believe what happened! First, I go to get in my car and the battery is dead. So I call road service and have to wait 45

EXERCISE 6-4   Employing Clarification Skills

Directions: For each of the following consultee messages, develop a sample clarification response. Before responding, ask yourself:

- What has the consultee told me?
- What parts of the message are either unclear, vague, or maybe missing?
- How can I request information, focusing the consultee on the part I want clarified?

Discuss your response with a colleague or classmate. If you have selected different points for clarification, why? What might be the effect of such different focusing?

1. **Consultee:** Gads, I've really screwed up! My butt's in a sling, and the time line is totally blown!

   Consultant: _____

2. **Consultee:** OK, so I ran over budget on the project. The boss is ragged out and the staff about to jump ship. Big deal. I got things under control!

   Consultant: _____

3. **Consultee:** That group is just a bunch of babies. They are always on my back complaining about something. I'm their foreman, not their mother.

   Consultant: _____

---

minutes until they get there. I get a jump and now I'm off (late of course) for the meeting. Well, traffic is bumper to bumper on the expressway. So I'm now a good hour and a half late for the meeting. You can just imagine how Alice must be reacting.

Oh, but it doesn't end there. Sitting in traffic the car starts to overheat. Do you believe this? This car is the absolute worst. I've had nothing but bad luck since I got it last year. The damn thing cost me $16,000...

***Consultant** (interrupting): It appears that you have had a number of problems with the car. Sounds frustrating, but in spite of all of that you did have your meeting with Alice. Perhaps you could tell me how that meeting went?*

The consultant's brief summary of the ongoing discussion of the car invites the consultee to end the discussion of that particular topic and focus on a more thorough presentation of the experience of the meeting with his employee, Alice.

In addition to closing a discussion or focusing on an aspect to develop, summarization can be used to focus the consultee's scattered thoughts and feelings. As the consultee's story unfolds, the consultant needs to attend to certain consistencies or patterns—of feelings (e.g., anger, sadness), behaviors (e.g., avoidance, procrastination), and experiences (e.g., abandonment, rejection) shared by the consultee. These consistent patterns, or *themes,* will be repeated or referred to over and over as the consultee shares her or his story. For example, imagine that in talking with a consultee, you become aware that they have provided four separate instances, with four different students, where he (the consultee) has lost his temper. Further, you discover that each time he loses his temper, he "blames" the students in an almost victim-like tone. You could use a summarization to pull together these various experiences around this single theme of victimization. You may suggest: "As you have been talking, I have become aware that you have spoken consistently about being an innocent victim, feeling as if the students do things to you and only you and that you have no control or role in the interaction. Perhaps this issue of being an innocent and powerless victim is one which you may want to focus on?"

Inviting the consultee to consider the possible existence of a pattern or theme in his or her experience may begin to move that person to a more full understanding of him- or herself, as opposed to simply attending to a discussion of what at first appears to be a set of separate, unconnected events. Further, it may help the consultee to more accurately identify and define the nature of the problem.

As evident in the examples provided, summarization requires the consultant to:

1. Attend to and recall varying verbal and nonverbal messages presented by the consultee
2. Identify specific themes, issues, and feelings conveyed by the consultee
3. Extract the key or core ideas and feelings expressed and integrate them into a concrete statement

As with many of the skills of helping employed in consultation, summarization is not an easy skill to develop or employ. It is one, however, that becomes easier and more effective with practice. Exercise 6-5 is provided to assist you in that practice.

Communication Knowledge and Skills Essential to Collaboration

Effective communication will not only serve as the means through which the consultant identifies the nature of the problem and the resources available for intervention, but it will also be the tool through which the collaborative relationship is established and maintained.

As noted previously, a collaborative relationship is one in which there is a mutual, nonhierarchical relationship in which both the consultant and consultee participate and co-equally own the results of the interaction. Maintaining this mutual, nonhierarchical and co-participative relationship is not always easy. The effective consultant will be aware of potential pitfalls, as well as the forms of communication that facilitate a collaborative interaction.

Communicating to Foster Mutual Involvement

Clearly, the consultant, as an expert in the specific form of problem solving desired by the consultee, is responsible for the direction of the interaction. However, while retaining this control, the effective consultant employs nonverbal and verbal communication techniques aimed at developing and maintaining a sense of mutuality within the relationship.

EXERCISE 6-5   Developing Summarizations

Directions: For each of the consultee presentations consider the following questions and develop a simple, concrete summarizing statement. Share your summaries with a colleague or classmate and discuss points of similarity and difference. In your discussion identify the possible impact each summarization may have on the direction of the consultation interaction. Questions to consider in preparing your summaries are:

1. What is the message the consultee is sending? What are the key elements (feelings? content?)?
2. Is there a recurrent message (i.e. patterns, themes)?
3. Which of the consultee's words can I incorporate into a summary statement?

Consultee 1: I've tried to speak with him but he just won't listen. It is so frustrating. I describe what I expect him to do, but he ignores me. It's like he has his mind made up and what I say just isn't important. Hell, I am his boss. Should I just fire him?

Summarization: _____

_____

_____

Consultee 2 (This is the third time you have met, and each time you come up with a plan of action, the consultee comes up with an excuse as to why she can't do it): Boy, I bet you are going to be really angry! I know we decided last week that I would contact Mr. and Mrs. Spellman about Colleen, and begin to problem solve around her difficulty with completing assignments on time, but I had so many projects to do this week that I just couldn't get around to calling them. I know that I had some problem doing it the last two weeks as well, but this is really a busy time. You know we had the Christmas play, midterm exams, and parent meetings all over the past few weeks. It can really get overwhelming.

Summarization: _____

_____

_____

Consultee 3: I really feel like such a wimp, I can't seem to assert myself. I am at work, I've been made the project manager and I am supposed to keep every body on task. Al and Harry are deliberately bucking me. They refuse to hand in their budgets or their time lines. They come late to our team meetings. It is going to make me look pretty bad if this project comes in late or over budget. I just wish they would cooperate.

Summarization: _____

_____

_____

The Nonverbals of Mutual Involvement

One interviewing technique suggested by Gerald Caplan (Caplan & Caplan, 1993) is to sit beside, as opposed to opposite to, the consultee. This positioning gives nonverbal support to the psychological tone the consultant is trying to attain. In sitting side by side, the message conveyed is that this consultation will be an "elbow-to-elbow" mutual problem-solving venture. Rather than sitting across from one another in a role of problem teller (the consultee) and problem solver (the consultant), the side-by-side posture suggests a mutuality to both the understanding and resolution of the problem.

The Verbals of Mutual Involvement

In addition to directly asking and encouraging the consultee to freely and actively contribute to the consultation process, the consultant can actively engage the consultee by the judicious use of questions.

The use of questions is a primary tool for engaging the consultee in the consultation (Caplan & Caplan, 1993). Rather than giving immediate advice and direction, the consultant seeking to maintain a collaborative relationship will attempt to engage the consultee in joint "pondering" over the nature of the problem at hand, as well as the options available for intervention. This invitation to the consultee to join with the consultant in pondering, reflecting, and considering the issues at hand is extremely important to the development of the collaborative relationship. The consultant, seeking collaboration, must resist the tendency to provide solutions, directions, and/or answers. Rather than directing and resolving, the consultant seeking collaboration will ask questions. Asking questions such as: "I wonder...?", "Do you have any ideas...?", or "Any suggestions...?" elicits active consultee participation and creates the sense of mutuality within the relationship.

While it may be therapeutically sound and effective for a counselor to sit in silence as a client or a patient discloses his or her personal story, such longstanding silence can disrupt the nonhierarchical balance of a collaborative consultation. Allowing the consultee singularly and unilaterally to disclose while the consultant sits in silence suggests that the consultant is absorbing all that is shared and will in return offer his or her sage-like advice. To maintain mutuality and nonhierarchical relationship, the consultant should parallel, or mirror, the level of involvement of the consultee. That is, the consultant should balance consultee disclosure with consultant disclosure, question with question, direction with direction.

One theory that appears to have particular value in this area of mutuality is that originally presented by Gregory Bateson (1935, 1958) and discussed in relationship to consultation by Parsons and Meyers (1984). According to Bateson, communication occurs in one of two patterns—symmetrical or complementary. A *symmetrical* communication pattern is one in which the relationship is equalized through equivalent behavioral exchanges: A dominant type of communication (e.g., directing) would be responded to with a dominant-type communication. Similarly, a submission-type communication (e.g., asking for affirmation) would be met with a similar submission-type response. A *complementary* interaction is characterized by exchanges that are dissimilar in terms of control. In complementary exchanges, one person's efforts to control are accepted by the second person, such that dominance by one is met with submission by the other.

The consultant seeking to develop and maintain mutuality within the consultation would be advised to be aware of and employ symmetrical communication patterns. While others, such as Ericson and Rogers (1973) and Sluzki and Beavin (1965, cited in Erchul, 1992) have developed sophisticated coding systems for identifying relational patterns, the position taken here is that the collaborative consultant should attempt to mirror the consultee's pattern of communication in order to maintain symmetry and mutuality. Thus, a consultee's assertion should be followed by a consultant's assertion (e.g., giving advice or direction). Similarly, a consultee submissive type communication (e.g., asking for support, affirmation, or assistance) should be followed with similar types of consultant responses. The following two case illustrations will demonstrate the difference between complimentary and symmetrical communications (Case Illustration 6-1).

It is evident from the illustrations that complimentary communication, where the consultee is submissive and responsive to the consultant's request for information, justification, or action, as was the situation in Case 1, interferes with the sense of mutuality experienced by the consultee in terms of control of the direction of the interaction.

Communicating to Promote a Nonhierarchical Relationship

With complimentary interactions a consultant not only risks interfering with the sense of mutuality within the relationship, but such a communicational pattern can also create a hierarchical arrangement (dominance–submission) to the consultation. Creating a nonhierarchical relationship is essential if collaboration is truly to be developed. But developing and maintaining such a nonhierarchical relationship may be difficult.

The Nonverbals of Nonhierarchical Relationships

A number of decisions and actions can serve as nonverbal threats to nonhierarchical relationships. The consultant can suggest a power differential by physically positioning himself or herself above the consultee, as in the case of standing over the consultee while discussing the case. Thus Caplan's suggestion (Caplan & Caplan, 1993) to sit beside the consultee works to avoid this posturing for power. Posturing of power can also be achieved by positioning oneself behind large desks or at the head of a large conference table (Meichenbaum & Turk, 1987).

Perhaps one of the strongest ways to communicate power differential is through one's manner of dress. Dressing for power, or in ways that attempt to give evidence of the consultant's greater income and/or prestige, can interfere with the creation and maintenance of nonhierarchical relationship. Establishing one's referent power can be increased by presenting in manner of dress and style in ways mirroring that of the consultee. When it is impossible or artificial to hide or distort the natural perks of the consultant's position, the consultant would do well to make behavioral adjustments to de-emphasize these elements. For example, the consultant who is more formally dressed than the consultee may need to take off his or her blazer and roll up his or her sleeves. Consider Case Illustration 6-2.

While it certainly would have been advisable for our consultant, Tom, to have done some homework regarding the culture and manner of dress for the setting to which he was about to consult, it becomes clear that even when artifacts of power and status are present, the consultant can do some things to de-emphasize the power differential they may suggest.

The Verbals of Nonhierarchical Relationships

In addition to becoming sensitive to the possible nonverbal cues that may signal power differential, the effective consultant will be sensitive to avoid those communication processes that highlight power differential. For example, communication that overemphasizes the consultant's expert power without a concomitant demonstration and evidencing of the con-

---

CASE ILLUSTRATION 6-1   A Look at Communication Control

Case 1 **Complimentary Interaction**

In the following dialogue the consultant dominates and controls the interaction direction by asking questions, giving advice, and giving direction; whereas the consultee responded with complimentary answers—requests for support and direction.

Consultant: Hi, Tom. Did you get the data I requested?
Consultee: Yes, here it is.
Consultant: Is this all you were able to get?
Consultee: Yes, isn't that enough?
Consultant: No, it's fine, but it is always useful to gather as much information as we can. Now if you look here, on Tuesday's information you will begin to see the problem.
Consultee: I'm not sure what you mean.
Consultant: Okay, look at these numbers as compared to what you collected on Friday. It appears that what you will need to do is go back and get the data on sales from last month.

Case 2 **Symmetry**

In this exchange the same consultant attempts to mirror the consultee's attempts to assert and direct the interaction with his own assertion. Similarly, when the consultee takes a more submissive stance seeking support or demonstrating lack of direction or clarity, the consultant attempts to parallel that submission in order to maintain the sense of mutuality.

Consultant: Hi, Tom. Did you get the data I requested?
Consultee: Yes, here it is. This is interesting stuff, I think we can use it.
Consultant: Hopefully! It could show us some trends to sales. Is this all you were able to get?
Consultee: Yes, isn't that enough? There is data from last month, but we originally agreed just to look at this month.
Consultant: No, you're right, it's fine, but it is always useful to gather as much information as we can. What do you think of this—look here—on Tuesday's information?
Consultee: The chart really drops off. I'm not sure what it means, do you have any clue?
Consultant: I'm not sure.
Consultee: Maybe we need to compare it last Tuesday?
Consultant: OK, or maybe we could look at these numbers as compared to what you collected last month.
Consultee: That shouldn't be a problem. I have the data for each of the months for the entire past year.

---

sultee's expertise can prove detrimental to the nonhierarchical nature of the relationship. The use of professional jargon should be held to a minimum in order to reduce its potential negative effects (Meichenbaum & Turk, 1987). Further, recommendations presented by the consultant should be made with a tentative, rather than an absolute, or dictatorial tone (Parsons & Meyers, 1984). For example, rather than stating: "OK, now here is what you do," it would prove more nonhierarchical to state: "Do you think it would help if we . . ." or, "Perhaps it would be valuable to . . ." The intent is NOT to destroy the consultant's expert power, but simply to open an avenue for the consultee's mutual involvement. In those situations

---

CASE ILLUSTRATION 6-2   Handling Power Differentials

Background

Tom is a very successful lawyer and organizational consultant who has been hired by the board of directors of a national accounting firm to work with a new, young CEO of the regional headquarters for that firm.

For the first meeting, Tom wore a $1000 handmade suit, Italian shoes, and exquisite gold jewelry. Tom parked his European sports car in the visitor's spot. He exited his car carrying his monogrammed Gucci attaché case.

Entering the building, Tom noted that while everyone was neatly groomed, the dress was informal. All the members of the firm were dressed in sweaters or casual blouses and slacks. The chief financial officer was wearing jeans and a flannel shirt, and the CEO exited his office wearing a corduroy sport coat, open-collar shirt, and jeans.

Decisions to enhance status and power differentials:

1. Make physical gestures, such as straightening French cuffs on shirt, in order to highlight the fact that the shirt was handmade and the cuff links had real diamonds.
2. Place the Gucci attaché on top of the table.
3. Make gestures to point out personal manicure, gold Rolex watch, and gold pen.
4. Others? Can you provide additional ways to emphasize the hierarchical nature of the relationship?

Actions aimed at diffusing power differential:

1. Remove coat ASAP, undo tie, and roll up sleeves.
2. Place attaché on floor and bring materials up to table without the gold pen and the leather binder.
3. Cross leg over knee in a 90-degree angle to give the appearance of being casual.
4. Others? Can you provide additional ways to de-emphasize the differential power dressing?

---

where the consultant's expertise is both evident and needed, the balance of power can be maintained by emphasizing the consultee's value and expertise as the case archivist providing the consultant with the content and details of the current case.

Caplan (1970) noted that often the consultee will attempt to test the consultant's assertion of the coordinate nature of this relationship by seducing the consultant into a position of superiority. For example, the consultee may state that he or she is deferring to the superior expertise of the consultant, or the consultee may simply "play dumb" and fail to offer input or suggestions into the problem-solving process. Such a process of deference may prove seductive to a consultant who rushes in to "save the day" with his or her superior knowledge and/or skill. When such consultee deference is encountered, the consultant needs to respond in kind. If the consultee responds with deference, the consultant should answer with deference. Consider the following exchange.

Consultee: *I am really sorry that I can't be more helpful. I know there is probably much more I could share with you, but I just can't think right now.*

Consultant: Actually, I'm the one feeling a bit apologetic for having to rely so heavily on your input, but you have such a wealth of experience with this situation that I would probably be much less effective without your help.

Or, consider the following exchange:

Consultee: Well, it is clear that the things I tried didn't work. I am sure you have much better ideas.

Consultant: To be honest, the two things you told me you tried were going to be my first two recommendations. I guess we think alike. Perhaps we could put our heads together and come up with a third strategy?

Caplan (1970; & Caplan, 1993) suggests that in addition to highlighting the consultee's value to the consultation process, a consultant may need to deflate his or her own contribution in a process he called *one downmanship.* The consultant does not want to completely diffuse his or her expert power when employing one-down maneuvers, but he or she may need to at least convey to the consultee that in this setting, and with this consultation, they are meeting as equals, and that the consultant's expertise is different, not greater.

Summary

Consultation has been presented within this text as a problem-solving process. It should now be apparent that consultation involves two separate yet interdependent problems to which the consultant must attend. The one problem served as the reason for the consultation, that is, to resolve a specific work related problem. However, given the need for a collaborative interaction with the consultee to fully understand the presenting concern and the realities of the resources available, the consultant will also need to attend to the "problem" of establishing and maintaining a helping, collaborative relationship.

As with many forms of helping, the process and outcome of consultation will be impacted by the quality of the communication occurring within the consultation relationship. The effective consultant, like all effective helpers, will be proficient in the communication skills of helping, including active listening, questioning, probing, clarifying, and summarizing. Further, the effective collaborative consultant will be knowledgeable and skilled in the use of those verbal and nonverbal techniques, such as one downmanship and symmetry of communication direction and control, which will help to make the relationship one that is nonhierarchical and mutual in nature.

The importance of the relationship to the quality and outcome of a consultation cannot be overstated. However, as previously suggested, building and maintaining the working relationship is but one of the problems that confronts a consultant. With the beginnings of the relationship established and an initial understanding of the depth and breadth of the problem acquired, the consultant and consultee now begin to approach the *problem definition and intervention* stages of consulting. The next three chapters will begin to address the specific techniques, approaches, strategies, and tools for moving the consultation to a concrete and detailed understanding of the nature of the problem so that specific intervention and prevention steps can be taken.

Chapter 7

Client-Focused Consultation

Once the consultant has gained *entry* to a system and has established a rudimentary relationship with the consultee, the process of *problem identification* becomes the focus for the consultation (Meyers, Parsons, & Martin, 1979; Parsons & Meyers, 1984). Even though the consultant has most likely "heard" the presenting complaint, perhaps along with the consultee's analysis of the situation, she or he should not be too quick to embrace that portrayal of the problem.

One of the major tasks of the consultant during this phase of problem identification is to determine the real target for intervention. Clearly, the goal is to impact that client and the client's functioning. However, as noted previously, the focus in consultation is broader than simply this client at this time. The model proposed within this text promotes both a preventive focus as well as the more typical remedial orientation. The consultant needs to step back and consider the most effective (in terms of intervention and prevention potential) focal point for the intervention. The specific diagnostic and intervention strategies will vary significantly, depending on whether the consultant chooses to respond by focusing on the client, the consultee, or the system.

The current chapter will discuss those strategies for diagnosing and intervening when the client is the focal point and the ultimate target. Chapters 8 and 9 will provide a look at those strategies for impacting the client by targeting diagnosis and intervention on the consultee (Chapter 8) or on the System (Chapter 9).

In the discussion to follow the reader will be introduced to an expanded view of consultation—a view that allows for direct contact with the client and one that promotes a broad-based, multimodal model of diagnosis and intervention. Specifically, the reader will:

1. Understand the differences between a restricted direct service model and a consultation approach that allows for direct contact.

2. Be introduced to a diagnostic/intervention model that views the client's behavior as a function of the interaction between the client, the specific task, and the environment in which the the client functions.

3. Be provided with a expansive multimodal approach to diagnosis and intervention in case-focused consultation.

Expanding Consultation to Include Direct Client Contact

As noted previously, a distinction has typically been made between direct services (e.g., counseling, therapy, and psychological assessment) and what was typically viewed as an indirect form of service (consultation). The position presented within this text is that such a dichotomy is both artificial and overlimiting.

Direct Clinical Services

In traditional clinical services, the mental health professional would meet with the client and employ a variety of techniques or approaches to evaluate or assess the client and the client's problem. This process of evaluation typically took place in isolation from the natural setting in which the client performed his or her duties. Further, the evaluation typically involved the specialized skills and instruments of a trained clinician and/or psychometrician. These data collected through the skilled use of psychological assessment tools and trained interviews can prove extremely valuable in both understanding the nature of the client's concerns and the possible paths of intervention.

However, as a sampling of client behavior, attitude, and cognition, such an assessment regimen may have its limitations in terms of both its prescriptive value and generalizability to the work setting. It is possible that these data revealed through such an assessment, while being of value for the clinician, may fail to directly translate to usable information for the consultee. It is not uncommon for teachers, managers, and support healthcare professionals to complain that while the psychological assessment has resulted in the application of a diagnostic label or the creation of somewhat idealistic recommendations, neither appear that useful for the person directly impacted by the client (the consultee).

Traditional Consultation—An Indirect Mode of Service Delivery

To remedy this shortcoming, many clinicians moved from behind the psychometrician's desk to gather information indirectly through the consultee's observation and data collection procedures. This extension of the diagnostic intervention process to include naturalistic observation and the indirect delivery of remedial procedures through the consultee has both increased the utility and validity of the data gathered, and also introduced the consultee to the process of diagnosis and intervention planning. The utilization of the consultee as data collector and interventionist is based upon the following rationale:

1. The consultee has knowledge about the client that may be difficult if not impossible to obtain in the brief focused encounter with the psychometrician.

2. Problems are to some degree situationally defined and thus are best understood within the context in which they occur. The consultee can provide information regarding the uniqueness of that context.

3. A clinician's naturalistic observation of the client in the work environment is most likely impossible without consultee cooperation and support.

4. Intervention plans will prove more effective if they can be applied both within the clinical setting and within the work environment. Such spread of intervention will be more accepted if the consultee was involved in its development.

5. Assessment techniques need to emphasize the linkage between the assessment and the intervention as such knowledge of the work environment and task demands is essential for such linkage to occur.

6. The client's current level of functioning is assumed to be a result of the client interacting with a particular task and within a particular environment. Understanding and intervening with the task and the environment is best achieved with consultee involvement.

An Expanded, Collaborative Approach

For many the distinction of direct service from such indirect consultation services hinged on whether the clinician had direct contact with the client. Traditionally, consultation viewed as an indirect service model required that the consultant avoid direct client diagnostic or remedial contact. Under this schema, the consultant would assist the consultee in the development of the data collecting procedures, but the actual client contact fell within the realm of the consultee. Following appropriate data collection, the consultee would bring this information back to the consultant for analysis, diagnosis, and intervention planning. For example, a consultant employing a behavioral approach may assist the consultee to operationalize the problem and/or goals and support the consultee as the consultee gathered baseline data. The consultant and consultee would most likely discuss and analyze the data and develop an intervention plan that the consultee will implement.

Previously within this text it was argued that such a dichotomization of direct (i.e., clinical) and indirect (i.e., consultation) services was artificial. Further, in a previous text, this author, with Joel Meyers and Roy Martin (Meyers, Parsons, & Martin, 1979), argued that consultation could be carried out even when the consultant had direct access to the client. Rather than viewing direct services and consultation as mutually exclusive, we demonstrated that it was more useful to view consultation as a continuum of more or less direct services. It was argued that consultation could occur whether the consultant gathers data directly from the client or through the efforts of the consultee (Meyers, Parsons, & Martin, 1979) or some combination of both. However, for direct service to be accurately considered consultative it must:

1. Include an interaction not just with the client but also with the consultee;

2. Involve interaction with the consultee which entailed a process of give and take in which the expertise of the consultant is integrated with expertise and experience of the consultee in order to understand and employ the data collected by the consultant, and;

3. Focus on producing change in the environment in which the client functions.

Client-focused consultation involves the full collaboration of consultant and consultee in both the diagnostic and intervention processes and allows for the possible direct contact between client and consultant in addition to the more typical consultee-client contact. Such consultative collaboration provides a number of potential benefits. First, by incorporating varied perspectives (consultant and consultee) on data collection and interpretation, the potential bias of either perspective is checked and the validity of data collected may be increased. Secondly, by employing data on the specific elements of the task and environment with which and in which the client is operating, the possibility of achieving an assessment-intervention linkage has been increased. Finally, the collaborative exchange can serve an educative and thus preventive function for the consultee, increasing his or her knowledge of the influencing effects of task and environmental demands.

Client Diagnosis—A Collaborative Effort

From this consultation frame of reference not only are the diagnostic and intervention planning processes expanded to include consultee collaboration, but the approach has been expanded to insure both remedial and prevention effects. This expanded approach is based on the assumption that behavior is a function of the interaction between the unique characteristics of the client, the task the client is asked to accomplish, and the environment in which this occurs (Behavior = f[client-task-environment]). Consider, for example, the case of Charles M. Charles is a 35-year-old Caucasian male who has just recently been diagnosed as having an Attention Deficit Disorder without hyperactivity. The identification of his ADD has helped Charles to understand his tendency to be inattentive, or forget what other people are saying, and even his tendency to be somewhat accident prone. While the ADD is clearly a client variable, the effect of that ADD will certainly be amplified or mollified as a function of the task Charles is asked to perform (e.g., watching the operation dials of a nuclear power plant versus loading and unloading a lumber supply truck), or even the setting in which he performs this task (i.e., the degree of alternative stimulation or distraction available). The assumption that is operative within this text is that understanding the nature of a problem as well as identifying possible strategies for intervention can be maximized by considering each of these variables (i.e., client-task-environment) along with the potential effects of their interactions.

Therefore, in addition to employing a diagnostic model to assess the individual client's profile, the collaborative, consultative model attempts to assess the specific requirements of the tasks with which the client is exhibiting difficulty and the unique characteristics of the environment within which the difficulty is exhibited. Such an expansion not only leads to a more comprehensive evaluation of the influencing factors, but incorporates the expertise of the consultee regarding those task and environmental variables with which he or she is familiar.

Further, this client-task-environment focus results in the identification of multiple points of intervention that are easily accessed by the consultant and consultee alike—multiple interventions that not only increase the possibility of effective intervention but also decrease the likelihood of future problems for that client (i.e., the preventive potential). The analysis of the task demands and environmental presses and the way they can impact this client helps the consultee to begin to consider modification of these variables as a way of avoiding similar problems with other clients in the future.

Collaboration of the consultant and consultee during the diagnosis can occur in a number of ways and at a number of points along the process. The consultee might be invited to be present during the evaluation and even participate in the interviewing process, assuming that such co-interviewing would both be appropriate and acceptable to the client. The consultee might even observe the testing process and share observations about the client's behavior while he or she is engaged in the testing. These observations can be compared to those of the consultant and used to illustrate the types of problems or behaviors encountered by the consultee in the work setting.

Collaboration can also occur when the consultee and the consultant engage in their own unique form of data collection without the other being present. Under these conditions the consultant and the consultee need to discuss the rationale for the diagnostic methods employed. Further, the specific variables or factors that are being assessed need to be concretely defined so that the data collected through these various methods can be compared to find points of similarity.

Assessing the Task

It is clear that the difficulty a client is exhibiting may be a result of some unique personal problem that he or she may be experiencing. For example, Liz is currently in a very heated divorce process. She is physically stressed and finds it hard to concentrate at work. Liz's supervisor reports that Liz has been making an extraordinary amount of errors in her paperwork. In this situation the source of Liz's work difficulty may be her physical and emotional exhaustion, which are the results of a very hostile divorce process.

But, consider Sally. Sally's supervisor also reported that Sally has shown an increase in the amount of errors in her paperwork. It was discovered that the timing of the appearance of the increased errors correlated to the initiation of a new process for completing the forms. With further investigation it was determined that the new procedure had increased the eye fatigue of all of the workers and also resulted in a decrease in accuracy for all of the clerical staff. In this case, it was most likely the unique demands of the task itself, rather than any personal problem, that were the source for the poor work performance.

Thus, while it is clear that the difficulty a client may be exhibiting may be the result of some unique personal problem that the client is experiencing, it is also possible that the specific demands of the task with which the client is having difficulty may be augmenting the effects of the personal problem, or perhaps may even be the primary source of the work-related problem. Thus it is important to include an assessment of the task demands as part of an expanded diagnostic process.

The process of task analysis is far from new or novel. Task analysis was originally develop by R. B. Miller (1962) as a process aimed at facilitating the training of armed services personnel. The basic concept is that a task, be it performing rudimentary mathematics or computer skills or running a sales meeting or supervisory session, involves a number of subtasks, each requiring specific abilities and skills. Further, it is assumed that successful completion of these subtasks are preconditions to the successful completion of desired final task. A task analysis gives a picture of the logical sequence of the necessary steps for performing some final process or achieving some ultimate goal. Further, the specific analysis of the task into subunits assists the consultant and consultee in identifying the unique demands placed on the consultee by each subtask, as well as the unique skills or knowledge required to successfully perform that task. Such a microanalysis of the task may identify the source of the client's work-related problem. By analyzing the task that appears to be involved with the client's problem, and reviewing the specific demands such a task places upon the person attempting to complete it, the consultant and consultee can identify those areas mastered by the client, as well as those areas causing the most difficulty. Perhaps the client is having a problem because he or she lacks the necessary prerequisite skills. This could certainly be the case of a student who has been incorrectly placed in an advanced mathematics class without having had training in the prerequisites. The frustration experienced by the student, along with the potentially disruptive behavioral manifestations of that frustration, can best be understood and remedied by the realization of this lack of prerequisite skill acquisition.

In addition to possibly lacking the skills required to successfully complete a particular unit or subtask of the task, there may be something unique in the task demands that interacts with the client's own current psycho-social-emotional resources in such a way as to produce or elicit an interfering response. Consider the case of Keith, found in Exercise 7-1.

Assessing the Environment

The setting or psycho-social-physical environment in which the client is functioning (or dysfunctioning) can serve an active role in creating and/or supporting this dysfunctionality. Thus, an expanded model of diagnosis involves the analysis of the environmental conditions potentially impacting the current problem. While the following sections briefly discuss the nature of some of those environmental factors that have the potential to effect the client, a more in-depth presentation of these variables will be found in Chapter 9.

Physical Environment

Research (see Dunn, Beaudry, & Klavas, 1989; Dunn & Dunn, 1987; Tharp, 1989; Torrance, 1986) would suggest that an individual's learning and performance are impacted by the social-physical environment in which he or she is asked to perform. This research suggests that an individual's performance can be significantly affected by variables such as the amount of light, noise, temperature, formality, or mobility found within the performance or learning environment. Further, space utilization (Hall, 1966), the arrangement of materials, the physical layout, and forms of stimulation (e.g., noise and colors) have all been considered as environmental elements that can impact an individual's level of performance and thus should be considered when diagnosing a client.

Social/Cultural Climate

In addition to the physical elements of an environment, research has demonstrated the potential impact of social/cultural elements on learning and performing. Rudolph Moos (1974) has developed a series of survey instruments aimed at assessing the social-psychological climate of an organization. Factors such as the degree to which workers feel supported and involved, or the degree to which autonomy is encouraged, are all found to be

EXERCISE 7-1   The Case of Keith—Focusing on the Task

Directions: In this exercise you will be given a brief statement of the problem, provided by Keith's teacher, Dr. Hagerstown, along with some background information on Keith. In Part I, you are asked to read the referral information. Your task is to identify the particular tasks causing Keith some problems. More specifically, you are to identify five factors involved in performing the task. In Part II, you are asked to identify five personal issues or experiences that may interact with these components of the task to inhibit Keith's performance. Through discussion of your response with a colleague, mentor, or supervisor, you will begin to see the value of task analysis to the diagnostic process.

Part I Problem Statement

Dr. Hagerstown, Keith's creative writing teacher, has noted that "Keith's performance in class has become simply unacceptable. I am not sure what happened. He has been an excellent student up to this point and he is certainly a compliant youth, but he is simply not producing the creative work that is required and expected of one so talented. Since the beginning of the second marking period (November 8), his essays have been short and not descriptive; his personal journal writing has been sporadic and his verbal contribution during our class creative roundtable are simply sterile! Keith is simply not putting himself into his work."

According to Dr. Hagerstown, his class is run like a college seminar. Students are assigned a theme at the beginning of each marking period. Their assignments (all of which will vary in form and genre) reflect aspects of that theme. The theme for this marking period has been "Family—Community—Belonging: Essential to Our Human Existence."

Students orally present their creations to their study group for peer feedback before correcting and presenting to the class as a whole. Students' presentations to the class are somewhat formal, with the presenter standing at a podium. Following each presentation the presenter will answer questions about the process he or she employed in producing this work.

While other teachers have noted a drop in Keith's overall performance, most have attributed it to "senioritis." Further, his math, science, physical education, and art teachers feel Keith is performing at expected levels.

Part II

In column A identify five separate task demands. In column B suggest five unique personal characteristics or experiences that may be negatively interacting with the task demand to reduce Keith's performance.

Column A
Task Analysis

Column B
Personal Characteristics

(sample):
Knowledge and comfort with theme   Parents currently in divorce process

1) _____   _____

2) _____   _____

3) _____   _____

4) _____   _____

5) _____   _____

associated with the degree of success experienced within a work environment. This point will be expanded upon in Chapter 9.

Another line of research emphasizes the importance of social climate and organization as a factor differentially impacting the learning and performance of individuals from different cultures. For example, Vasquez (1990) emphasized the family- and group-oriented view of the Hispanic culture, and suggested that Hispanic American students would prefer a more cooperative learning environment than one promoting competition. This same author (Vasquez, 1990) noted that Navajo students sometimes show strong preferences for learning privately, through trial and error, rather than having their mistakes made public. Similar unique preferences for learning and performance environments were reported with African American populations (Bennett, 1990; Hale-Bensen, 1986) and Asian Americans (Suzuki, 1983).

Thus, learning to view the presenting concern in the context of the physical and social/cultural environment in which it occurs provides both an expanded framework for diagnosis and added directions for intervention and prevention. Let's return to the case of Keith (see Exercise 7-2).

Assessing the Client

Our discussion of the client has been placed last in order to emphasize the extrapersonal focus of the consultation model employed. However, this is not to suggest a linear approach to assessment—that is, first assess the task, then the environment, and then the client. Clearly, in assessing each of the previous focal points for diagnosis (i.e., task and environment), consideration has been given to the client. Thus, assessing the client has already begun. Now, we turn our attention to a fuller understanding of the client and the elements she or he brings to the task and to the environment.

While there are many interesting and varied models for assessing a client and his or her problem, one found to be comprehensive and which this author feels leads to concrete conceptualization about solutions, is that presented by Arnold Lazarus (1971). Lazarus presents a model he terms *multimodal.* The essence of his multimodal approach is that a person's functioning or dysfunctioning can be defined as manifesting within seven areas, or modalities. These seven areas are: **B**ehavior, **A**ffect, **S**ensations, **I**mages, **C**ognition, **I**nterpersonal relationships, and **D**rugs (or biological functions)—**BASIC ID.**

Using the acronym BASIC ID to represent these various modalities, Lazarus argues that a complete identification of one's problem must account for each modality of this BASIC ID. Because of the potential value of this model (Lazarus, 1989) for the consultant, each modality, with the type of questions to be posed and considered by the consultant in attempting to define client functioning, is presented below.

B: Behavior. For Lazarus (1981) it is important to be mindful of areas of behavioral excess (e.g., client drinks too much? interrupts too often?) and deficit (e.g., doesn't initiate conversation, fails to do homework, etc.). Thus, it is important to begin to identify how it is that the client acts. What does he or she DO and what are the conditions under which they act or behave differently?

EXERCISE 7-2   Keith—An Environmental Analysis

Directions: As with Exercise 7-1, your task is to review the data provided. The additional data highlights a number of unique factors of the physical-social-psychological environment found in Dr. Hagerstown's classroom. After reading the five pieces of information provided, identify two possible ways these unique physical and/or psycho-social environmental factors could negatively impact Keith's performance. Discussing your conclusions with a colleague, mentor or supervisor will help you to expand your awareness of the possible interactions between environment and client.

Classroom Observation

In observing Keith in his creative writing class you collected the following observations:
1. Classroom arranged in major sections—what appears to be an area for small peer groups and one for large class discussion (20 students)
2. Classroom is very bright, cheery, many decorations, both commercial and student created. According to the teacher, the decorations reflect the theme of the marking period and therefore change four times throughout the year.
3. When students are working in their small groups, they review each other's written work, rough notes, and any graphics or pictures that accompany the work.
4. Keith's peer group (five students) includes himself and four females. There are eight other boys in class besides Keith.
5. Keith's group meets in the rear left corner of the room and Keith sits in a seat facing the back of the larger room.
6. You understand from one of the students that the girl directly facing Keith (in his small group) is his ex-girlfriend.

Possible Impacts
1. (example):The pictures placed around the room show happy families in both commercial products and snapshots of the students' families on vacation, at home, and in other settings. The pictures are very upsetting to Keith and he has trouble focusing on his work, being pulled to fantasize about his "once happy family."

2. _____

_____

3. _____

_____

Regarding to the client's presenting concern: What behaviors does she or he exhibit or fail to exhibit that appear part of the problem experienced? Asking the client and/or the consultee questions such as: "What would you (the client) like to do, or stop doing?" or "If you (the client) were performing the way you wished, what would you being doing, that you are not doing currently?" will help to identify habits or behaviors which need to be targeted for change.

Consider Keith's situation. Dr. Hagerstown suggested that Keith's performance has dropped off drastically. He describes the problem behaviors as:

1. Writing short essays
2. Not being descriptive in his journal writing
3. Not being personal in his classroom discussions

In looking at the client's behavior, we must also consider what events (antecedents) lead up to the client acting a certain way and similarly, what are the results (consequences) of these actions. Oftentimes, one's behavior is heavily influenced (if not caused) by these antecedents and consequences. For example, if every time Keith attempted to enter into the classroom discussion he began to cry and feel sick to his stomach, it might be hypothesized that lack of participation is a way of avoiding these painful consequences. Such an understanding not only clarifies the nature of the problem but also may help the consultant and consultee identify other ways of gaining Keith's participation in a way that results in less upsetting consequences.

Those interested in more fully understanding the relationships between behavior and antecedent and consequential events are referred to the work of behavioral theorists such as Mahoney and Thorensen (1974) and Cormier and Cormier (1991).

A: Affect.   When most people think of helping another person, they generally envision someone asking the client, "How do you feel about that?" Feelings are important aspects of the human experience and thus need to be identified, especially as they are tied to a presenting complaint. However, identifying feelings in and of themselves is not sufficient. The consultant and consultee need to be attentive to both those feelings that are reported and those that are never or rarely noted. The consultee and the consultant will need to consider the degree to which the client's feelings appear appropriate to the situation, as well as the degree or intensity with which the feelings are experienced. Questions such as: "Are these emotions overdone and the client too sensitive?" or, "Are the client's feelings being blunted, somewhat insensitive, or underdone?" need to be considered. Also, the consultant and consultee need to consider the degree of control (too much, too little) the client exhibits in the expression of his or her feelings.

Perhaps the "sterility" of expression exhibited by Keith is a reflection of his own grieving of his parents' marriage. It may be appropriate following such a loss, but is it proportional to the actual loss? Does Keith experience the loss in other ways, other than sadness? Does he feel depressed, hopeless? Does he find any pleasure in the activities he liked prior to the divorce? Finding the answers to these type of questions not only clarifies the depth and breadth of the problem but begins to identify goals and outcomes desired.

S: Sensation.   When considering client sensations, we are obviously concerned about their five major senses and the degree to which they are accurately receiving the signals around them, but we also need to listen to the degree to which their problem is presented in the form of body sensations (e.g., sick to the stomach, dizziness, headaches, etc.) For example, when Keith speaks of being upset, does he also mean that he feels sick to his stomach, has headaches, or muscle tensions?

The sensations the client reports may be valuable for two reasons. First, as with the other modalities, identifying sensations associated with the concern more clearly defines the nature of the problem and how it is experienced. Secondly, the identifications of such sensations may even provide us with an early diagnostic-warning system, as when a person experiences a muscular tension (in neck) before becoming very angry. Such an early warning system could be useful in developing strategies for early intervention.

I: Imagery.   For Lazarus, imagery involves the various mental pictures that seem to influence our life. For example, the student who "sees" himself as being laughed at may tend to withdraw from volunteering an answer in class. Or, the person who may "see" him- or herself as fat, even after losing weight, may still act and feel fat. Having a better understanding of the way the client "sees" him- or herself and his or her world is useful information. It not only reflects a part of the client's concern, but it can also suggest a helpful goal to be achieved. Questions such as: "What bothersome dreams or memories do you have?" "How do you view yourself?" "How do you view your future?" may begin to reveal such imagery. Again, consider Keith.

As noted, Keith has withdrawn from active participation in the classroom discussion. In fact, he reports feeling sick to his stomach when he attempts to participate (sensation). In interview with Keith, the consultant learns that he "sees" himself starting to talk about his family and completely losing control in class. The others in class he sees as being disgusted by his emotional outburst. He especially envisions his ex-girlfriend making fun of him. Further, Keith reports that he can hardly get the image of his mom crying out of his mind, especially with all the family pictures around the room.

Clearly these images play an important role in the overall problem Keith is experiencing. Further, helping Keith remove or reshape these images would be a very valuable goal for the consultation.

C: Cognition.   The "C" in Lazarus' BASIC ID stands for cognition. Cognition is comprised of our thoughts, beliefs, or ways of making meaning out of our experience. Often, the way we interpret our experience is inaccurate. We need to learn to identify when our thinking is distorted and thus learn to correct it.

The effective consultant needs to unearth the client's cognitive patterns as a part of the overall experience of the problem. Seeking the answers to questions such as: "What does this mean to the client?" "What assumptions about him- or herself, his or her world, is the client making?" will provide a clearer picture of the client's cognitive orientation.

For example, while the loss that Keith is experiencing is one that is both undesirable and disappointing, it is not unbearable, nor does it provide evidence of his failure. In reviewing Keith's journal, it becomes clear to Dr. Hagerstown that Keith blames himself for his parents' divorce; in fact, in one section he wrote: "If I had been more like the son my dad wanted, he would never have left my mom! It is all my fault!" Concluding that his parents' divorce is his fault is certainly a distortion of reality. Such a distortion exaggerates the importance of his role in the marriage and leads to an inordinate amount of guilt tied to a decision over which he had no control. Further, correcting such a distorted interpretation would prove to be a very useful and helpful goal and relieve much of what is most likely debilitating guilt.

I: Interpersonal Relationships.   As "social animals," how we behave, or do not behave, with others is an essential element of our human experience. We need to begin to assess how the client approaches others, responds to others, and communicates with others.

In assessing the interpersonal modality, the client may come to understand how this component both reflects the problem experienced and may in fact contribute to it. Again, in the case of Keith, we come to understand that he becomes overly withdrawn when emotionally upset. This tendency to withdraw from friends and family can certainly increase the experience of anxiety and concern over the demise of his intact family by removing him from other possible sources of support. Further, his social withdrawal in class has created a situation in which his grades are declining and this in turn has compounded his feelings of guilt. Thus, a useful goal for this consultation would be to assist Keith to learn to use appropriate disclosure and reliance on friends and families as way of adjusting to the emotional crisis he is experiencing.

D: Drugs/(Biology).   While the "D" certainly does complete the acronym, it may be a bit misleading. Lazarus is not focusing only on drugs. He is suggesting that we consider the nonpsychological aspects of a person's experience. We need to consider the client's diet, general health, and well being, and overall general physiology (hormones, nervous system, and so on).

The consultant and consultee are most likely not trained to intervene with organic conditions, but they need to increase their awareness of the affect of substances (such as chemicals, food additives, or even natural substances such as caffeine) and physiology (e.g., hormones) in creating problems in our lives. In the case of Keith, the consultant and consultee need to consider whether Keith's reaction may be associated with his lack of sleep, or change in eating (which may result from the disruption of the family patterns at home). Does Keith's emotional response pattern have any possible connection with any medicine he may be taking, or has stopped taking? Again, seeking the answers to such questions not only gives the consultant and consultee a more complete picture of the depth and breadth of the problem but also begins to provide clarity about the goals to be achieved.

While the purist may wish to define a client's problem in terms of each of these seven modalities, what is being suggested here is that the BASIC ID model is a useful template or guide for systematically assessing the client's situation. Whether the consultant and consultee employ seven or fewer modalities, such a model enables them to more specifically and more concretely define the nature and scope of the client's concern as the first step to formulating useful and achievable goals and outcomes.

Exercise 7-3 will help to demonstrate the use and value of problem defining using the model of the BASIC ID.

Intervention—Collaborative Effort

Expanding the diagnostic process to include assessment of the task, the environment, and the client, along with the way these three elements interact and contribute to the work-related problem, results in a wide base understanding of the nature of the problem. Further, the inclusion of the task analysis and environmental assessment into the diagnostic process makes possible a collaborative dialogue between the consultant and consultee around the identification of intervention strategies that not only remediate the current problem but can also prevent it from occurring in the future.

EXERCISE 7-3   Keith—Assessing the Client
BASIC ID

Directions: After reading the case material, use the BASIC ID to identify the various components or modalities involved in Keith's experience.

Case Presentation

In an interview with Keith, the consultant discovered the following information. Since the beginning of the second marking period he has found himself daydreaming a lot in class. He sometimes sees himself on a small boat like a dinghy with the big boat is going off into the sunset. He doesn't feel very energetic in creative writing (and says he seems and feels okay in other classes).

Keith admitted that he is not spending much time on his creative writing assignments, he seems to get distracted with thoughts about his mom and his dad, thinking that "... I can't make it without them!" When he thinks like this he finds it hard to concentrate on the various writing tasks. In fact, sitting down to write seems to make this daydreaming and thinking happen. So he simply avoids the tasks.

Keith also noted that he has split up with his girlfriend (Laura), who is in the same creative writing class. As a result, he just doesn't feel like he can talk to anyone.

Keith noted that he is losing weight and has some difficulty getting to sleep. He finds himself feeling sad, and nervous, like sometimes his body is tingling.

Analysis of the Client

B-EHAVIOR: _____

_____

A-FFECT: _____

_____

S-ENSATION: _____

_____

I-IMAGERY: _____

_____

C-OGNITION: _____

_____

I-NTERPERSONAL: _____

_____

D-RUGS (DIET, ETC.): _____

_____

In working with a client, the consultant and consultee will need to (1) identify the nature of the problem and the desired goal(s), (2) prioritize the goals or issues to be addressed, (3) develop intervention strategies, and (4) select and implement the strategy (ies).

Identifying Problems and Goals

The utilization of task and environmental analysis along with the widespread view of the client (i.e., BASIC ID) will increase the utility and validity of the intervention processes in a number of ways. First, by the inclusion of the consultee as task and environmental expert, the consultant has not only increased his or her breadth of solution but has also tailored the understanding of the nature of the problem and the intervention steps to be taken to the specific needs of that client, with that specific consultee.

In addition, the focus on the specific task that appears to be the primary arena in which the difficulty is manifesting itself provides the consultant and the consultee the opportunity to develop specific remedial steps that are not only clearly relevant to the needs of the consultee but are tied specifically to the client's task-related deficiencies. Together the consultant and consultee can use the data from the task analysis, environmental analysis and client assessment to

1. Develop additional training or intervention processes to assist the client with developing the skills needed to perform the subtasks
2. Identify the components of the task or the environment that may be manipulated or modified in order to facilitate and cue the desired behavior, or, at a minimum reduce or eliminate those components that interfere with the desired behavior

Returning to our case of Keith, the linkage of assessment to intervention becomes clear. One point of problem definition was that Keith experienced a number of intrusive and upsetting images that interfered with his attending and concentrating on his classwork. Keith needs to understand that these images, while being responses to his own personal fears surrounding the divorce of his parents, are also responses to the visual stimulation found around the classroom (i.e., pictures of happy, intact families).

In this situation the professional counselor may attempt to employ strategies such as rational emotive imagery training (Ellis & Harper, 1975) to help Keith reduce the debilitating effect of his imagery. As a collaborating consultant, this professional counselor would not only employ such imagery training techniques but assist the consultee to reconsider the posters and pictures which decorate the classroom. Through a collaborative dialogue the consultee may choose to reduce the emphasis on dual parent family photos, and include additional happy single parent images.

In addition to this form of intervention, the professional counselor working with Keith may employ a variety of Gestalt-type techniques, such as the empty chair technique (Perls, 1969) to assist Keith to identify and express his feelings of anxiety, anger, and guilt. This may be seen as the first step to problem solving. While such a strategy would not be appropriate within the classroom, the utilization of journal writing as a way to express feelings, or even a project on creative problem solving, would be appropriate to Dr. Hagerstown's class and may prove therapeutic for Keith.

Setting Priorities and Finding a Place to Start

After establishing a wide-based diagnostic profile of the client, task, and environment, it will become quite obvious to both the consultant and consultee that it is not possible to intervene at each diagnostic point, simultaneously. The consultant needs to narrow the focus and prioritize the strategies. In selecting both the focal point or target and the nature of the intervention plan, the consultant should consider the following general guidelines.

Breadth of Impact

One of the first points to be considered in selecting a point and process of intervention is the breadth of impact. The consultant should attempt to select an intervention strategy that provides the broadest impact for the effort. Intervention strategies that impact a variety of client modalities and/or task and environmental elements may have a greater chance of being successful and thus should be first considered for implementation. Further, since the goal of consultation is twofold (i.e., remediative and preventive), the consultant needs to consider the remedial and preventive value of each intervention in hopes of identifying the intervention with the broadest (both remedial and preventive) impact possible.

In our case illustration, it becomes clear that expanding the subject matter of the pictures decorating the classroom will not only help Keith, but will also allow other students living in single-family conditions a point of personal reference. This single intervention would therefore not only impact Keith, but all students "distracted" by the exclusion of their family experience in the models presented.

Causes Least Strain

While breadth of impact is clearly an important consideration as a selection criterion, it needs to be tempered by the cost of implementing the intervention.

As noted throughout the text, consultation implies change, and change, by its very nature, is costly. For the interventions to have a chance of succeeding they must be implemented and maintained. Thus it is important to select intervention strategies that cause the least strain or costs for the consultee or the system's resources. For example, if a consultant can choose between an intervention that requires the consultee to learn new skills and acquire some additional resources (e.g., materials, supplies, etc.) versus an intervention where the consultee has the needed ability and resources, it is generally more effective to consider the latter, as least costly. The consultant needs to collaboratively dialogue with the consultee regarding the perceived level of adjustment and strain to be encountered while implementing a particular intervention. The consultant should attempt to provide as much support as possible (time, energy, resources) to reduce the strain experienced by the consultee, especially during the early phases of the intervention process when success (i.e., "pay-offs") may not be as apparent.

Similarly, in selecting an intervention strategy, the consultant needs to consider those approaches that best suit the consultee's goals, needs, and expectations. Thus, suggesting that a consultee employ extinction procedures to reduce an undesirable student behavior may be theoretically sound, but this same intervention may be contrary to a particular consultee's need to feel responsive or to actively engage with students. Under these conditions, extinction may be perceived as a passive approach and thus more costly. A more active and directive intervention may prove more effective under these conditions.

Address the Immediate Pain

Strategies or intervention plans that address the immediate pain being experienced by the consultee and client will most likely be those embraced and accepted. These are the issues that the client and the consultee would be most motivated to do something about and thus be least resistant to the intervention process.

For both Dr. Hagerstown and Keith, Keith's inability to elaborate within his writing is the most concerning aspect of his current problem. Thus, focusing the intervention plan to provide a rapid solution to this difficulty would be met with acceptance by both the consultee (Dr. Hagerstown) and the client (Keith). Perhaps the degree of personal disclosure will increase if Dr. Hagerstown could assure Keith that his writing would not have to be presented publicly until he was ready. With such an assurance and sense of control, Keith may be willing to risk some vulnerability and personal disclosure with Dr. Hagerstown, thus enriching his written work.

Start Where Invited

In selecting intervention strategies, it is useful for the consultant to focus on the issues that the consultee and/or client feel are important and have stated an interest in addressing. Having the client and consultee demonstrate a willingness to work is a prerequisite to maintaining their involvement in the intervention process.

Thus, while the consultant may feel that the issue that needs to be addressed is Keith's irrational feelings of guilt about the divorce of his parents, it would be better to address the quality of his writing, assuming that is the point with which Keith and Dr. Hagerstown have sought assistance. It is hoped that in working where initially invited, the consultant can move (i.e., shape) the relationship and the intervention to other areas of concern that may have been initially less apparent to the consultee and/or client.

Create Success

Both the consultee and the client are entering the intervention after having experienced a problem, and perhaps a series of failures, for some time. This can be a somewhat costly experience. It is important, therefore, that they experience a payoff as soon as possible. It is important to experience success in goal achievement as evidence of both the hopefulness of the situation and the helpfulness of the consultation.

It is useful, therefore, to begin with a problem or an issue that is manageable. Thus it might be important to attempt to break the larger problem down into more manageable subparts that can be addressed one at a time. Once this is accomplished, start with the task that appears to have the most likelihood of success.

Again, while it is desirable to have Keith expand on his formal writing projects, what might be needed first is to assist Keith to first feel comfortable with elaborating on his journal writing.

Developing and Employing Intervention Strategies

Once the target for intervention has been identified, the consultant and consultee need to engage in the process of intervention planning and implementation.

While no one person can be truly a master of all intervention strategies, it is important that the consultant have a well articulated model of intervention (e.g., behavioral, cognitive, multimodal, dynamic, etc.). Further, the consultant needs to work with the consultee in a collaborative effort to translate the therapeutic steps to be taken in a way that they can be incorporated into the task or environmental experiences provided by the consultee. Thus, as noted previously, imagery training, while clinically appropriate, becomes much more consultatively effective when translated in ways that can assist the consultee in promoting more positive, facilitative images, or at a minimum reduce the stimulation for negative imagery.

While it is not the intention of this author to promote or encourage a single form of intervention planning, nor is it possible to identify all the successful strategies for dealing with specific problems in a text of this sort, Table 7-1 presents a brief list of references that may prove useful in addressing specific problem areas. The interventions have been organized around the acronym BASIC ID. It must be noted that the authors referenced and the techniques identified are not the only appropriate resources for those working within that modality, nor are they intended to be mutually exclusive. It is quite possible that the mate-

TABLE 7-1   Treatment Directory

Modality	Procedures
Behavior	Cormier & Cormier (1991) Kanfer & Goldstein (1991) Bellack, Hersen, & Kazdin (1990) Wolpe (1990)
Affect	Perls (1969) Gardner (1972) Goode (1992) LeShan (1972)
Sensation	Zahourek (1988) Smith (1990) Cautela (1978) Nigl (1986)
Imagery	Ellis & Harper (1975) Cormier & Cormier (1991) Hampson, Marks, & Richardson (1990) Lusebrink (1990) Goode (1992)
Cognition	Hughes (1988) Burns (1981) Beck & Emery (1979) Ellis & Grieger (1986) Kuehlwein & Rosen (1993)
Interpersonal	Goldstein, Glick, Zimmerman, & Coultry (1987) Alberti & Emmons (1978) Harris & Harris (1985) Kelly (1982)
Drugs/Diet	Wurtman & Wurtman (1979) Gerson (1984) Pennington (1991) Gelenberg, Bassuk, & Schoonover (1991) Julien (1992)

rial listed in one modality can effect change in another modality. The intent here is to simply to encourage the reader to begin to develop a personal database of techniques, strategies, and approaches that have demonstrated utility for effecting change within a particular modality or with a particular problem.

This database needs to be actively updated and consistently tested for utility and validity. The effective consultant needs to be aware of the current research demonstrating the validity of various therapeutic interventions and problem-resolving strategies. It is essential, as with all professional activity, that the effective consultant continue to engage in professional development activities and remain abreast of the literature and research.

Putting It All Together—A Case Exercise

Prior to proceeding to the next chapters in which the focus for data collection and intervention switches from client focus to consultee focus (Chapter 8) and system focus (Chapter 9), it may be useful to attempt to pull together the unique, integrated, and multifocused approach discussed within the current chapter. The exercise provided (Exercise 7-4) will assist the reader in applying the task-environment-client model to the case of Todd (Exercise 7-4).

Summary

While all consultation could be said to be client targeted—having a remedial and hopefully preventive effect on the client—not all consultation involves client diagnosis and or direct client intervention. Client-focused consultation is a form of consultation in which diagnostic and intervention efforts center on the client as he or she interacts with a specific task within a specific environment. In client-focused consultation, the consultant is free to interact directly with the client, and/or gather diagnostic information and implement intervention strategies indirectly, using the consultee as the conduit for such activities.

The current chapter presented an expanded model for assessing and intervening with a client, from within a collaborative consultation framework. As discussed within this chapter, the consultant can increase the validity and utility of the diagnostic information by expanding the focus to include not only specific information about the client, but also information regarding the nature and requirements of the task, and the unique characteristics of the environment in which the task is performed. Such an expanded view also facilitates the development and maintenance of a collaborative relationship between the consultant and consultee. The consultee is the expert when it comes to understanding the task and the environment in which the client is currently functioning or dysfunctioning. Blending the consultee's diagnostic perspective with that of the consultant not only expands the data available but also facilitates the linkage of assessment to intervention.

Because of the large possible number of intervention focus points that may be identified using this integrated multifocal approach, a number of guidelines for selection of intervention target points were presented. It was suggested that the consultant prioritize possible targets based on: breadth of impact, degree of strain, felt pain, expectations, and chance for success.

EXERCISE 7-4   Case of Todd: A Client-Focused Consultation

Directions: This exercise is best performed in consult with a colleague, mentor, or supervisor. Read the case information (Part 1) and answer the questions found at the end of the case presentation (Part 2).

Part 1:

Referral: Todd was referred by his tenth-grade teacher because of his cheating in class. Mr. Elmwood wrote on the referral form: "I have waited for several weeks before sending this referral. Todd is in my tenth-grade language arts class, and I have suspected that he has been copying homework and cheating on quizzes since the beginning of the year. It is not my style to accuse anyone, so I gathered information carefully. Todd is sneaky—but I got him. When I confronted him, he first appeared angry, as if I had no right catching him cheating, and then to my surprise he started to tear up like a big baby. I suggested he should talk to you, since obviously he has some real problems. I hope you can help him start to take responsibility for his own life and do his own work."

Teacher Interview:

In an interview with Mr. Elmwood, the consultant discovered the following:

- Mr. E has been teaching for 12 years.
- Mr. E enjoys his work. He tries to teach class on a college level, having the students take responsibility for their own deadlines, topic choices, work, and so on. He lets the students work without his hovering over them. He feels that is the way to teach independence.
- Mr. E noted that his class was somewhat "loose," in that the students could sit where and when they wanted to. He even allowed them to walk around if they could think better that way.
- Mr E stated that the kids in his class are very competitive. They love to do "challenge bees" in which he will give a prize for the row that completes the assignment the fastest and most accurately. He requires that everyone in the row be finished before he counts that row as complete. The students appear to like this activity. He noted that sometimes the very competitive members of a row get upset if someone in the row is taking too long or not getting correct. And he added, "This happens to Todd almost all the time—he never knows what he is supposed to be doing, or he loses his place and the kids jump all over him!"
- Mr E related that Todd is oldest of three adopted children of Mr. and Mrs. S. His parents, according to Mr. E, are well educated and somewhat renowned in their respective fields (father, chemist; mother, nuclear medicine).

Teacher Observations:

Mr E reported that he has observed Todd at lunch and during free-hall (a free period where kids can be in a student lounge). He reported that Todd appears to have difficulty sitting, he moves around a lot, like he is "hyper" or "tense" or "something." He doesn't seem to get along with the others and appears teased because of his weight. Todd is approximately 35 pounds overweight, which Mr. E certainly understands, since as he described it: "Todd only eats junk and cokes for lunch. That kid puts more sugar, chocolate, and soda in his mouth than the remainder of the sixth period lunch group."

Interview with Todd:

In an interview with Todd, the consultant was able to support Mr E's observations. Todd is obese and overly tense (complaining of headaches and neck muscle cramps). He presents as a child with very low self-esteem. He complained of peer rejection, sibling rivalry, and expressed concerns (bad dreams) of being rejected (abandoned) by his parents.

Continued

Continued

Part II: Diagnosis and Intervention

1. Define Todd's problem, employing two separate modalities (BASIC ID).
    Sample:

    > **Drugs:** Todd is 35 lbs overweight, tends to be sedentary, and ingests a lot of sweets and caffeine (soda and chocolate).

    First Modality _____

    _____

    _____

    Second Modality _____

    _____

    _____

2. Identify two specific task demands that may have relevance to the understanding or intervention of Todd's problem.

    Sample: Bees require concentration under competitive tension and rapid response under stress of competition.

    First demand _____

    _____

    _____

    Second demand _____

    _____

    _____

3. Select two environmental characteristics or factors that may have relevance to the understanding of and intervention with Todd's problem.

    Sample: The atmosphere is relaxed and as a result is filled with a lot of visual and auditory stimulation and distraction as students mill about.

    First element _____

    _____

    _____

    Second element _____

    _____

    _____

4. Using the criteria presented to guide prioritization of targets and goals, which one of the two target modalities listed in question 1 would you select as having priority?

    _____

    _____

    _____

5. Develop one specific intervention strategy for use with each of two modalities in question 1 and state how the task and the environment could be modified to augment the intervention.

Modality	Intervention	Task adjustment	Environment modification

Chapter 8

Consultee-Focused Consultation

As emphasized in the previous chapter, the position taken here and elsewhere (e.g., Meyers, Parsons, & Martin, 1979; Parsons & Meyers, 1984) is that extrapersonal factors play an important role in the creation, maintenance, and eventual alleviation of the client's work-related problem. One of the environmental factors that is certainly positioned to play a central role in the current client problem is the consultee and the manner in which the consultee approaches his or her role in relationship to that client. As will be demonstrated, it is not uncommon to find that the most effective and efficient approach to remediating and preventing client related problems is to improve the consultee's knowledge, skill, and objectivity.

The consultee's level of professional expertise, skill, and objectivity and the impact these have on the consultee's interaction with the client is often central to the understanding of the current problem. At a minimum, these factors, along with the consultee's interactional style, are important factors to consider in the development of remedial and preventive programming. In consultee-focused consultation, the consultant attempts to increase the work-related functioning of the client by focusing the diagnostic, remedial, and preventive processes on the consultee in hopes of increasing the professional development of the consultee.

Focusing diagnostic and intervention efforts on the consultee is both delicate and complex. Consultee-focused consultation employs many of the same observational and interpersonal skills previously discussed, but it will also rely heavily on skills of confidentiality, self-monitoring techniques, direct and indirect confrontation, and educational programming. While consultee-focused consultation will most likely result in the consultee gaining personal insight along with the intended gain in skills and knowledge related to his or her job performance, it is not intended to serve as personal counseling or psychotherapy for the consultee. The consultant engaged in consultee-focused consultation must be alert not to cross this boundary between personal consultee counseling and consultee-focused consultation. The following chapter will help the reader to:

1. Understand the nature and value of consultee-focused consultation.
2. Identify when the consultee's level of professional knowledge, skill, or objectivity are pivotal to the creation, maintenance, and eventual amelioration of a client work-related problem.
3. Develop appropriate confrontational skills as the base for intervention at the consultee-focused level of consultation.
4. Understand a variety of techniques employed in consultee-focused consultation, including didactic information giving and theme interference reduction strategies (Caplan, 1970).

The Consultee: A Significant Extrapersonal Variable

In Chapter 7 much attention was given to the fact that a client's behavior is assumed to be a result of the interaction between certain client factors, the task characteristics, and the environment within which the task is being performed. Further, it was suggested that the most efficient form of intervention, both in terms of rapidity and permanence of effect, would be one that was widespread in its impact. Thus, consultation aimed at effecting change within the client, the tasks assigned and the environment within which the client operates would not only prove more beneficial to that client, but would also set the stage for prevention of future client-related problems. What was implied in that previous discussion was that one of the primary elements operating within the client's environment, and therefore most often directly tied to the characteristics of the task, was the professional style and personal interpersonal mannerisms of the consultee.

It can be demonstrated that it is often the consultee's own response to the client that, if not causing the current client-related problem, is exacerbating the situation. Consider the Case of Al, a 63-year-old second-shift supervisor for a electronics producer. Al approached the human relations director of the company complaining of the "attitude and general negative behavior" of Malcolm, a new line worker. According to Al, Malcolm has had "a chip on his shoulder from day one." Al noted that "(I) have tried everything with this young black man, I know how important it is for him to succeed and to begin to dig himself out of his environment. I have tried to talk with him. I have tried to offer him my help—after all, I have been doing this now for well over 41 years. I even invite him to coffee break. I told him that I really care about my boys on my line and I want them all to make it. After all, they are like my own!"

The human relations director interviewed Malcolm and discovered that Malcolm is a very achievement-oriented individual. Malcolm shared that this was his first real job after dropping out of high school and after spending two years on the street. Malcolm shared that his life has really turned around since he turned to Islam and became a Muslim, and that he "really wants to do his best for himself and his people." Malcolm, who is 20 years old, has over the course of the past year become much more involved in his faith and the ethnic/cultural origin and pride of his African heritage. It appears that with Malcolm's increased focus on personal and ethnic pride and heritage, he finds Al's habit of touching, kidding with his "boys," and his general "paternal" style as offensive and demeaning. While being sensitive to Malcolm's experience, the human relations director attempted to increase Malcolm's understanding of Al's style as originating from good intentions. But the real source of intervention (and prevention) rested with increasing Al's awareness, sensitivity, and respect for Malcolm's experience in relationship to Al's style. Through discussion with the consultant, Al increased his understanding of Malcolm's concerns and consequently began to reduce his own paternal style and language. More importantly, with this new understanding, Al began to speak with Malcolm both about his own interest in religion and his general ignorance of the Muslim faith. The openness of Al's communication along with his apparent sincerity in wanting to know more about Malcolm and Malcolm's faith experience provided a base for developing a better relationship and reducing of the inadvertent antagonism that had developed.

While it may have been possible to work only with the client in an attempt to desensitize him to the supervisor's behavior, it was clearly more efficient, both in terms of remediating the current condition and preventing future similar situations, to focus the consultant's efforts on increasing the consultee's (Al's) understanding of his own behavior and the potential impact this form of supervision could have on one such as Malcolm.

In the previous example, the focus of the consultation was on increasing the consultee's level of understanding. Once accomplished, the consultee had the needed skills and professional level of objectivity to adjust his own style in order to more effectively supervise his client. There are times, however, when increasing the consultee's level of understanding and knowledge are not sufficient. The consultant working in a consultee-focused consultation will encounter situations in which the salient characteristic of the problem situation may be either the consultee's limited knowledge, the consultee's lack of skill, and/or the consultee's lack of professional objectivity. Each of these targets presents special opportunities and concerns for the consultant and therefore each one is discussed in further detail.

When Knowledge Is Needed

As with the case of Al, the electronics supervisor, it is not unusual for a consultee to draw erroneous conclusions about the meaning and cause of the client's behavior. Under these conditions the consultee may begin to implement what he or she feels are remedial steps. For example, when Al assumed Malcolm was reacting negatively simply because of feeling somewhat "new" and "outside" of the "second shift family," Al increased his paternal approaches and playful touches, hoping to demonstrate Malcolm's inclusion. However, because of the misunderstanding of the situation, the remediation implemented by the consultee proved ineffective and may even have exacerbated the situation.

In such situations it is not the lack of goodwill or even professionalism that serves as the base for the consultee's involvement with the client's problematic behavior. Rather, it is simply the consultee's lack of a clear understanding about the nature of the situation. To further clarify this point, consider the case of Mrs. H (Case Illustration 8-1).

As suggested in Case Illustration 8-1, there are times when a consultee may simply lack the proper understanding of the principles of human development, management processes, or even interpersonal dynamics. As a result a client's behavior that was both understandable and at its point of origin was well within the normal limits for a particular stage

---

CASE ILLUSTRATION 8-1 Mrs. H—Lacking Information

Mrs. H has been a teacher for the past 38 years. Her health, particularly her hearing and eye-sight, is not as good as it used to be and her speech is sometimes slurred. She is very afraid of losing her job through forced retirement and is very defensive about any suggestion that she may no longer be fit to teach. She has sent two boys to the guidance counselor's office stating on the referral form "Please help these two disrespectful, disruptive hooligans!"

In speaking with the two boys, the counselor begins to discover that contrary to the comments from Mrs. H, neither of the youths is disrespectful nor does either have any history of acting out in class. In fact, the direct opposite has been the case with the two in question. In reviewing the records, the counselor finds that the boys have excellent academic histories and are very interested in pursuing careers in education. Further, it appears that their talking to each other during Mrs. H's class is the result of their need to check their understanding of Mrs. H's lectures. They stated that they really have a difficulty understanding her sometimes and they check with each other to validate that what they heard was accurate. Further, it appears that what Mrs. H interprets as "disrespectful" is the fact that these two often ask questions of Mrs. H that may appear off the topic. Through observations of the class interaction, the consultant soon realized that the questions asked were a result of the boys misinterpreting what Mrs. H said, a misinterpretation created by Mrs. H's tendency to sometimes slur her words. It was clear, through the observation, that the boys were not intending to disrupt or embarrass Mrs. H, but were only seeking clarification.

The consultant working with this case could certainly assist the boys (the clients) to develop more effective styles of coping with this environment, but a more effective approach, both in terms of immediate remediation and potential prevention, would be to focus the consultant's efforts on providing Mrs. H additional understanding of the nature of and motivation for the boys' behaviors.

In this situation a fuller understanding of the dynamics of the classroom and the true motivation behind the boys' talking with each other and asking questions may assist Mrs. H to reduce her negative perception of them. Further, her increased understanding of the nature of the situation may result in her adapting her own style, for example, by employing lecture outlines and printed handouts. Such a change in her own teaching approach would not only reduce the boys' need to interrupt with questions or to dialogue with one another, but would also prevent other students from needing to engage in similar actions.

---

of development or a particular environmental situation, may become aggravated by the consultee's reactions or attempted remedial steps, which in turn were the result of the consultee's limited understanding of the "normalcy" of the client's initial behavior.

The impact of a consultee's lack of understanding may be most clearly seen in those situations in which the consultee is faced with a changing client population. In situations where the population with whom the consultee is called to work has changed, and the unique talents and needs of the client population are different than those for whom the consultee was originally trained, the lack of consultee knowledge and understanding can be significant factors in the development and maintenance of the client's work-related problems. Perhaps one of the clearest examples of this comes as a result of the movement to educate exceptional students in regular classrooms, a process sometimes referred to as mainstreaming (Woolfolk, 1993). The impact of this change in educational planning and programming is demonstrated in Exercise 8-1, which provides an opportunity to more fully understand the impact of a consultee's limited understanding on a client work-related problem.

Mainstreaming could certainly create problems for both the regular classroom teacher and the child who is mainstreamed, if the teacher is ill-informed or lacking in knowledge

---

EXERCISE 8-1   Mainstreaming

Directions: Read the following case scenario. For Part I of this exercise develop two hypotheses regarding the possible point of connection between the consultee's level of understanding and the referral problem. Further, identify ways you, as consultant, could develop the data required to support either of your hypothesized connections and engage the consultee in this validation process. You may find this exercise more effective if performed with another, such as a classmate, a colleague, or a supervisor.

Case Presentation

Referral: Timothy was referred to your office by his fifth-grade teacher, Ms. Ellison. Ms. Ellison reported that Timothy, a new student to your school, is "constantly getting out of his seat, tormenting other children, and almost never on the page or the worksheet that he is supposed to be doing." Ms. Ellison reported that Timothy has been doing this "since day one, and it is only getting worse each day." Further, she noted that she cannot tolerate it anymore, and is truly "beginning to dislike this boy!"

Classroom Observations: In observing the classroom, you note that Ms. Ellison, a third-year teacher, is highly energetic and enthusiastic in class. She moves rapidly around the room, speaks loudly and employs a lot of animation in her communication patterns. Ms. Ellison's is an activities-driven classroom. She has her class set up in learning stations that are very stimulating, both visually and auditorially, and she has the children moving around the class, going from one learning center to another. The classroom is very active, very stimulating, and very energetic. It is clear that there is much opportunity for students to be engaged in the learning process.

Additional information: In looking at Timothy's records you find that he had been diagnosed as having Attentional Deficit Disorder with Hyperactivity. Further, you find that Timothy has been recently mainstreamed into your school, coming from a self-contained program for ADDH children where he spent the last three years.

Part I: Connecting Ms.Ellison's lack of information to Timothy's behavior.

Hypothesis 1:_____

_____

Hypothesis 2:_____

_____

Part II: Supporting your hypothesis.

What type of data would you attempt to gather to support either of your hypotheses and how would you engage Ms. Ellison in this process?

as to what to expect and how to respond to the child's special needs. Another phenomenon that may increase the negative impact of the consultee's limited knowledge occurs as a result of the increased focus on inclusion of culturally diverse populations within the work environment. Many managers, supervisors, teachers, coordinators, and so on simply lack the awareness of the unique cultural practices and values of many of their employees and thus offend or fail to be sensitive to those particular needs and practices.

It is not just the rapidly changing composition and profile of the clients with whom the consultee is called to work that may necessitate the consultee's acquisition of additional information and knowledge. The rapid increase in technology and research regarding professional practices can also create conditions in which the consultee is asked to work without truly possessing the knowledge needed. Consider the case of Rose L, the senior engineer for a small environmental engineering firm (Case Illustration 8-2).

CASE ILLUSTRATION 8-2   Rose—The Need for Technical Knowledge

Rose has been an engineer for the firm for the past 18 years and for the last five, she has served as project manager. In her role as project manager she was to assign specific tasks, time lines, and resource priorities to the various engineering groups working on projects. Her job required that she understand the engineering project and have the ability to analyze and assign the parts to the project to the groups best able to deal with that component. Within the last year, the owner and president of the company instituted a process of decentralized decision making and collaborative project development. This process differed from that which was previously employed and which provided top down communication, direction, and decision making. The new system made each engineering group responsible for the development of its own operational plan and time line. Each group was to analyze a project, identify its role, and outline its process. The project manager's task was to work with team leaders from each group and facilitate the various groups' collaboration.

Rose sought outside assistance because project details were beginning to fall through the cracks, budgets were being overrun, and tension and conflict existed between many of the groups. Rose felt that the problem was that the various groups were simply taking advantage of this new system and her limited "authority" to tell them what to do.

In discussion with the various group leaders it was discovered that they were unclear about what their new role was supposed to be and they really wanted direction from Rose. However, they reported that she appeared passive and uninvolved at their meetings and thus they were unsure who was coordinating the various projects. Through consultee-focused consultation, the consultant was able to identify that Rose falsely assumed that this new model meant that she should not try to direct the groups. It became clear that much of the initial confusion and lack of efficiency being experienced was a result of her limited understanding of the collaborative model being employed and the role she was now supposed to play. She had falsely interpreted her role to be one of a laissez-faire leader, rather than an active facilitator. Once her authority to manage people (rather than projects) had been clarified, Rose was able to take ownership of the process and become more actively engaged in facilitating the group coordination. This was a case where the new role of decentralized authority and collaborative management was simply something that the consultee did not completely understand, but once understood, was able to implement thus reducing the problems previously experienced.

In situations where the consultee is responding to people and processes without the proper understanding and knowledge, the consultant needs to serve as a source for informational dissemination and education.

Diagnostic Model

Interview and observational skills will prove invaluable tools in diagnosing the lack of consultee knowledge. In discussing the client, the consultant needs to be sensitive to the consultee's accuracy of understanding of the client's functioning and the interpretation of such client's behavior as compared to normative developmental or job related behavior.

For example, consider the situation with Sr. Patrice, an eighth-grade teacher at a local parochial school. Sr. Patrice had over 12 years of teaching experience, but prior to this year, all of her experience was with first graders. Sister contacted the consultant extremely upset over the overly hostile behavior of one of her male students. Sister described Paul as "apparently having some real anger toward women!" She noted that Paul liked to tease the girls in the class, but more importantly he liked to run up behind them on the playground and give them bear hugs "sometimes picking them up off the ground." Sr. Patrice thought it was important for the consultant to work with Paul. After observing Paul's behavior on the playground it became apparent that what Sr. Patrice saw as hostility was actually adolescent sexual play. Paul, and many of the other boys and girls, would find ways to come into physical contact—touching, poking, grabbing, or even bear hugging each other. While Sister may have identified an area where some instruction might be useful, to approach it as if Paul had a serious problem would have only exacerbated the situation. What was needed was for Sister to become somewhat more familiar with preadolescent and adolescent behavior.

Sometimes it is not the consultee's comprehension of the client's behavior that is at issue. There are times when the consultee may need to develop a more accurate understanding of his or her own response style as well as the degree to which that style is congruent with standards of professional practice. Consider, for example, Helen, a teacher in a community daycare center. Helen reported having an unusually difficult time managing one particular 4-year-old. Helen was very aware of what typical 4-year-old children like to do and she was even knowledgeable about the use of reinforcement as a means of shaping behavior. She simply could not understand why she was unable to manage Theo, the 4-year-old in question.

The center had been used for some university research and was equipped with a one-way mirror and a video recorder. The consultant asked the consultee, Helen, if he could tape the children at play so that together they could attempt to understand what might be going on with Theo. As they observed the tape, Helen almost embarrassingly exclaimed, "Gads, look at me, I look so serious! I don't seem to be enjoying myself and it has been 45 minutes and I have yet to provide any child with a word of praise!" It became apparent to both the consultant and the consultee that even though she was quite knowledgeable about child development and classroom management techniques, Helen was somewhat less knowledgeable about her own teaching style. As they continued to view the tape Helen quickly identified that Theo's behavior was really quite normative and that his limit testing appeared to be in attempt to gain her attention.

In diagnosing the existence of a consultee's lack of knowledge or understanding, the consultant will attempt to answer three separate questions (Meyers, Parsons, & Martin, 1984). The consultant needs to determine if the consultee (1) accurately perceives his or her behavior in relationship to the client, (2) sees his or her behavior as congruent to what he or she wishes to do, and (3) understands what is generally presented as the standards of practice for his or her role.

Accuracy of Self-Knowledge

First, the consultant needs to identify the degree to which the consultee is aware of his or her professional behavior. The question to be addressed is whether the consultee possesses accurate self-knowledge and reality-based perception of his or her behavior with the client. In order to answer this first question, the consultant needs to systematically observe the consultee in interaction with the client. The consultant needs to have the consultee estimate his or her behaviors and compare these estimations against the data collected. The feedback provided must be objective and nonevaluative. In the previous case involving Theo and the preschool teacher Helen, the availability of the videotaped proved efficacious in that the data could be presented in an objective and nonevaluative manner and the incongruency between the way Helen thought she acted and how in fact she behaved was quite apparent.

Congruency of Behavior with Consultee's Expectations of Professional Practice

Assuming that the consultee demonstrates an accurate awareness of his or her response style, the consultant proceeds to the second question. The consultant now needs to determine whether the consultee's observed and self-defined behaviors are congruent with the consultee's attitudes about how he and she should professionally function. That is, the consultant wants to be sure that what the consultee is doing is what the consultee desires to do.

Consultee's Understanding of Professional Practice Standards

The final question to be addressed is whether what the consultee is doing and wishes to do is congruent with what is known to be the accepted form of professional practice. Clearly, discrepancies along any point of the questioning need to be confronted and accurate information provided as the potential remedial steps increasing knowledge and understanding.

Exercise 8-2 provides another example where the consultee's lack of understanding may be the primary reason for the current client-related difficulty. Exercise 8-2 will also provide the reader with the opportunity to apply each of the previous diagnostic questions to a case example.

Interventions

Clearly, when knowledge is needed, the intervention of choice is to provide the consultee with the information needed. As noted, the consultee may need specific information about the client, about the developmental or theoretical principles operating, or even information about his or her own response style. Providing the consultee information may allow him or her to more accurately understand the client's responses and perhaps open for the consultee a variety of options that were not apparent previously.

EXERCISE 8-2   Jennifer—Too Much Attention

Directions: Read the following presentation and

1. Identify the source or specific form of the consultee's lack of understanding.
2. Identify the specific consultee reaction that may be augmenting if not creating the client work-related problem.

Case Presentation

Mr. J is a teacher of high school social sciences and has been for the past 7 years. Mr. J is generally well liked and has a good reputation with the students and fellow teachers. Mr. J have been "very concerned" about the emotional state of being exhibited by Jennifer, one of his students. Mr. J perceives that Jennifer is very unhappy, feels unloved, and is confused and vulnerable to being used by the males she encounters. He has tried to "support her" by paying special attention to her in class, providing her with unconditional approval, and even intervening to protect her when he sees her confronted by boys. According to Mr. J, Jennifer appears to be getting worse—"She is even withdrawing from (me)!"

In speaking with Jennifer, you find that she is new to the school, having transferred from another state. As you talk, you come to feel that Jennifer is a typical adolescent, with ups and downs. She feels that Mr. J is a really nice guy, but she is embarrassed by all the attention he gives to her. "It really makes me stick out from the others and I really just want to blend in!"

Interventions employed, while tailored to the specific needs of the consultee, involve two steps. The first step of an intervention aimed at a consultee's need for information is to confront the consultee with the need for more information. The second step would be for the consultant to serve as an informational resource and to collaboratively develop an educational program for the consultee. It is obvious, but this form of feedback and didactic instruction requires the consultant to be both directive and confrontational. Because of the possible resistance encountered, it is important for the consultant to be sure to have developed a collaborative relationship with the consultee PRIOR to implementing such consultee-focused consultation. Further, the consultant needs to remind the consultee of the confidential, nonevaluative nature of the relationship.

The goal for the intervention would be to provide the consultee with nonevaluative feedback about his or her current level of knowledge and the degree of congruence that knowledge has with that of current research or expert opinion. Further, the feedback needs to highlight the impact that this lack of information has had on the consultee's choices of response in working with the client and how these choices have contributed (if not caused) the current client work-related problem. Once the need has been identified and embraced by the consultee, the second phase of intervention would be to provide an educational program for the consultee.

As a first step to this second phase of intervention, the consultee and consultant need to establish concrete goals. The specific needs and nature of the goals will thus help to determine the specific form of information dissemination and education. It is essential that the consultant maintain the collaborative relationship, so that there is clear ownership of both the goals and the process on the part of the consultee.

When Skills Need Developing

There are times when the consultee is both clear and accurate in his or her own self-observation and is also very aware that such behavior is NOT that prescribed as professional practice. This would be the case in the situation where a teacher is quite aware of the limited effectiveness of the use of mild reprimands and other forms of punishment and is committed to the concept of employing positive reinforcement within his classroom. The teacher in question finds that his habitual style is to ignore the desired behaviors, simply being happy that the student is doing what is expected, and to reprimand the child when not performing. While understanding the inefficiency of his classroom management style, the consultee in question is having difficulty shedding the old habit. In a situation such as this, the consultant would be called upon to assist the consultee in increasing the habit strength and skill in using positive reinforcement within his classroom. Another example of such a consultee need for skills development would be the case of a team leader who is attempting to move his work team to a collaborative form of project management. While fully appreciating the benefits of such a collaborative team model, the consultee finds it difficult to facilitate team development and collaborative exchange, having never been trained in the specifics of small group leadership. Under both of these situations it is skill development rather than information acquisition which is needed.

Diagnosing the Need for Skill Development

Using data acquired from systematic, nonevaluative observation and interview of the consultee's skill application, the consultant, in collaboration with the consultee, needs to:

1. Perform a task analysis, identifying the specific skills needed to successfully perform the consultee's role.
2. Highlight specific areas for skills development.

While the specific skills to be developed are task-, person-, and culture-dependent, a number of general areas for training have been identified in the literature. For example, a number of specific training targets have been proposed to assist consultees to develop discreet skills to enhance their problem-solving and management skills (e.g., Bergan & Kratochwill, 1990). Anderson, Kratochwill, and Bergan (1986) found that an inservice training program was effective in increasing teacher understanding of behavior modification principles and the frequency with which they used specific verbal behaviors in a simulation situation. In a review of the literature, Zins (1993) concluded that "the consultee's ability to benefit from consultation can be increased by directly training them in relevant problem-solving, communication, and intervention techniques" (p. 188). And, Robinson and Wilson (1987) found that counselor-led human relations training for teachers not only increased the teachers' skill levels but also indirectly affected student achievement in the classroom. Thus, any of these skills (i.e., problem solving, management, behavior modification, and human relations) would appear to be fruitful ground for consultee skill development.

When attempting to diagnose the specific consultee skill development need the consultant must be extremely sensitive to the need to maintain a collaborative relationship. Specific professional practices may be more related to individual preferences and professional cultures than to theoretical models (Caplan & Caplan, 1993). Therefore, full and complete agreement on both the need and the specifics is essential. Further, since in most situations there are a number of behaviors, actions, regimens, or skills that can be employed, it is important for the consultant in collaboration with the consultee to identify those viewed by the consultee as desirable, reasonable, and possible to develop. Establishing goals for development of skills that are either beyond the reach of the consultee or inappropriate for use by that consultee or within that culture would only discredit the consultant's value and disrupt the working relationship.

Intervention When Consultee Skill Development Is Needed

When the goal involves increasing the consultee's skill, practice is essential. Skill development is not typically accomplished by one or two inservices, but generally requires a system of practice and corrective feedback. Because of the need to be systematic in such skill training, it is first suggested that the consultant attempt to link the consultee to any of the training programs, or mechanisms (such as inservices, workshops, etc.) that are offered as part of the typical operation within that system. Connecting the consultee to the system's natural mechanism for training will ensure longevity of the process. When no such resource exists within the work setting, the consultant, along with the consultee, will need to develop an individualized program of training and skill development. It has been this author's experience as well as that of others (e.g., Caplan & Caplan, 1993) that when programs have to be developed it is best to attempt to offer such training on a group basis rather than on an individual basis. The use of a group training format has a number of pedagogical benefits (e.g., the availability of a variety of practice partners and alternative view points), psychological benefits (reducing the consultee's feelings of inadequacy by demonstrating the widespread need among his or her colleagues), and consultation benefits (helping to spread the effect and thus increase the preventive impact). For example, in working with one teacher who was demonstrating some difficulty in applying good classroom management skills, the consultant developed a five-week training inservice for teachers interested in developing and employing assertive discipline (Canter & Canter, 1976; Canter, 1989) within their classroom. The receptive response to the invitation helped the consultee feel less defensive about her own limited classroom management skills and also provided an ongoing support group for skill development once the inservice was completed.

Program Development
The specific form of the training program needs to be shaped by the nature of the skills to be developed, the unique needs and resources of the consultee, the available resources of the consultant, and the training environment. However, even with this mandate to tailor the learning experience, the following general principles should be followed in developing a training program.

1. *Establish clear objectives.* It is important that all participants understand what the purpose of the training experience is and is not. Establishing clear objectives will not only facilitate the learning process but will also assist in keeping the activities in line with the desired goals.

2. *Specify evaluation procedures.* It is important to ensure that the learning experience is for professional development and not job evaluation. All forms of assessment should be created with the purpose of remediating and prescribing rather than simply labeling. Using a number of clear, concrete criterion reference measures (Woolfolk, 1993) will help the participants know when they are mastering the basic skills as well as to assist them in knowing which skills need continued development.

3. *Design the specific learning activities.* Since the focus is on the development of skills and not simply increasing the consultee's knowledge, a general guideline for learning activities is that they should employ demonstration or modeling (either in vivo modeling or video presentations), the opportunity for application and practice (e.g., role play opportunities), and the use of corrective feedback. It is important that the consultant and consultee approach this task of skill development as an opportunity for professional development and not one of job performance evaluation. With such an orientation the consultee will approach the corrective feedback with more receptivity. For the training to come full circle it would be useful for the consultant to observe the consultee applying the skills within the work setting and again provide the needed corrective feedback. From this point additional training could be considered. As an alternative to the use of actual practice when such hands-on practice is not possible, the consultant could use pencil and paper simulations. This simulation approach is less desirable since it may demonstrate a consultee's ability to "know" what to do, yet fail to increase his or her ability to do it (Parsons & Meyers, 1984).

When Objectivity Is Lost

A final target for consultee-focused consultation is the consultee's level of professional objectivity. There are situations in which the consultee is both knowledgeable and skilled at efficiently managing the client and the client's work-related behavior and yet the consultee has become ineffective. Often, such ineffectiveness is the result of the consultee's loss of professional objectivity or the fact that his or her own emotional needs and particular psychosocial history is interfering with the performance of his or her professional duties.

This would be the case where a supervisor is who is currently going through a divorce process finds that he is more curt, less attentive, and extremely poorly organized while supervising the client. As a result, the client's own work has begun to deteriorate. Clearly the added stress of the divorce and the emotional interference this may be causing the consultee is negatively impacting the consultee's supervisory skills, and thus in turn negatively impacting the client's job performance. It is also possible for the consultee's professional functioning to be impeded because of his or her emotional involvement with the client or some emotional theme or issue surrounding the client. Under these conditions a consultee may become either too close or perhaps too removed from the client to be effective in responding to the client's particular needs. The consultant's task, therefore, would be to assist the consultee to become aware of this loss of objectivity and to begin to establish means by which the consultee can regain a professional, objective distance from the client.

Gerald Caplan (Caplan, 1970; Caplan & Caplan, 1993) has been an important contributor to consultation theory and practice regarding this issue of loss of objectivity. Caplan and others (e.g., Parsons & Meyers, 1984) have noted that working in the arena of loss of objectivity truly taxes the consultant's ability to maintain a collaborative relationship and can become perilously close to the boundaries of psychotherapy or individual counseling. Working with a consultee who has lost objectivity is a challenge for the consultant seeking to maintain a collaborative relationship. Thus, while the intervention will at some basic level involve a confrontation of this loss of objectivity, the manner and style must be one that allows the consultee the ability to retain a sense of professional competence and self-esteem. It is important that the intervention attempt to keep the focus on the consultee's current level of professional functioning in relation to the client, while avoiding any indepth discussion of the personal issues or experiences that may have contributed to this loss of objectivity. Such a discussion would clearly be a flirtation with the boundaries of psychotherapy and, if needed, is better done by the consultee in the context of therapy.

As will be demonstrated, some forms of loss of objectivity will require more than can be provided by a consultant. In some circumstances the consultee is in need of professional mental health services; the role of the consultant would be to assist the consultee to come to this realization. Under these conditions the consultant needs to be prepared to provide referral information while being alert not to engage in directive service with the consultee. There are other forms of loss of objectivity where the consultant can play a more active role in the intervention. Thus, the first step for the consultant is to discern the nature and source of the loss of objectivity before proceeding with intervention processes.

One model for understanding the different forms or causes for loss of objectivity has been developed by Gerald Caplan (1964). This model has been adapted and employed by this author and others (e.g., Meyers, Parsons, & Martin, 1976; Parsons & Meyers, 1984; Caplan & Caplan, 1993) and will be used here to understand the nature and impact of loss of professional objectivity along with the steps needed to be taken by the consultant.

Caplan and Caplan (1993) suggest that in most cases loss of objectivity can be classified into five overlapping categories: (1) direct personal involvement, (2) simple identification, (3) transference, (4) theme interference, and (5) characterological distortions. Each of the these categories will be discussed in some detail.

Direct Personal Involvement

It is not unusual for a consultee, who has the professional role of superior, teacher, supervisor, or manager of the client, to also share a personal relationship with that client outside of the professional setting. For example, perhaps the teacher is also her student's aunt or next door neighbor or even her mother's best friend. Or consider the situation where a supervisor is also best friends and bowling partner with a line worker, or even situations where a professor falls in love with his graduate student. In each of these situations the personal relationships the consultee has with client outside of the work environment could interfere with the consultee's objectivity and ability to respond professionally to the client within the work setting.

Certainly, it is harder for each of the aforementioned to professionally discipline the client, given the positive personal relationship and feelings they share. And while the examples presented all point to positive relationships outside of the work arena, it could also happen that a negative personal experience outside of work results in the consultee being overly punitive or restrictive to the client within the work setting. This point becomes clear when considering the impact on the client's work assignment, job performance, or even evaluations in a situation where he or she is supervised by a consultee who also was his or her "jilted lover."

According to Caplan and Caplan (1993), the consultee with a loss of objectivity due to his or her personal involvement with the client may be more or less aware of this distortion of his or her professional judgment. However, even with such an awareness the consultee may be unwilling to publicly admit this distortion of his or her professionalism because of his or her own sense of guilt or shame. Clearly, the consultant will need to foster a conscious awareness and acceptance of this distortion of professional objectivity prior to providing any strategies for assisting the consultee to separate his or her personal needs from his or her other professional duties and responsibilities.

Interventions employed with such a loss of objectivity will all entail some form of confrontation. The goal of this confrontation will be to assist the consultee not only to regain his or her professional relationship with the client, but to discover ways to replace the satisfaction of his or her personal needs with appropriate satisfaction found in professional goal attainment. Thus the consultee who is unable to reprimand his friend for a job poorly done will have to reframe his reprimand as an attempt to help his friend maintain and perhaps advance in his job. Similarly, the jilted lover would need to focus his or her energy on developing new relationships outside of the workplace, thus neutralizing the emotional ties to his or her coworker.

Simple Identification

A second form of loss of objectivity occurs when the consultee relates or identifies with the client or one of the other significant individuals within the client's situation. This could occur in a case where the consultee, having just come through a bitter divorce process, may begin to be overly protective and solicitous of a coworker who is just beginning a similar process. The consultee in this situation is not placing himself or herself completely in the position of the client or this significant other person, but has focused on some isolated aspect of the situation that does have personal and emotional relevance to the consultee. Thus, in terms of the divorced consultee, the recognition that the coworker is about the begin the divorce process may be significant enough to encourage the consultee to identify with that element and generalize from his or her own experience to that to be encountered by the client.

Often, this process of simple identification is easy to recognize in that the point of connection, or similarity, may be quite apparent. For example, the consultee and client may share physical similarity, ethnic backgrounds, unique behavior (e.g., tics or stuttering), or share common social experiences (e.g., recently divorced, moved out of the house, have an overbearing parent). The consultee's description of the client or client's current situation will oftentimes highlight these similarities. It is not unusual for the consultee to refer to the

---

**CASE ILLUSTRATION 8-3   The Simple Identification
of Divorced Consultee**

In the initial conversations, the consultee presented the client with a sense of urgency and desperation.

Consultee: Tom, I want you to see Helen immediately!

Consultant: Immediately? What's wrong?

Consultee: She's falling apart. She can't focus on her work—I'm afraid for her! She's a wreck!

Consultant: Helen? I don't understand. I was just speaking to her yesterday and she told me that she may have to use a few of her personal days to go to court regarding this damn divorce. I told her it was no problem and she seemed fine.

Consultee: SEEMED FINE? You have no clue. I've been there—she is going through hell and is just putting up a good front. You don't know what it is like. I'm telling you, she is in the midst of a major crisis and you have to help her NOW!

Following this initial request, the consultant attempted to gather additional information from the client, a step demonstrating that the consultee's concerns were perhaps exaggerated and reflective of his own loss of objectivity.

In follow up interaction with Helen (the client), it becomes very clear to the consultant that Helen is handling the divorce without any major emotional upset or job disruption. It is clear from the consultant's discussion with Helen that:

1. Both she and her husband are seeking this divorce, having recognized that they married too young and that they really are not as compatible as they thought.
2. She enjoys her work and sees herself focusing on her professional development over the course of the next year.
3. Financially, she is very well equipped to support herself.
4. Most of her family and friends are sad to see the couple have to go through this process, but most had suggested that they reconsider getting married when they first announced it.

---

client in very positive and sympathetic terms, speaking as if it were from personal experience. This sense of personal involvement was evident in the case of our divorced consultee (see Case Illustration 8-3).

As demonstrated in Case Illustration 8-3, Helen's clarity about the reasons for this divorce as well has her understanding of the consequences (at least some) of the divorce, gave evidence that the consultee's feelings of urgency were not truly warranted. In this situation, the consultant reframed the problem as one reflecting the consultee's loss of objectivity as a result of identifying with the situation and not a reflection of Helen's reality.

As with all forms of loss of objectivity, the consultant will need to confront the consultee about this distortion of professional objectivity. Using skills of confrontation, both direct and indirect forms (to be discussed later within this chapter), the consultant will attempt to raise the consultee's level of consciousness around the emotional identification he or she feels regarding this particular client or client situation. Further, the consultant will try to help the consultee to recognize the ways such identification may be distorting the

---

EXERCISE 8-3   Loss of Objectivity Due to Simple Identification

Directions: This exercise continues with the case of the recently divorced consultee and the divorcing client. Review the initial dialogue presented previously and then read the dialogue occurring in the next consultee-consultant session. This second session followed a consultant-client observation and interview. After reading the exchange, answer the questions that follow. Again, it is generally a useful strategy to discuss your responses with a colleague, peer, mentor, or supervisor as a way of benefiting from varied perspectives.

Session 2:

Consultant: Hi, I'm glad we could get back together. After our conversation I went to observe Helen during her shift and even spent about 30 minutes with her during lunch asking her about the job, her divorce, and so on. I am actually pretty amazed about how well she is handling it. From her perspective, her work has not been affected and in general she feels she is handling it very well.

Consultee: Sure, she does NOW, but she has no idea what is going to happen.

Consultant: So from your perspective she is doing OK at the present time?

Consultee: Yeah . . . but, I'm telling you all hell is going to break loose. I know!

Consultant: You really seem to be able to anticipate what often can or perhaps could happen as a result of getting a divorce.

Consultee: Well, you know what I went through last year. Not only does it cost you time—you know how many days I had to take off work—but it can cost you a ton of bucks, and this is just the beginning. Your friends and family start to look at you differently, you know, like it was your fault or something, and even here at work, people don't know if they should include you in after-work social activities. It's hell! She has no idea. I'm really worried about her.

Part I: From the specific information presented by the consultee and the client, identify those points for which there is clear evidence—factual information—regarding the current impact of the divorce on Helen.

Part II: Given the consultee's concerns, what are the possible impacts that a divorce process may have on Helen?

Part III: What information has been revealed that suggests that Helen's experience may be different than that of the consultee, and as such may in fact reduce the probability of the occurrence of some of the consultee's predicted outcomes (those listed in Part II)?

---

consultee's professional judgment and behavior. The consultant will need to help the consultee identify the reality base for his or her assumptions, and, where needed, identify professionally appropriate ways to respond to the client's needs, should such truly exist. Exercise 8-3 is provided to further clarify this process.

Transference

Transference is the third form of loss of objectivity discussed by Caplan and Caplan (1993). In many ways transference is similar to identification, excepting that it involves more distortion of reality by the consultee. Transference has been found to occur in the context of an intense helping relationship. It is the process wherein the client places his or her own feelings from past events and relationships onto the therapist or others within his or her current life situation. This same form of transferring of feelings can occur between the consultee and the client for whom the consultee is accountable (Caplan, 1970).

The consultee who is acting out of transference will project onto the client a set of attitudes, expectations, and judgments that more accurately reflect the experience of the consultee (rather than the client's own experience), and that will distort the consultee's accurate and objective evaluation of the client and the client's life experiences. Under these conditions the consultee will respond from the transferred feelings rather than react to the actual conditions of the client and the client's life. The following case of Conrad (Case Illustration 8-4) will highlight this process.

In most settings, transference as a process is discouraged by the very fact that the consultee and the client remain emotionally detached. In most situations, the consultee has separated his or her professional interactions from his or her private life, and thus the boundaries of the profession serve as a reality check to hold in place transferential distor-

---

CASE ILLUSTRATION 8-4   Conrad—An Example of Transference

Conrad, the unit director for a small mental health service center, approached the consultant seeking assistance with one of his therapists. Conrad explained that Elsie, the therapist with whom he had concerns, was new to the center. Elsie, according to Conrad, just moved to this area with her husband and two boys, having lived in Georgia for the past 36 years. Conrad noted that Elsie had a good resume and appeared to be qualified to do the job. Even though it was hard for Conrad to pinpoint his concerns, he simply "felt that there was something just not right with Elsie" and he wanted the consultant to "check her out." After meeting with Elsie and having her assess her experience with the move and the new job, the consultant returned to Conrad.

As the consultant entered the second session with the consultee, Conrad met him at the door with a big smile, and stated, "What do you think, a religious fanatic?" Caught somewhat off guard, the consultant was unsure how to respond. In the silence that followed Conrad continued, stating, "You've got to watch these Bible belt people, they'll jam it down your throat. You have a problem, well, that's God's way of saying you are a sinner and dammed. I can hear her now—a client walks into the room and she yells, 'REPENT, you sinner!'" The consultant reflected Conrad's feelings and asked if he or the other staff have noticed any such behavior. Conrad responded "Oh, no, I was just having a little fun, you know, the Georgia thing, the southern Bible circuit, you know, just having a little fun."

In follow-up conversations with both the therapist, Elsie, and the consultee, Conrad, it became clear that there was no truth to Conrad's concerns. Elsie was raised as a Roman Catholic and, while attempting to live a good, value-based life, was not very active in her church. Further, it became obvious that Conrad had some very old, unresolved issues regarding his own faith stance and in particular his own feelings of guilt surrounding some of his earlier choices in life. It appeared to the consultant that Conrad was allowing his own fears of condemnation and sense of guilt to interfere with his assessment of Elsie's professional practices. Further, his concern for her clients appeared to be more a projection of his own fear of being discovered as a "sinner."

tions. However, as noted by Caplan and Caplan (1993), the possibility of blurred boundaries can be a significant issue for administrators and supervisors, and—this author would add—teachers, since they are all responsible for maintaining close observations and connections with those clients, particularly those who are having the most difficulty functioning. In these situations, the characterization of the client as weak, immature, or ill-prepared for the job can encourage the consultee to provide emotional support or guidance. Along with this invitation to provide emotional support comes the invitation to engage at a psycho-emotional level with the client and thus become more vulnerable to the opportunities for transference.

As suggested in Case Illustration 8-4, the existence of a transference reaction can often be identified by the somewhat stereotyped or prejudged nature of the consultee's reaction to the client. This was certainly the case with Conrad's assumptions about Elsie simply because she relocated from Georgia. When transference is identified, it must be confronted and the transferential issues elevated within the consultee's consciousness. Because transference typically reflects events or experience with significant personal relevance, working with a consultee around these transferential issues is extremely difficult if one is attempting to maintain a collaborative consultation relationship and avoid moving into a psychotherapeutic contract. Because of this delicate balance, it is often preferable for the consultant to employ less direct forms of confrontation (see Indirect Confrontation, below) in order to allow the consultee the opportunity to retain a sense of personal privacy while at the same time making the connections between his or her own personal experience and the current distortion of the client's reality. Further, there may be times when the consultee is so defended from his or her own awareness of the transferential issues that the best the consultant can hope for is to be able to successfully refer the consultee for additional therapeutic support and individual counseling.

Theme Interference

According to Caplan (1970), transference reactions, as described above, occur with severely disturbed individuals or in work settings that lack adequate support and control. However, it is his contention that minor transference reactions can occur even among healthy workers and within settings with sufficient supervisory or administrative involvement. Such minor transference occurs when the consultee displaces his or her own unresolved personal problems onto the job-related task. Such minor transference Caplan (1970) termed "theme interference."

Theme interference can usually be recognized by the fact that the consultee who had typically worked both effectively and professionally now presents as unable to handle a particular work-related issue, and as a result appears both confused and upset. The difficulty that the consultee is exhibiting is also confusing to those who supervise the consultee, since it is the type of situation where he or she has both the knowledge and skills needed to professionally respond. The consultee experiencing theme interference appears blocked in his or her response to the work situation and may appear unaccountably sensitive to some facet or aspect of the work situation (Caplan & Caplan, 1993). Case Illustration 8-5 highlights this process.

CASE ILLUSTRATION 8-5   Theme Interference

Theme interference appeared to be operative in the situation with a young floor nurse who was promoted to the position of night supervisor. While being knowledgeable about the procedures to be employed and skilled in supervisory and managerial tactics, the consultee expressed some frustration and concern with her inability to get her shift to accurately and completely file reports. In presenting the concern to the consultant, the consultee shared not only her concern and frustrations over the work issue (i.e., completing reports), but also emphasized that she hates being supervisor and the fact that she now has to be a "real bitch" to the people on her shift, some of whom she has been friends with for years.

Consultant: You seem very concerned about how the others are reacting to you?
Consultee: Well, you can just imagine what they must be thinking.
Consultant: I am not sure.
Consultee: Well, they know that I am the "boss"—the "supervisor"—and now have to be a real bitch. I hate being the authority. Now that I am in this position I can't be friends with them any more. They must hate me.

According to Caplan and Caplan (1993), what happens in a situation such as this is that a conflict related to the consultee's experience has not been satisfactorily resolved and now persists as an emotionally toned cognitive constellation, called a "theme." For the consultee in the illustration, there are some real concerns or issues regarding the role of a supervisor and the position of authority. A consultee with theme interference exhibits some distorted or dysfunctional and rigid thinking that links two, separate thoughts or interpretations without empirical bases. Thus, one thought that may be reflected in the particular situation—for example, being the supervisor—is inevitably linked to a second thought—for example, "Supervisors are bitches and lose all friends." Thus, finding herself in the supervisory role stimulates the inevitable conclusions regarding her loss of friends and her change in style (becoming bitchy). This conclusion, which is both unpleasant and unacceptable, blocks her utilization of effective, assertive supervisory techniques to have her staff comply to the job requirements regarding reports.

The rigid almost syllogistic thinking found in theme interference and demonstrated in Case Illustration 8-5 generally leads the consultee to jump to conclusions about the client's reactions, which in the case presented would be to dislike the supervisor and terminate the previous friendship. Thus the consultee's own reaction would be in response to this anticipated client behavior, rather than in response to the reality of the client's work.

Caplan and Caplan (1993) suggest that typically the theme is adequately repressed or otherwise defended against but may become active when the consultee's equilibrium is upset. Thus, even though our consultee has had this theme throughout her life, it has not been disruptive since she has always operated from a role of nonauthority. However, once promoted to a position that by definition involved authority, the theme was aroused and the disruptive conclusions began to influence her job-related responses and her perceptions of her staff. In response to the surfacing of the theme, the consultee will redirect her energies from dealing with the underlying conflict around authority and authority experience to concerns regarding her staff's report writing.

Unresolved themes can lead the consultee to not only draw invalid conclusions about a particular client, but also may lead the consultee to respond in an impulsive, nonfunctional way as an attempt to intervene with the perceived client problem. Exercise 8-4 is provided to further clarify this point.

Intervention with Theme Interference

Intervention with such theme interference can take two forms. First, the consultant can attempt to "unlink" the referral problem, or client behavior from "category A" of the consultee's syllogistic thinking. Assisting the consultee in re-examining his or her perception of the client may help the consultee to understand that his or her perception of the client's situation was not accurate. Thus, in the case of the latchkey child, helping Ms. Roberts understand that Liz's mother works at a local elementary school and that her schedule parallels Liz's, may help her to reframe her initial impressions regarding Liz as a latchkey child.

EXERCISE 8-4   Theme Interference

Directions: Read the following case presentation, being especially sensitive to identify elements of the client's situation that appear to have an unusual emotional tone or charge for the consultee. Next, identify those consultee responses that appear to be an artifact of the theme rather than an objective response to the client's need.

Case

Ms. Roberts is a sixth-grade teacher. She is a recent college graduate and this is her first professional teaching assignment. Ms. Roberts has invited the consultant to help her with one particular child in her class, Liz. According to Ms. Roberts, Liz needs to be watched very closely. Ms. Roberts stated that Liz is a child "just waiting to explode." Ms. Roberts is unable to point to anything specific that Liz is doing or not doing, but she wants the consultant (the school psychologist) to begin to counsel Liz. From her position as teacher Ms. Roberts will keep a "tight control on Liz, giving her a lot of structure and being sure to check up on her daily." Ms. Roberts continued: "I have made time in my day where I can meet with Liz and let her know I'm available if she needs to talk, but I know she needs more than I can provide. She is really a neat kid, it's a shame to see her throw it away and start to get out of control."

When the consultant questioned the need for the counseling and the extreme control, Ms. Roberts avoided the questions and turned the discussing the fact that "Liz's mom is newly divorced and has since returned to work. Liz is obviously going to be one of those latchkey kids and you know what happens to them! You sometimes have to wonder why people like that have kids."

Questions

1. What possible theme or themes are operating to block Ms. Roberts' utilization of her skills as a classroom manager?
2. What is the syllogistic conclusion from which Ms. Roberts appears to be responding?
3. Which responses appear tied more to Ms. Roberts' issues rather than client need?

Similarly, providing the consultee with additional data regarding the client or the client's situation may facilitate the consultee's attempt at reframing the client's experience so that it can be unlinked from the inevitable conclusions drawn from the syllogism of the consultee's theme. Providing Ms. Roberts information regarding Liz's after-school activities—such as her involvement with Girl Scouts, peer tutoring, and church youth group—and the very loving and close-knit relationship that Liz has with both her father and her mother may help her to reduce the feeling that Liz will inevitably become a problem child. This form of intervention may assist the consultee to give up on displacing his or her own conflictual issues on the client, since the client no longer is perceived as fitting the logic of the initial category. However, this unlinking, while assisting the consultee to relate more objectivity to this client, does little to reduce the possibility that linking may occur in the future. In order for this to occur the basic irrationality of the consultee's thinking must be identified and reformed. The second form of intervention aims to reduce or remove the theme.

Caplan (1970) recommend a process of theme interference reduction to test the logic of the consultee's thinking. One such method would start with the consultant's "accepting" the client and/or the client's situation as fitting into category A—for example, Liz is a latchkey child. However, in so doing the consultant is attempting to set up a cognitive dissonance that will eventually lead to the reformulation of the consultee's logic. That is, if we accept the client or the client's problem as fitting the category A (i.e., Liz is a latchkey child), then we are to assume B (i.e., Liz will become a problem) to follow. The consultant needs to assist the consultee to gather objective data around the specific occurrence of B. For example, asking Ms. Roberts to gather "evidence" or point out data that would demonstrate Liz's problematic behavior may help her identify that her prediction—that Liz would be out of control as a result of the latchkey experience—is not supported by the data, and therefore the connection between these two ideas is not supported. When the existence of B is not evidenced by the data, the inevitable linkage and the validity of the logic question is challenged. It is hoped that such dissonance will cause a reformulation of the consultee's thinking. Further, it is assumed that the weakening of the certainty of the linkage between the two events will result in a lessening of the interference due to the theme. Once the theme interference is reduced, the consultee will move from the crisis-oriented response pattern that has most likely aggravated, if not caused, the current client problem and return to his or her effective level of professional functioning.

Readers interested in developing more specific skills in the process of theme interference reduction are referred to Chapter 8 in Gerald Caplan and Ruth B. Caplan's *Mental Health Consultation and Collaboration* (1993).

Characterological Distortions

There are times when the work-related problem experienced by the consultee is not a result of the dysfunctionality of the client, but rather the enduring emotional problems of the consultee. Most often the consultee exhibiting exaggerated distortions of reality or enduring psychological disturbances is easily identified and responded to through normal administrative and supervisory channels. As noted elsewhere (Caplan & Caplan, 1993; Parsons & Meyers, 1984), it is not impossible, however, for less-than-obvious disturbances to go unnoticed by those within the consultee's system until they begin to impact the functioning of the client population. Consider the situation of the junior high school teacher who was constantly sending his male students to the disciplinarian because of various "perverted sexual acts." When the consultant followed up on one such referral, she heard the consultee complain about the general immorality of these students. "Sex is the only thing on their minds. I have to watch them like a hawk. They are constantly touching themselves, placing their hands in their pockets, and we know what that means." The consultee expressed his fear that if these boys were not identified and helped they would end up "attacking and molesting some poor little girl!"

As might be assumed, the behaviors that the teacher was identifying were most often nonsexual, and those that might have some sexual overtone were well within the normal developmental limits for that population. Further, much of the consultee's behavior during the interview suggested to the consultant some vicarious pleasure being derived by the consultee as he discussed the students. The consultee, while voicing concern about the "perverted sexual acts," did so while smiling and inviting the consultant to share her own feelings about such actions. The consultee even appeared somewhat seductive in response to the consultant, making statements regarding her attractive blouse and flattering shoes. Each of these comments occurred out of context to the discussion at hand and all were inappropriate to the professional nature of the relationship.

It is not the suggestion here that the consultant become a clinical diagnostician after meeting with the consultee only one or two times. However, consultants must be aware that the possibility exists that the work-related difficulty identified by the consultee may in fact be a reflection of the consultee's own emotional problems and not a response to a client's behavior.

Caplan and Caplan (1993) suggest that there are times where a brief consultative contract may be sufficient to enlist the consultee's adaptive controls in order to return the consultee to a reasonable level of professional objectivity and job performance. Thus, in the situation previously described a consultant who could provide the consultee with information that accurately described the client's behavior and its interpretation as occurring within the boundaries of normal development would be sufficient to return the consultee to his performance of his professional duties. This has not been this author's experience, however.

Consultees who because of a complex and long-standing set of experiences have ongoing distortions of reality require more direct intervention both for the safety of the consultee and the client alike. The consultant can attempt to support the consultee's defenses while at the same time lowering his or her level of anxiety so that a therapeutic confrontation can occur. And while the role of the consultant is NOT one of therapist, it is suggested that the consultant attempt to identify for the consultee the areas of intense personal concern that the consultee may be experiencing and invite the consultee to seek out and contract for professional services so that he or she could regain the professional objectivity needed to perform his or her job.

However, in addition to such a direct intervention, the consultant should provide appropriate feedback regarding the work functioning of the consultee (not the personal, emotional history) to those in direct responsibility for the consultee's supervision and work assignments. The goal here would be to provide the consultee with the support needed for controlling his or her emotional needs within the work setting. The consultee needs support in regaining professional distance from clients who arouse these distortions and the clients deserve protection from the further deterioration of the consultee's professional objectivity.

Confrontation—An Essential Intervention Ingredient

While the specific forms and strategies for intervening with consultee-focused consultation will vary according to the unique needs of the consultee, the form of loss of objectivity, the depth and nature of the consultation relationship, and the unique characteristics of the consultant, two generic elements are involved in all interventions. First, the consultant needs to confront the consultee, elevating his or her awareness of the nature of his or her contribution to the client's problem, be it via limited knowledge or skill or loss of objectivity. Secondly, the consultant and consultee should problem solve strategies aimed at increasing the consultee's immediate professional need for knowledge, skill, or distance and ensuring long-term return and stabilization of his or her level of professional functioning. Implied within the intervention process and key to its success is the consultant's ability to effectively confront the consultee. The remainder of this chapter will look at appropriate methods of direct and indirect confrontation.

Methods of Direct Confrontation

When attempting to understand the value and use of confrontation in consultation, the consultant must overcome the general tendency to equate the word "confrontation" with a destructive, aggressive, hostile act. Confrontation, when used within a helping context, does not take the form of lecturing, judging, or punishing. These are examples of the abuse of confrontation. Within the context of a helping relationship, confrontation represents an *invitation* by one participant to have the other participant look at, discuss, clarify, or reconsider some event occurring within the helping exchange. It is truly an invitation to explore all the facets of what is being presented. Such an empathic invitation to self-exploration has been found to facilitate another's self-exploration (Pierce & Dragow, 1969).

For example, we have all had occasion, while talking with a friend, to question a point made where we had contradictory information. Imagine the following dialogue between two teachers:

> **Ted:** *Gads, how will we ever get through this assignment for our accreditation visit, especially when we have to go on that training seminar this weekend?*

> **Mary:** *Gee, I may be wrong, but I thought the memo said that the training seminar was next weekend.*

The interaction, while not a hostile, attacking, or destructive exchange, is nonetheless confrontational. In fact, it reflects a particular type of confrontation called a *didactic* (informational) confrontation—a confrontation in which one member of the dialogue invited the other member to reconsider his or her position in light of this more accurate information. A consultant may find didactic confrontation useful when he or she experiences:

1. An inconsistency between what the consultee says and how he or she behaves. For example, perhaps the consultee states that he or she is excited about trying the new techniques discussed in the consultation, yet week after week the consultee notes that he or she forgot to use the strategy.
2. A discrepancy between what the consultee "knows" to be true and the evidence or facts as the consultant knows them. This was the case with the previous example regarding the training weekend.
3. A contradiction between the verbal and nonverbal expressions of consultee's emotions. This may be the case when a consultee states that he or she is fine with the recommendations of the consultant and yet exhibits a frown and/or worrisome look.
4. An inconsistency between two pieces of information the consultee verbally presents. This would happen in the situation where a consultee states that he or she understands and values the use of positive reinforcement, and yet the consultant notes that his or her primary technique for controlling the class is through verbal reprimand.

While these are four situations in which a consultant should seek clarification of the inconsistencies, contradictions, or discrepancies, in reality confrontation occurs anytime we call to question another's behavior, attitude, or feelings. Since confrontations are inevitable, the effective consultant will need to understand the elements that make a confrontation productive, facilitative, and relationship-building, rather than destructive and attacking.

Guidelines for Effective Confrontation
In attempting to confront a consultee, the effective consultant will consider each of the following guidelines:

1. **Present Conclusion as Tentative.** In presenting our confrontation we must present the apparent discrepancy or inconsistency in a tentative manner. The issue or discrepancy with which we wish to confront the consultee reflects our perception and may not necessarily reflect absolute facts. Thus, we need to present our confrontation as our tentative conclusions about the event. What appears to us to be an inconsistency may in fact be totally consistent from the consultee's point of view. This need to be tentative in our conclusions is especially important when confronting a consultee in the early stages of the consultation relationship. During the early stages, the consultant may not have a full grasp of the consultee's world and thus misread experiences they share.

2. **Keep a Motive of Understanding.** It is important for the consultant to keep a clear sense of the motive for his or her confrontation. Pointing out a discrepancy or an inconsistency in hopes of embarrassing or humiliating another will certainly be confrontational, but not helpful. The confrontation, to be helpful, needs to be presented from a helping, caring, supportive intention or motive. It should reflect the consultant's desire to clarify and understand rather than exhibit power or oneupmanship.

3. **Use a Descriptive, Nonjudgmental style.** The helpful confrontation is presented in language and tone that is descriptive, rather than judgmental and labeling. The consultant

is not trying to evaluate the consultee. Rather the consultant's goal is to describe his or her own experience and points of confusion with hopes that the consultee provide clarification.

4. Be Empathic. In presenting the confrontation the consultant should consider how it will be received. The confrontation should be presented in a way that maximizes the consultee's ability to receive it. While the above characteristics will assist in this process, it is also important to provide the confrontation from a perspective of empathy for the other. The consultant needs to consider how the confrontation will appear to the consultee. The consultant needs to ask himself or herself how receptive or open would he or she be to receiving this confrontation if he or she were in the consultee's shoes at this time. Keeping this perspective of the consultee as a guideline, the consultant may find that it is more helpful to present the confrontation in small specific steps, rather than to dump one large, general blast of issues on the consultee.

The consultant who, from a perspective of empathy with the consultee, can *descriptively* and *tentatively* point out areas of consultee misinformation or mixed and confusing messages can constructively move the consultation relationship to a greater level of accuracy, clarity, and collaboration. For example, the confrontation presented in the example regarding the training seminar moved the interaction to more clear, accurate communication and common agreement. However, that confrontation could have been less productive and much more destructive to the relationship if Mary had stated: "You are really a space shot! You never read anything! The memo said the training seminar is NEXT weekend. WAKE UP!"

Even when we attempt to follow the guidelines for appropriate confrontation, our confrontation may be less than productive or effective. The real proof of effectiveness is not in the degree to which all the "correct" elements were present, but rather the degree to which the desired effect was achieved. If the consultee attempts to discredit the statement, argue the point, or devalue the importance of the confrontation, he or she may be giving evidence that the confrontation was too much for him or her to accept.

Remember that the purpose of the confrontation is to move the relationship to greater clarity and accuracy. When this happens the consultee is likely to openly accept and consider the confrontation, rather than deny or defend against it. So the proof of the effectiveness of the confrontation is in the response of the consultee. Exercise 8-5 will assist you in employing the previous guidelines to formulate your confrontation. As you formulate the confrontations consider the possible impact your comment may have on the consultee.

Methods of Indirect Confrontation

Prior to employing direct confrontation the consultant must determine the degree to which this relationship is established as an open, honest, trusting helping exchange. The consultant needs to consider the extent to which the consultee has demonstrated an openness to the consultant's inquiries, a willingness to be open to the consultant's ideas and feedback, and a willingness to explore a variety of issues and topics. When the consultee appears to be somewhat closed and protected within the consulting relationship, indirect forms of confrontation may prove more productive.

Indirect methods of confrontation allow the consultee to maintain his or her defenses and protective stance while at the same time opening the consultee to new and potentially

---

EXERCISE 8-5   Effective Confrontations

Directions: Complete an appropriate confrontation for each of the following. As with other exercises, it is useful to compare your responses to those of a classmate, colleague, or supervisor.
In writing a confrontation be sure to:

- Consider the perspective of the consultee
- Use descriptive language
- Provide small steps of confrontation
- Have your tone reflect your helping intentions

1. **Consultee:** I really like what you are saying and I am sure it will help (looking anxious).
   Consultant: _____

2. **Consultee:** These workers have a real bad attitude, I have to be on their backs every moment in the day.
   Consultant: _____

3. **Consultee:** I'm really going to develop a sense of teamwork on my shift, so I told them that they have to come to the meeting next Friday—or else. You know I got to get them there.
   Consultant: _____

4. **Consultee:** NO! There is NOTHING wrong! Get off my back!
   Consultant: _____

5. **Consultee:** I know Timmy called Tommie a name, but Timmy is so frail I just know the bullies in the class are always picking on him.
   Consultant: _____

---

conflicting material. The goal is provide the consultee with enough psychic safety that he or she may be receptive to the confrontation. Directly revealing the loss of objectivity may require the consultee to respond overtly to the consultant and in some situations this is simply too threatening. It is under these conditions that a less direct form of confrontation may prove effective. Two forms of indirect confrontation to be discussed are (1) modeling and (2) talking around the issue and the use of the parable.

Modeling
One somewhat indirect form of confrontation occurs when the consultant acts as a role model of the consultee, interacting with the client or the client's situation in ways that are conflictual to that anticipated as necessary by the consultee and yet demonstrate a level of professionalism. Consider the consultee presented in Scenario 5 of Exercise 8-5. Assuming that Timmy is not as helpless or as fragile as the consultee may perceive, the consultant could indirectly confront the consultee's loss of objectivity by interacting with Timmy in a somewhat bantering manner. The experience of having Timmy "hold his own" with the consultant and possibly tease back would be in direct confrontation to the consultee's per-

ception that Timmy needs to be protected from such interaction. Or consider the supervisor who uses an abrasive style when confronting his coworkers. In this situation, the consultant may model appropriate confrontation techniques that results in a more productive exchange with one of the consultee's workers. It would be hoped that the consultee, in observing the positive outcome of the confrontation, will incorporate some of the consultant's confrontational style and thus reduce his own abrasive approach.

The use of modeling as an indirect form of confrontation allows the consultee the psychic room to not publicly admit to the consultant his or her own loss of objectivity or the detrimental effects of that loss, while at the same time experiencing something that will "force" him or her to reconsider his or her own perception and actions in relationship to the client.

Specific guidelines on effective modeling can be found within the early work of Bandura (1977, 1982), Meichenbaum (1977), and Brown and Schulte (1987).

Talking around the Issue and the Use of Parable
Talking around the issue and the use of parable are additional forms of indirect confrontation. As with all indirect confrontation techniques, these techniques when employed successfully will allow the consultee room to keep personal ego intact while providing information that may create enough personal dissonance to motivate a change in the consultee's perception and behavior.

Talking around is a technique in which the consultant describes similar situations—for example, with other consultees, him- or herself, or even other clients. Thus, rather than directly suggesting that the consultee has loss objectivity in this case, the consultant may simply share a story about another consultee or client that on some level reminds him of the current situation. Thus the consultant working with Timmy's case may note for the consultee, "You know, Timmy is very tiny. He reminds of me of my nextdoor neighbor's child. Rob is kind of small for his age but he is very quick. All the kids like him on their team when they play tag since he is so fast and elusive. But, you know, he is quite a con. When he gets caught in tag, he often kids the bigger kids about picking on this little kid (referring to himself)." Under this situation the consultant hopes to alert the consultee to his possible loss of objectivity with Timmy by demonstrating the potential to misread the situation with Rob.

A similar approach, the use of parables, was suggested by Gerald Caplan (1970). In using a parable, the consultant "invents" an anecdote that is similar to that currently experienced by the consultee. Embedded within the parable is the message of overinvolvement and the role it played in creating the situation experienced by that consultee. The elements of a parable are characters and situations that are possible identification objects and behavior and outcomes that convey a moral. The task for the consultant is to find a parable that, while portraying the essential features of the current case, is sufficiently different to allow the consultee's defenses to remain intact. The consultee can "risk" accepting the moral of the parable and choose to apply the moral to his or her own experience, or if too threatened, can privately refuse to embrace the moral without risking admonition from the consultant. From this perspective the parable must balance being far enough removed from the current situation so as to not be threatening while at the same time having enough relevance and "realness" that it can prove instructional. Thus, for a consultant to share a story about

"Tina," who is pale and sickly and yet always the instigator of the problems in the classroom, may be too obvious and direct for Timmy's teacher. Expanding on the neighbor's child who on first perception appeared too small to keep up with the neighborhood kids, however, may provide enough distance that the consultee could dismiss the case as irrelevant to the classroom, but close enough to extract the moral—that the child may be more competent and responsible than first appears.

Summary

The current chapter noted that while a consultant may be called in to assist a consultee with a client and a work-related situation, it is not unusual to find that the client is simply the "symptom" signaling that something is wrong. Further, with additional information the consultant may discover that the source of the problem may actually rest not with the client but with the consultee.

It was pointed out that there are times when the consultant may fail to have accurate knowledge of the client or the professional practice needed to work with that client successfully. Under these conditions it is essential that the consultant employ a variety of information dissemination techniques. It is also possible that while understanding both the client and the process for professional practice, the consultee may lack the needed skills. Again, under these conditions the task of the consultant is to elevate the consultee awareness of this skill deficit and to assist the consultee to develop a training regimen through which these skills can be developed.

One of the most sensitive forms of consultee-focused consultation is that which attempts to address the problems created by the consultee's loss of objectivity. The current chapter presented a number of forms such loss of objectivity can take, noting that while confrontation is essential, such confrontation must be administered appropriately and focus only on the specific work-related issues. The danger for consultant's attempting to confront a consultee's loss of objectivity is that he or she must be sure not to step into an individual counseling or therapeutic relationship. The techniques discussed were aimed at facilitating that confrontation while at the same time maintaining the collaborative boundaries of consultation. In order to focus the reader on the material presented within the chapter, we will close the chapter with Exercise 8-6.

EXERCISE 8-6   Redirecting the Focus onto the Consultee

Directions: For each of the following situations:

1. Identify the type or form of loss of objectivity exhibited by the consultee
2. Provide an example of a direct confrontation that could be used
3. Describe an example of an indirect confrontation that might prove useful

Situation A

Ms. H is very concerned about Lisa's home life. According to Ms. H, Lisa appears to be un-cared for, is often "tired looking," has only minimal lunches (a sandwich and a piece of fruit), and lacks personal hygiene ("she never does her hair up!"). Your observations and those of the social worker are that Lisa has a good, yet modest home life. Lisa presents as both a happy and well-cared-for child. In discussion with Ms. H, you discover that as a child she was neglected, and at the age of 7 was placed in a foster home. You sense that Ms. H continues to have personal fears of abandonment.

Situation B

Henry is in his first year of teaching. Henry is currently teaching twelfth-grade English. He came to you because he is having problems with controlling his seventh-period class. In discussing the situation with you, Henry notes that he doesn't understand it—"the guys in my seventh period are really cool...I don't know why they treat me this way. I really like them. I don't know what to do—after all, I don't want to come across like some kind of ogre!"

Situation C

Paul is very upset with the way the kids are teasing Jerome and rejecting him, just because he is "Orthodox." Paul lets you know in no uncertain terms that he "just knows" how horrible it is for Jerome, after all he (Paul) "was also the only Jewish boy attending his public school." Your observations suggest that Jerome's interactions with his classmates are age-appropriate and Jerome appears quite accepted by his peers.

Chapter 9

System-Focused Consultation: Working to Prevent Problems Systemwide

Previously it was suggested that the effective consultant would familiarize himself or herself with the culture of the system in which he or she was consulting. This recommendation reflected the reality that without such knowledge and sensitivity many forms of direct service or consultant prescription might be blocked as antithetical to the nature and functioning of that system or system's culture. For example, the consultant attempting to employ extinction procedures in a system where direct control is the norm may find his or her recommendation met with resistance. The consultant who has a sense of the system's culture will be able to tailor the recommendations so that they are culturally compatible and thus minimize resistance. Understanding the organization within which one is consulting is clearly an important element in the diagnostic-prescriptive process, even when attempting to provide direct forms of service.

The need to understand the role and influence of the system extends far beyond this concern for treatment compatibility. There are times when what has been identified as the client's "problematic behavior" is really a symptom of a larger, more pervasive system problem. Under these conditions all attempts to remedy the client behavior may prove ineffective. The nature and functioning of the system itself needs to become the focus of a consultation, because it may be the source of the problems identified. Consultants who consider the social and technical forces in the work environment have been reported to produce superior interventions when compared to nonsystem forms of intervention (Guzzo, Jette, & Katzell, 1985). In addition to proving more effective in remediating the problem at hand, a systems-focused approach offers the most promise for prevention. Changing the system's goals, framework, and method of operation is a better predictor of lasting change than is the practice of changing people as an independent variable (Kurpius, 1985).

It is clear, therefore, that a consultant without a full grasp of the system within which he or she is operating may provide approaches that are not only counter to the culture of that organization but may in fact provide inadequate assessment and short-sighted, ineffectual, and incorrectly targeted interventions. The current chapter will focus on both the special demands and unique opportunities of systems-focused consultation.

In addition to providing an increased awareness of the value and need for systems-focused consultation, this chapter will provide the reader with guidelines for implementing such an approach and highlight the unique skills required for systems-focused consultation.

Certainly many of the skills previously described (e.g., relationship-building skills, active listening skill, etc.) are useful in systems-focused consultation. However, the unique characteristics and special dynamics of a system require that a consultant possess additional diagnostic and intervention skills. This chapter will focus on developing the knowledge needed for identifying those unique characteristics of a system and the special consultation skills and expertise required to navigate a consultation exchange with a systems focus. Specifically, the chapter will:

1. Provide the reader with a review of the definition and operation of organizations as systems
2. Review the various manifestations of the character or culture of a system
3. Provide a model for organizing diagnostic focus as system analysis
4. Assist the reader in developing diagnostic skills, including observational skills essential to system-focused consultation
5. Offer a model for introducing innovation and change within systems

Fundamental Knowledge of System Functioning

When a systems-focused consultation is targeted, the consultant explicitly attempts to consider the multiple contexts of the manifested problem, and from this viewpoint considers the options available for problem resolution (Wynn, McDaniel, & Weber, 1986). Consultation focused on the system has several purposes. First, the consultant hopes to increase awareness of those within the system of the current nature and status of their organization. Secondly, the consultant attempts to assist system members to identify and highlight those factors maintaining the current form of operation and to enumerate alternative natures/statuses for the system to consider. Thirdly, the consultant will help the members articulate and implement the means of achieving this alternative form. And, finally, the consultant will facilitate the system's capacity to continue this process of self-awareness and renewal (Parsons & Meyers, 1984).

A prerequisite to achieving the goals of a system-focused consultation is for the consultant to understand the dynamics of the organization. Such an understanding could start with a definition of a system.

System Defined

According to Kurpius (1985), a system is the "an entity made up of interconnected parts with recognizable relationships that are systematically arranged to serve a perceived purpose" (p. 369). Thus, whether we are engaged in a school system or a manufacturing plant, understanding the dynamic relationship between those engaged in the system (administrators, teachers, staff, and students, or stockholders, managers, and line workers) along with the various resources (money, machinery, physical plant, and material) and processes (curriculum, support programs, decision-making structures, and manufacturing process) as they operate both independently and interdependently in hopes of achieving some common goal (educating a community's youth or production of a product) is essential.

A number of theorists have offered models for understanding this dynamic interrelationship as well as explaining when and why systems fail (Beer, 1980; Kast & Kahn, 1978; Kast & Rosenzweig, 1974; Kurpius, 1985). One theory in particular, open systems theory, has been extensively applied as a framework for consultation (Dougherty, 1990; Gallessich, 1982; Kurpius, 1985).

Systems: Open and Closed

Open systems theory postulates that organizations take life in response to a perceived need and that resources are placed into simple and complex processes and structures aimed at satisfying that need. An open system remains accountable and responsive to its consumers and the perceived changes in needs. Thus the open system is flexible in structure and open to innovation and change as response to the ever-changing needs of the consumer. As an example, one could consider the small neighborhood grocery store. The owner/manager of the store will undoubtedly monitor the products in high demand and those rarely selected and manage his or her inventory accordingly. But even beyond such a product tracking, this manager may also have formal (e.g., suggestion box) or informal (being on the floor chatting with customers) means for understanding the changing interests, needs, and tastes of his consumers, and in turn responding by acquiring new products. This open flow between the changing needs of the market and the product provided is a keystone of an open system.

Open system theory also postulates that a social system can run down and die (i.e., entropy) unless it imports energy from the environment. Thus an open system tends to move toward growth and expansion. Our small corner grocery store may need to develop additional aisle space to house the new products, employ more staff to order and dialogue with suppliers, and require the store owner/manager to spend more time in the office and off the floor. With this growth, the system begins to increase in differentiation and elaboration of specialized interdependent subsystems. Now our corner store has a produce department (and manager), a meat and poultry department (and manager), and a variety of other organizational departments (e.g., payroll and marketing). Because each subsystem tends to develop autonomy with its own processes and technologies while at the same time needing to function interdependently for the good of the system, tension results.

Open systems will experience tension, or inherent conflict between the various subsystems as they go about carrying out their tasks. A system will also experience tension between itself and the ever-changing environment in which it exists. One cannot, nor even need not, prevent this tension. But for the system to successfully continue to operate, structures and processes need to be developed and employed to anticipate and adjust to these tensions (Kurpius, Fuqua, & Rozecki, 1991).

In the process of this evolution of functional structures and processes, what starts out as a dynamic, interactive entity can in its attempt to manage its internal conflicts become entrenched—fixed and nonadaptive—in a particular way of operating. As in the case of our example, where once product decisions were made with flexibility and oftentimes spontaneously as a result of the owner/manager directly dialoguing with his or her consumers, now a more formal and somewhat routine process of accepting new products from suppliers, retaining the "usual order," and keeping products in the same locations for ease of monitoring, becomes "THE way." This entrenchment in our tried and true methods can occur even when shifts in the internal and external environments make such a pattern of behavior obsolete or even destructive to the organization's well being (Argyris, 1990; Beer & Spector, 1993; Senge, 1990; Solomon, 1991). Under these conditions a system is considered to be closed. No longer is responding to the consumer needs the driving force; rather, a closed system is invested in the status quo, is inflexible and nonadaptable, and generally operates impervious to the ever-changing needs of those within and without the system.

In a world such as ours, where changes in the external environment (i.e., shifts to transnational marketplaces, increases in social mobility, the introduction of educational voucher systems, managed healthcare, etc.), along with changing internal environments (due to technological advances, increased diversity of workforce, etc.), a system's openness and ability to be flexible and adaptable is keystone to its survival. Breaking old rigid patterns of organizational behavior appear essential to the insured health of organizations in the twenty-first century. But beyond the system's survival, being flexible in addressing the needs of those within the system appears essential to the health and well being of system members.

Client Symptoms: System Problems

Historically, those involved with the study of organizational development identified the source of many of the problems found within organizations to be the result of the ever-increasing bureaucratic "machine" model of organization (Meyers, Parsons, & Martin, 1979). That is, the highly specialized and fractionated organization of role isolated the worker from the success of working on the whole and thus reduced his or her sense of accomplishment and achievement. Further, it was assumed that the increased layering of authority generally resulted in decision making and prescriptive communication becoming one-way, top down, as was all responsibility for important changes in procedure, processes, and priorities. Such structural impacts have resulted in a sense of worker disenfranchisement and what one author (Argyris, 1970) termed adaptive antagonistic activities on the part of the worker.

Adaptive antagonistic activities can take many forms, such as workers exhibiting passive aggressive behaviors (e.g., damaging machinery and "forgetting" important details), general apathy, and feelings of alienation from the company. Argyris (1970) suggested that all such client behavior is more accurately attributed to the disenfranchising structure of the system as a whole, rather than a manifestation of a person's internal dynamic. Because of this, focusing on the client in the absence of system change would prove fruitless.

System Diagnosis

While there may be a variety of models, approaches, and techniques to be employed in system diagnosis, it appears that there are some commonly agreed upon activities that are needed to insure an effective diagnostic process. It is typically agreed (Beer & Spector, 1993) that the diagnostic process

1. Is most often triggered once the system or members note that a problem exists
2. Involves data collection by a combination of internal and external agents attempting to identify the problem source
3. Is targeted to data perceived by organizational members to be valid
4. Concludes with the results being fed back to organizational members

System Analysis: A Demanding Process

This process of system analysis is a time-consuming, demanding process that requires a number of unique talents and skills on the part of the consultant. Prior to beginning such a system-focused appraisal the consultant would be wise to take note of the following observations.

1. **System Analysis Requires Multiple Skills.** As Kuh (1993) noted, system analysis demands a biographer's discipline, perseverance, and eye for detail and the therapist's insight, intuition, and interpersonal skills. The consultant involved in system-focused consultation will need to perform content analysis of written materials as well as clinical interview of the systems "historians." The consultant will certainly need to develop collaborative relationships and be able to employ and maintain a team approach to the evaluation process.

2. **System Analysis Is Both Time and Energy Consuming.** Because of the wide array of units and focal points that need to be evaluated, as well as the many forms of data to be collected (e.g., material to be read, events to be observed and interpreted, people to be interviewed), systems-focused consultation is time and energy draining. Further, since appraisal of the system's character cannot be conducted by outsiders alone (Kuh et al., 1991), collaboration is essential. The development and maintenance of such collaborative relationships will also take time, energy, and skill on the part of the consultant.

3. **System Analysis Will Incur Resistance.** While the system may wish to grow and respond to the input of the consultant (open orientation), systems are also self-protecting and self-maintaining (closed orientation) and thus may resist change. Because change is a critical process, it may be perceived as threatening to the current state of the system and thus be a serious violation of the self-preservation, cultural norms (Kuh, 1993).

4. **System Analysis Is More Than Data Gathering, It Is Intervention.** Diagnosis is a process of gathering information about the various subsystems of an organization, along with the processes and patterns of behavior that take place within that organization (Beckhard, 1969). But system diagnosis is not simply for identification or data gathering only. System analysis as a diagnostic step is done for the purpose of mobilizing action on a problem (Block, 1981). It is not only essential as the first step of problem solving, but it may in fact be the first step of intervention. System analysis can actually be part of a process of

large-scale organizational revitalization (Beer & Spector, 1993). It is a process that can serve to motivate organizational members to engage in change (Alderfer & Brown, 1975)

When done effectively, system diagnosis is a process that can assist the organization by

1. Enhancing capacity to assess and change the culture of the organization
2. Providing opportunity for members to acquire new insights into the dysfunctional aspects of their culture, and patterns of behavior as a basis for developing a more effective organization
3. Ensuring that the organization remains engaged in a process of continuous improvement (Beer & Spector, 1993)

Steps in the Diagnostic Process

According to Beer and Spector (1993), the effectiveness of the diagnostic process as a source of mobilizing change is influenced by the manner in which the diagnostic/intervention process is conducted. This author has found the process articulated by Peter Block (1981) to be effective. Block provides a number of steps for the consultant to utilize in moving from the identification of a problem through to the implementation of the intervention. A slight modification of the process as originally presented by Block (1981) is described below.

It will be noted that the process is presented and discussed as being linear, that is, one step proceeding to the next step, and so on. This is for ease of discussion and does not accurately reflect the lived experience. Since the diagnostic process is a collaborative venture, characterized by mutual understanding and ownership, it most often does not proceed in a linear fashion but rather may go back and forth across these steps in order to ensure that the consultant and the consultee are fully collaborative and in tune with one another. With this as a caveat the following six steps are presented.

Step 1: Identify the presenting problem. Any diagnosis begins with a description of the problems. Systemically, it can be suggested that the presenting problem is usually only a symptom of the real problem and the purpose of data collection is to elaborate and broaden this initially identified issue.

Step 2: Make a decision to proceed. The consultant needs sanctioning to proceed in the diagnostic process. This sanctioning is one way of removing a possible source of resistance. It is important for the consultant to collaborate with the consultee's system when proceeding. Further, this sanctioning must be done with the system's understanding that the process in which the consultant is engaged is ultimately for the purpose of impacting change.

Step 3: Select the dimensions to be studied. While using a broad brush, it is important to restrict the number of areas that will be analyzed so as to not overwhelm the consultant or the consultee with too much data.

Step 4: Decide who will be involved. Involving people in the data collection also implies that they will be informed as to the findings. The systems-focused consultant needs to identify the levels and types of representatives to be involved in the actual collection, as well as those who will provide the data to be collected. Questions regarding whether the entire staff of a unit, subsystem, or organization will provide the data need to be resolved.

Step 5: Select the data collection method. The selection of the data collection method is usually dependent upon the scope and nature of the consult. The methods employed should not only fit the problem, but should also reflect the resources of the system, the time available, and the motivation and abilities of those involved. To minimize the perceived threat of such data collection the consultant may want to proceed from less structured forms of data collection (e.g., unstructured observations and individual interviews) to the more structured methods employing surveys and questionnaires.

Step 6: Collect the data. At this step it is important that the consultant NOT overcollect data. That is, it is important to reduce redundancy where possible. The data collection phase can prove highly motivating (Nadler, 1977) and a way of initiating a desire to move from the status quo. The consultant does not want to lose this enthusiasm through overburdening or redundancy.

Involving organizational members in the data collection will not only increase commitment but can also serve as a training process (teaching observation and interview skills) and a way of including data collection as an ongoing process to the culture of that organization.

Focusing the Diagnosis

A system is a complex entity with many dimensions, structures, processes, and elements. Each of these many components could be an appropriate target for the diagnostic process. Thus a consultant interested in system-focused consultation would be ill-advised to enter the process without an understanding of the difficulty to be experienced and a model to guide the process. There are a number of excellent models or frameworks that can help the consultant organize data and diagnose organizational functioning (e.g., Beer, 1980; Parsons & Meyers, 1984; Tichy, 1983; Waterman, Peters, & Phillips, 1980).

The scope of the diagnostic process can either be narrow, involving a quick look at the easily identified trouble spots in an organization, or a more indepth analysis of the intricate workings of the system. If change is to be long term and permanent, then a more systematic review of the interactivity and interdependence of the various system components will be necessary. It is important to understand that multiple interactive elements are operative within and without a system that may impact its functioning. It is important for the systems consultant to understand each of these components, since they are interrelated and interdependent and thus play some part the system's presentation.

In diagnosing a system, the consultant must, at a minimum, identify the inputs, processes, and outputs of a system. The inputs generally include the resources necessary to maintain various operations of the system, including personnel, tangible goods, space, budget, time, information, and raw materials. The consultant also needs to consider the impact of the specific processes employed by the system as it attempts to reach its particular goals. These processes include such things as specific programs implemented, organization structure, and methods of communication, decision making and evaluation. Finally, the system-focused consultation should consider the system output. What is the mission of the system and how is it reflected in the outcomes it achieves? How successful is the system at attaining its goals and do these goals meet the needs of the those the system wishes to service?

Using this very simplistic view of a system (input—process—output) as your framework, consider Exercise 9-1.

Analyzing the Systems: Elements, Forces, and Culture

A somewhat more elaborate, broad-based, eclectic model for conceptualizing the many forces and potential targets for systems-focused consultation has previously been presented

---

EXERCISE 9-1   The Tale of Two Schools

Directions: As with most of the exercises presented, this exercise is best completed either with another or in a small group. Read the brief descriptions of two neighboring schools. As you read the descriptions attempt to identify the unique inputs, processes, and desired outputs present in both schools. Finally, answer and discuss the questions that follow the presentation.

School on the Right

Constructed in 1951, the School on the Right is a private, religious-sponsored elementary school, grades K–8. The school is staffed by clergy and members of a religious community. Values teaching, by instruction and by model, is keystone to the curricular experience. The school is financially supported by the archdiocesan department of education, the particular parish in which the school is located, and tuition paid by parents who send their child(ren) to the school.

School on the Left

Constructed in 1961, the School on the Left is the public elementary school, grades K–6, for this local community. The school is one of four elementary schools in this district, which is directed by a single elected school board, a superintendent, three assistant superintendents, a principal, vice principals, and a host of support personnel (including guidance staff, nursing staff, crisis interventionist, and drug and alcohol counselors). The school receives funding through local taxes and a number of federally funded programs. The professional staff are all certified and the district is a union shop. Academic excellence and social responsibility are the driving values for the curriculum.

Reflections:
1. Identify the unique **inputs** for each system. How would these inputs reflect the desired **product?**
2. How would the identified inputs impact the internal **processes** and **structures** for each system?
3. Identify one unique demand placed on a student in each of the system; on a teacher in each system; on an administrator.
4. Describe the relationship of the system to its consumer population. What limits to power—interactive influence—unique opportunities, or limitations, exist?
5. For each of the following behaviors, discuss how each system would (a) respond to it or be impacted by it; and (b) contribute to its creation. Stealing, fighting, requests for special Saturday makeup days, preadolescent sexual concerns, parent advocacy groups, faculty–staff input.

by this author (Parsons & Meyers, 1984). That model, in a somewhat elaborated and adapted form, will serve as the foundation for the discussion to follow.

The model to be presented focuses the system diagnostic process on the identification of the system's salient elements, impacting forces, and unique organizational culture as they independently and interactively contribute to the system's current level of functioning and dysfunctioning.

Elements

In analyzing a system, the system-focused consultant needs to consider the unique characteristics and impact of the *people* involved, the *physical environment,* and the *product* the system is attempting to produce. Each of these elements plays an essential role in the function and possible dysfunction of a system.

People: In assessing the people composing the system, the consultant needs to consider the unique values, skills, and orientations presented by these individuals. Whether the consultant is targeting the client(s), staff, or administrators, the unique values, skills, and orientation they bring to the system can prove significant to system functioning.

Referring to the examples provided in Exercise 9-1, consider the values and religious community affiliation of the staff and faculty of School on the Right. Consider how those unique characteristics of the people element of that system will impact the consumer (i.e., student) and product (i.e., curriculum). Understanding both the uniqueness of this people element and its impact is essential for effective system-focused consultation.

In addition to describing the individuals, the systems-focused consultant will identify the unique grouping of individuals and the specific nature, character, and influence each group has on the other and the system as a whole. Again referring to the examples found in Exercise 9-1, consider the potential impact of group affiliation of either union or nonunion on the day-to-day atmosphere and functioning of the School on the Left, especially during contract discussion time.

Physical Environment: A second class of elements operative within a system are all of those facets of the physical environment in which the people of the system function. This dimension includes the system's physical layout (including the use of space); the arrangement of various departments, units, resources, and the overall condition and feeling of the physical work space. One very real example for this author is that this chapter is currently being written at a time when my geographic area is under a heat and humidity wave, with temperatures over 100 degrees. How different my attitude, my focus, my productivity would be in an environment without air conditioning or in one with an overabundance of people. The physical environment is a significant variable in the overall operation of a system. Clearly the experience of facility convenience or crowding can enhance efficiency or result in frustration that in turn can impact behavior and attitudes of those involved.

Product: The final class of elements to be considered is the product or output desired by the system. The output desired by the system is the reason for its existence and is most typically found as the mission of the system. Welzenbach (1982) defined mission as the "broad, overall long-term purpose of the institution" (p. 15).

As the rationale for what the system aspires to be, the mission represents the ends that the system hopes to attain. The product will help determine who will use the system, how often it will be used, and what procedures and resources the system may need to function effectively (Parsons & Meyers, 1984). The mission of an institution would therefore guide institutional priorities and practices.

Assessing both the product desired and the product produced will not only provide insight into the special character, structure, and process of the system but also some of the unique demands placed upon the system and system resources. Exercise 9-2 will further clarify this point.

In assessing the system product, the consultant needs to consider questions such as: Does the actual product reflect the mission defined desired product? How have the consumer needs been addressed by this product? How does the product reflect the needs of the external system and/or the internal needs of the system's population? How have these goals been operationalized into objectives? What unique structures and processes have been instituted to facilitate the system's achievement of these goals? What are the indicators and processes employed to demonstrated objective achievement?

EXERCISE 9-2   The Impact of Mission on Structure and Process

Directions: For each of the contrasting organizational missions, assess the subtle or perhaps not-so-subtle influence of the organization mission on the development of system structures and processes for day-to-day operations. Further, consider the resources needed to fulfill the mission and the unique demands placed on the members operating within that system. It would prove useful to share and discuss your perspective with a colleague, mentor, or supervisor.

System	Mission (Product)	Impact
Set 1: An emergency unit in a metropolitan area		
A wellness clinic in a resort town		
Set 2: An inner city public school		
An inner city private preparatory school		
Set 3: A social service agency such as a community mental health clinic		
A stock brokerage firm		

Assessing Forces Impacting the System

In addition to knowing where the system wishes to go (i.e., mission/product) and the physical and personnel resources it has available, the systems-focused consultant needs to understand the forces that may be affecting its current level of operation.

June Gallessich (1974) differentiated among the many forces that may prove significant to the understanding and assessment of a system. She identified three classes of such forces: *internal, trajectory,* and *external.*

Internal: The internal forces are those operating within the climate or culture of the organization. These would be forces created by the structures and processes existing within the organization (i.e., the system of authority, the rewards employed, decision making processes, etc.) and these will be discussed in more depth in the next section.

Trajectory: In addition to internal forces, Gallessich (1974) noted that a system is impacted by its own history and developmental direction (i.e., trajectory). The trajectory of a system reflects both its history and its trend. While it is not suggested that the projection of movement need be a predeterminer of system function, it is clear that past trends—as reflective of current and future realities—can impact the nature, character, and performance of a system and thus should be considered by the systems-focused consultant.

External: The final class of forces that Gallessich (1974) discussed are those external to the system. The consultant must be careful not to limit his or her system analysis to the internal operations of the system. Rather, to be effective the systems-focused consultant need be mindful of the powerful force and resource that the suprasystem offers (Ridley & Mendoza, 1993). In analyzing the external forces impacting the system, the focus is on both the adversarial and supportive role played by the external environment.

The systems-focused consultant needs to understand both the individual characteristics of the population (community) that may support the system via input of resources (e.g., tuition, taxes, or purchases) as well as the unique characteristics of those who will consume the services of the system. In addition to understanding the individual characteristics of the population, the consultant needs to be sensitive to significant trends (e.g., economic, political, social-cultural) that may impact the system. Aplin (1978) noted a number of external trends that could impact a system's operations:

1. Economic pressures leading to downsizing or rightsizing that organization
2. Business trends pushing for decentralization of authority and the use of total quality management
3. Technological innovations and increasing government regulations
4. Social political pressures for increased egalitarianism, diversity, and equity within the workplace

Beyond simply identifying the external forces operating, the effective consultant needs to assess the organizational capacity to collaborate and build supportive networks and healthy interdependencies with other systems in the external environment. Unless the organization is both aware of the changing environment and able to respond, it will have problems being effective.

Assessing the System Character and Culture

Perhaps one of the most difficult yet most salient components of a system to assess is that of the system culture. A system's culture could be defined as the unique, collective, mutually shaping patterns of institutional history, mission, physical settings, norms, traditions, practices, and beliefs that influence the behavior of individuals and groups (Kuh & Whitt, 1988). A system's culture provides a frame of reference within which to interpret the meaning of events and actions within and without the system (Kuh & Whitt, 1988). Kuh (1993) provides an interesting illustration describing a consultant offering a debriefing session to a representative body of a college. The membership at the meeting included the president of the college, the academic and student affairs deans, four faculty members, and three students. Kuh (1993) noted that the consultant, after exchanging pleasantries, reminded those in attendance about the purpose of the meeting (i.e., to solicit feedback on the report) and then asked for comments. As described by Kuh (1993), the consultant's request for comments was followed by three minutes of absolute silence. Following this extended silence, the president finally began to speak.

Many of us may have felt uncomfortable with this apparent lack of response to the consultant's invitations to ask questions. We may have been tempted to interrupt the silence as a means of stimulating exchange and dialogue. However, in this instance, the consultant was familiar with the culture of the system and expected a protracted period of silence. The system that Kuh (1993) was describing was a Quaker college. It was a system where people listened at meetings, reflected, and thought carefully before speaking. This process of listening—reflecting—considering and responding was a reflection of the Quaker philosophy that assumed that such a process allows "the light of truth" to emerge (Krehbiel & Strange, 1991). Thus the period of silence is part of the cultural process and need not, nor even should be, interfered with by the consultant. But a consultant without an understanding and appreciation of the operative culture may have missed this point and indirectly interfered with the process required by the system.

Various researchers have articulated concepts and approaches that are useful in the analysis and intervention within an organizational culture (e.g., Borum & Pedersen, 1990; Gagliardi, 1990; Hatch, 1993; Pedersen, 1991; Turner, 1990; Young, 1989). However, Edgar Schein (1981, 1983, 1984, 1985) has developed perhaps the most enduring and comprehensive conceptual framework from which to analyze and intervene in organizational cultures—a framework that will be utilized for the discussion to follow.

Schein saw the organization's culture as:

> *a) a pattern of basic assumptions, b) invented, discovered or developed by a given group, c) as it learns to cope with its problems of external adaptation and internal integration, d) that has worked well enough to be considered valid and therefore e) is to be taught to new members as the f) correct way to perceive, think, feel in relationship to those problems (Schein, 1990, p. 111).*

According to Schein (1985), organizational cultures exist on three simultaneous yet separate levels: *artifacts, values,* and *basic assumptions.* Each of these levels can serve the systems-focused consultant as a target for assessing the climate and culture of an organization and thus will be discussed below. However, prior to further discussing these elements, the reader is referred to Exercise 9-3.

EXERCISE 9-3   A Look at One System's Culture

Directions: In order to make the following discussion more meaningful and understandable, it is suggested that you attempt to apply the concepts, as they are discussed, to one of the specific systems with which you are involved. This could be your work environment, or if you are a student it could be the educational institution in which you are enrolled or the specific program. In order to gain a full appreciation for the power of a system's culture it is suggested that you follow the steps provided. Complete Step 1, then follow the instructions for reading additional sections before completing Steps 2, 3, and 4. Then complete Step 5.

Step 1: Briefly identify the system you have targeted. As you describe, attempt to identify the mission, purpose, and global goals for that system.

_____
_____
_____
_____
_____
_____
_____
_____

Step 2 (To be completed ONLY after reading the section on Artifacts): After observing your system, identify the unique physical artifacts, special spaces, special stories, myths, logos, rituals, and ceremonies.

_____
_____
_____
_____
_____
_____
_____
_____

Step 3 (To be completed after reading the section on Values): Identify the widely shared values and assumptions, many of them tacit, about human nature and the process of doing what it is the system is created to do. These values will be reflected in the system's view of the importance of certain activities, relationships, and goals.

_____
_____
_____
_____
_____
_____
_____

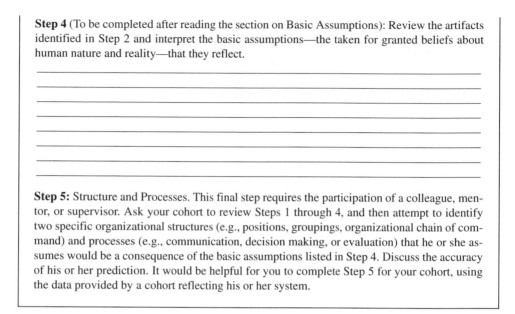

Step 4 (To be completed after reading the section on Basic Assumptions): Review the artifacts identified in Step 2 and interpret the basic assumptions—the taken for granted beliefs about human nature and reality—that they reflect.

_____

_____

_____

_____

_____

_____

_____

_____

Step 5: Structure and Processes. This final step requires the participation of a colleague, mentor, or supervisor. Ask your cohort to review Steps 1 through 4, and then attempt to identify two specific organizational structures (e.g., positions, groupings, organizational chain of command) and processes (e.g., communication, decision making, or evaluation) that he or she assumes would be a consequence of the basic assumptions listed in Step 4. Discuss the accuracy of his or her prediction. It would be helpful for you to complete Step 5 for your cohort, using the data provided by a cohort reflecting his or her system.

Artifacts: On the surface of any organization are the visible, tangible, or concrete manifestations of the organization's varied activities. These products Schein (1985) termed *artifacts*. Artifacts can be divided into three groups—physical (i.e., those things that surround people, such as space, architecture, or technical machinery), verbal (e.g., stories, written and oral histories, or special words), and behavior (e.g., rituals and ceremonies). Artifacts would include items such as an organization's symbols, logos, slogans, images, and metaphors in addition to its formal organizational charts, rites, and rituals (Kuh, 1993).

To understand or "know" a system, therefore, a consultant must be somewhat of a cultural researcher or anthropologist. It is in analyzing the system's shared symbols, ideology, values, myths, rites, rituals, customs, language, legends, logos, design, and even architecture that the system's culture begins to be known (Kuh et al., 1991). Before proceeding to the next section, it is suggested that you return to Exercise 9-3 and complete Step 2.

Values: The second level, according to Schein (1985), below artifacts is the *values* or social principles, philosophies, and standards of the organization. The philosophy of the system is the manifestation of widely shared values and assumptions, many of them tacit, about human nature and the process of doing what it is the system is created to do (e.g., for education systems, to teach, and to promote learning). The values of a system present that system's view of the importance of certain goals, activities, relationships, and feelings (Kuh & Whitt, 1988). By reviewing the way those within the system traditionally and continually address specific problems posed by the situations they face in common, the systems-focused consultant can begin to understand the system's values (Van Maanen & Barley, 1985).

The values, which are often in the form of some assertion about how the system should function, can be different than those observed. Often it is the enacted values—the way people and the system actually prioritize and function—that shape policies, decision making, and other operations. The systems-focused consultant must therefore be mindful of both the espoused and the enacted values along with the possible impact of any discrepancy between these two forms. Before proceeding to the discussion on Basic Assumptions complete Step 3 of Exercise 9-3.

Basic Assumptions: The final level of a system's culture, according to Schein (1985), is the system's *basic assumptions,* which reflect the organization's taken-for-granted beliefs about reality and human nature. These assumptions form the unquestioned, nondebatable truths and reality of people within the system. As Schein (1985) noted, when a solution to a problem works repeatedly, it comes to be taken for granted to the point where what was once only a hunch starts to be treated as a reality, as if this is the way nature really works. These basic assumptions then serve as the foundation from which the system defines structures and processes to guide its operations.

It is this deepest level, the level of basic assumptions, which Schein felt held the key to understanding and thus changing the culture of an organization. What organizational members assume to be true shapes what they value and the form these values take. Thus if the assumption is that human beings are lazy and resist work, managers will have expectations of laziness, which will color their perceptions of workers. Thus a worker who is taking a deserved break or taking time to contemplate a problem will be perceived as avoiding his or her work responsibility.

These assumptions will also shape management procedures and evaluation. For the system in which workers are assumed to be lazy and resistant to work, management procedures or evaluation processes that reward sustained effort, activity, and restriction of worker autonomy (since lazy people would use freedom to goof off) will be evident, and artifacts of management control (e.g., time clocks, daily productivity reports, and other forms of accountability measures) will be plentiful. Returning to Exercise 9-3, review the identified artifacts as reflections of the underlying basic assumptions and philosophy that drive your identified system, then complete Step 4.

The Linkage of Artifacts, Values, and Assumptions: The links among a culture's artifacts, values, and assumptions are central to the organization's operations. To understand the systemic influence of the culture of an organization one must analyze the nature and interaction between the system's artifacts, values, and assumptions (Dyer, 1985; Kuh, 1993; Kuh & Whitt, 1988; Schein, 1985). A number of procedures have been suggested for accomplishing these tasks.

For example, Schein (1987, 1991) and others (e.g., Finney & Mitroff 1986) suggest the use of interpretation of the artifacts and values as they reveal basic assumptions. It is also important to listen to the stories of the system about heroic figures and critical events. Such stories can offer insights into the morale of staff, as well as those behaviors that are valued or negatively sanctioned. Reviewing rituals and ceremonies along with traditions and celebratory events can also provide a look at the means through which a system's character is not only formed but perpetuated (Masland, 1985; Whitt, 1991).

This author has found that interviewing organizational members is a useful approach to understanding the basic operating assumptions of the system. Through such an interview process, the consultant can identify how business is conducted, which in turn reveals the basic assumptions guiding the organization. Identifying the rules of behavior or the norms of the system can assist the consultant in knowing the underlying values and assumptions operative within that system. But beyond facilitating the consultant's own understanding, the interview process can also be used to elevate the conscious awareness of these assumptions for organizational members.

Diagnostic Tools and Techniques for Systems-Focused Consultation

The diagnostic process is an essential first step in system intervention. As part of an intervention strategy, the diagnostic process can elevate system members' awareness of the current level of system functioning and can also serve as a model for a process of ongoing open communication and nondefensive appraisal. It is important that all techniques employed respect the appropriate privacy of those within the system while at the same time encouraging open dialogue and collaborative ownership. Involving system members in the diagnostic process can reduce resistance and educate the members to the value and nature of ongoing evaluation and system adjustment. This last point is essential if the intervention is to continue to impact the organization with a preventive payout.

A number of techniques, such as ethnographic observation (Aurora, 1988; Barley, 1986) and interviews (Botti & Pipan, 1991), have been suggested as useful diagnostic tools for systems-focused consultation. The systems-focused consultant may also choose to employ survey or questionnaire formats to gather data regarding the cultural climate and/or system operations. Numerous survey techniques are available. Rudolph Moos (1973, 1974) has developed a number of specific scales aimed at assessing a variety of system and organizational climates. A modification of one of his scales, the Community Oriented Programs Environment scale (Moos, 1974) was presented by this author in a previous work (Parsons & Meyers, 1984, p. 191). Areas of focus for this scale included conflict among staff, communication and problem-solving patterns, felt support and involvement, order and organization, rules, and use of staff time. The systems-focused consultant should familiarize himself or herself with the various packaged scales available, as well as the dimensions that they assess.

The reader interested in a more developed presentation of the theory of organizational culture and the analysis of its dynamic is referred to an excellent article written by Mary Jo Hatch, entitled "The Dynamics of Organizational Culture" (1993). Other sources of detailed information regarding the process of analyzing the character/culture of a system can be found in the work of Austin, Rice, and Splete (1991) and Whitt and Kuh (1991).

A technique that this author feels is essential to systems-focused consultation is *naturalistic observation.*

Naturalistic Observation
Through unstructured observation the consultant can develop a sense of the unique structure, dynamics, and "feel" of a system. Such naturalistic, participant-observation proce-

dures require special consideration in order to maximize the validity of the data observed. A number of recommendations should be followed when functioning in such a naturalistic observational role (Parsons & Meyers, 1984).

1. *Distinguish Fact from Interpretations.* The consultant needs to clearly delineate what is truly observed from what he or she feels is meant by that phenomenon.
2. *Observe from a Perspective of the System.* The consultant should attempt to place him- or herself in the perspective of those involved, rather than imposing his or her values and perspective on the analysis.
3. *Separate Supported from Unsupported Hypotheses.* The consultant needs to keep conclusions that are supported by the data separate from conjectures or unsupported hypotheses.
4. *Employ Extensive Record Keeping.* It is useful for the consultant to attempt to observe and record everything. What might at first appear to have minimal relevance or significance may prove key to the understanding of some other important facet of the system's operations. The consultant should take extensive notes on all that is observed.
5. *Concretize Data.* The consultant should gather quotes, examples, work samples, products, and other artifacts that appear to clarify and support his or her observations and conclusions.
6. *Be Respectful.* As a visitor to the system it is important that the consultant demonstrate respect for the privacy of those observed. Therefore, treat all data collected with appropriate professional sensitivity and consideration of confidentiality. Operating as an ethical, respectful observer should take precedence over data collection.

System Intervention

With a systems approach it is very likely that the consultant may discover numerous places where intervention could prove useful. Selecting the target(s) to approach and the technique(s) to employ must take into consideration the specific characteristics of the system. The selection of the intervention target and approach must be guided by the unique needs, requirements, and resources on the part of system targeted for intervention (e.g., personnel, policy, structure).

General Guidelines

With the realization that all intervention needs to be system specific as a backdrop to the following discussion, the consultant operating within a systems-focused model may find the following general guidelines useful in the development of an intervention plan.

1. **Use diagnostic data as an intervention step.** Interventions that maximize diagnostic data should be used first when the situations are not completely known to the consultant or consultee.
2. **Interventions need to be understandable and acceptable.** It is important that the consultee or the parties responsible for implementing and maintaining the intervention understand the intervention and embrace the potential value of this intervention.

3. **Consider the success potential.** While research is still needed to validate the effectiveness of the various techniques, strategies, or interventions that are possible, some interventions do have empirical support for their effectiveness in particular situations. It is prudent to employ these proven approaches rather than unproven or untested approaches. Interventions should be prioritized in terms of expected effectiveness.

4. **Consider the efficiency potential.** Interventions should be ordered in a way to better use the current organizational resources (e.g., time, money, energy). From this perspective interventions should be ordered in a way to maximize the speed with which the system attains organizational goals.

5. **Consider the cost of intervention.** All other things equal, the approach that requires the least expenditure of resources (personal and system) should be considered. Since resistance may be increased as a function of resource expenditure, the systems-focused consultant would be wise to select the appropriate and least disruptive form of intervention. The position taken here is that interventions which minimize psychological and organizational strain should take priority.

6. **Consider the cost of impact.** The interdependence of the various components of a system means that impacting one will surely affect others. Thus, the selection of an intervention should also be done with consideration of the possible impacts on other parts of the system (Davis & Sandoval, 1991). The consultant must attempt to be mindful of this potential for multiple effects and where possible inform those involved within the system of this possibility. The consultant needs to be concerned that improvement in one area does not have a negative effect in another area. Interventions that minimize such cost of impact should be considered first.

7. **Seek longevity and spread of impact.** Again, all things equal, an intervention of choice is one that will have a great spread of effect. Priority should be given to interventions that not only impact this client or consultee, but may impact other and future such individuals or lend to preventive changes.

Using these guidelines as a framework, the following three classes of system intervention—(1) the use of data gathering and feedback, as intervention; (2) fine tuning current system structures and processes; and (3) changing the system's character and culture—will be presented.

Feedback: The First Level of Intervention

Often the problem presented by the consultee has not been resolved simply because those involved really do not have a clear picture of the nature of the problem. This lack of clarity may be a function of their limited or biased perspective of the nature of the problem, or the very fact that they lack the information needed to clearly understand the problem and thus the possible resolutions. Therefore, an essential first step to systems intervention is for the consultant to provide a clear, focused view of the nature of the problem and its likely causes. Often this first step is sufficient in itself to be remedial.

This was the situation at a hospital in which the oncology department was experiencing increased stress and tension among staff, open conflict across shifts, and a general lowering of morale. Through observation and interview the consultant discovered that the root of this tension was the fact that the procedures used for documenting medical activity and filling patient reports was modified for the evening shift but was not for the day shift. The new procedure was part of an experimental program implemented with the evening shift, using the day shift as a control. However, the nature of the changes and the specific reasons for this new procedure were not communicated to the department members. This lack of communication created a condition in which those at night were upset and angry at the inconsistency of the day reporting, and similarly, those in the day felt burdened by the absence of certain data that they had come to expect to be documented by the evening shift and that were no longer included.

Simply identifying the disparity of documentation approaches and communicating the reason for the change was sufficient to reduce the negativity and strain encountered. No additional interventions were required.

Under these types of situations where a particular subgroup or unit of a system is in crisis simply because it lacks the information and knowledge about a process or practice within the system, the provision of feedback can be a sufficient form of intervention. Even in those situations where data collection is but the first step of a more elaborate intervention plan, it does still mark the beginning of an action phase of consulting.

Preparing for Feedback

Once the data is collected, its value as both an informative and formative (in terms of facilitating the system's effort to adjust) vehicle is dependent upon the consultant's ability to convey these data to those empowered to take action. The process of data feedback is therefore a very important and sensitive part of the systems-focused intervention process.

The primary goal for data feedback is to reach consensus regarding those components or aspects of the organization that appear to be interfering with goal achievement. Once such consensus has been achieved, the consultant needs to facilitate the members' commitment to action. The last phase assists those in power to provide feedback of the discovery process and the plan of action to all organizational membership who have participated in the process (Beer & Spector, 1993). This feedback not only encourages additional validation and provides support for the process (closure), but strengthens commitment via public disclosure. In structuring data collection so that it can be useful as an intervention process, the systems-focused consultant should consider each of the following guidelines.

1. **Keep it focused.** The consultant should narrow the diagnostic process, condensing the data to that which is both important and usable by those within the system.
2. **Employ everyday language.** To be useful, the data collected needs to be translatable into action by those within the system. Using language understandable to those within the system can facilitate this process.
3. **Collaborate in design and implementation.** Joint ownership will prove essential if the consultant expects the members of the system to accept the implications and direction provided by the data.
4. **Include data on the specific problem and system response.** Block (1981) noted that if adjustments are to be effective, they should consider not only the nature of the problem itself, but also how the system is functioning or managing the problem.

5. **Avoid collusion.** The role of the consultant is to remain an objective reporter of the data. It is important for the consultant not to support a stance that reduces the system's ability to solve the problem. As Block (1981) noted, if the issues are essential—even if they are sensitive and to this point avoided by the consultee—it is important that the consultant not collude with their resistance by failing to focus on them as well.

6. **Confirm and confront.** The skilled consultant will present the data in ways that reduce consultee resistance and maximizes the consultee's ability to productively respond. This requires a skillful blending of feedback that is both confirming and confronting.

   The consultant should provide data that confirms those things the system is doing well. While confirming those aspects of the system that are functional, the consultant needs to also point out those things within the system that are self-defeating. The consultant must avoid "protecting" the consultee from the reality reflected in the data.

The Process of Providing and Managing the Feedback

Feedback of the data can be handled exclusively by the consultant and there are times when such feedback may, at least initially, need to fall within the domain of the consultee. However, in order to maximize system involvement and ownership, it is useful, when possible, to engage a system representative (supervisor, administrator, manager, etc.) in co-presenting the feedback. One process, the waterfall procedure, facilitates such involvement and has been presented by this author and others (Meyers, Parsons, & Martin, 1979). In this procedure the data is presented to small groups consisting of a supervisor and his or her immediate subordinates, proceeding from top of the organization's structure to the bottom. In the waterfall procedure, subordinates in the first meeting provide feedback to their subordinates in the second meeting, and so on until all members have received feedback (Meyers, Parsons, & Martin, 1979).

   Regardless of the method employed, it is essential that the consultant maintain a level of control over the feedback. For the data to prove useful it needs to be structured and delivered in a clear, cogent, and focused manner. One sequence of presentation that has been found useful is the following:

1. Restate the original reason for the consultant's involvement.
2. Set the tone for this feedback session by structuring the meeting agenda.
3. Provide data descriptively (not interpretatively).
4. Provide data interpretation (referring back to summarized data for support).
5. Present recommendations referring to the specific data points addressed.
6. Solicit reaction to data. Keep control and focus on the data, not the interpretation or recommendation that will be discussed later.
7. Seek reaction to recommendations. It is important to have those attending consider the implications for their own units or their own role and functioning.
8. Review purpose (originally) and seek feedback to be sure the process is meeting the consultee's needs and specification of the original contract.
9. Discuss decision to proceed and develop initial next step(s), having each of those attending consider the steps they can and/or need to take.
10. Plan followup and provide support and encouragement for what they are doing and what they can do.

Fine Tuning: A Second Level of Intervention

A second level of intervention involves making adjustments to the existing structures and processes within the system. There are situations in which the system has the processes and structures needed for effective functioning. However, it is possible that these structures and processes may not be operating optimally for some reason. Under these conditions the consultant will attempt to facilitate system members' understanding of how and why the system is not working optimally and initiate steps to bring all system processes up to running order. For example, consider Case Illustration 9-1.

While the case presented highlights two targets (job descriptions and work assignment processes) for fine tuning a system, there may be many possible targets for such fine tuning. Some of these targets require only minor adjustment—such as that of adjusting the way work schedules are assigned and/or announced—while others require a bit more preparation and energy, such as might be the case in developing leadership training and skill development programs for current managers. Even though the target for fine tuning will be situation specific, it has been this author's experience that three general areas (i.e., role definition, communication, and skill level) are often involved in the system's dysfunctionality and will be discussed as arenas for fine tuning interventions.

CASE ILLUSTRATION 9-1   When System Fine Tuning Is Needed

This case involves a small engineering firm. The consultant was invited by the CEO because of an increase in tension among many of the staff and "open conflict" between two divisional managers. The CEO felt that the two divisional directors were antagonistic to one another and that this conflict was upsetting and disrupting to the work of the staff. While the CEO had spoken to both directors, the conflict continued, and as a result the tension within the company was high and the staff morale was low. After interviewing the two directors and a representative group of the staff, the consultant discovered that the company had just recently redesigned its organizational structure. Where previously there were two separate and somewhat autonomous divisions, each consisting of a director, six technical staff, and four clerical support staff, the new structure, while increasing the total compliment of employees, reduced the composition of each division. Each division now had a director and two project coordinators. The technical and support personnel were pulled from the division and placed in a resource pool consisting of sixteen technical members and ten clerical support members. This resource pool was housed in central location and was to be shared by the two divisions. In the process of the redesign, the job descriptions of the directors—including their specific responsibilities and lines of authority—were never clearly developed or communicated. Further, the procedures for prioritizing projects and utilizing the resource pool were not fully communicated (even though it was clearly developed).

It appeared that the conflict, along with the low morale and frustration being experienced, was a result of the directors operating as if still under the old, more independent structure, and because those in the resource pool were never informed about the process for setting job priorities. The consultant felt that the best solution to the experienced tension was to establish better and more clearly defined job descriptions for each director and to communicate to all involved the very clearly established procedures for employing the shared resource staff.

Role Confusion/Role Conflict

As was suggested in the previous case of the conflicting directors, it is possible that the system's experience of dysfunctionality is the direct result of role confusion or even role conflict. As a system grows, sometimes additional duties and responsibilities are either informally assigned to system members or simply fall through the cracks and are not assigned. Without clear lines of authority and responsibility, members may inadvertently cross role boundaries and fail to perform needed functions, duplicate efforts, or more seriously, offend another by operating within the realm of that person's authority. The resulting frustration, inefficiency, or experienced antagonism will drain energy from system functioning. Thus role confusion and/or role conflict when occurring needs to be a target for a finetuning intervention.

A review of job definitions and delineation of responsibilities may be needed in situations where there is conflict over domains of authority or confusion about responsibilities and areas of accountabilities. In this situation, role defining and clarifying activities would be useful. One exercise this author has used and reported elsewhere (Parsons & Meyers, 1984) is the "Announcement." In this technique the members involved in the confusion or role conflicts meet as a group. As a first step the members are asked to develop an "Announcement" in which they introduce the other members to their role titles and responsibilities. Specifically they are asked to identify and share: (1) one aspect of their current role that they find satisfactory and that they wish would remain the same, (2) one aspect of their role that is good but needs to be implemented in a different manner or to a greater extent, and finally, (3) one aspect of their role that they would like to reduce or eliminate. These announcements are exchanged, read, and discussed. The consultant's role is to facilitate the discussion with the primary goal being to educate about the role each plays within the system. However, a secondary goal, depending on the nature of the conflict, would be the refining or, if needed, the redefining of the roles, with responsibilities shifting to make them more efficient and enjoyable to those occupying the roles.

Communications Processes

In reviewing the communication processes, the focus for the consultant is on how information flows within the system and between the system and the external marketplace. The goal for such a review would be the identification of the internal communication network and the communication network between the system and suprasystem. It should include a look both at the formal mechanisms (i.e., line staff, organizational chart) as well as the informal processes by which information and feedback are exchanged and decisions made.

There are times when the system's method and/or mode of communication (e.g., newsletter, morning announcements, memo, or staff meetings) and/or the competency of those developing and delivering the communication is simply inadequate. Under these conditions, the consultant will attempt to introduce alternative modes of communication and/or increase the current level of communication skills through the initiation of member training experiences. Exercise 9-4 can help to further clarify the way method and mode of communications could serve as a target for systems-focused consultation.

In addition to fine tuning the communication processes so that they convey accurate information with relative ease and efficiency, as might be the need in each of the scenarios presented in Exercise 9-4, the systems-focused consultant should also attempt to maximize the degree to which the system's communication is characterized by each of the following.

1. **Congruency of action to message.** The focus here is on the degree to which managerial actions parallel the official messages conveyed.
2. **Communication as dialogue.** The consultant assisting the system in its effort to fine tune its communication processes may focus on the degree to which internal communication is a two-way process. Assisting the system to engage in a dialogue with managers trained in feedback techniques as well as techniques that encourage upward communications will facilitate the quality of communication.
3. **Face-to-face in form.** In order to increase accuracy of communication while also conveying messages of employee value, methods of face-to-face communication—especially between top management and employees—should be emphasized. This may entail the inclusion of more face-to-face meetings rather than relying on printed forms of communication.

EXERCISE 9-4   Fine Tuning Communication Processes

Directions: This exercise is best completed with another or in a small group. For each of following brief scenarios, (1) identify the way in which the mode or method of communication is contributing to the manifested problem, and (2) discuss how the communication processes can be finetuned to alleviate the problem.

Scenario 1: **Morning Announcements**

In Marion elementary school the announcements of activities and schedules for the day are presented immediately after the bell rings signifying the beginning of school. The announcements are read by a student and presented over the public address system. Students have complained about missing club meetings and sporting events because they "never heard the announcement" and teachers have noted the disruptive influence of some readers.

Scenario 2: **The Weekly Meeting**

A small mental health clinic has weekly meetings of all clinical staff and supervisors. The original purpose of the meetings had been to staff cases, receive supervision, and discuss therapeutic procedures. However, because of a number of organizational changes and the addition of many new clinical staff meetings, most of the weekly meeting time goes to providing information about administrative details around telephone usage, procedures for completing insurance forms, reviewing staff schedules, and the like. Staff have complained about the lack of supervision and case staffing opportunities.

Scenario 3: **A Bark Louder Than a Bite**

The graveyard shift of a telephone answering service has begun to complain and threaten to file sexual harassment claims because of the supervisor, Al. Al was just recently transferred to the position of supervisor for the operators after working for five years as a successful supervisor of building operations and maintenance. The operators have complained of Al's "offensive language," his "sexist references," and his "angry-sounding criticisms."

While structured, prepackaged training programs aimed at increasing the communication skills of employees, supervisors, and managers abound, these have been found to be less effective than some other more process-oriented approaches (Fiedler & Garcia,1985). Fiedler and Garcia (1985) expressed concerns that such training programs can become too didactic with limited involvement on the part of system members and thus little ownership and desire to change. Rather than a consultant as expert model for fine tuning, in a process focus, the consultant works as a facilitator, assisting work teams and management groups to identify their difficulties with the communication processes and solve the various problems identified. The process nature of this intervention increases the likelihood of member ownership and motivation for implementation.

Sometimes the system's philosophy of decision making and communication needs to be challenged and the mechanisms and processes supporting this philosophy need to be revamped. Under these conditions, the consultant is seeking a more involved form of intervention than that included here as fine tuning. The goal under these conditions is not to simply fine tune the delivery system but to reframe a new philosophy about communication and to develop or reconfigure the processes and mechanisms employed in the communication process. Such a major revamping will be discussed below, as a third level of intervention.

Skill Acquisition and Development

The changing nature of the marketplace along with the impact of technological or regulatory shifts may require system members to develop new knowledge and/or skills. Similarly, the changing character of the internal membership of the system as a result of expansion, merger, or new hiring practices may place those in managerial roles in positions where their management skills may be inadequate. Under these conditions, training programs targeted to the development of specific competencies would be useful.

The consultant in this situation can take on a provisional role by directly offering the training experiences or operating more prescriptively, directing those within the system responsible for such staff development to the resources available and the programs needed. A number of companies and professional organization offer prepackaged training materials, but the use of such materials should be done with the following caveat: For a program of skill development to be effective, it is important to identify the specific skills needing development and match the didactic and experiential material presented with that particular skill need. In addition to this obvious matching of program to audience need, the consultant should also attempt to match the program to audience resources.

Once the topic or area of skill development has been identified, it is useful for the consultant to attempt to assess the current level of competency as the entry point from which to provide the program of development. Without such a tailoring to the competency and needs of the audience, the consultant risks the possibility of underestimating the competency of those in attendance and presenting what is already known and practiced rather than that which is needed. Conversely, without an accurate understanding of the current level of competence, the consultant may overestimate audience entry level skills and thus begin training at a level too advanced to be useful.

In addition to providing programs tailored to audience need and skill level, the consultant needs to employ principles and practice of good pedagogy. As a general guideline, programs aimed at skill training should include each of the following elements.

1. *Learning Objectives:* Provide objectives that will help the participants to focus on the purpose of the training.
2. *Overview:* Provide an overview to the presentation, highlighting steps or stages to be followed.
3. *Didactic Presentations:* Basic information should be organized and presented clearly and simply. Use familiar terms, and situationally relevant examples and illustrations.
4. *Modeling:* The principles and skills presented should be modeled—either via film presentation or in vivo demonstration—and analyzed and discussed.
5. *Guided Practice:* In order to move beyond simple comprehension to skill development, a sequence of guided practice exercises should be employed.
6. *Corrective Feedback:* For the practice to be effective, the participant needs to have available a coach or mentor to monitor the practice response and give clear, concrete corrective feedback when needed.
7. *Independent Practice and Self-Monitoring Techniques:* Participants need to be encouraged to apply the new skills on their own within the work setting. In addition to practicing the skills, the participants need to develop methods for self-monitoring the adequacy of their application as a method for maintaining the learning and skill development outside of the formal training program.

The Third Level of Intervention: Changing the Character and Culture of a System

It is possible that the problems experienced by the system are a direct reflection of the basic character and culture of that system. As noted previously, patterns of behavior found within a system arise from the underlying culture (i.e., values and assumptions) of that organization. Therefore, when problematic patterns are noted, it may be the basic values, assumptions, or culture of the system that needs to be addressed (Beer & Spector, 1993). Opening a system and moving it to change its fundamental character is far from an easy process and requires much knowledge and skill on the part of the consultant.

Opening a System to Change

When improving an organization's effectiveness necessitates changes to the system's structure, processes, basic character, and configuration, resistance is to be expected. An organization is geared to avoid, deflect, and defend the culture and the patterns of behavior embedded within its culture (Argyris, 1990) and as such resist change. Knowing what to expect and how to work within a system's reaction to change may assist the consultant in his or her level three intervention. One model or theoretical framework that can prove helpful in facilitating system change is that offered by Kurt Lewin (1958).

Lewin (1958) suggested that change occurs in three phases—unfreezing the system, moving the system (change), and refreezing the system.

Unfreezing the system.   A system's fundamental character and culture is perceived by the members as a valid condition of the organization, created and maintained by those currently operating within the system. Thus, the first task that a consultant needs to address when attempting to change the culture of a system is to reduce system resistance by getting the system to accept both the diagnosis and the need for such a level of system intervention.

The consultant can reduce resistance and begin to unfreeze the system by assisting the members of the organization to see that while the way things were done was useful, the reality is that the environment (internal and/or external) has changed dramatically and these ways are no longer as useful. An essential first step in unfreezing the system is to heighten the members' awareness of their current form of functioning and the ineffectiveness of this approach. To achieve this heightened awareness requires that the consultant gain and maintain the system's commitment to the diagnostic process and outcome and provide appropriate data collection and feedback. The goal is to sensitize the system to the need to change and the need to modify its current structure and processes, in order to more effectively achieve its goals and fulfill its mission.

Quite often the role of the consultant during this unfreezing stage of system change is to be somewhat countercultural. The process of asking questions and collecting data around issues that others within the system have taken for granted is the beginning of this counterculture response. It is as if the consultant is willing to both ask questions about the "emperor's new clothes" and report the data that suggest the clothes are nonexistent. While such data reporting will not automatically change the character or culture of the organization, it is the beginning of the introduction of new observations, ideas, suggestions, or values not reflective of the operative culture.

Beyond the introduction of these new observations, ideas, suggestions, or values, for change to occur the consultant, through collaborative dialogue, needs to move those empowered within the system to embrace these new views. To facilitate this process it is important for the consultant to assist those in the system to see that adjustment in the way the system operates can lead to increased efficiency in this changed environment.

This last point (i.e., increasing efficiency) is essential to the process of reducing resistance and unfreezing the system. Beer, Eisenstat, and Spector (1990) noted that motivation to change is increased when the change process addresses the critical strategic tasks of the organization. That is, the consultant attempting to adjust the character/culture of a system needs to employ, as his or her starting point, the demonstration of the possibility of increased effectiveness once system adjustment has been made. Resistance will be reduced by increasing the organizational dissatisfaction with the status quo and the increased awareness of the connection between current behaviors and reduced effectiveness.

Schein (1985) suggested that assumptions can be altered by the introduction of new values (usually by top management) and the experience of success attributed to them. Schein (1985) argued that if new values lead to successful outcomes then they will be maintained, and over time they will be taken for granted—thus becoming a core assumption. Hatch (1993) noted that this process is one of conflict and dissonance. That is, if the new values take hold, they will at first be at odds with existing assumptions and thus it could be assumed that resistance will be experienced. But as success is experienced, the dissonance will diminish and the new will become the standard.

Moving the System (Change).   The second step in the process involves making the actual changes in the system's way of operating. This may involve the introduction of new expectations, job definitions, or skill applications at the level of the employee. It also could mean the development of a new structure or set of operating procedures. In some rare circumstances it may even involve the development of an entirely new system of operation.

Refreezing. The final step in the process is what Lewin (1958) termed refreezing. This refreezing involves institutionalizing and thus stabilizing these changes. The institutionalization of these changes takes root when the organization's recruitment, training, and evaluation processes have been modified to reinforce the new philosophy and values. With these changes, support structures and processes will also be modified to reflect and service the new values and assumptions.

Refreezing begins with the public acceptance of the new structure and processes and continues through the inclusion of these changes into the formal documents of the system (including new organizational chart, job descriptions, procedures, etc.)

This process of moving from unfreezing through change to refreezing a change in a system's fundamental character and culture is exemplified by the following case illustration and exercise (Exercise 9-5).

EXERCISE 9-5 A Mental Health System in Need of Change

Directions: The following exercise is most effectively completed by working either with another person or in a small group. While many of the concepts and variables discussed within this chapter are present within the brief description of the case of the Mental Health System in Need of Change, your task is focus upon the following questions and concerns:

1. How did the system's trajectory contribute to the current experience of dysfunctionality?
2. How did the external environment contribute to the current problem?
3. Where did unfreezing start, and what stimulated the unfreezing?
4. Where is refreezing being evidenced?
5. What else do you feel could be done to move this system in the direction of increased adaptability?

Case Description

The consultant was invited by the CEO of a large, metropolitan mental health service organization to come in to work specifically with one unit in the system that, according to the CEO, was experiencing "extensive bickering, back stabbing, and general in-fighting." Through discussion with the CEO the original focus of the problem was expanded to include all of the employees in the organization.

The CEO stated, "I know that the problem is most notable in the sexual dysfunction unit, but really there is and has been for some time now increasing tension and antagonism among all the employees across units. In fact, I think there is a real significant overall drop in employee morale and motivation. I am also very frustrated by the reduction in the quality of their work, as well."

Through a process of direct interview of the employees, the consultant began to understand that the organization had been experiencing a number of significant changes in terms of staff composition and responsibility. Because of their declining market share, the system had reduced its professional staff by 20 percent and its support and clerical staff by 30 percent. This reduction forced a realignment of task assignments, with professional staff required to not only cover more hours but also perform some duties that had previously been assigned to other unit professionals or the support personnel. The increased workloads, the redefinition and blurring of professional/staff lines, and the anticipation that things "might get worse" resulted in the identified "symptoms" of tension, hostility, and low morale.

After gathering additional data regarding the internal environment of the system, including information on its mission, philosophy, and previous modes of operation, the consultant gathered data regarding the external environment and marketplace. What emerged from these data was that the current "symptoms" of those in the system, while directly attributable to the changes within the system, was actually a response to the system's inability to adapt to a changing external environment.

The history and current operating philosophy of this mental health organization could be best described as one of providing long-term, intensive, dynamically oriented treatment aimed at providing significant personality adjustment for all clientele. Historically, outpatient clients were scheduled for a minimum of two sessions a week. The average length of a client's treatment was two years. Such an approach appeared to be working as evidenced by the previous financial success of the organization.

In reviewing client records, intakes, and marketing efforts it became evident that the nature of the local community had changed over the last three years. Where previously individuals who would come to the center would most often pay for their treatment directly, within the last three years the number of direct payers had declined to the point where now over 98 percent of those currently in treatment submitted some form of third party (insurance) payment.

This reliance on third-party payment added a number of new demands upon the system. In addition to the additional recording and paperwork, the organization began to experience a number of challenges to its therapeutic model and approach. The external environment—as reflected by the orientation of insurance companies and other third-party payers—was shifting toward an emphasis on managed healthcare, cost controls, and brief-time limited forms of mental health services. Thus the number of individuals for whom a therapeutic regimen of twice a week for two years was a possibility was drastically reduced.

Following the presentation of the data to the executive body (i.e., the CEO, the vice president of clinical services, the vice president of organizational management, and the comptroller), they became very aware that the difficulty currently experienced was not simply the result of the cutbacks within the organization, or the personal makeup of the current employees. As noted by the vice president of organizational management, "our problem is that we are too damn rigid and nonadaptable. We saw this coming and we thought we were above it!" This somewhat rigid, and nonadaptable system character—in light of the changing external environment—was clearly the source of their current difficulty and if not addressed may be the source of the organization's demise. The most efficient approach (while at the same time perhaps the most difficult) was for the consultant to assist the system to open its boundaries to the demands and opportunities presented by the new external environment and to adjust its own internal environment (i.e., structure and processes) in order to be responsive to this changing marketplace.

The intent of the data feedback was not to force the system to change its original mission but rather to invite those within the executive committee to consider the relationship between their current mission, their history of previous practice, and the needs of the marketplace. Using the data collected, the consultant assisted the planning group to:

Continued

Continued

1. Identify the specific ways the mission of the organization is manifested in its structures and day to day processes.
2. Review the opportunities and limitations within the current marketplace as a result of the changing orientation of the various third-party payment sources.
3. Identify those areas within the system's culture, as reflected in the structures and processes operating, that appear no longer useful or efficient given the changing external environment.
4. Identify those aspects of the organization's mission, philosophy, structures, and processes that remained useful even in light of the changing external environment.

This process of data feedback and analysis provided the executive committee with a clear understanding that maintaining the current approach would lead to further reduction of marketshare and thus lead to further cutbacks and eventual shutdowns. This awareness helped the members accept the need for fundamental change and increased their willingness to undergo the draining process that such change would entail.

As a result of the data collected, the planning body was expanded into strategic taskforce with inclusion of representatives from across all areas of the organization. The charge for this taskforce was to begin to identify strategies for improving the organization's efficiency and effectiveness. The consultant introduced a force field model for identifying:

1. The system's goals
2. The forces (internal and external) that would facilitate achievement of those goals
3. The forces (internal and external) that would inhibit achievement of those goals
4. Specific strategies for maximizing the facilitating forces and reducing the inhibiting forces

A result of the strategic task force was the realization that the current long-term, intense model of treatment needed to be reevaluated and reconfigured. As part of the process, the strategic planning body identified the projected increase in revenue that would be available to the system as a result of reconfiguring their treatment model and also identified a new, previously unserved market (employee assistance programs) that would further increase revenues. With this awareness of the benefits of such a significant modification to the culture and character of the organization, the taskforce began to identify and implement strategies to move the system to a time-limited form of treatment that was more congruent with the managed care requirements of the third-party payers who supported the system's clientele.

Committing to the change in treatment orientation resulted in a number of significant structural and process changes. For example, staff selection and training procedures had to be modified in order to bring those on board up to running speed with the new orientation, and to bring new people on board who already had such a therapeutic orientation. Procedures (including those governing supervision and employee evaluation) had to be modified, promotional material had to be developed, and additional support staff had to be added to allow for the additional paperwork required by a managed care environment.

The consultant in this case believed that he should not only assist the consultee to address the presenting problem (i.e., tension and low morale) but should do so in a way that would leave the consultee better able to cope in the future. With this preventive focus in mind, the consultant assisted the system to institute and formalize the strategic planning group. Moving the system from a long-range planning model to a more responsive strategic planning focus would keep the system more open to the changing character of the internal and external environment and provide a structure and process that would facilitate ongoing adaptation to these changes.

Summary

The need to understand the nature and dynamic of the system within which a consultant is working is a must, if for no other reason than to ensure that the recommendations and/or interventions proposed are compatible to the culture of that system. However, the current chapter attempted to demonstrate that the need to understand the role and influence of the system extends far beyond this concern for treatment compatibility.

In this chapter, situations in which what has been identified as the client's "problematic behavior" was only a symptom of a larger, more pervasive system problem were highlighted. It was proposed that under these conditions all attempts to remedy the client behavior will prove ineffective unless the system problem is identified and remedied.

As should be obvious from the chapter, it is this author's belief that systems-focused consultation, while serving as the vehicle for a consultant to have the broadest remedial and preventive influence, is also one of the most demanding and time-involving forms of consultation. It is a focus for consultation that requires special diagnostic and intervention knowledge and skill. To assist the consultant seeking to increase his or her ability to engage in systems-focused consultation, the current chapter provided a review of the unique dynamics of a system's culture, offered a model for organizing the diagnostic information essential to understanding a system, and suggested a general model of introducing change to a system.

Specifically, the position presented here was that diagnosis can either be narrow—involving a quick look at the easily identified trouble spots in an organization—or a more in-depth analysis of the intricate workings of the system. The bias presented within this text, however, is that for change to be long-term and permanent, a more systematic review of the interactivity and interdependence of the various elements, structures, processes, and forces will be necessary. The model offered allowed for multiple foci for analysis and multiple skills and techniques to be employed. But regardless of the focus or the technique, systems analysis requires that the consultant have a biographer's discipline, perseverance, and eye for detail, as well as the therapist's insight, intuition, and interpersonal skills.

In closing the chapter, a model and detailed explanation of three classes or levels of system intervention—(1) the use of data gathering and feedback as intervention, (2) fine tuning current system structures and processes, and (3) changing the system's character and culture—was presented. While the depth of change required varied across the three levels, for each the task of the consultant remained the same. Through a process of opening the system to change (unfreeze), introducing the innovation (movement), and attempting to institutionalize or stabilize the change (refreeze), the systems-focused consultant was attempting not only to remediate the current problem but also to assist the system to increase its adaptability and flexibility, thus making it more responsive to future internal and external demands.

Chapter *10*

Ethical Concerns
and Considerations

For those already working in the helping profession, it is extremely clear that *helping*—whether as a counselor, therapist, or consultant—is a powerful, awesome process that carries with it equally powerful and awesome responsibilities. As is true for other professional caregivers, consultants need to be sensitive to those issues and practices that may interfere with the welfare of their clients and the performance of their professional duties. Consider the issues and concerns confronting the consultant depicted in the following brief scenario (Case Illustration 10-1).

Asking for assistance on a classroom management issue appears to be straightforward enough, but more information reveals that what appears to be a simple matter is packed with a number of areas of ethical concern. In responding to the request and the information

---

CASE ILLUSTRATION 10-1   Helping as an Ethical Venture

Pat was requested to assist Bob with one of his first-grade students, Alice. According to Bob, Alice is quite an active child and appears to be either unable or unwilling to follow the classroom rules. Bob was very concerned about coming to Pat, since he was a first-year teacher and was afraid that perhaps his needing help may be perceived by the principal as a sign of incompetency.

In discussing the situation further, Pat discovered that Bob employed "the board of education" (a small flat stick) as a means of enforcing the class rules. Bob stated that the principal had given him the suggestion to create and employ the "board," and for most of the students it seemed to be working. He would paddle the children on the bottom when ever they violated one of the "serious" classroom rules. But as Bob noted, even this approach was not working with Alice, and he was at his wits' end.

ascertained about the previous methods employed, the consultant will need to make a number of ethical decisions around issues such as:

- Who is the client?
- What is the responsibility of the consultant for the child's welfare and safety?
- What is the consultant's responsibility and ethical response to the use of the "board of education"?
- What are the limits of confidentiality?
- What values and possible value conflicts may exist between the consultant, the consultee, and the system (i.e., the principal) and how will these impact the consultant's response?

As is suggested by the brief scenario, consultants face numerous ethical issues in their delivery of services (Ferris & Linville, 1985). Further, the unique nature of consultation and the consultation relationship often makes the resolution of these ethical concerns somewhat more complex than might be the case in the more traditional direct service model of helping. The triadic nature of consultation, the possibility of multiple clients, and the issues surrounding advocacy and innovation, offer many unique ethical challenges for the consultant (Dougherty, 1990).

It is clear that consultants, like other professional help providers, need standards of practice and guidelines for making the many complex ethical decisions encountered in the practice and performance of their duties. Some have called for the creation of a separate code of ethics (e.g., Gallessich, 1982), while others suggest revisions of existing codes of professional behavior to include the unique needs of consultants. However, even with such a clear and present need for an ethical code of professional practice, very little has been written or offered within the professional literature (e.g., Dougherty, 1992; Dougherty 1990; Ferris & Linville, 1985; Newman, 1993).

Professional organizations such as the American Counseling Association (ACA), the American Psychological Association (APA), the National Association of Social Workers (NASW), and the National Board of Certified Counselors (NBCC) all provide guidelines for ethical practice and help giving. These codes, while providing the structure for general professional practice, currently provide little guidance in terms of the specific and unique needs of the practicing consultant (Newman, 1993).

The current chapter addresses a number of specific issues that have special import to the practice of consultation. Specifically, the chapter will:

1. Highlight the need for the ethical consultant to (a) be competent and skilled, (b) be aware of his or her own operative values, and (c) demonstrate cultural awareness and sensitivity.
2. Emphasize the ethical concerns and considerations involved with (a) establishing and maintaining confidentiality, (b) gaining informed consent, (c) maintaining professional boundaries, and (d) utilizing influence and power within the consultation relationship.
3. Sensitize the reader to the ethical issues involved in (a) the identification of the client in a consultation process, (b) the utilization of efficient and effective treatment procedures, and (c) the need for consultants to demonstrate accountability.

It must be noted that the discussion and the concerns raised are not intended to be *the* definitive, all-inclusive statement on the issue of ethics in consultation practice. What follows is simply one attempt to sensitize the practitioner to the unique ethical challenges potentially encountered in the practice of consultation.

Guides, Not Fixed Directives

The first guide recommended for the ethical practice of consultation would be for each consultant to become familiar with the specific principles of practice developed by the professional organization of which he or she is a member. In fact, the discussion to follow draws on the recent positions taken by a number of the professional organizations previously cited.

In reviewing the codes of practice provided by any one professional organization, we must remember that the codes are developed as guidelines for practice. They are not written as, nor intended to be, clear-cut, absolute recipes or directives for action. The guidelines are provided so that each individual can regulate his or her own behavior. Because of the generality and the general inadequacy and limitations of these guidelines when applied to the practice of consultation (see Brown, Kurpius, & Morris, 1988; Brown, Pryzwansky, & Schulte, 1987; Dougherty, 1992), there will be many instances and experiences encountered by the professional consultant that do not neatly fall into any one guideline. Decisions regarding one's professional behavior will ultimately depend upon the personal values and ethics of the consultant.

A second general recommendation for the ethical consultant, in addition to becoming familiar with the formal standards of professional practice, is for the consultant to have and maintain access to updated professional literature, information, continuing education, peer interaction, and supervision. It is through the ongoing professional dialogue around issues of common concern that judgments become articulated and clarified and professional practice standards take shape.

Basic Ethical Concerns

While each specialty in the helping field may emphasize one or another ethical principle of practice, it would appear that a number of guidelines are common and fundamental to all professional groups. Brown and Srebalus (1988) identified seven basic ethical principles found in most codes of ethics and professional practice. These common principles can be clustered into three primary categories: (1) those concerning consultant issues, (2) those involving issues regarding nature of the relationship, and (3) those concerning the process of consulting.

These three general categories will serve as the outline for the remainder of this discussion. Specific ethical concerns and issues found within each of the general categories will be presented below.

Consultant Issues

The consultant's level of training, personal values, and cultural sensitivity are factors that shape and guide his or her professional practice. The way these variables influence a consultant's professional practice and the ethical consideration emanating from them will be the focal point for this section.

Consultant Competence

A fundamental ethical principle upon which all professional groups agree is that a helper must be aware of the limitations of his or her own professional competence and not exceed those limitations in the delivery of service. For example, the American Psychological Association's *Ethical Principles of Psychologists* (1992) notes: "Psychologists recognize the boundaries of their competence and the limitations of their techniques. They only provide services and only use techniques for which they are qualified by training and experience" (p. 2).

It is all too easy for consultants to be seduced into providing services or attempting to engage in problem solving in areas for which they are ill prepared. In the field of professional practice, a consultant operates free of mentors, supervisors, or even peers. In this environment, with the pressing request for service, it may be difficult for the consultant to either say no to the request or to seek support and assistance as he or she ventures into new areas of practice. But when the problem is beyond the scope of the consultant's competency, saying no and/or seeking support is the ethical response.

This concern over professional competency is one that is felt and expressed in many areas of the helping professions. However, it is perhaps even more of an issue in the area of consultation, since the specific activities, skills, and competencies deemed essential to consultation are simply not universally defined. Further, as suggested by the research in the area of counselor preparation and training, few educational programs attend to the training of consultants (e.g., V. B. Brown, 1983; D. Brown, 1985; Brown, Pryzwansky, & Schulte, 1991; Brown, Spano, & Schulte, 1988; Dougherty, 1990).

Because of this failure of the profession to provide a set of formal competencies and the limited preservice training that many have received in the cognates and skills required to practice as a professional consultant, it becomes incumbent upon each consultant to conscientiously seek ongoing appropriate education, training, and supervision and to practice within defensible ethical parameters. Given this guideline of competence, it can be suggested that the ethical consultant will:

1. Know and embrace the limits to his or her competence
2. Seek ongoing training and supervision
3. Know when to seek support and consultation from a colleague
4. Make referrals to another consultant when the needs of the client will be best served through that referral

Consultant Values

According to Warwick and Kelman (1973), ". . . ethical responsibility requires a full consideration of the process and probable consequences of intervention in the light of set of guiding values" (p. 416). While it could be argued that the guiding values referred to are those explicated in the professional code of ethics, it is also true that the professional consultant needs to be aware of the impact that his or her own personal values have in the professional decisions he or she makes.

Because the consultant is entering a situation in which numerous parties (consultee, client, system-units) will be involved, conflict of values is to be expected. In being sensitive to the value of the diversity to be encountered, a consultant must first be aware of his or her own operating values and how these influence his or her decisions as a consultant. To assume a consultant can be value-free, or to simply attempt to ignore the role played by values within the practice of consultation, could be "naive at best, and from an ethical perspective, dangerous" (Newman, 1993, p. 151). Thus, for the consultant presented in our opening vignette, her personal values regarding the use of corporal punishment—the obedience model of teaching and a "stick" approach to motivation—need to be identified and clarified as they influence her own thinking and decision making within this consult.

It is not a matter of *if* a consultant's values will influence his or her decisions, but a question of when, where, and how. Thus, it is an ethical imperative that the practicing consultant clarify, and where possible articulate, his or her personal and professional values and the role they may play in the consultative process. While the specific values to be clarified will most often be situationally defined, as a first step to such clarification it may be useful to simply begin to identify the values that motivate one's desire to be a consultant. Exercise 10-1 is offered as a first step to such clarification.

The existence and impact of personal and professional values cannot be ignored. And while the consultant does not have the right to impose his or her values on the consultee, it needs to be noted that the consultant should not abdicate his or her values and attempt to present as totally value free. This author would agree with the position taken by Gallessich (1982) that the discussion of the operative values, to the extent that they are identified and understood, prior to formal engagement in the consultation relationship may be the most effective, responsible, and ethical way to handle the potential impact of differing values. As an individual with expertise called into assist the consultee, the ethical consultant needs to

1. Understand the range of options available
2. Identify those options most in line with his or her own value structure
3. Attempt to help the consultee and consultee system identify their own operative values and the relationship of each option to that value structure
4. Through collaboration determine both the intervention goals and strategies to be employed that are most aligned with the operating values of the consultee, the consultee's system, and the consultant's orientation

The one value operative throughout the discussion within this text is that of collaboration. It is important to note that as an operative value, collaboration needs to be explained to the consultee prior to engaging in the diagnostic and intervention processes. Assuming the acceptance of this mode of operation and guide for decision making, collaboration would be employed throughout the consultation process and would then allow for the mutual resolution of future value conflicts.

While it would be ideal to find the system and the consultee for whom the consultant's values are absolutely compatible, such universal agreement is not necessary. However, where significant incompatibility exists—or the values of the system or consultee are clearly unethical in light of the consultant's personal and professional standards—contracts, when initiated, should be terminated—or better yet, not initiated or consummated.

EXERCISE 10-1   Identifying Operative Values

Directions: While it may be hard for you to anticipate the type of consultee problems you will be invited to work with, and thus hard to determine how your values may help or hinder your effectiveness, this exercise will assist you to at least begin this process of self-awareness of values and bias. As with each of the exercises, it is suggested you respond to the items presented and discuss your response with your colleagues, mentors, or classmates. This will be a two-part exercise.

Part 1
For each of the following identify your belief, attitude, or value about the issue presented.

1. Equality of genders _____

2. The need and value of unions _____

3. Children's rights _____

4. The recreational use of drugs _____

5. The use of the "carrot" and/or "stick" as motivators _____

6. The Horatio Alger viewpoint—pulling yourself up by your bootstraps _____

7. The trustworthiness of people _____

8. Quota systems (for hiring)_____

9. Inclusion (of those with special needs into the work place and/or classroom)_____

10. Alternative life styles _____

11. The absolute right of privacy _____

12. The value of competition versus cooperation _____

13. The importance of power _____

Part 2
Through personal reflection and discussion of your responses to Part 1, identify those items for which you have strong opinions, attitudes, or values.

Next, identify the types of consultee problems or consultee systems for which some of these values may hinder your ability to remain objective, nonjudgmental, and collaborative.

For example, how might a consultant with very strong opinions about a women's need to place the role of mother and wife before that of her professional career work with a consultee who is a female CEO of a major corporation? Or, what impact might the consultant's strong belief in "inclusion" and "mainstreaming" children with special needs into the regular classroom have on his ability to collaborate with a regular classroom teacher having a problem adapting his or her curriculum to a student with special needs?

Consultant Cultural Sensitivity

The topic of multiculturalism, while not a mainstay of the consultation literature (Jackson & Hayes, 1993), is certainly a hot topic in direct service (i.e., counseling, psychotherapy) literature. And while the research or discussion of multiculturalism has not been central in consultation literature, it would appear that what has been accepted, almost as a matter of fact in the practice of consultation, is just now becoming a felt reality in the direct service market. Consultants have known and operated from the awareness that providing help to another, be it a direct, counseling form of service, or the indirect forms of service found in consultation, occurs within a cultural context. Human behavior—human problems—and the process of helping occur within a social, cultural context. For a human service professional to view individual concerns or a person's problems as separate from that person's social, cultural context is to misunderstand them. To realistically understand the experience of another, we must view that person within the context of the society, the culture, the system in which he or she exists.

While perhaps something of a new idea to some direct service providers, the reality of the importance of cultural awareness and sensitivity should not at all be unique or insightful for the consultant. As noted throughout this text and elsewhere (e.g., Hansen, Himes, & Meier, 1990), being sensitive to the culture and values of the system and the specific consultee is a prerequisite for effective consultation—from point of entry through problem definition and intervention implementation.

However, even beyond the practical implications and value of being sensitive to the cultural context in which we consult, the ethical requirement of providing for the care of those to whom we serve demands that we be sensitive and valuing of another's culture. The ethical consultant is one who engages in consultation for the care of the client, the consultee, and the consultee's system. Such care demands that the consultant become sensitive to the cultural makeup of the system in which he or she is consulting and the role this cultural element plays in the creation and resolution of the problem presented.

In addition to being sensitive to the unique values and cultural influences impacting a client's life, being culturally sensitive is an essential ingredient if we, as consultants, hope to understand the true nature of the clients' problems. It is essential that as human service professionals we understand and appreciate the unique "tinting" of perspective that comes as a result of one's culture. To see what the client, consultee, or members of the system see and experience as a result of their cultural lenses rather than to simply assume that their viewpoints are the same as our own is both a challenge and an ethical responsibility.

Being insensitive to another's worldview and imposing one's own cultural meaning on the experience of another and believing that what is needed is the same, regardless of tradition or heritage, is not only ineffective but an unethical demonstration of our lack of care for the client.

Perhaps it could be suggested that the solution to a consultant's ethnocentrism is to ensure that all consultants only consult to clients, consultees, and systems with similar cultural backgrounds. However, the evidence for ethnic matching in the counseling literature is generally less than convincing (Atkinson, 1983) and it is nonexistent in the consultation research. Further, such an approach is simply unrealistic. It is incumbent upon all of us to increase our own cultural sensitivity and to develop the skills and the attitudes needed to effectively and ethically work with a culturally diverse population.

To be a culturally sensitive consultant one must (1) be aware of his or her own culture and its influence, (2) understand the limits of a single-culture, "mainstream" approach, (3) be sensitive to alternative worldviews, and (4) employ approaches that reflect the respect and sensitivity for other cultures. Because of the practical and ethical importance of each of these categories, they will be discussed in some detail.

Awareness of One's Own Culture and Its Influence

In addition to being sensitive to the unique value of the culture of those to whom we consult, a consultant must also be aware of his or her own worldview and the impact that such a worldview may have on his or her consultative interactions. The effective and culturally sensitive consultant is aware of how his or her own cultural background and experiences, attitudes, and values influence his or her definitions of normality and abnormality and his or her approach to the process of helping. Further, the culturally sensitive and competent consultant understands and accepts that his or her worldview is but one (of many) valid and valuable sets of assumptions, values, and perspectives from which a person may effectively function.

Awareness of the Narrowness of a Single Mainstream Perspective

The ethical and culturally sensitive consultant is aware of the limitedness and narrowness of any one single cultural perspective, even if, and perhaps especially when, that perspective represents the cultural mainstream.

The ethical and skilled consultant is aware that the "truth" is culture colored. The ethical and culturally sensitive consultant needs to be sensitive to a a larger worldview. This consultant needs to understand and appreciate how relative and nonabsolute any one cultural view may be, including his or her own, and thus avoid functioning from an ethnocentric perspective.

Understanding and Valuing an Alternative Worldview

It is not the intent to suggest that each consultant must be skilled and knowledgeable in all cultures, or that a person abandon his or her own cultural perspective. It is suggested that the ethical consultant will accept and *value* as legitimate the culturally diverse perspective presented by those with whom he or she works. Further, as was suggested throughout the text, the effective and ethical consultant will allow this sensitivity and valuing of the others' unique cultural circumstances to color his or her decisions through the collaborative process exhibited at each stage of the consultation.

Employing Culturally Sensitive Approaches
to Diagnosis and Intervention

While it may be argued that there are human universals, the one universal is that variation exists. People while similar are also clearly different. The cultural medium in which we operate and develop affects our values, our goals, our behaviors, and will also affect the decisions we make, or should make within the consulting context.

The ethical and skilled consultant continues to assess his or her goals and consulting strategies to insure that they are relevant and appropriate to the culture in which they are consulting. Problem definitions and goals occur within cultural context. For example, in discussing the diagnostic models for assessing pathology in individuals, Pederson (1991) noted that the assessment of healthy behavior in one cultural context may be diagnosed as deviant in another. This point should not be lost on the culturally sensitive consultant.

The consultant must be aware and accepting of the fact that there can be wide variation of cultural definitions of normative and normal. The consultant in attempting to define what is dysfunctional needs to be sensitive to the culture of the system in which he or she is working and how that culture defines acceptable, desirable, and normal or functional. As the professional help provider, the consultant may have assumptions about what constitutes conflict and problems as well as what defines solutions and health. However, the ethical consultant will be mindful that these definitions are culturally impacted and will place his or her goals and concerns within the context of the client/consultee and system's culture. The pervasive, sometimes subtle, influence of culture can be demonstrated through Exercise 10-2.

Relationship Issues

At its most fundamental root, the process of consultation is a form of helping in which the professional consultant attempts to offer a service of caregiving to the client, the consultee, and the consultee's system. As a caregiver, the consultant must remember that the consultation relationship exists for the benefit and care of the client, consultee, and consultee's system and NOT for the personal needs or benefits of the consultant.

It is in placing the rights and needs of the client, the consultee, and the system as primary that a consultant begins to establish the general framework for ethical practice. The ethical consultant enacts this principle of professionalism ensuring that any one consultation relationship is characterized by 1) informed consent, 2) confidentiality, 3) professional boundaries, and 4) the ethical use of power.

Informed Consent

The ethical consultant must demonstrate a respect for the right of the consultee to be fully informed. Consultees must be provided with information to enable them to make informed choices. However, undertaking this can be quite delicate and difficult.

Providing the information needed for informed decision making at a time and in a manner that the consultee can understand and optimally use can be a real challenge. Too much information too soon can prove overwhelming, anxiety provoking, and even be destructive to the consultation process. The goal of informed consent is to promote cooperation and participation of the consultee in the consultation process. The ethical consultant will attempt to provide the consultee with information that can assist that consultee in deciding if he or she wishes to enter, continue, or terminate the consultation relationship.

The consultee will need to understand both what consultation *is* and *is not.* The consultant should inform the consultee about the nature and responsibilities of collaborative

EXERCISE 10-2   Events in Multicultural Context

Directions: Below you will find a number of variables that may be important to the consultation process. For each variable you will be provided a specific culture's response. Your task is to identify your perspective on that variable. When your perspective varies from that presented, identify the potential impact of these varying cultural viewpoints on your consultation relationship with a consultee who presents that cultural perspective.

Variable	Cultural View	Personal View	Impact of Differences
Time	Time is NOT linear; time is when something is happening. Thus, lunch is when our work is at a good point to stop or work begins when you get here. On time is when the events happen rather than according to predetermined schedule.		
Contracts	A verbal contract and a handshake are more important than written structured contracts. Organizations are personally and informally structured, not driven by organizational charts.		
Responsibility	The top individual shoulders all the responsibility for positive and negative outcomes, regardless of where the action was initiated.		
Values	Cooperation, respect, and interdependence are valued rather than individual achievement and autonomy.		
Listening	A person shows respect and attending by listening without giving acknowledgment (not even a nod or an "uh huh") and with eyes downcast.		
Learning Style	The person has a global, visual preference in learning. When hearing "a story" he or she prefers to receive the entire "picture" all the way through to the end before asking questions.		
Sociolinguistics	After providing feedback or asking a question, the presenter may experience no immediate response from the listener; in fact, a delay of up to a few minutes may occur before the listener responds.		

consultation. The consultee needs to understand the role that consultant is to play, the role the consultee is to play, and the anticipated nature and character of the relationship as it unfolds through the various stages of the consultation process. Further, it is important for the consultant to highlight as much as possible the projected impacts (both positive and negative) of engaging in consultation.

In addition to these general concerns, the consultant needs to continually update the consultee on the process and progress of the consultation, the anticipated steps to be taken next, and the unfolding consequences of each action, so that the consultee can actively engage in the process of consultation from the perspective of understanding.

Confidentiality

In seeking help, the consultee should be able to expect a relationship that is trusting, honest, and safe. For consultation to be effective, consultees must feel free to disclose and share their private, professional concerns. For such a sense of freedom to exist, the consultee needs to feel that the interaction is one that is *confidential.*

Confidentiality involves an individual's fundamental right to privacy (Newman, 1993) and is the foundation upon which the consultant builds a trusting, honest, safe, and effective relationship. Confidentiality is both an ethical and legal issue. As with other guidelines for practice, the issue of confidentiality is not absolute, nor are decisions to hold in confidence always black and white. The use of confidentiality requires professional judgment.

While there has been elaborate discussion on the limits of confidentiality when applied to the more traditional, directive forms of helping, less clarity has been offered to those working within a consultation relationship. For example, Newman and Robinson (1991) highlight the difficulty encountered by the practical limits on the consultant's ability to protect the confidentiality of information gathered. A modification of the suggestions made by these authors (Newman & Robinson, 1991) to assist with this difficult issue of confidentiality are presented below. It is felt that the consultant concerned with his or her limited ability to protect the privacy and confidentiality of those engaged in the consultation should:

1. Remember that in organizational contexts, maintenance of confidentiality depends not only on the consultant, but also on the cooperative efforts of perhaps many organizational members as well.
2. Engage in information disclosure on a need-to-know basis. Since levels of participation by members are often variable, so too must access to information be variable.
3. Explain and negotiate the limits of confidentiality with each new consultation contract, since these limits are situationally defined and not inherent in any given consultation relationships.
4. Publicly delineate these boundaries and limits to ensure that all parties know who has access to what information.
5. Encourage all parties involved to be respectful of the rights of all others engaged in the consultation and request that all information be treated appropriately.

The ethical consultant, while attempting to instill a sense of trust in the consultee and create a atmosphere conducive for disclosure, must accept the limits to his or her ability to maintain privacy and protect confidentiality. Further, these limits MUST be conveyed to all of those involved in the consultation.

In addition to informing the consultee as to the limits with which the consultant may be able to protect confidentiality, the consultee needs to understand the conditions under which the consultant will, in fact, break confidentiality. While the situations under which confidentiality must be broken can vary as a function of many variables (e.g., state laws, organizational procedures, and age of participants), it is generally agreed that within a direct service relationship, such as counseling, the counselor MUST break confidentiality when it is clear that a client might do harm to himself or herself or to another, as might be the case in suicide, child or elderly abuse, or homicide. The determination of when a person is in clear and imminent danger to himself or herself or to another is a professional judgment and is not always absolutely clear.

When viewed within the consultation relationship, the conditions of clear and imminent danger to the client or others (consultee or system) may be even harder to detect. Nonetheless, the principle should still be employed. While clearly responsible to protect, the consultant must remember the multiple levels of client (i.e., consultee and system) for whom she or he is responsible. Thus, when the issue of a consultee's privacy conflicts with the protection of the client or others within the system, confidentiality may have to be breached. Under these situations it would appear that open discussion of concerns with those empowered within the consultee system appears to be the most warranted response, with additional, responses considered in light of the costs and benefits to be accrued (Newman, 1993). When the consultant is uncertain whether confidentiality should be maintained, he or she should consult with colleagues, whenever possible, to assist in that determination. As demonstrated in Exercise 10-3, the decision to maintain or breach confidentiality is not always easy, nor are the conditions dictating the decision always clear.

Establishing and Maintaining Professional Boundaries

It is generally agreed that someone seeking help has a right to expect a *professional* relationship with the helper. Media focus and sensational stories have brought to the attention of the public and the professions the sad reality of the many examples of unprofessional misuse and abuse of the power of other forms of helping, such as counseling and psychotherapy. For instance, therapists engaged in sexual misconduct with their clients is a primary cause for malpractice action against mental health providers. All of the professional codes of ethics identify sexual intimacy with a client as unethical, and yet it continues.

The opportunity to cross professional boundaries, while perhaps not as seductive as that found within the intimate confines of a therapist's office, does exist in consultation. The ethical consultant, therefore, needs to be able to recognize his or her own personal feelings and needs and distinguish those feelings from the professional needs and concerns of the consultee. It must be remembered that the purpose of this relationship is to assist the consultee, and NOT to meet the consultant's own personal needs.

Each of the professional organizations specifies the importance of keeping clear boundaries as a way of ensuring that the relationships remain professional. For a consultant, professional boundaries may be difficult to maintain, especially when the consultant finds

---

EXERCISE 10-3   Maintaining Confidentiality?

Directions: Below you will find a number of consultation scenarios. With a colleague, mentor, or supervisor identify the specific factors in the scenario that may make confidentiality difficult to maintain, or require that confidentiality be broken. Discuss the specific steps you, as consultant, would take in response to each situation.

Situation 1: You have been invited to provide organizational consulting to a large, executive search firm. The president of the firm has two specific agendas:

1. He wants you to identify the employee's needs for in-service training; and
2. He wants you to identify which employees may have drinking and drug problems, sexual hang-ups, and problem marriages.

Further, he wants you to provide him with a written report on your findings, including names, and specific quotes from the employees.

Situation 2: As a counselor in the university counseling center you have been invited to work with the RAs (residence assistants) in-servicing them on the identification of drug and alcohol abuse. You begin working with the director of the RAs in developing the program to be delivered. As you work with the director, you discover that he is having an affair with one of the RAs, and he is concerned that this may "blur boundaries" and make it hard to supervise her like the other RAs. The director is 38 years old, married with two children, and the RA is a 19-year-old sophomore.

Situation 3: You have been requested by the nurse supervisor to work with a group of oncology floor nurses. Apparently their work has been becoming increasingly less professional (e.g., poor record keeping, incomplete charts, etc.) with evidence of much interpersonal conflict among the eight nurses. Through interviewing the nurses you find out that two have been drinking on the job and on occasion smoking marijuana. On more than one occasion, the two drinking have become so incoherent that they simply went to a room and fell asleep. The nurses all report that they like these two people and "are working to help them." They ask that the consultant give them some time to work out their problems rather than tell the supervisor.

Situation 4: You are an elementary school counselor who was invited to work with a fifth-grade boy because of his "irritating, disrespectful behavior in class." In gathering additional information, the consultee (his science teacher) states the following, "I need you to do something immediately! I have had kids like this before—in fact, I lost my last job because a kid like him got me so mad, I beat the kid up. Hey, this is confidential—nobody knows about that—you are NOT allowed to tell anybody. But I'm telling you, you've got to get this kid to straighten up—he's REALLY getting to me!"

---

him- or herself engaged in a dual relationship with the consultee, or when the consultee attempts to blend consultation with therapy.

A consultant's professional boundaries and objectivity may be compromised when the consultant and the consultee are engaged in relationships outside of the consultation. Situations in which there exists a dual relationship between consultant and consultee (i.e., when the consultant and consultee have a personal relationship, such as lovers or neighbors, outside of the work setting) threaten the principle of professional contact. Such dual relationships can impair the consultant's level of objectivity and professional judgment and thus need to be avoided whenever possible. The reality, however, especially for those functioning as internal consultants, is that it is sometimes impossible to avoid consulting with a consultee with whom other professional and personal relationships have been formed. Under these situations the consultant must be sensitive to threats to professional objectivity that may exist, and even share these concerns with the consultee. Further, under these conditions it may be helpful to discuss the situation with other professional colleagues or supervisors in order to develop ways to monitor the professional relationship and identify strategies that may help ensure that professional boundaries are maintained.

A second threat to the professional boundaries of the consultation contract involves the crossing into personal counseling with the consultee. As noted throughout this text, consultation is a process that focuses upon work-related issues and not the personal, psychological needs and concerns of the consultee. The clear, work-related boundaries must be articulated and agreed upon. Further, it needs to be made clear that this is NOT counseling for the consultee, and personal, non–work-related issues will NOT be addressed. When such personal needs are interfering with the consultee's performance of his or her work responsibilities, then the consultant will attempt to refer the consultee for personal counseling, but will NOT offer to provide that counseling.

Assisting the consultee to understand these boundaries, as well as maintaining the integrity of the boundaries, is an ethical responsibility of the consultant.

Power

In discussing the issue of entry and the development and maintenance of a collaborative relationship, emphasis was given to the value of the use of expert and referent power to influence the nature of the relationship. Other strategies of influence, such as one downmanship techniques, the use of parable, and spontaneous proximity, were offered as techniques for increasing the collaborative nature of the relationship and increasing the possible successful outcome of the encounter. As should be evident the role of consultant is by its nature a role of potential power and influence.

The power to influence another's attitude or behavior is a natural consequence of interpersonal dynamics. The reality is that all consultants by the definition of having expertise and being requested to assist another to reach a heretofore unachieved goal, have power and are in the business of influencing (Newman, 1993). Thus, it is not the reality of power nor its use that is at issue, it is the potential for misuse or abuse that needs to be considered.

The focus of this text has been on developing a collaborative relationship in which the consultee has the right to accept or reject the consultant's suggestions and recommendations at anytime. This right includes the right to terminate the relationship, anytime. Consultation as presented within this text is a voluntary decision on the part of the consultee, and the consultant's actions to fully inform and collaborate should be geared to protect this voluntary nature of the relationship.

The right to voluntarily participate can be jeopardized by the consultant who unethically employs threats or sanctions to manipulate the consultee, or even who unethically employs the various forms of interpersonal influence or power to restrict the consultee's freedom to choose. It is hoped that the techniques suggested within this text are used to balance the distribution of power between the consultant and consultee, moving the relationship to true collaboration. The development of a truly collaborative, informed, and voluntary relationship may be the best means to insure that power is NOT abused.

Process Issues

In addition to the ethical concerns involving consultant training, values, and cultural sensitivity and the unique demands and characteristics of the consultation relationship, the actual dynamic or process of consulting brings with it a number of additional ethical concerns. Questions surrounding the identification of the client, the selection and implementation of intervention, and the evaluation of outcome and process are discussed below.

Identification of the Client

The characteristic of consultation, as a triadic relationship, raises a number of unique ethical concerns. Albeit the roles of consultant, consultee, and client may be clearly defined, the question of who is in fact the client for the consultant may remain an ethical concern. Is the consultant's client ultimately the system, as suggested by some (e.g., Fannibanda, 1976), or may it be the specific consultee with whom the consultant works, or the client for whom the consultee expresses concern? How does the consultant address the special need to know, when often the specific client is excluded from the consultation processes (Robinson & Gross, 1985), as may be the case in system-focused or consultee-focused consultation? While many agree that the consultant shares responsibility for the welfare of the client (Brown et al., 1991; Newman, 1993; Newman & Robinson, 1991), what are the ethical limits to that responsibility when that client is most often not included in the deliberations of the consultation process (see Robinson & Gross, 1985; Snow & Gersick, 1986)?

The ethical consultant must consider the impact of his or her presence and structured interventions on all those potentially involved, as well as all those specifically targeted for intervention. The welfare of members of each level of problem identification—the client, the consultee, and/or the system—needs to be protected. One way this protection of the welfare of those to be impacted may be achieved is for the consultant to expand the involvement and "informed" understanding of the processes to all those (or their representatives) who may be impacted by the consultation.

Efficacy of Treatment

Consultants are professional service providers. They present themselves as having particular expertise, which they provide to others in need of that expertise. Implicit in this definition of a professional service provider is that the service provided is both valid and effective.

Granted, no one professional can guarantee success in each and every situation, but as an ethical practitioner, the consultant should, where possible, ensure that the services he or she provides have both technical and ethical adequacy (Newman, 1993).

The fact that the consultant is "competent" is the first step in ensuring this efficacy of treatment. But beyond the ethical requirement that one provide services for which one is both knowledgeable and competent, the consultant needs to provide those services for which some research (empirical and/or clinical) has been found to support their efficacy.

While there is an ever-increasing empirical database across multiple disciplines—such as psychology, organizational development, educational research, social services (e.g., Armenakis & Burdg, 1988; DeMeuse & Liebowitz, 1981; Golembiewski, Proehl, & Sink, 1981; Gutkin, 1980; Huczynski, 1987; Kellogg, 1984; Knoff, McKenna, & Riser, 1991; Margulies, Wright, & Scholl, 1977)—that can be used to assess the relative efficacy of differential approaches and techniques for consulting, no one set of efficient, effective, operating procedures has been identified. Thus, the ethical consultant needs to be alert to update his or her own professional knowledge and skill, as well as to keep abreast of the ever-increasing research supporting specific intervention strategies. The ethical consultant needs to incorporate these research findings into his or her own decisions regarding intervention strategies (Gibson & Froehle, 1991).

Because the existing research on the efficacy of various intervention strategies is still somewhat lacking, the consultant needs to not only be informed as to these findings, but also function as his or her own "practitioner-researcher." In order to insure efficacy, the consultant needs to both employ empirically validated forms of intervention when known and possible, AND employ outcome and process evaluation measures as part of his or her own consultation process.

Evaluation—A Stage of Consultation and an Ethical Consideration

Evaluation of the consultation relationship and its impact is very often viewed by practicing consultants as superfluous or as only tangential to the primary function of consulting. This is not unique to consultation, since as Hackney and Cormier (1988) noted in their discussion of counseling and therapy, one of the primary abuses to these forms of helping is the failure to monitor and evaluate the effects of the intervention strategies.

It is clear that a similar lack of attention has been given to the process of evaluation of consultation outcome and process (Armenakis & Burdg, 1988; Erchul, 1992; Fuchs, Fuchs, Dulan, Roberts, & Fernstrom, 1992; Kratochwill, 1991; Witt, 1990). The position presented here is that knowing how to monitor and evaluate one's consulting activities is not only an essential step in the consulting process, but is also an ethical requirement used to ensure accountability and effectiveness.

Having a system of evaluation in place serves a number of valuable and ethical functions. A system of evaluation can

1. Serve as ongoing reminder that the consultation relationship is not one upon which the consultee can remain dependent
2. Provide the criteria needed for knowing when decisions and actions need to be reconsidered
3. Provide a means for monitoring and adjusting the nature of the relationship
4. Provide a rationale base from which to determine if and when closure is appropriate
5. Provide the means to justify the consultant's "expense" and market his or her value, for the client, the consultee, and the system.

Forms of Evaluation

Evaluation, as an ongoing part of consultation takes two forms: formative and summative evaluation.

Formative evaluation is used at strategic points throughout the consultation to assist in the ongoing decisions to continue or modify the action plan and to check on the perceived level of collaboration and mutual satisfaction with the process. The overall purpose of such formative evaluation is to gather data that expedite decision making about the upcoming steps, procedures, and processes to be implemented in the consultation relationship. Such evaluation provides the basis on which to better form the process for attaining desired outcomes.

Formative evaluation can often be achieved by simply setting aside time for the consultant and the consultee to process or discuss the relationship and the procedures employed up to that point (Parsons & Meyers, 1984). Often an informal procedure, such as asking the consultee for his or her feelings about the plan or the progress they have made to date, will serve the purpose of formative evaluation. Informally, the consultant can assess progress by the oral response of the consultee. Having the consultee discuss his or her feelings about the nature of the relationship and the consultation interaction, the strategies employed, and the problems they experienced are ways to gather soft information about the consultation process.

As a formative process, this type of evaluation should begin with the first session. Consider the exchange between a consultant and a consultee found in Case Illustration 10-2. The exchange took place at the end of the first session.

Even though this was only the first session, Dr. P employed formative evaluative questions to assess Tom's comfort with the interaction, the collaborative process, and even the first steps of data collection. The formative evaluation not only helps Dr. P assess the consultee's level of understanding but also provides the consultee with one other opportunity to be an active contributor—a collaborator—in this consultation process.

While a simple set of open questions can serve as the format for ongoing formative evaluation, those seeking a more formalized way of assessing the process and progress may wish to employ a checklist or Likert-type survey scale to be filled out by the consultee. Readers interested in reviewing samples of such questionnaires and surveys should refer to Brown, Kurpius, and Morris (1988) work or that of Parsons and Meyers (1984).

Summative evaluation addresses the issue of goal attainment. The specific intent of summative evaluation is to show that the action plan has reached its original objectives. A summative evaluation may attempt to answer the following questions:

1. Were the objectives/goals attained?
2. What factors in the action plan contributed to goal attainment or inhibited it?
3. What is the value of this action plan in contrast to alternative plans?

On a more structured or formal level, the consultee can be assisted to actually collect data that would be used to assess the degree to which progress has been made toward his or her goal. The establishment of such a formal or structured form of evaluation is greatly assisted if during the problem identification stage and goal setting stage, the goal was specified in concrete, quantifiable terms. It is easier to know when consultation has achieved

---

CASE ILLUSTRATION 10-2   Formative Evaluation

Dr. P (human resource director): Well, Tom, I certainly appreciate your willingness to come in and spend the time with me discussing your concerns about Tina's reduced performance. It is clear from our discussion that you are not only concerned with performing your job as Tina's supervisor, but you are truly concerned that unless something is done, Tina may be jeopardizing her job. I feel like we covered a lot of information today, and I like our idea about charting Tina's productivity over the next two weeks. That should give us some very solid data that may help us (and Tina) to eventually understand what is happening and what should be done.

Before we end today I would be very interested in receiving your feedback about how you felt our session went. What are your feelings about today's session and the plan we have established?

Tom: When I first came, I was a bit nervous. I was anticipating that somehow you were going to blame me for Tina's lack of performance. But I was surprised how comfortable I felt with you. You made it very easy to talk to you. In fact, I am surprised how much I did talk—usually I am pretty quiet.

Dr. P: Well, I appreciate your willingness to risk with me and trust opening up. Thank you. It is clear to me that you are really concerned about Tina. Also, without your valuable insights it would be hard for us to know where we need to go next! How did you feel about the direction the session took?

Tom: Well, I wish I had an immediate answer as to what I should do, but I know that's not very realistic. I am also a bit surprised that you are not going to talk to Tina—I thought I was just going to come in and tell you I had a problem and you would take care of it. But I understand the idea of collaboration, and even though it is more than I originally bargained for, I feel good that I might learn some things that can make me a better supervisor. So I guess to answer your question, I feel like it was a real productive session.

Dr. P: Me, too, Tom. Before we stop, is there anything that you would like me to clarify? Are you okay with the data we want to collect? Anything you would like to ask me?

Tom: I'm fine with the data collection—I know exactly how to do that. In fact I'm kind of excited to see what it looks like. I am sure there are things I should be asking, but I can't think of anything right at this point. But, hey, I know how to find you if anything comes up!

---

the goals specified when those goals have been clearly and concretely articulated. A goal stated vaguely—such as: "We will get student A to study more"—is much more difficult to assess than one that is placed in observable, quantifiable terms—such as: "For each day of the remainder of this month, student A will spend 2 hours reading and outlining his chemistry notes."

Learning to quantify the consultee's goals is an essential step in the evaluation process. Exercise 10-4 is designed to provide you with practice in this phase of the evaluation.

In addition to concretely defining the consultee's desired goal, it may be a useful procedure, even during the problem identification phase, to have the consultee attempt to quantify the frequency or level of the undesirable behavior, or even a count of the degree to which the desired goal was present, prior to treatment. Such baseline data will serve as a reference point against which to estimate the effectiveness of our treatment strategy.

EXERCISE 10-4   Operationalizing Goals

Directions: For each of the following presenting complaints identify two concrete, quantifiable forms of the implied, desired goal.

Presenting Complaint	Goal 1	Goal 2
1. (Sample) Kristian is such a pain, he never listens.	Each day, Kris will show me that he has correctly listed his homework in his book.	At the end of each homeroom period, Kristian will repeat to me the specific assignment for the next day.
2. Karen simply refuses to fill out her time sheet.		
3. This is the class from hell—they walk all over me.		
4. Lori is a mess—you've got to help me.		
5. The morale around here is horrible.		

For example, in one case, the consultee Karen was asked to keep a daily record of the number of minutes Peter (the district one truck driver) was late picking up his deliveries as well the time he punched out at the end of the day. Peter had an excellent driving record and was generally a very good employee, it was just that his tardiness was setting a bad example for the other drivers.

These data were collected and it was discovered that Peter was late each day, with the average being 22 minutes a day. Further, the data revealed that even though he started his day later than expected, he typically punched out at the exact end of his shift. As a preliminary goal, the consultant and consultee decided to reduce Peter's tardiness by 50 percent. Such baseline data not only helped in establishing a workable goal but also proved to be a reference point from which to judge the progress that was being made. Following the introduction of the intervention plan, it was noted that Peter's tardiness was not only reduced in both frequency (i.e., two out of five days) and duration (the average was 10 minutes) but that on those days that he was late, he stayed after punchout time to compensate for his time lost.

Such monitoring will not only assist the consultant and consultee in identifying when the goal had been reached, but it will also allow them to finetune the action plan (i.e., formative evaluation). In addition to serving a diagnostic function, such a formative evaluation can provide encouragement to the consultee, when additional time and work may be needed to achieve the terminal goal. This was the situation with Karen and Peter in the case just described.

Karen was becoming very frustrated with Peter and the data, even as he improved on his tardiness. The data collected helped Karen to not only feel more hopeful that Peter's lateness could be modified, but it also helped her develop a more positive attitude toward Peter, seeing him as conscientious employee, since he not only completed his work but was willing to stay later to compensate for his late starts.

In addition to providing encouragement about progress, a summative evaluation can also be used to define that point at which the consultation can terminate. When the initial problems have been eliminated or sufficiently reduced, and the consultee is currently coping better with these problems, then termination appears appropriate and the closure process can begin. Similarly, when the data reveal that the terminal goal has not been achieved, closure to the original contract may be appropriate and the need to reenter may be signaled.

It should be noted that since consultation aims at having both a specific remedial value and a broad-based preventive impact, the consultant seeking to perform a summative evaluation should identify multiple and broad-based outcomes. Thus, not only did the consultant working with Karen wish to reduce and/or eliminate Peter's tardiness, but from a preventive perspective the consultant may have hoped to (1) increase Karen's effective confrontation skills, (2) reduce Karen's negative and somewhat hostile attitude toward Peter, (3) institute effective self-monitoring techniques from all drivers, and (4) begin to move the company (system-focus) to consider a flextime approach to the work schedule. Assuming that these points would also be identified as desired outcomes, data should be collected to demonstrate the degree to which these goals were also achieved. By employing multiple outcomes and broad-based assessment, the consultant may be better able to demonstrate the more subtle, preventive benefits of a consultation approach.

While most practitioners shy (perhaps run) away from anything that suggests research and statistics, the utilization of the principles of good research as applied to consultation evaluation is essential (Meyers, Parsons, & Martin, 1979; Parsons & Meyers, 1984). Concerns about validity and reliability must be applied to our consultation evaluation. A number of authors (e.g., Brown, Kurpius, & Morris, 1988; Gallessich, 1982; Meyers, Parsons, & Martin, 1979; Parsons & Meyers, 1984) have reviewed the issue surrounding the need and means of evaluating consultation outcomes and process. One excellent explication of the issues confronting an ethical practitioner seeking to employ reliable, valid, and yet practical approach to evaluation has been presented by Frank Gresham (1991) and should be referred to by each ethical consultant. Gresham (1991) provides a brief look at both the major factors limiting the use of conventional methods of performing and reporting outcome research while at the same time providing three alternative methods (i.e., social validation, single case experimental designs, and reliable change indices) that have value and practical utility to those consultants in the field of professional practice. Exercise 10-5 provides one more opportunity to conceptualize the process and procedures to be employed in the initiation of formative and summative evaluation. As with most of the exercises presented within the text, it is useful to work with a colleague, mentor, or supervisor in performing Exercise 10-5.

EXERCISE 10-5   Developing Formative and Summative Evaluation Strategies

Directions: Below you will find a brief set of descriptors for the consult in which you are about to engage. This is first meeting with the consultee, and without any additional information your task is to complete the questions posed under the subheadings of formative and summative evaluation.

Description of Situation

Ms. Sayers is a first-year teacher, very committed to the profession, very anxious about working with you, the school counselor, and very frustrated with Suzie, one of her students. Suzie is a third-grade student, who, since the first day of school, has talked aloud even as she sits and performs her assigned seat work. The principal has expressed some real concerns about Ms. Sayers' ability to manage her classroom.

Formative Evaluation:

Identify three elements (variables) you would like to introduce into the relationship or process of the first encounter. How would you assess the impact of these elements?

   Sample:

   Variable = Demonstrate nonjudgmental style, to build a trusting relationship

   Assessment = Watch to see if the consultee began to physically relax and begin to freely disclose the information requested

   a) **Variable** =

   Assessment =

   b) **Variable** =

   Assessment =

   c) **Variable** =

   Assessment =

Summative Evaluation

For each of the following targets, develop a concrete description of the outcome to be achieved and a means of demonstrating that outcome achievement. For example, one of the outcomes desired may be to increase Ms. Sayers' knowledge of the behavior modification process of shaping. This could be assessed both by her ability to describe how she will use shaping with either the referred child or another child in her class, and through observation of her employment of that process.

   Target 1: Client, Suzie

   Outcome =

   Assessment =

   Target 2: Consultee, Ms. Sayers

   Outcome =

   Assessment =

   Target 3: System (Principal)

   Outcome =

   Assessment =

Summary

The unique characteristics of the consultation relationship and dynamic make for the identification and resolution of the typical ethical concerns encountered by others in the helping professions even more complicated. Those intending to work as professional consultants must be aware of and employ a set of standards for guiding the ethical practice of their trade. As a first step toward such ethical practice, each consultant must be familiar with the ethical standards created by his or her own specific professional organization. Further, those working as consultants must be constantly alert to the articulation of specific principles of ethical practice that may be unique to the role and function of the consultant.

Specific guidelines to the ethical practice of consultation will continue to evolve and develop. It is imperative for the effective, ethical helper to keep abreast of these developments. But in addition to these specific guidelines there are a number of common guidelines that can serve as ethical beacons for the consultant throughout his or her careers. These include the following general guidelines:

- Ethical consultants are aware of their own needs and how these may be active in the consultation relationship.
- Ethical consultants do not meet their own needs at the consultee's or client's expense.
- Ethical consultants are aware of their own biases and cultural orientations and are sensitive and respectful of diverse cultural orientations.
- Ethical consultants employ techniques, models, and frameworks of consultation that are recognized and accepted as effective and efficient.
- Ethical consultants seek to increase their competence and contract to provide services only in those areas in which they are competent.
- Ethical consultants continue to develop their professional skills and knowledge through formal training, professional membership, and peer consultation and supervision.
- Ethical consultants appreciate the power of the consultation relationship and use it for the benefit and care of the consultee.
- Ethical consultants protect against the possible misuse of power by developing a voluntary, collaborative working relationship with the consultee, one characterized by informed consent.
- Ethical consultants are concerned with issues of accountability and efficacy and employ formative and summative evaluative methods.

Yet, regardless of the formal statements and standards or the ethical beacons a text may provide, being ethical demands a personal decision and choice on the part of the consultant. The ethical consultant needs to not only remain in tune with his or her profession, but also remain open and reflective of his or her own choices and decisions as well as the bases upon which they were selected.

Exposure to a set of professional ethical guidelines is not sufficient. The ethical consultant must make ethical practice an internal value. It is important to enthusiastically and energetically set out to learn and assimilate the ethical principles. It is recommended that the reader seek structured—behavioral—case-oriented materials that will help in this effort (e.g., Eberlein, 1987), and continue in his or her own professional development through formal education, collegial interaction, and professional membership.

Chapter 11

Putting It All Together— An Integrated Approach

As with most forms of helping, consultation is a developmental phenomenon. The focus for the interaction and the nature of the tasks accomplished will change over the length of time and interaction between the consultant and consultee. While there is no one definitive conceptualization of the form these changes take or the stages through which consultation develops, it is generally agreed that the consultation proceeds from (1) a point of initial contracting, through (2) the identification of a problem and the associated goals, to (3) the implementation of goal-achieving processes (e.g. Tindall, Parker, & Hasbrouck, 1992; Polsgrove & McNeil, 1989; West & Idol, 1990).

The model and case illustration to be presented within this chapter will employ a modification of the conceptualization originally presented by this author with others (Meyers, Parsons, & Martin, 1979). While highlighting the three salient tasks noted above, the model to be presented provides a stage of problem identification in which the specific focus for the consultation (i.e., client, consultee, or system) is discerned. Further, the model emphasizes the importance of process and outcome evaluation and the tasks to be achieved in closing the consultation relationship.

While each of the stages to be described have been implied throughout the previous chapters, they will be briefly defined within this chapter, along with the identification of the specific tasks to be accomplished at each stage. It is expected that the reader, upon the completion of this chapter, will

1. Understand one model for conceptualizing the stages of consultation
2. Be sensitive to the unique demands presented at each stage of the consultation process
3. Understand the unique tasks that need to be achieved and supported through each stage of the consultation process

4. Be able to apply this knowledge as a guide to his or her decision making as a consultant to two specific case simulations

It should be emphasized that although the stages will be presented and described as if they were separate, discrete experiences, such is not the case in the world of application. In the practice of consultation, the consultant will experience the stages sometimes occurring in neat, linear order, while at other times the experience will suggest that the consultation process is cycling in and out of various stages almost simultaneously. Thus, while the discrete, linear presentation makes it easier for a textbook presentation, it is not to be assumed that these stages will occur in neat, discrete or invariant order within the real world of practice.

The Stages of the Consultation Process—A Dynamic Flow of Interpersonal Exchange

Consultation is a dynamic process—cycling through the processes of contracting (entry), problem identification and definition, intervention planning, evaluation, and decision making. As the reader is most certainly aware, the approach taken within this text is that the consultant, while employed to assist with a specific client-related problem, approaches the consultant with an expanded diagnostic orientation (i.e., behavior = f[task-environment-client]). This expanded focus allows the consultant to be alert to the possibility of focusing the intervention on the consultee and/or the system, as well as with the client. This expanded view requires that the consultant employ an integrated model that will allow him or to consider problem defining and intervening at multiple levels.

Figure 11-1 depicts an integrated view of the stages of consultation. The model presented in Figure 11-1 represents an adaptation of that presented originally by Gerald Caplan's (1970) and previously discussed by this author and others (Meyers, Parsons, & Martin, 1979). The graphic highlights the stages of an integrated approach to a multifocused form of consultation.

The uniqueness of the model is that it provides for a system of consultation services that focuses on prevention and intervention and emphasizes the extrapersonal factors involved in the client-related problem. Thus, while continuing to target the client for remediation and prevention, the focus for any one consultation, as noted in the approach to problem definition, could be the client (client-focused consultation), the consultee (consultee-focused consultation), and/or the system (system-focused consultation).

One bias that is presented within the graphic is that this model gives priority to the diagnosis and possible intervention at the extrapersonal level (i.e., system and consultee). This bias of emphasizing the least direct form of service is based on the assumption that when such forms of indirect intervention are remedial, they also bring with them the greatest potential for prevention planning. Thus, in an effort to maximize the consultant's effect the least direct form of service is prioritized. This decision to work within a systems-focused or consultee-focused consultation will be determined by a number of things, including the needs of the client, the nature of the consultation contract, and the strength of the collaborative relationship.

FIGURE 11-1   Stages of Consultation

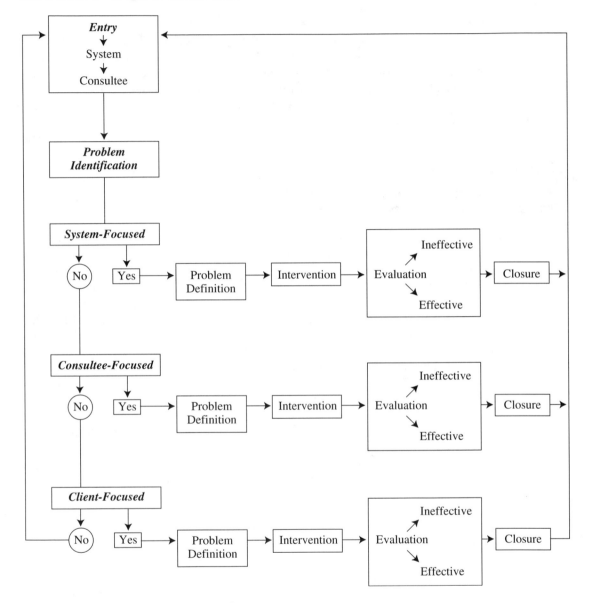

The Stages of Consultation

Entry: A Two-Step Process

As emphasized in Chapters 3 through 6, consultants, while needed and requested by the systems in which they are employed, and the consultees who seek their assistance, are often actively resisted by the same. The primary stage of consultation involves developing a working—useful—relationship both formally, within the system (i.e., contracting), and informally and interpersonally, with the consultee (i.e., developing a collaborative relationship). The nature of both of these relationships will set the foundation and the limits to (1) the types of problems the consultant will be invited (allowed) to work, (2) the approaches or specific techniques to be employed, and (3) the levels (i.e., client-focused, consultee-focused, or system-focused) from which the consultant can approach the client's difficulty. Thus entry, both at the systems level and at the consultee level, is pivotal for the entire consultation process.

When negotiating a contract to provide consultative services it is important to identify the parties to be involved, including the identification of the specific "client." It is also important to elicit the system's expectations of the consultant and to be able to contrast that with what it is the consultant is able and interested in doing. While it is gratifying to be offered a contract to work as a consultant, as is evident in Chapter 10, one must function ethically. When the task requested or the nature of the contract violates the consultant's ethical principles (as may be the case when asked to do something that is well beyond the consultant's training and competence), that contract must be refused. This does not mean, however, that the consultant could not still attempt to redefine the contract to be both of service to the system and within the boundaries of the consultant's competencies. In negotiating a contract—be it the formal one at the systems level, or the more informal contract occurring each time one works with a consultee—the consultant should be mindful of achieving several specific goals. The goals are described below.

1. **Negotiate Wants:** The consultant needs to identify what is envisioned, desired, and sanctioned by the highest level administrator to whom you will be responsible (when negotiating the formal contract) and with the consultee.
2. **Identify Culture, Frame of Reference, and Points of Resistance:** Begin to identify concerns regarding exposure, loss of control, and change, for example, as well as forms of service that may be experienced as alien to the specific culture or personal frame of reference.
3. **Explain the Expanded Model:** Explain the collaborative, expanded, integrated model of consultation in order to surface mixed feelings and concerns and to educate as to the rationale and value of such an approach.
4. **Address Both Remedial and Preventive Focus:** Present a contract that addresses immediate felt needs, while at the same time providing freedom to operate in a more preventive manner.
5. **Identify Goal:** Identify as concretely as possible the terminal goal expected as a result of the consultation.
6. **Define Role:** Describe the specific roles to be played (i.e., consultant and consultee), the nature of the relationship (i.e., collaborative), and elicit specific concerns or confusions around these two factors.
7. **Obtain Mutual Consent:** Whether it be at the formal level of contracting or informally with the consultee, successful entry requires that all parties freely enter the contract understanding the explicit nature of the contract, the demands of the contract, the ex-

pectations and limitations of the contract, and anticipation that all will receive something of value.

8. **Understand That Contracts Are Renegotiable:** Finally, it is crucial that all parties involved understand that contracts can be renegotiated at any time during the consultation process. It is important for each party to feel the freedom to redefine needs, wants, and expectations for the consultation, as they may change over the course of the consultative process.

Focusing the Consultation Problem Identification

After a general identification of the presenting concerns, history of the problem, and the attempts at resolution has been acquired, and the consultant begins to establish a feel for the system's culture and points of both system and consultee resistance, a decision regarding the focus for the consultation is to be made. Since the actual definition of the problem, along with the specific forms or strategy for remediation, will vary greatly depending on the focus of the consultation (i.e., client, consultee, and system), the identification of both the optimal and possible level of consultant focus is essential to the successful outcome of the consultation. The consultant needs to look beyond the consultee's original conceptualization of the problem and solution in order to test whether other more indirect and thus more preventive approaches could be employed. When attempting to identify the possible level of focus, the consultant needs to consider a number of factors such as (1) the level of immediate crisis (system, consultee, or client), (2) the nature of the system's culture, structure, processes, and history, and (3) the consultee's expectations and openness to the collaborative exchange. Clearly in the situation where the system expects and has rigidly employed a direct service, provisional orientation to dealing with client problems and the consultee is highly defensive and anticipates a provisional form of consultation, a consultant may find entering at any level of focus other than client-focused quite difficult, if not impossible. Thus, while recognizing that the optimal value of the consultation may be accrued by working at the systems level or consultee level, the reality of this consult dictates that the consultant enter and work at a client-focused level, in hopes of beginning to shape the consultee and the system to consideration of allowing more indirect services in the future.

Tasks to be accomplished during this stage of consultation are

1. *Become Aware of System's Culture and Climate:* The consultant needs to establish a clear sense of what is allowed or not allowed within the system as well as what is anticipated and valued so that the processes employed can at a minimum be culturally compatible.

2. *Assess Sensitivity to Consultee Orientation:* The consultant needs to assess the degree of openness and willingness within the system to work with the consultant at the various levels of focus, as well as the consultee's resources for working at each of the different focus levels.

3. *Expand the Initial Hypothesis of Presenting Concern:* The consultee will oftentimes present both the nature of the problem and a proposed general approach to its resolution. The consultant needs to be cautious NOT to embrace this initial presentation or

to jump in with a rapid problem definition and solution plan. In light of the integrated model, it is more important for the consultant to provide the consultee with three re-definitions of the presenting concern, one highlighting each of the different possible focal points. For example, the consultee may claim that the client is simply a "sick person" needing therapy (i.e., direct service). The consultant, while accepting this as a possibility, should attempt to broaden the consultee's orientation by suggesting that while this may be one valid view, perhaps the person could be responding to something or someone else in the environment (expanding the focus to include extrapersonal variables).

4. *Invite the Consultee to Collaborate on Testing the Hypotheses:* If the consultant was able to reframe or reconceptualize the possible nature and cause for the client's problem, he or she can elicit the consultee's assistance (thus building collaboration) to gather additional "evidence" to test one or another of the hypotheses. Rather than jumping into a locked definition of the problem, the consultant has begun to educate the consultee to the collaborative nature of the relationship and the expanded problem-solving focus to be employed. Further, the additional information gathered may suggest a need to focus at a level different than what was first presented.

5. *Select the First Point of Operation:* The consultee and consultant should come to agreement on the level of entry and focus to be employed. The consultant needs to use his or her expertise to assist the consultee to identify the focus that holds the most promise for success and breadth of impact (i.e., intervention and prevention). Further, it is important to assist the consultee to view this as "our" first point of operation and that reconsideration and renegotiation can occur at any time as additional information presents itself.

Defining the Problem—Operationalizing Goals

Once a focus and level of entry have been agreed upon, the next step in the consultation process is to begin to gather diagnostic data that will concretely, and in detail, identify the nature and scope of the problem, and to begin to operationalize the desired goal(s) to be achieved. Throughout this process the consultee must be reminded that the model employed assumes that the client's behavior is a function of interaction between the unique characteristics of the client, the task requested, and the environment in which the client is to function. Thus, all attempts to define the problem and the desired goals should include components of each of these factors (i.e., the client, the task, the environment). The specific tasks to be completed at this stage will be to

1. *Distinguish Levels:* The consultant needs to help the consultee distinguish between presenting concerns and underlying problems.
2. *Expand the Focus:* The consultant needs to support the consultee in his or her understanding of the expanded view taken within this model that emphasizes the problem to include client, task, and environmental elements.
3. *Collect Data:* The consultant needs to identify the strategies or techniques to be employed in the data collection process. The consultant needs to assist the consultee in the articulation of his or her own data collections processes and how these can be used

to cross validate that of the consultant, and/or train the consultee in the valid application of the consultant's strategies for data collection.

4. *Involve the Consultee in Interpretation:* The consultant needs to assist the consultee in organizing the data collected; identifying points of similarity and dissimilarity in data collected; extracting the consistent, salient factors; and drawing conclusions about the nature, scope and causative elements to the observed problem.

5. *Keep Centered on Purpose:* The data collection is for the purpose of moving toward action (the assessment-intervention linkage) and not for research. Thus, the consultant needs to assist the consultee to keep the data collection clear, simple, and meaningful. The consultant needs to help shape the data so that it provides a clear and simple picture of what is causing and maintaining the client's problem (including client, task, and environmental elements).

6. *Treat the Problem Definition Process as Primary Opportunity for Collaboration:* The consultant needs to use this problem definition stage as an arena to highlight the consultee's valued role in this collaborative effort. Including the consultee at every point in the data collection and problem definition process is important as is providing the consultee with evidence of the perceived value of his or her contributions.

Intervention Planning

While presented here as a separate stage in the consultation process, it must be noted that interventions and intervention planning have been an essential thread in the fabric of entry, problem identification, and problem definition. The simple process of clarifying the problem or identifying goals can be sufficient to establish a direction for the consultee, and thus serve as an intervention. Similarly, the act of contracting the services of a consultant is often enough to have those involved within the organization begin to reconsider the current forms of operation and make needed adjustments on their own. In this case the process of entry would have an intervening quality.

However, consultation as a problem-solving process typically involves the articulation and application of an intervention strategy. It is this more formal process of developing and applying interventions that is the focus of this stage of consultation.

The specific form of intervention is determined by the nature of the problem, the unique expertise of those involved, the resources available to effect change in that defined problem area and the degree to which the intervention is owned or embraced by the consultee and consultee's system. Therefore, the specifics of intervention development will not be addressed here. However, as a subprocess in the larger process of consultation, the development and implementation of intervention requires that the consultant attend to a number of specific tasks. These tasks are

1. *Achieve the Assessment-Intervention Link:* Help the consultee (and/or consultee's system) connect the data collected (defining the problem) with the intervention proposed.

2. *Provide a Multiplicity of Strategies:* The consultant needs to attempt to assist the consultee to identify multiple strategies for impacting the defined problem.

3. *Maximize Payoffs, Minimize Costs:* With the consultee, the consultant needs to identify the intervention that will maximize impact while at the same time keep costs (physical, social, psychological) to a minimum.

4. *Gain Mutual Agreement:* As with all aspects of the collaborative process it is important for the consultant to gain agreement (sanction) from the consultee and consultee's system that the process should proceed.

5. *Develop Evaluation Plan:* As part of the process of developing an intervention the consultant and the consultee need to develop a plan and a process by which the effectiveness of the intervention can be assessed.

6. *Assign Tasks:* Identify the tasks that each party (i.e., consultant and consultee) will be responsible to implement.

7. *Work with Resistance:* Recognize that resistance occurs even at this stage of consultation, and thus the consultant will need to recognize, identify, invite, and reframe the resistance for the consultee should it occur.

8. *Maintain Collaboration throughout Implementation:* In light of the preventive goal and the collaborative nature of the relationship, the consultant needs to resist the temptation to jump in and take on more responsibility for intervention implementation. Sharing equally in the process of implementation, as well as its success or failure is still a goal for this collaborative process.

9. *Provide Support:* Support the consultee through the implementation with special attention to remaining open to the possible need to recycle through the process of redefining the problem and/or generating alternative strategies should a blockage be encountered in the intervention plan.

Evaluation

As noted above, during the stage of intervention planning and implementation, the consultant must attempt to identify the criteria and mechanisms by which the success or failure of the intervention plan can be evaluated. This evaluation should target both the degree to which the desired outcomes were achieved as well as the degree to which the collaborative process was maintained. The consultant should complete the following tasks:

1. *Establish Criteria:* Assist the consultee to identify multiple criteria to assess the success of the outcome and process of the consultation.

2. *Target Process as well as Outcome:* Employ some measures that will allow the consultant and consultee to recognize the positive impact of the relationship even if the terminal goals or outcomes were not achieved.

3. *Target Success and Limitations:* Target measures that will help the consultant and the consultee to identify the value (to both the consultee and the consultee's system) of the consultation model.

4. *Employ Valid Designs:* While focusing on the practical utility of the evaluation process, the consultant should consider employing simple, valid, structured designs that will increase the validity of the conclusions drawn from the evaluation (see, for example, Brown, Kurpius, & Morris,1988; Meyers, Parsons, & Martin, 1979; Parsons & Meyers, 1984).

Closure

While termination of the consultation relationship can occur at any time throughout the process, closure as an anticipated stage occurs at the completion of the entire process of consultation (i.e., entry through intervention implementation and evaluation). Regardless of whether the desired outcomes were achieved, the initial contract is closed once the intervention has been applied and the outcomes evaluated.

Closure When Successful

Under those circumstances where the consultation intervention has proven successful, the consultant will need to attend to a number of final tasks. These closure tasks are important, not only as marketing strategies for future consultation contracts, but as a learning experience for both the consultant and consultee. When handled effectively, the process of closing the consultation contract (i.e., closure) can serve as a means to solidify the changes introduced and the preventive elements initiated. Following upon the successful completion of the consultation contract the consultant should:

1. *Review Contract:* Review the elements of the original contract and the specific steps incurred as the consultant and consultee moved through the process
2. *Share View of Experience:* The consultant should share his or her sense of how the working relationship developed and his or her level of satisfaction with the outcomes
3. *Invite Consultee Disclosure:* Invite and support the consultee in sharing his or her view of the working relationship and the degree of satisfaction with the outcomes
4. *Reinforce Consultee Value:* Reinforce the consultee's valuable involvement, highlight the knowledge and skill that the consultee has both contributed and developed as a result of the consultation.
5. *Review Current Needs:* Help the consultee to identify his or her current needs and the way the consultant might be of continued service.
6. *Establish Availability:* Make clear the consultant's availability to work with the consultee in the future.

Closure When Unsuccessful

Even the most effective consultant-consultee collaboration may result in unsuccessful or less than successful outcomes. When the evaluation process demonstrates that the interventions have been unsuccessful, the tendency may be to simply "run and hide." Effective closure is perhaps even more important under conditions when the intervention proved unsuccessful than when success was achieved.

While the tendency may be to reduce the personal and professional vulnerability by reducing the focus on the lack of success, reviewing our efforts and processes is essential for both the consultant's and consultee's learning and growth, and the possibility of successfully resolving either this specific problem, or similar problems in the future. Providing effective closure when the intervention has been unsuccessful requires that the consultant achieve a number of the tasks previously noted along with a special few additions. Specifically, the consultant will need to:

1. *Convey a Sense of Hopefulness:* Approach the data revealed in the evaluation as important and valuable pieces of the puzzle to be considered as we reapproach the problem. The message to be conveyed is not one of failure, but one of success, success in identifying something that doesn't work, and information that may help us better identify what may work.
2. *Review Original Contact:* Review the elements of the original contract and the specific steps incurred as the consultant and consultee moved through the process.
3. *Share Personal View:* The consultant should share his or her sense of how the working relationship developed and his or her level of satisfaction with the outcomes.
4. *Invite Consultee Disclosure:* Invite and support the consultee in sharing his or her view of the working relationship and the degree of satisfaction with the outcomes
5. *Resist Patching:* Resist the temptation to simply modify the intervention plan or jump back in and try again. Rather than simply continuing on the same path with a different tool, it is important for the consultant and consultee to step back and reconsider the situation given this new information. With such stepping back, alternative levels of focus may be selected, or the problem may take on a new definition. New intervention will also be generated.
6. *Recontract and Recycle:* Invite the consultee to recontract (entry). With a return to entry and recontracting, the consultant and consultee will employ the new data to again consider the problem at hand (problem identification) and the level of focus for the consultation process that appears to be needed. Once the level of focus has been selected, the additional information from the previous efforts will assist in clarifying the problem.

Practice, Practice, Practice

As the story is most often told, a young child interested in gaining directions asks a man, "How do I get to Carnegie Hall?" The man responded, "Practice, practice, practice!"

Perhaps the same prescription applies to each of us wondering how to ever feel comfortable and competent with this consultation paradigm. We need to practice, practice, practice. As a new paradigm or frame of reference for understanding presenting concerns and formulating approaches to working with those concerns, the model presented within this text may at first feel artificial and somewhat alien. With continued use it will become a more natural and comfortable part of your professional identify.

This text will conclude with two opportunities to practice. Two somewhat detailed cases will be presented for your consideration and guided practice. As you read the cases you are invited to mentally superimpose the stages of consultation and the tasks and concerns to be accomplished at each stage as a guide or framework from which to make meaning out of the data provided and direct your own decisions regarding the steps you would take in working with this case. In an attempt to assist with this application of the model, the first case is accompanied by a number of consultant reflection questions that may assist you in viewing the data through an integrated, multidimensional collaborative consultative paradigm.

As with many of the previous learning exercises, it is suggested that you not only work through these cases on your own, but that you share your conclusions, your insights, and your experience with a colleague or a mentor in order to benefit from the insight and experience of another. In Practice Case 1(Exercise 11-1), a school-based consultation regarding Ellen, a tenth-grade special education student, is presented. As you read through Practice Case 1 you will note questions a consultant may want to consider as he or she processes the information gathered, and conclusions drawn that in turn guide the consultant's decisions. It is this process of questioning, hypothesizing, and testing that should guide your own practice of consultation. Practice Case 2 (Exercise 11-2) is offered without these interjections so that the reader can begin to practice his or her own reflection and decision making.

EXERCISE 11-1   Practice with a School-Based Consultation

Original Referral

As the counselor for all tenth-grade students, you were given a referral by Dr. L. S. Jameson, the assistant principal. The referral requested that you see Ellen, a tenth-grader for whom he had some serious concerns. The referral read as follows:

Please see Ellen M. immediately! I am very concerned about her safety. I worked with Ellen quite a bit last year (because of her tendency to inappropriately talk out in class) and I thought we had a good relationship. Well, yesterday I bumped into her in the hall after school. I began to talk to her and noticed she looked upset. She wouldn't look me in the eye. When I asked her if something was wrong, she looked down said "No," and then stated she had "to get home, right away!" Physically, she looked fine to me, in fact she has lost some weight and looked as if she was giving more time to her hair and makeup. I know I don't have a lot to go on, just a feeling, and therefore I don't want to do anything official yet, but I think maybe she is being abused or doing drugs or something pretty serious. You need to check this out!

Consultant Reflections

- I don't know Ellen, other than seeing her in the hall. This is potentially very serious I need to respond quickly and see her.
- It appears that Dr. Jameson anticipates a provisional, direct service approach from the counseling office. I will need to see Ellen, but parallel to contact with her, contact and collaboration with Dr. Jameson. This is a good opportunity to introduce the collaborative, triadic nature of consultation by employing a client-focused consultation.
- I know Dr. Jameson at a professional level only. He seems to be a concerned educator. He seems to be concerned for the students, although he is generally presented in a negative light by the students. Perhaps that's because he is the disciplinarian.
- I have heard that he seems to want to step into the role of counselor when working with the students.
- Without any other indications (e.g., physical changes, behavioral changes, other teachers' reports) I wonder if Dr. Jameson is overreacting or responding to something else (perhaps lack of information or loss of objectivity).
- I want to see Ellen immediately, but go slow, and I want to go to see Dr. Jameson as soon as possible to propose how we can work together (collaborative consultation contract) and to begin to gather his perspective and cross validate it with my own information.
- I need to give him some immediate payoff (thank him for his concern and let him know about the meeting I scheduled with Ellen today).

- I need to reduce the cost of his talking with me. Dr. Jameson is always on the move, so rather than formally invite him to the office, or schedule to meet with him I think I'll go roam the halls to see if I can "spontaneously" connect with him.
- I must remember Dr. Jameson's tendency to want to probe into students' personal issues and watch for boundaries and confidentiality issues.
- I must remember that the entire school just went through extensive training on the laws and responsibility governing child abuse reporting, and there is a real heightened sensitivity right now, both regarding professional duties and anxiety regarding litigation issues. But I also wonder if that is what is happening here and that perhaps it is a matter for consultee-focused consultation.
- I need to gather additional information on Ellen. I'll check the records, speak with Dr. Jameson and others (i.e., the nurse, homeroom teacher, etc.) and interview her. I may want to observe either her social interactions with her peers or in a class.

Client (information gathered through review of the cumulative record, interview with Ellen, Dr. Jameson, and Ms. Blue, the resource room teacher).

Ellen is a 15-year-old student in the tenth grade. She has a Full Scale IQ WISC IV Score of 78 (Verbal IQ: 84; Performance IQ: 76). The school espouses adherence to the values and practice of inclusion (that is, providing all students with the needed education in the least restrictive environment). So, there are no special education classes within the school, although a resource room is available and some students are programmed into the room for individual assistance, as recommended by their subject teachers. Ellen has struggled through school since first grade. Up to this point her grades have generally been Ds and Cs. She has not failed any courses up to this point and is in fact on track to graduate. It has been very difficult, however, for her to keep up with the work, and it appears that it is getting harder as she progresses through high school.

In the ninth grade, after a review of her progress, she was assigned to work in the resource room for mathematics. Ellen was very upset with that decision and hated being assigned to what she called "the dummy room." However, through discussions with Dr. Jameson, she finally agreed, noting that while it may help her now, "she would get out of it—real quick!"

Ellen lives with her mother (an accountant), father (an elementary school teacher in a neighboring system), and a younger sister (age 8, grade 2). The family has been in this school district for eight years, having moved from neighboring state when Ellen was in second grade.

The counselor/consultant is new to the school this year and has had only superficial contacts (e.g., saying "Hi" in the hall) with Ellen. The initial contact with Ellen was somewhat strained. She presented as somewhat guarded and stated that "everything is fine . . . except for that dummy class!" Ellen stated that school is going okay, with the exception of resource room, which "(she) really hates." She stated that she feels like she is wasting her time in that "dummy room" and is totally embarrassed when she has to go there. In the interview Ellen stated that she "is not very popular and has only a very few good friends." She noted that she "would like more friends," but it isn't really bad since most of the students in her class seem to treat her in a friendly manner.

Ellen, while appearing guarded in her disclosure, maintained appropriate eye contact and generally demonstrated mature social behavior. When asked about home and her parents, she was quick to respond that "everything is fine." Ellen went on to share that she and her mom and dad had recently become members of the church choir and she is real excited

Continued

Continued

about singing in the choir and even began to think that she would like to go to college to become a music teacher. When questioned about drug or alcohol use, Ellen shared her feelings about how she believes that God gave her a body that she must care for, and that drugs, or excessive drinking, or even smoking cigarettes damages the body and as such she feels it is wrong. Her response appeared natural and genuine. She shared with the counselor that her mom and dad were going to come in to talk with the principal about moving her out of the resource room and she wanted to know if (the counselor) could help her with that.

Overall, while being a private person, Ellen appeared nondefensive about her family, her Christian values and church involvement, and her anti-drug stance. Further, she appeared healthy, well cared for, and gave no evidence of physical abuse.

Consultant Reflections

- Ellen is certainly private yet appears appropriate in her interaction with this new adult (i.e., the counselor).
- There is no evidence of abuse and she appears willing to have the principal and the counselor talk with her parents.
- Her church involvement appears to be developmentally appropriate and is nonsupportive of any drug involvement or family abuse.
- I am concerned about the issue of friends. I need to find out more about the extent of her social isolation both in school and perhaps at home to see if that is something with which I could be of assistance.
- I need to get a better feel for the resource room and the appropriateness of this placement. This may be the thing I can connect and contract with Ellen about.
- I need to try to establish a relationship with Ellen in order to help her develop realistic career goals.
- I need to try to share my observations with Dr. Jameson and try to better understand what it is he is sensing or seeing that I am not picking up.
- I wonder if Ellen's reaction to Dr. Jameson had something to do with the resource room. Was she angry at him? Maybe she was embarrassed knowing he knows she's in the "dummy class?"

Resource Room

Ellen has always had particular difficulties in math. She barely got Ds in her mathematics classes and although she might be expected to do better in the resource room setting, she is struggling just as much. Ellen is teamed with three other students in the resource room. They are doing word problems. The tasks for doing these problems entail: (1) Converting the written words into mathematical symbols and equations, (2) going to the board with answers, and (3) group work.

Ellen spends 90 minutes a day in the resource room with three other students. The teacher uses a token economy to keep the kids on task. While Ellen is able to function without this high level of external motivation, she is comfortable with it. The lighting in the room is dim, it is fairly noisy, and Ellen sits on the side of the class away from the window. She stated that she is accepted by the others in the class and is in fact somewhat looked up to as one of the smarter kids.

Ellen's teacher, Mrs. Blue, is the only resource room teacher in the school. She is generally liked by her students, but she is viewed as ineffective by parents and her peers. Most believe that while she is supportive and enthusiastic with the students, she lacks the skills to focus her students on task behavior. The implementation of the token economy came at the suggestion of the principal as a way to assist Mrs. Blue in keeping the students on task. However, Mrs. Blue feels that setting up and maintaining the economy has taken more energy than she suspected and she hasn't been able to attend to teaching the students as much as and the way that she should. Ellen is not particularly close to Mrs. Blue. In fact, she is not very trusting of most of the adults at school.

Mrs. Blue did state that Ellen is active in class and is the best student in the resource room. In fact, Mrs. Blue was questioning the value of Ellen's placement in the resource room. She felt that perhaps hooking Ellen up with a tutor would be a more effective way to help her with the mathematics. Mrs. Blue also noted that she was considering returning Ellen to her regular math class at the end of the marking period, although Dr. Jameson seems to be resistant to that idea. Mrs. Blue noted that each time she approached Dr. Jameson with the idea, he insisted that Ellen needs additional support.

Consultant Reflections

- Ellen's concerns about the inappropriateness of her placement seem supported by Mrs. Blue.
- Mrs. Blue's suggestion about returning Ellen to her regular classroom with the additional support of a tutor appears appropriate.
- What is Dr. Jameson reacting to? Does he know something I am still missing? Is something going on within him, perhaps interfering with his level of objectivity?
- Does Ellen know Dr. Jameson has been resisting her return to the regular class? If so, maybe that explains her reaction to him in the hall.

Consultee

Although Dr. Jameson made the referral and was willing to meet with the consultant, he appears curt in his dealings with the consultant. He assumes a negative physical stance toward the consultant, crossing his arms and appearing to be ready to walk away, not squaring his shoulders. When presented with the counselor's observations, he responded by saying, "Boy, you are green! She's got you snowed. I know her and there is definitely something serious going on here!" When informed that Ellen's mom and dad wanted to come in for a conference, Dr. Jameson appeared to become more agitated, stating, "You really don't expect that they are going to come in! They don't care." When asked to explain what he meant, Dr. Jameson simply stated, "I know their type."

The counselor found out that what appears to be antagonistic or belligerent style has been experienced by others (e.g., Mrs. Blue) but appears to be more noticeably directed to the counselors.

While he is fair with the kids, he is generally perceived by students and faculty as not very approachable or personable. According to Dr. Jameson, he worked with Ellen off and on throughout her ninth-grade experience. He expressed a sense of pride with the work he did, noting: "If it wasn't for me, she probably wouldn't have made it through the year." From Ellen's perspective, Dr. Jameson always treated her fairly, and while she has no interest in spending

Continued

Continued

time within him, she states that she does like him and he did help her. She feels that sometimes he gives her "too much attention," however.

Consultant Reflections

- Dr. Jameson appears to be defensive around the counselors and manifests that defensiveness by becoming abrasive and antagonistic.
- It appears that Dr. Jameson becomes defensive when directly confronted; I will need to continue to build referent and expert power, and use indirect forms of confrontation.
- Dr. Jameson does not appear to have many personal or professional relationships with the staff at school.
- Dr. Jameson is generally viewed in a negative light by the students since he is in the role as disciplinarian.
- Dr. Jameson appears to have success with Ellen both in terms of assisting her with a classroom problem and in developing a personal relationship.
- I wonder if Dr. Jameson has lost some professional objectivity in relation to Ellen and is overinvolved with being her caretaker. Or perhaps even concerned that if "she doesn't need his help," she won't call on him or continue to relate to him?

System Observations

The high school is in a supportive, white, middle-class rural community. The school is rather small (300 students for four grades), with a low teacher-to-student ratio. With so few in the school, most students know each other and each other's families. Most of the families whose children are in the school have lived in this community for generations. Further, most of the teachers and staff live in this community, with many having attended this school. The counselor and Dr. Jameson are the only two professional staff members who are not originally from this area.

The consultant is the first and only full-time counselor the school has had. Two teachers also work in the counseling department as 25 percent of their load. Prior to hiring the full-time counselor counseling was performed by part-time "teacher-counselors" and Dr. Jameson.

While the economy of the community is primarily agricultural, the mission of the school is to prepare students for post-secondary education. Most of the students go to college and most return to this environment to work and live.

Counselor Reflections

- As an outsider (to this community), I need to go slow and be sensitive to their culture and ways of doing things. Maybe being an outsider may elicit system and community resistance.
- Since I am the first full-time counselor, the faculty and administration are unclear about how the counselor should function. But being a small school they are used to collaborating. So a collaborative approach may be acceptable even though Dr. Jameson sent Ellen for direct service.
- To be effective I need to develop referent power with Dr. Jameson. Perhaps working on the issue of being "outsiders" and the difficulty involved in connecting with a closed, somewhat private community may give us some point of common reference.
- With Dr. Jameson's limited connections within the community at large and within the school community, is it possible he is using his relationship with Ellen as a way of establishing himself or meeting his own needs for relationship?

- With the focus on post–high school education, is Ellen feeling additional pressure to get out of the resource room? Is it possible that the resource room is a social stigma, as suggested by Ellen? If so, that may be an area for future systems-focused consultation.
- I would like to enter at the consultee-focused level of consultation, working with Dr. Jameson around possible loss of objectivity, while at the same time assisting him to find a balance between being the disciplinarian and the supportive administrator by demonstrating increased approachability to all students (and staff).
- I think being new to the setting, along with Dr. Jameson's apparent negativity toward counselors, that entering at the consultee-focused level may be difficult. Perhaps the first step is to redefine the process to be more collaborative, and he and I can work with Ellen around the issue of the resource room. Perhaps he would understand that, since that is something with which she wants help. It may serve as the means to get her to work with us and allow us to test the hypothesis regarding abuse or drug involvement.
- Further, by working with Dr. Jameson around Ellen's resource room concern, I may be able to provide some indirect confrontation (via modeling and parable presentations) to confront Dr. Jameson's perceptions of Ellen as needing to be rescued from a much larger issue.
- Working directly with Ellen on the issue of abuse and/or drug involvement appears ineffective, thus the original contract is closed. Attempt to reenter with Dr. Jameson around the new issue of Ellen's resource room placement, and redefine the service to be a collaborative working a the level of a client-focused consultation.
- At some point in the future I may want to see if I can reorganize the career counseling program and look at the way the resource room in utilized (system-focused consultation).

Case Postscript

Assuming that the relationship can be redefined from one of counselor provisional service to collaboration, and the focus of service can be redefined to be one of indirect consultation intervention at the client-focused level, then the process will proceed. The consultant in this case needs to clearly educate the consultee (Dr. Jameson) to the extended focus for the service being one of prevention and intervention and thus focusing on the role played by extrapersonal factors (including Dr. Jameson, the school environment, curriculum, etc.). The redefinition and recontracting will require that the consultant be extremely sensitive to the points of resistance both within the system and emanating from Dr. Jameson, and be attentive to developing a reduced-cost, immediately gratifying relationship with a balance of referent and expert power.

EXERCISE 11-2   Practice with a Business-Based Consultation

Directions: Below you will find the initial referral and additional data collected by the consultant. As you read the case, consider each of the following questions:

1. What are the expectations regarding the consultant's role and job definition? Do the expectations, the job contract, place limits on the things the consultant is free to do?
2. What unique system factors must be considered as a means of reducing system resistance?
3. What unique consultee variables or factors must be considered and responded to in order to reduce consultee resistance to collaborative consultation? What special relationship

Continued

Continued

considerations should I be aware of in order to develop and maintain a collaborative consultee relationship?

4. What appears to be the optimal level for consultation intervention? (i.e., client-focused, consultee-focused, system-focused).

5. What is the feasible level of consultation at this time? If different from the optimal, what elements prevent it from operating at the optimal level? What steps can be initiated to move to recontracting at the optimal level at a later time?

6. What is the specific focus for consultation intervention (i.e., problem definition)?

7. What intervention techniques or strategies appear appropriate and possible for this problem?

8. How will I know that the consultation was successful, both in outcomes and process, and how could I demonstrate that success to the consultee or others?

Original Referral

You are the human resource person for a small (100 employees) manufacturing company. John, the manager of the product development division of your company comes to you because of a problem he is having with one of his department members, Alan, one of his product engineers.

As John explains to you, Alan is a product development engineer. Over the last 2 months he has missed several very important deadlines. His failure to keep to schedule has totally disrupted product development deadlines and in one instance forced our company to miss a new products show. Further, when Alan has been given some corrections to make on a product design, he often either fails to implement the changes or makes changes on his own that were not requested. The end product was not only incorrect, but was also not up to the company's quality standards. The CEO is getting on John's case about the delays and missed deadlines and he is afraid his "head is going to roll if something isn't done." He wants you to either straighten Alan out, or tell him (John) what he has to do to "fire this clown" without running into legal problems.

> **Consultant Reflections** (e.g., special concerns, hot points, hypotheses? consultee expectations? crisis level? etc.) _____
>
> _____
> _____
> _____

The System

You, John, and Alan work for W & C Johnson Manufacturing Enterprises. The company was originally established in 1945 by two brothers, William and Charles Johnson. Not only was the firm successful, but it cornered the market for the production of fabric die casts by the 1980s. The company's product was used by most textile manufacturers in the world.

In 1990, the brothers decided to semi-retire. What was previously a two-man form of governance changed and the brothers instituted a number of separate departments (e.g., product development, marketing, customer service, production, finances, and personnel). For each of these departments, they selected a manager and "empowered" these managers to run the business on a daily basis. They continued to oversee the yearly plans and monthly statistics and they retained the power to make all final decisions.

Recently the company has been losing business to smaller, more cost-efficient firms. It appears that over the course of the last five years a number of significant changes in technology have occurred and the company has not kept pace, nor has it retooled its own production procedures to incorporate this faster and less costly technology. The Johnson brothers, not understanding the loss in business, attribute it to the incompetent managers they chose to run the business. As a result, they are coming to work more often and intervening in day-to-day operations, often acting impulsively and reactively. Their actions most often cause delays and interruptions in the manufacturing processes, since they are not completely aware of the process that has been put into place. Further, they have placed much more pressure on management and over the course of the past two years, and the brothers have become quick to remove a manager when a problem emerges. The feeling at the management level is one of apprehension, tension, and limited job security. This "threatening" atmosphere is quite new to the company, starting with the reconfiguration following the brothers' "retirement." Prior to the brothers' retirement, the firm had always valued employee loyalty and prided itself on low turnover and the philosophy that employees took precedence over profit.

> **Consultant Reflections** (e.g., system factors that may be contributing to Alan's behavior. John's response? Points of possible resistance? Opportunities for systems-focused consultation, on this problem or other potential problems? etc.) _____
> _____
> _____
> _____

Consultee

John has been manager of the product development division for the past six months. Prior to his promotion, John worked for the past six years as a product engineer for the company. His father had worked for the firm years ago and was both an asset to the company and a close friend of the two brothers. Prior to his promotion, John had worked with Alan as peers on many of the product development projects. John has had no management experience prior to this, and finds it difficult to be confrontational and directive with Alan and the other members of his division.

As John noted, even though managers have been let go, very few employees (below management) have been terminated at the company. John is worried how it will look if he is the first manager to fire someone and he is hoping that you can change Alan's current work behavior.

Up to this point, John has taken no real steps to confront Alan about his job performance. John said he tried to motivate Alan by sending him notes and reminders, "you know, things like . . . hope the project is almost completed; remember the deadline is tomorrow at 5 PM." He stated that he even "tries to let him know that we are losing business and with that new house of his he needs to be concerned about what that might mean."

John made it very clear that he doesn't want to be an ogre or a bad guy: "Gads, I'm really just a product engineer. I know all those guys and I have worked with Alan since I got here. So I don't want to come across like Mr. Big Shot. In fact, I always kid with them that if we don't shape up, it could be pink slips all around."

> **Consultant Reflections** (possible limited skill, knowledge, objectivity? Areas of resistance to collaborative consulting? Openings for establishing a collaborative relationship? etc.)
> _____
> _____
> _____

Continued

Continued

Client

Even though the division uses a matrix approach to resource allocation—that is, each engineer is project manager for his or her project and each is then empowered to assign work to the draft pool, CAD operators, and even, when needed, other engineers. Alan, because of seniority (having worked with the company for the longest time, seven years) is viewed as the senior engineer and all projects are first given to him for distribution to the specific project manager. Alan has had a very good job history, being one of the most creative and productive engineers in the division. In fact, many people felt that Alan would be the one selected to head up the division, rather than John.

Six months ago, Alan and his wife purchased a home in the suburbs and while they are thrilled with the move, it has placed a significant strain on their budget. Alan has two children, ages 7 and 4, and he just found out that his wife is pregnant with their third child. To help bring in extra money to maintain their lifestyle, Alan has begun to freelance some independent projects, working at home late at night and on weekends.

Although lucrative, this extra work is draining his energy reserves and he has become short-tempered and lethargic, both at home and at work. Alan often complains of headaches and nausea, which results in his calling in sick. His doctor believes that Alan has developed severe allergies to dust, mold, and animal hair.

As part of the new realignment of the company, all managers were moved away from the actual manufacturing and design activities and placed in offices located on the third floor. The product development division is located in the renovated basement of the three-story building. The work space for the product development division is new (having been only created within the last eight months), bright, and open. Each engineer, draftsperson, or CAD operator has his or her own desk, but the desks are spread out in one large open room, not separated by any walls or doors. As a result privacy is quite low, and noise level is quite high.

Communication between John, as manager, and the rest of the division is most often via numerous memos delivered by way of John's new secretary.

Consultant Reflections (e.g., reconfigure problem in terms of interaction of person-task-setting. Unique characteristics of Alan, unique task or setting demands and how they may interact with Alan's characteristics? Level of emergency or crisis? Point of least resistance to innovation and client change, etc.)_____

_____

_____

_____

Summary

While consultation is a dynamic process that takes shape in response to the unique characteristics of the participants and the nature of the task at hand, it can be conceptualized as developing through a series of stages, each involving a number of a specific tasks or focus points. The current chapter briefly discussed the tasks to be achieved at each of the following consultation stages:

- Entry (both system and consultee)
- Problem Identification (level of consultation: client-focused, consultee-focused, system-focused)

- Problem Definition
- Intervention
- Evaluation
- Closure

    Although the stages were presented as somewhat discrete, static points in the consultation process, it must be remembered that in practice the process of consultation is active, and therefore will not occur in a neat, invariant, static order, but will move back and forth across the various stages.

    The chapter emphasized the need to practice implementing the knowledge and skills outlined in the text, and concluded with the presentation of two cases. In the first case, the reader is provided with both the case material and the consultant's internal and guiding concerns. It was suggested that as the reader reviews the second case, he or she should employ similar internal reflections to guide himself or herself through the consulting process.

A Concluding Thought: Not an End, but a Beginning!

Throughout the text, various methods and strategies for diagnosing problems, engaging in consultation relationships, and implementing intervention strategies have been discussed. It must be emphasized, however, that as with other forms of helping, it is the quality of the person, the helper, or in this case, the consultant that is far more important than any skill or strategy. As a skilled, effective consultant, it is essential that one be first and foremost an authentic, ethical, and caring helper.

    While this is the end of this text, it is really only the beginning of an ongoing and continuing process of becoming a skilled, effective, and ethical consultant. There is and will always be much more to learn, much more to practice, if one is to truly be a skilled consultant.

Bibliography

Abidin, R. A. (1972). A psychosocial look at consultation and behavior modification. *Psychology in the Schools, 9,* 358–364.

Abidin, R. A., Jr. (1975). Negative effects of behavior consultation: "I know I ought to but it hurts too much." *Journal of School Psychology, 13,* 51–56.

Albee, G. W. (1967). The relation of conceptual models to manpower needs. In E. L. Cowen, E. A. Gardner, & M. Zax (Eds.), *Emergent Approaches to Mental Health Problems.* New York: Appleton-Century-Crofts.

Alberti, R. E., & Emmons, M. L. (1978). *Your perfect right: A guide to assertive behavior* (3rd ed.). San Luis Obispo, CA: Impact.

Albrecht, K. (1982). *Organizational development: A total systems approach to positive change in any business organization.* Englewood Cliffs, NJ: Prentice-Hall.

Alderfer, C. P., & Brown, L. D. (1975). *Learning from changing: Organizational diagnosis and development.* Beverly Hills, CA: Sage.

Altrocchi, J. (1972). Mental health consultation. In S. E. Golann & C. Eisdorfer (Eds.), *Handbook of community mental health.* Englewood Cliffs, NJ: Prentice-Hall.

American Association for Counseling and Development. (1983). *Ethical Standards.* Alexandria, VA: Author.

American Association for Counseling and Development. (1988). *Ethical Standards* (Rev. ed.). Alexandria, VA: Author.

American Psychological Association. (1990). *Guidelines for providers of psychological services to ethnic and culturally diverse populations.* Washington, DC: Author.

American Psychological Association. (1992). Ethical principles of psychologists and code of conduct. *American Psychologist, 47,* 1597-1611.

American School Counselor Association. (1990). *Professional development guidelines for elementary school counselors: Self audit.* Alexandria, VA: Author.

Anderson, C. M., & Stewart, S. (1983). *Mastering resistance: A practical guide to family therapy.* New York: Guilford Press.

Anderson, T. K., Kratochwill, T. R., & Bergan, J. R. (1986). Training teachers in behavioral consultation and therapy: An analysis of verbal behavior. *Journal of School Psychology, 24,* 229–241.

Aplin, J. C. (1978). Structural change versus behavioral change. *The Personnel and Guidance Journal, 56,* 407–411.

Apter, S. J. & Conoley, J. C. (1984). *Childhood behavior disorder and emotional disturbance.* Englewood Cliffs, NJ: Prentice Hall.

Argyle, M. (1967). *The psychology of interpersonal behavior.* Baltimore: Penguin.

Argyris, C. (1970). *Intervention theory and method: A behavioral science view.* Reading, MA: Addison-Wesley.

Argyris, C. (1982). *Interpersonal competence and organizational effectiveness.* Homewood, IL: Dorsey.

Argyris, C. (1990). *Overcoming organization defenses: Facilitating organizational learning.* Boston: Allyn & Bacon.

Argyris, C. (1991). Overcoming client-consultant defensive routines that erode credibility: A charge for the 90's. *Consulting Psychologist Bulletin, 43,* 30–35.

Armenakis, A. A., & Burdg, H. B. (1988). Consultation research: Contributions to practice and directions for improvement. *Journal of Management, 14(2),* 339–365.

Aronson, E. (1980). Communication in sensitivity-training groups. In E. Aronson (Ed.), *The Social Animal*. New York: W. H. Freeman.

Aronson, E., Willerman, B., & Floyd, J. (1966). The effects of a pratfall on increasing interpersonal attraction, *Psychonomic Science, 4,* 227–228.

Artise, J. (1984, June). Management development in the United States: A new era in human resources development. Paper presented at World Congress on Management Development, London, England.

Asbury, F. R. (1984). The empathy treatment. *Elementary School Guidance and Counseling, 18,* 181–187.

Atkinson, D. R. (1983). Ethnic similarity in counseling psychology: A review of the research. *The Counseling Psychologist, 11(3),* 73–92.

Atkinson, D. R., Morten, G., & Sue, D. W. (1979). *Counseling American minorities: A cross-cultural perspective.* Dubuque, IA: Brown.

Aubrey, R. F. (1969). Consultation, school interventions, and the elementary counselor. *The Personnel and Guidance Journal, 56(6),* 351–354.

Augsburger, D. W. (1992). Cross cultural pastoral psychotherapy. In R. Wicks & R. D. Parsons, *Clinical handbook of pastoral counseling* (Vol. II) (pp. 129–143). Mahwah, NJ: Paulist Press.

Aurora, S. L. (1988). No tickee, no shirtee: Proverbial speech and leadership in academe. In M. O. Jone, M. D. Moore, & R. C. Snyder (Eds.), *Inside organizations: Understanding the human dimension* (pp. 179–189). Newbury Park, CA: Sage.

Austin, A. E., Rice, R. E., & Splete, A. P. (1991). *The academic workplace audit.* Washington, DC: Council of Independent Colleges.

Bakker, C. B. (1975). Why people don't change. *Psychotherapy Theory, Research and Practice, 12(2),* 164.

Bandler, R., & Grinder, J. (1982). *Reframing.* Moab, UT: Real People Press.

Bandura, A. (1977). Self-efficacy: Toward a unifying theory of behavioral change. *Psychological Review, 84,* 191–215.

Bandura, A. (1982). Self-efficacy mechanisms in human agency. *American Psychologist, 37,* 344–358.

Barak, A., Patkin, J., & Dell, D. M. (1982). Effects of certain counselor behaviors on perceived expertness and attractiveness. *Journal of Counseling Psychology, 29(3),* 261–267.

Barley, S. R. (1986). Technology as an association of structuring: Evidence from observations of CT scanners and the social order of radiology departments. *Administrative Science Quarterly, 31,* 78–108.

Barra, R. (1983). *Putting quality circles to work.* New York: McGraw Hill.

Bartunek, J., & Moch, M. (1987). First-order, second-order and third-order change and organizational development interventions: A cognitive approach. *The Journal of Applied Behavioral Science, 23(4),* 483–500.

Bartunek, J. M., & Louis, M. R. (1988). The interplay of organization development and organization transformation. In W. A. Pasmore & R. W. Woodman (Eds.), *Research in organizational change and development* (Vol. 2) (pp. 97–134). Greenwich, CT: JAI press.

Bates, R. J. (1987). Corporate culture, schooling and educational administration. *Educational Administration Quarterly, 23(4),* 79–115.

Bateson, G. (1935). Culture contact and schizomogenesis. *Man, 35,* 178–185.

Bateson, G. (1958). *Noven* (2nd ed.). Stanford, CA: Stanford University Press.

Beck, A. T., & Emery, G. (1979). *Cognitive therapy of anxiety.* Philadelphia: Center for Cognitive Therapy.

Beckhard, R. (1969). *Organization development: Strategies and models.* Reading, MA: Addison-Wesley.

Beckhard, R., & Harris, R. T. (1977). *Organizational transitions: Managing complex change* (1st ed.). Reading, MA: Addison-Wesley.

Beer, M. (1976). The technology of organizational development. In M. D. Dunnette (Ed.), *Handbook of industrial and organizational psychology.* Chicago: Rand McNally.

Beer, M. (1980). *Organization change and development: A system view.* Glenview, IL: Scott, Foresman.

Beer, M., Eisenstat, R. E., & Spector, B. (1990). *The critical path to corporate renewal.* Boston, MA: Harvard Business School Press.

Beer, M. & Spector, B. (1993). Organizational diagnosis: Its role in organizational learning. *Journal of Counseling & Development, 71,* 642–650.

Beer, M., & Walton, A. E. (1987). Organizational change and development. *Annual Review of Psychology, 38,* 339–369.

Beisser, A., & Green, R. (1972). *Mental health consultation and education.* Palo Alto, CA: National Press Books.

Bellack, A. S., Hersen, M., & Kazdin, A. E. (Eds.). (1990). *International handbook of behavior modification and therapy.* New York: Plenum Press.

Bennett, C. I. (1990). *Comprehensive multicultural education: Theory and practice* (2nd ed.). Boston: Allyn & Bacon.

Bennis, W. G. (1969). *Organizational development: Its nature, origins and prospects.* Reading, MA: Addison-Wesley.

Bennis, W. G. (1973). Theory and method in applying behavioral science to planned organizational change. In A. Bartlett & T. Kayser (Eds.), *Changing organizational behavior.* Englewood Cliffs, NJ: Prentice-Hall.

Bennis, W. G., Benne, K. D., & Chin, R. (Eds.). (1969). *The planning of change.* New York: Holt, Rinehart & Winston.

Berenson, B. G., & Carkhuff, R. R. (1967). *Source of gain in counseling and psychotherapy.* New York: Holt, Rinehart & Winston.

Bergan, J. R. (1977). *Behavioral consultation.* Columbus, OH: Charles E. Merrill.

Bergan, J. R., & Kratochwill, T. R. (1990). *Behavioral consultation and therapy.* New York: Plenum.

Bergan, J. R. & Tombari, M. L. (1976a). The analysis of verbal interactions occurring during consultation. *Journal of School Psychology, 13,* 209, 226.

Bergan, J. R. & Tombari, J. L. (1976b). Consultant skill and efficiency and the implementation and outcomes of consultation. *Journal of School Psychology, 14,* 3–14.

Beutler, L. E., Crago, M., & Arezmendi, T. G. (1986). Research on therapist variables in psychotherapy. In S. L. Garfield & A. E. Bergin (Eds.), *Handbook of psychotherapy and behavior change* (3rd ed.). New York: Wiley.

Blake, R. R., & Mouton, J. S. (1976). *Consultation.* Reading, MA: Addison-Wesley.

Block, P. (1981). *Flawless consulting.* San Diego, CA: Pfeiffer & Comp.

Bloom, B. L. (1973). *Community mental health: A historical and critical analysis.* Morristown, NJ: General Learning Press.

Borum, F., & Pedersen, J. S. (1990). Understanding the IT people, the subcultures and the implications for management of technology. In F. Borum, A. L. Friedman, M. Monsted, J. S. Pedersen, & M. Risberg (Eds.), *Social dynamics of the IT field: The case of Denmark* (pp. 105–120). Berlin: Walter de Gruyter.

Botti, H., & Pipan, T. (1991). Civil servant, service idea? Paper presented to the 8th International SCOS conference, Copenhagen, Denmark.

Brack, G., Jones, E. S., Smith, R. M., White, J., & Brack, C. J. (1993). A primer on consultation theory: Building a flexible worldview. *Journal of Counseling & Development, 71,* 619–628.

Brammer, L. M. (1988). *The helping relationship.* Englewood Cliffs, NJ: Prentice-Hall.

Brammer, L. M., Shostrom, E. L., & Abrego, P. J. (1989). *Therapeutic psychology: Fundamentals of counseling and problem-solving skills.* New York: Haworth Press.

Brehm, J. W. (1966). *A theory of psychological reactance.* New York: Academic Press.

Brehm, J. W. (1972). *Responses to loss of freedom: A theory of psychological reactance.* Morristown, NJ: General Learning Press.

Brehm, J. W., & Cohen, A. R. (1962). *Explorations in cognitive dissonance.* New York: Wiley.

Brehm, S. S. (1976). *The application of social psychology to clinical practice.* New York: Wiley.

Brown, D. (1985). The preservice training and supervision of consultants. *The Counseling Psychologist, 13,* 410–425.

Brown, D. (1987). A systematic view of psychological consultation in schools. *Canadian Journal of Counseling, 21,* 114–124.

Brown, D., Kurpius, D. J., & Morris, J. R. (1988). *Handbook of consultation with individuals and small groups.* Alexandria, VA: Association for Counselor Education and Supervision.

Brown, D., Pryzwansky, W. B., & Schulte, A. C. (1987). *Psychological consultation: Introduction to the theory and practice.* Boston: Allyn & Bacon.

Brown, D., Pryzwansky, W. B., & Schulte, A. C. (1991). *Psychological consultation: Introduction to theory and practice* (2nd ed.). Needham Heights, MA: Allyn & Bacon.

Brown, D., & Schulte, A. C. (1987). A social learning model of consultation. *Professional Psychology: Research and Practice, 18,* 283–287.

Brown, D., Spano, D. B., & Schulte, A. C. (1988). Consultation training in master's level counselor education programs. *Counselor Education and Supervision, 27(4),* 323–330.

Brown, D., & Srebalus, D. J. (1988). *Introduction to the counseling profession.* Englewood Cliffs, NJ: Prentice-Hall.

Brown, D., Wyne, M. D., Blackburn, J. E., & Powell, W. C. (1979). *Consultation: Strategy for improving education.* Boston, MA: Allyn & Bacon.

Brown, V. B. (1983). Implementing block grants in mental health services: How consultants can help. *Consultation, 3(1),* 27–31.

Bundy, M. L., & Poppen, W. A. (1986). School counselors' effectiveness as consultants: A research review. *Elementary School Guidance and Counseling, 2,* 215–221.

Burns, D. (1981). *Feeling good.* New York: Signet Books.

Burrello, L. C. & Reitzug, U. C. (1993). Transforming context and developing culture in schools. *Journal of Counseling & Development, 71,* 669–677.

Campbell, D. (1992). The school counselor as consultant: Assessing your aptitude. *Elementary School Guidance and Counseling, 21,* 215–221.

Canter, L. (1989). Assertive discipline—More than names on the board and marbles in a jar. *Phi Delta Kappan, 71(1),* 41–56.

Canter, L., & Canter, M. (1976). *Assertive discipline: A take charge approach for today's educator.* Los Angeles: Lee Canter and Associates.

Caplan, G. (1951). A public health approach to child psychiatry. *Mental Hygiene, 35,* 235–249.

Caplan, G. (Ed.). (1955). *Emotional problems of early childhood.* New York: Basic Books.

Caplan, G. (1963). Types of mental health consultation. *American Journal of Orthopsychiatry, 3,* 470–481.

Caplan, G. (1964). *Principles of preventive psychiatry.* New York: Basic Books.

Caplan, G. (1970). *The theory and practice of mental health consultation.* New York: Basic Books.

Caplan, G., & Caplan, R. (1993). *Mental health consultation and collaboration.* San Francisco: Jossey-Bass.

Carkhuff, R. R. (1986). *The art of helping video series* (Tapes 2 and 3). Amherst, MA: Human Resources Development Press.

Carkhuff, R. R. (1987). *The art of helping VI.* Amherst, MA: Human Resources Resource Development Press.

Carkhuff, R. R., & Berenson, B. G. (1977). *Beyond counseling and therapy.* New York: Holt, Rinehart & Winston.

Casas, J. M. (1984). Policy, training and research in counseling psychology: The racial/ethnic minority perspective. In S. D. Brown & R. W. Lent (Eds.), *Handbook of counseling psychology* (pp. 785–831). New York: Wiley.

Casey, P., & Critchley, B. (1984, June) Second thoughts on team building. Paper presented at World Congress on Management Development, London, England.

Cautela, J. R. (1978). *Relaxation: A comprehensive manual for adults, children and children with special needs.* Champaign, IL: Research Press.

Chamberlain, P., Patterson, G., Reid, J., Kavanagh, K., & Forgatch, M. (1984). Observation of client resistance. *Behavior Therapy, 15,* 144–155.

Chandler, S. M. (1985). Mediation: Conjoint problem solving. *Social Work,* July-August, 346–349.

Chin, R., & Benne, K. D. (1969). General strategies for effecting change in human systems. In W. G. Bennis, K. D. Benne, & R. Chin (Eds.), *The planning of change* (2nd ed.), New York: Holt, Rinehart & Winston.

Cienki, J. A. (1982). An exploration of expert and referent power in consultation with elementary school teachers. Unpublished doctoral dissertation, School of Education, University of Pennsylvania.

Claiborn, C. D. (1982). Interpretation and change in counseling. *Journal of Counseling Psychology, 29,* 439–453.

Cohen, W. A. (1985). *How to make it big as a consultant.* New York: AMACOM.

Comas-Diaz, L., & Griffith, E. (1988). *Clinical guidelines in cross-cultural mental health.* New York: Wiley-Interscience.

Connor, P. E., & Lake, L. K. (1988). *Managing organizational change.* New York: Praeger.

Conoley, J. C. (1981). Emergent training issues in consultation. In J. C. Conoley (Ed.), *Consultation in schools: Theory, research, and procedures.* New York: Academic Press.

Conoley, J. C., & Conoley, C. W. (1982). *School consultation: A guide to training and practice.* New York: Pergamon Press.

Conoley, J., & Conoley, C. (1988). Useful theories in school-based consultation. *Remedial and Special Education, 9,* 14–20.

Cook, L. (1991). Preparing teachers to participate in collaborative activities. Unpublished manuscript, cited in M. Friend & L. Cook (1992). *Interactions: Collaboration skills for school professionals.* White Plains, NY: Longman.

Cook, L., & Friend, M. (1991). Principles for the practice of collaboration in schools. *Preventing School Failure, 35,* 6–9.

Cooper, S. E., & O'Connor, R. M., Jr. (1993). Standards for organizational consultation assessment and evaluation instruments. *Journal of Counseling & Development, 71,* 651–660.

Cormier, W. H., & Cormier, L. S. (1985). *Interviewing strategies for helpers: Fundamental skills and cognitive behavior interventions* (2nd ed.), Monterey, CA: Brooks/Cole.

Cormier, W. H., & Cormier, L. S. (1991). *Interviewing strategies for helpers* (3rd ed.). Pacific Grove, CA: Brooks/Cole.

Crego, C. A., & Crego, M. W. (1983). A training/consultation model of crisis intervention with law enforcement officers. In W. A. Cohen & C. D. Claiborn, (Eds.), *Crisis intervention.* New York: Human Services Press.

Crowfoot, J. E., & Chesler, M. A. (1974). Contemporary perspectives on planned social change: A comparison. *Journal of Applied Behavioral Science, 10(3),* 278–303.

Curtis, M., & Meyers, J. (1985). Best practices in school-based consultation: Guidelines for effective practice. In A. Thomas & J. Grimes (Eds.), *Best practices in school psychology* (pp. 79–94). Kent, OH: National Association of School Psychologists.

Curtis, N.J., & Zins, J. E. (Eds.) (1981). *The theory and practice of school consultation.* Springfield, IL: Charles C. Thomas.

Davis, J. M., & Hartsough, C. S. (1992). Assessing psychosocial environment in mental health consultation groups. *Psychology in the Schools, 29,* 224–228.

Davis, J. M., & Sandoval, J. (1991). A pragmatic framework for systems-oriented consultation. *Journal of Educational and Psychological Consultation, 2(3),* 201–216.

Deal, T. E., & Kennedy, A. A. (1982). *Corporate culture: The rites and rituals of corporate life.* Reading, MA: Addison-Wesley.

Deal, T. E., & Peterson, K. D. (1990). *The principal's role in shaping school culture.* Washington, DC: U.S. Department of Education, Office of Educational Research and Improvement.

DeMeuse, K., & Liebowitz, S. (1981). An empirical analysis of team building research. *Group and Organization Studies, 6(3),* 357–378.

Deutsch, A. (1946). *The mentally ill in America.* New York: Columbia University Press.

Deutsch, M. (1973). *The resolution of conflict.* New Haven, CT: Yale University Press.

Dinkmeyer, D., & Carlson, J. (1973a). *Consultation.* New York: Wiley.

Dinkmeyer, D., & Carlson, J. (1973b). *Consulting: Facilitating human potential and change processes.* Columbus, OH: Merrill.

Dixon, D. N., & Dixon, D. E. (1993). Research in consultation: Toward better analogues and outcome measures. *Journal of Counseling & Development, 7,* 700–702.

Dobbs, R. F., Primm, E. B., & Primm, B. (1991). Mediation: A common sense approach to resolving conflicts in education. *Focus on Educating Children,* Oct., 1–11.

Dorr, D. (1977). Some practical suggestions on behavioral consulting with teachers. *Professional Psychology, 8,* 96–102.

Dougherty, A. M. (1990). *Consultation: Practice and perspectives.* Pacific Grove, CA: Brooks/Cole.

Dougherty, A. M. (1992). Ethical issues in consultation. *Elementary School Guidance and Counseling, 26,* 214–220.

Dougherty A. M., Dougherty, L. P., & Purcell, D. (1991). The sources and management of resistance to consultation. *The School Counselor, 38,* 178–185.

Downing, J., & Downing, S. (1991). Consultation with resistant parents. *Elementary School Guidance and Counseling, 25,* 296–301.

Drucker, P. F. (1985). The discipline of innovation. *The Harvard Business Review, May/June,* 68–72.

Dunn, K., & Dunn, R. (1987). Dispelling outmoded beliefs about student learning. *Educational Leadership, 44(6),* 55–63.

Dunn, R., Beaudry, J. S., & Klavas, A. (1989). Survey of research on learning styles. *Educational Leadership, 47(7),* 50–58.

Dustin, D., & Ehly, S. (1992). School consultation in the 1990s. *Elementary School Guidance and Counseling, 26,* 165–175.

Dyer, W. G., Jr. (1985). The cycle of cultural evolution in organizations. In R. Kilmann, M. Saxton, R.

Serpa, & associates (Eds.), *Higher education: Handbook of theory and research* (Vol. II)(pp. 85–102). New York: Agathon.

D'Zurilla, T. J., & Nezu, A. M. (1987). The Heppner and Krauskopf approach: A model of personal problem solving and social skills? *Counseling Psychologist, 15,* 463–470.

Eberlein, L. (1987). Introducing ethics to beginning psychologists: A problem-solving approach. *Professional Psychology: Research and Practice, 18,* 353–359.

Eckerson, L. O. (1971). The White House conference: Tips or taps for counselors? *Personnel and Guidance Journal, 50,* 167–174.

Egan, G. (1977). *You and me: The skills of communicating and relating to others.* Pacific Grove, CA: Brooks/Cole.

Egan, G. (1990). *The skilled helper.* Belmont, CA: Brooks/Cole.

Ekstrand, R. E., & Edminister, P. (1984, October). Mediation: A process that works. *Exceptional Children,* 163–167.

Elliot, S. N. (1988a). Acceptability of behavioral treatment in education settings. In J. C. Witt, S. N. Elliott, & F. M. Gresham (Eds.), *Handbook of behavior therapy in education* (pp. 121–150). New York: Plenum Press

Elliot, S. N. (1988b). Acceptability of behavioral treatments: Review of variables that influence treatment selection. *Professional Psychology: Research and Practice, 19,* 68–80.

Ellis, A. (1974). *Disputing irrational beliefs (DIBS).* New York: Institute for Rational Living.

Ellis, A., & Grieger, R. (Eds.). (1986). *Handbook of rational-emotive therapy* (Vols.1–2). New York: Springer.

Ellis, A., & Harper, R. A. (1975). *A new guide to rational living.* North Hollywood, CA: Wilshire Books.

Erchul, W. P. (1987). A relational communication analysis of control in school consultation. *Professional School Psychology, 2,* 113–124.

Erchul, W. P. (1992). On dominance, cooperation, teamwork, and collaboration in school-based consultation. *Journal of Educational and Psychological Consultation, 3(4),* 363–366.

Erchul, W. P., Hughes, J. N., Meyers, J., Hickman, J. A., & Braden, J. P. (1992). Dyadic agreement concerning the consultation process and its relationship to outcome. *Journal of Educational and Psychological Consultation, 3(2),* 119–132.

Erickson, F. (1987). Conceptions of school culture: An overview. *Educational Administration Quarterly, 23(4),* 11–24.

Ericson, P. M., & Rogers, L. E. (1973). New procedures for analyzing relational communications. *Family Process, 12,* 245–267.

Eysenck, H. (1952). The effects of psychotherapy: An education. *Journal of Consulting Psychology, 16,* 319–324.

Fannibanda, D. K. (1976). Ethical issues in mental health consultation. *Professional Psychology, 7,* 547–552.

Ferguson, M. (1980). *The aquarian conspiracy: Personal and social transformation in the 1980s.* Los Angeles: J. P. Tarcher.

Ferris, P. A., & Linville, M. E. (1985). The child's rights: Whose responsibility? *Elementary School Guidance and Counseling, 19,* 172–180.

Festinger, L. A. (1957). *A theory of cognitive dissonance.* Evanston, IL: Row, Peterson.

Fiedler, F. E., & Garcia, J. E. (1985). Comparing organization development and management training. *Personnel Administrator, 30,* 35–37.

Finney, M., & Mitroff, I. (1986). Strategic planning failures: The organization as its own worse energy. In H. P. Sims (Ed.), *The Thinking Organization* (pp. 317–335). San Francisco: Jossey-Bass.

Fisher, R., & Ury, W. (1981). *Getting to yes: Negotiating agreement without giving in.* Boston: Houghton Mifflin.

Fitzgerald, L. F., & Nutt, R. (1986). The Division 17 principles concerning the counseling/psychotherapy of women: Rationale and implementation. *The Counseling Psychologist, 14,* 180–216.

Frank, J. D., Hoehn-Saric, R., Imber, S.D., Liberman, B.L., & Stone, A. R. (1978). *Effective ingredients of successful psychotherapy.* New York: Brunner/Mazel.

French, J. R. P., Jr., & Raven, B. (1959). The bases of social power. In D. Cartwright (Ed.), *Studies in social power.* Ann Arbor: University of Michigan Institute of Social Research.

French, W. L., & Bell, C. H., Jr. (1990). *Organization development* (4th ed.). Englewood Cliffs, NJ: Prentice-Hall.

French, W. L., & Hollmann, R. W. (1975). Management by Objectives: The team approach. *California Management Review, 17(3),* 13–22.

Frey, D. H., & Raming, H. E. (1979). A taxonomy of counseling goals and methods. *Personnel and Guidance Journal, 58,* 26–33.

Friend, M. & Bauwens, J. (1988). Managing resistance: An essential consulting skill for learning disabilities teachers. *Journal of Learning Disabilities, 21(9),* 556–561.

Friend, M., & Cook, L. (1988). Pragmatic issues in school consultation. In J. F. West (Ed.), *School consultation: Interdisciplinary perspectives on theory, research, training and practice.* Austin: Research and Training Project on School Consultation, University of Texas.

Friend, M., & Cook, L. (1990). Collaboration as a predictor for success in school reform. *Journal of Educational and Psychological Consultation, 1(1),* 69–86.

Friend, M., & Cook, L. (1992). *Interactions: Collaboration skills for school professionals.* New York: Longman.

Froehle, T. C., & Rominger, R. L. (1993). Directions in consultation research: Bridging the gap between science and practice. *Journal of Counseling & Development, 71,* 693–699.

Fuchs, D., Fuchs, L. S., Dulan, J., Roberts, H., & Fernstrom, P. (1992). Where is the research on consultation effectiveness? *Journal of Educational and Psychological Consultation, 3(2),* 151–174.

Fuqua, D. R., & Gibson, G. (1980). An investigation of factors related to the durability of organizational innovations in human service systems. Paper presented at the annual convention of the American Psychological Association, Montreal, Canada.

Fuqua, D. R., & Kurpius, D. J. (1993). Conceptual models in organizational consultation. *Journal of Counseling & Development, 71,* 607–618.

Fuqua, D. R., & Newman, J. C. (1985). Individual consultation. *The Counseling Psychologist, 13,* 390–395.

Gagliardi, P. (Ed.). (1990). *Symbols and artifacts: Views of the corporate landscape.* Berlin: Walter de Gruyter.

Gallessich, J. (1974). Training the school psychologist for consultation. *Journal of School Psychology, 12,* 138–149.

Gallessich, J. (1982). *The profession and practice of consultation.* San Francisco: Jossey-Bass.

Gallessich, J. (1985). Toward a meta-theory of consultation. *The Counseling Psychologist, 13,* 336–354.

Gardner, R. A. (1972). *Dr. Gardner's stories about the real world.* Englewood Cliffs, NJ: Prentice Hall.

Gelenberg, A. J., Bassuk, E. L., & Schoonover, S. C. (Eds.). (1991). *The practitioner's guide to psychoactive drugs.* New York: Plenum Medical Book Co.

Gelso, C. J., & Fretz, B. R. (1992). *Counseling psychology.* New York: Harcourt Brace Jovanovich.

Gerson, R. F. (1984). *The right vitamins.* Chicago: Contemporary Books.

Gibb, J. R. (1968). The counselor as a role-free person. In C. A. Parker (Ed.), *Counseling theories and counselor education.* Boston: Houghton Mifflin.

Gibb, J. R. (1978). *Trust: A new view of personal and organizational development.* Los Angeles: The Guild of Tutors Press.

Gibson, G., & Froehle, T. C. (1991). Empirical influences on organizational consultation. *Consulting Psychology Bulletin, 43,* 13–22.

Goldstein, A. P., Glick, B., Zimmerman, D., & Coultry, T. M. (1987). *Aggression replacement training.* Champaign, IL: Research Press.

Golembiewski, R., Proehl, C., & Sink, D. (1981). Success of OD applications in the public sector: Toting up the score for a decade, more or less. *Public Administration Review, 41,* 679–682.

Goode, C. B. (1992). *The mind fitness program for esteem and excellence: Guided stories for imagery in whole-brain learning.* Tucson, AZ: Zephyr Press.

Graden, J. L., Casey, A., & Bonstrom, O. (1985). Implementing a prereferral intervention system: Part II, the data. *Exceptional Children, 51,* 487–496.

Gresham, F. M. (1991). Moving beyond statistical significance in reporting consultation outcome research, *Journal of Educational and Psychological Consultation, 2(1),* 1–13.

Gresham, F. M., & Kendell, G. K. (1987). School consultation research: Methodological critique and future research directions. *School Psychology Review, 16,* 306–316.

Grieger, R. M. (1972). Teacher attitudes as a variable in behavior modification consultation. *Journal of School Psychology, 10,* 279–287.

Grieger, R., & Boyd, J. (1980). *Rational-emotive therapy: A skills-based approach.* New York: Van Nostrand Reinhold.

Gross, D. R., & Robinson, S. E. (1985). Ethics: The neglected issue in consultation. *Journal of Counseling and Development, 64,* 38–41.

Gurman, A. S. (1977). The patient's perception of the therapeutic relationship. In A. Gurman & A. Razin (Eds.), *Effective psychotherapy: A handbook of research.* New York: Pergamon.

Gutkin, T. (1980). Teacher perceptions of consultation services provided by school psychologists. *Professional Psychology, 11,* 637–642.

Gutkin, T. B., & Hickman, J. A. (1990). The relationship of consultant, consultee, and organizational characteristics to consultee resistance to school-based consultation: An empirical analysis. *Journal of Educational and Psychological Consultation, 1(2),* 111–122.

Guzzo, A., Jette, R. D., & Katzell, R. A. (1985). The effects of psychologically based intervention programs on worker productivity: A meta-analysis. *Personal Psychology, 38(2),* 275–291.

Hackman, J. R., Oldham, G. R., Janson, R., & Purdy, D. (1975). A new strategy for job enrichment. *California Management Review, 17,* 57–70.

Hackman, J. R., & Oldham, G. R. (1980). *Work redesign.* Reading, MA: Addison-Wesley.

Hackney, H., & Cormier, L. S. (1988). *Counseling strategies and interventions* (3rd ed.). Englewood Cliffs, NJ: Prentice-Hall.

Hale-Benson, J. E. (1986). *Black children: Their roots, culture and learning styles* (Rev. ed.). Baltimore: Johns Hopkins University Press.

Hall, E. T. (1966). *The hidden dimension.* Garden City, NY: Doubleday.

Hall, E. T. (1968). Proxemics. *Current Anthropology, 9,* 83–108.

Hall, E. T. (1976, July). How cultures collide. *Psychology Today,* 122–127.

Hampson, P. J., Marks, D. F., & Richardson, J. T. E. (Eds.) (1990). *Imagery: Current developments.* New York: Routledge.

Hanna, R. (1986). Personal meaning: A conceptual framework for organizational consultation. *Consultation, 5,* 24–40.

Hansen, J. C., Himes, B. S., & Meier, S. (1990). *Consultation concepts and practices.* Englewood Cliffs, NJ: Prentice Hall.

Harris, A. B., & Harris, T. A. (1985). *Staying OK.* New York: Harper & Row.

Harrison, R. (1970). Choosing the depth of organizational intervention. *Journal of Applied Behavioral Science, 6,* 181–202.

Hatch, M. J. (1993). The dynamics of organizational culture. *Academy of Management Review, 18(4),* 657–693.

Havelock, R. G. (1973). *The change agent's guide to innovation in education.* Englewood Cliffs, NJ: Educational Technology Publications.

Hawryluk, M., & Smallwood, D. (1986). Assessing and addressing consultee variables in school-based behavioral consultation. *School Psychology Review, 15,* 519–528.

Hein, E. C. (1980). *Communications in nursing practice* (2nd ed.). Boston: Little, Brown.

Heisler, W. J., & Shivley, R. W. (1980). Creative products: Intergroup conflict resolution. In J. E. Jones & J. W. Pfeiffer (Eds.), *The 1980 annual handbook for group facilitators.* La Jolla, CA: University Associates.

Hermansson, G. L., Webster, A. C. & McFarland, K. (1988). Counselor deliberate postural lean and communication of facilitative conditions. *Journal of Counseling Psychology, 35,* 149–153.

Hersey, P., & Blanchard, K. H. (1988). *Management of organizational behavior* (5th ed.). Englewood Cliffs, NJ: Prentice Hall.

Highlen, P. S., & Hill, C. E. (1984). Factors affecting client change in individual counseling: Current status and theoretical speculations. In S. Brown, & R. Lent (Eds.), *Handbooks of counseling psychology* (pp. 334–396). New York: Wiley.

Hinkle, A., Silverstein, B., & Walton, D. M. (1977). A method for the evaluation of mental health consultation in the public schools. *Journal of Community Psychology, 5,* 263–265.

Hollander, E. P. (1960). Competence and conformity in the acceptance of influence. *Journal of Abnormal and Social Psychology, 61,* 365–370.

Homans, G. C. (1950). *The human group.* New York: Harcourt Brace Jovanovich.

Hord, S. M. (1986). A synthesis of research on organizational collaboration. *Educational Leadership, 44,* 22–26.

Horton, G. E., & Brown, D. (1990). The importance of interpersonal skills in consultee-centered consultation: A review. *Journal of Counseling & Development, 68,* 423–426.

Huczynski, A. (1987). *Encyclopedia of organizational change methods.* Brookfield, VT: Gower Publishing.

Huefner, D. S. (1988). The consulting teacher model: Risks and opportunities. *Exceptional Children, 54,* 403–414.

Hughes, J. N. (1986). Ethical issues in school consultation. *School Psychology Review, 15,* 489–499.

Hughes, J. N. (1988). *Cognitive behavior therapy with children in schools.* New York: Plenum Press.

Hughes, J. N., & Falk, R. S. (1981). Resistance, reactance and consultation. *Journal of School Psychology, 19(2),* 134–141.

Huse, E. F. (1978). Organization development. *The Personnel and Guidance Journal, 56,* 64–74.

Hutchins, D. E., & Cole, C. G. (1992). *Helping relationships and strategies.* Belmont, CA: Brooks/Cole.

Idol, L., Nevin, A., & Paolucci-Whitcomb, P. (1986). *Models of curriculum-based assessment.* Austin, TX: PRO-ED.

Idol, L., Paolucci-Whitcomb, P., & Nevin, A. (1986). *Collaborative consultation.* Rockville, MD: Aspen.

Idol, L., & West, J. F. (1987). Consultation in special education (Part II): Training and practice. *Journal of Learning Disabilities, 20(8),* 474–497.

Ivey, A. E., & Gluckstern, N. (1976). *Basic attending skills: Participants manual.* Amherst, MA: Microtraining Associates.

Ivey, A. E. (1988). *Intentional interviewing and counseling* (2nd ed.). Pacific Grove, CA: Brooks/Cole.

Jackson, D. N., & Hayes, D. H. (1993). Multicultural issues in consultation. *Journal of Counseling & Development, 72(2),* 144–147.

James, M., & Jongeward, D. (1971). *Born to win: Transactional analysis with Gestalt experiments.* Reading, MA: Addison-Wesley.

Johnson, D. W., & Johnson, F. P. (1987). *Joining together: Group theory and group skills* (3rd ed.). Englewood Cliffs, NJ: Prentice-Hall.

Julien, R. M. (1992). *A primer of drug action: A concise, nontechnical guide to the actions, uses and side effects of psychoactive drugs.* New York: W. H. Freeman.

Kanfer, F. H., & Goldstein, A. P. (Eds.). (1991). *Helping people change: A textbook of methods* (4th ed.). Boston: Allyn & Bacon.

Karp, H. B. (1984). Working with resistance. *Training and Development Journal, 38(3),* 69–73.

Kast, K., & Kahn, R. L. (1978). *The social psychology of organizations.* New York: Wiley.

Kast, K., & Rosenzweig, J. E. (1974). *Organization and management: A systems approach.* New York: McGraw-Hill.

Kazdin, A. E. (1981). Acceptability of child treatment techniques: The influence of treatment efficacy and adverse side effects. *Behavior Therapy, 12,* 493–506.

Kazdin, A. E. (1989). *Behavior modification in applied settings* (4th ed.). Pacific Grove, CA: Brooks/Cole.

Kellogg, D. (1984). Contrasting successful and unsuccessful OD consultation relationships. *Group & Organization Studies, 9,* 151–176.

Kelly, J. (1982). *Social-skills training: A practical guide for interventions.* New York: Springer.

Kenton, S. B. (1989). Speaker credibility in persuasive business communication: A model which explains gender differences. *Journal of Business Communication, 26,* 143–157.

Killman, R. H. (1985). A complete program for organizational success. *Consultation, 4,* 316–330.

Knoff, H. M., McKenna, A. F., & Riser, K. (1991). Toward a consultant effectiveness scale: Investigating the characteristics of effective consultants. *School Psychology Review, 20(1),* 81–96.

Knoff, H. M., McKenna, A. F., & Riser, K. (1991). *Behavioral consultation in applied settings: An individual guide.* New York: Plenum.

Kolb, D. A., & Froham, A. L. (1970). An organizational development approach to consulting. *Solan Management Review, 12,* 51–65.

Kopel, S., & Arkowitz, H. (1975). The role of attribution and self-perception in behavior change: Implication for behavior therapy. *Genetic Psychology Monographs, 92,* 175–212.

Krasner, L., & Ullman, L. (Eds.). (1965). *Research in behavior modification.* New York: Holt, Rinehart & Winston.

Kratochwill, T. R. (1991). Defining constructs in consultation research: An important agenda in the 1990s. *Journal of Educational and Psychological Consultation, 2,* 291–294.

Kratochwill, T. R., & Bergan, J. R. (1990). *Behavioral consultation in applied settings: An individual guide.* New York: Plenum Press.

Kratochwill, T. R., & van Someren, K. (1985). Barriers to treatment success in behavioral consultation. *Journal of School Psychology, 23,* 225–239.

Krehbiel, L. E., & Strange, C. C. (1991). "Checking the truth": The case of Earlham College. In G. Kuh & J. Schuh (Eds.), *The role and contributions of student affairs at involving colleges* (pp. 148–167). Washington, DC: National Association of Student Personnel Administrators.

Krumboltz, J. D. (1966). Behavioral goals for counseling. *Journal of Counseling Psychology, 13,* 153.

Kuehlwein, K. T., & Rosen, H. (Eds.). (1993). *Cognitive therapies in action: Evolving innovative practice.* San Francisco: Jossey-Bass.

Kuehnel, T. G., & Kuehnel, J. M. (1983). Consultation training from a behavioral perspective. In J. Alpert & J. Meyers (Eds.), *Training in consultation.* Springfield, IL: Charles C. Thomas.

Kuh, G. (1993). Appraising the character of a college. *Journal of Counseling and Development, 71,* 661–667.

Kuh, G. D., Schuh, J. H., Whitt, E. J., Andreas, R. E., Lyons, J. W., Strange, C. C., Krehbiel, L. E., & MacKay, K. A. (1991). *Involving colleges: Successful approaches to fostering student learning and development outside the classroom.* San Francisco, CA: Jossey-Bass.

Kuh, G. D. & Whitt, E. J. (1988). The invisible tapestry: Culture in American colleges and universities. *AAHE-ERIC/Higher Education Report, No.1.* Washington, DC: American Association for Higher Education.

Kurpius, D. J. (1978). Consultation theory and process: An integrated model. *The Personnel and Guidance Journal, 56,* 335–338.

Kurpius, D. J. (1985). Consultation interventions: Successes, failures and proposals. *The Counseling Psychologist, 13,* 368–389.

Kurpius, D. J. (1993). Fundamental issues in defining consultation. *Journal of Counseling & Development, 71,* 598–600.

Kurpius, D. J., Brack, G., Brack, C. J., & Dunn, L. B. (1993). Maturation of systems consultation: Subtle issues inherent in the model. *Journal of Mental Health Counseling, 15(4),* 414–429.

Kurpius, D. J., & Fuqua, D. R. (1993). Introduction to the speed issues. *Journal of Counseling and Development, 71,* 596–697.

Kurpius, D. J., Fuqua, D. R., & Rozecki, T. (1991). The power of consultants' conceptual thinking: Paradigms, models and processes. *Consulting Psychologist Bulletin, 43,* 2–12.

Kurpius, D. J., Fuqua D. R., & Rozecki, T. (1993). The consulting process: A multidimensional approach. *Journal of Counseling & Development, 71,* 601–606.

Kurpius, D. J., & Robinson, S. E. (1978). An overview of consultation. *The Personnel and Guidance Journal, 56,* 321–323.

Kutzik, A. J. (1977). The medical field. In F. W. Kaslow & Associates, *Supervision, consultation and staff training in the helping professions.* San Francisco: Jossey-Bass.

LaClave, L., & Brack, G. (1989). Reframing to deal with patient resistance. *American Journal of Psychotherapy, 43,* 68–75.

Lambert, N. M. (1973). The school psychologist as a source of power and influence. *Journal of School Psychology, 11,* 245–250.

Lambert, N. M. (1974). A school based consultation model. *Professional Psychology, 5,* 267–276.

Lang, A. J. (1976). *Responsible assertive behavior: Cognitive/behavioral procedures for trainers.* Champaign, IL: Research Press.

Lazarus, A. (1971). *Behavior therapy and beyond.* New York: McGraw-Hill.

Lazarus, A. (1981). *The practice of multimodal therapy.* New York: McGraw Hill.

Lazarus, A. (1989). *The practice of multimodal therapy.* (2nd ed.). Baltimore: John Hopkins University Press.

Lazarus, A. A., & Fay, A. (1982). Resistance or rationalization? A cognitive-behavioral perspective. In P. L. Wachtel (Ed.), *Resistance: Psychodynamic and behavioral approaches* (pp. 115–132). New York: Plenum.

Lee, C. C., & Richardson, B. L. (Eds.). (1991). *Multicultural issues in counseling: New approaches to diversity.* Alexandria, VA: American Association for Counseling and Development.

Leonard, P. Y., & Gottsdanker-Willekens, A. E. (1987). The elementary school counselor as consultant for self-enhancement. *The School Counselor, 34,* 245–255.

LeShan, E. J. (1972). *What makes me feel this way? Growing up with human emotions.* New York: Macmillan.

Levinson, H. (1991). Diagnosing organizations systematically. In M. F. R. Kets de Vries & Associates (Eds.), *Organizations on the couch* (pp. 45–48). San Francisco: Jossey-Bass.

Levitt, E. E. (1963). Psychotherapy with children: A further evaluation. *Behavior Research and Therapy, 1,* 45–51.

Lewin, K. (1951). *Field theory in social science.* New York: McGraw-Hill.

Lewin, K. (1958). Group decisions and social change. In E. E. Maccobby, T. M. Newcomb, & E. L. Hartley, *Readings in social psychology.* New York: Holt, Rinehart & Winston.

Lewin, K. (1969). Quasi-stationary social equilibria and the problem of permanent change. In W. G. Bennis, K. D. Benne, & R. Chin (Eds.), *The planning of change.* New York: Holt, Rinehart & Winston.

Lippitt, G. (1982, August). Developing HRD and OD, the profession and the professional. *Training and Development, 36,* 67–74

Lippitt, R., & Lippitt, G. (1978). *The consulting process in action.* La Jolla, CA: University Associates.

Lippitt, R., Watson, J., & Wesley, B. (1958). *The dynamics of planned change.* New York: Harcourt, Brace, World.

Lundberg, C., & Finney, M. (1987). Emerging models of consultancy. *Consultation, 6,* 32–42.

Lusebrink, V. B. (1990). *Imagery and visual expression in therapy.* New York: Plenum Press.

Maeroff, G. I. (1988). *The empowerment of teachers: Overcoming the crisis of confidence.* New York: Teachers College Press.

Magnotta, O. H. (1991). Looking beyond tradition. *Language, Speech and Hearing Services in Schools, 22,* 150–151.

Mahoney, M. J. & Thorensen, C. E. (1974). *Self-control: Power to the person.* Pacific Grove, CA: Brooks/Cole.

Mannino, F., & Shore, M. (1975). The effects of consultation: A review of empirical studies. *American Journal of Community Psychology, 3,* 1–21.

Mannino, F. V., Trickett, E. J., Shore, M. F., Kidder, M. G., & Levin, G. (1986). *Handbook of mental health consultation.* (DHSS Publication No. ADM 86–1446). Rockville, MD: U.S. Department of Health and Human Services.

Margolis, H., & McGettigan, J. (1988). Managing resistance to instructional modifications in mainstreamed environments. *Remedial and Special Education, 9(4),* 15–21.

Margulies, N., Wright, P., & Scholl, R. (1977). Organization development techniques: Their impact on change. *Group & Organization Studies, 2,* 428–448.

Martin, R. (1978). Expert and referent power: A framework for understanding and maximizing consultation effectiveness. *Journal of School Psychology, 16(1),* 49–55.

Masland, A. T. (1985). Organizational culture in the study of higher education. *Review of Higher Education, 8(2),* 157–168.

McCarthy, M. M., & Sorenson, G. P. (1993). School counselors and consultants: Legal duties and liabilities. *Journal of Counseling & Development, 72(2),* 159–167.

McClelland, D. C. (1978). Managing motivation to expand human freedom. *American Psychologist, 33,* 201–210.

McClelland, D. C. (1989). How do self-attributed and implicit motives differ? *Psychological Review, 96,* 690–702.

McDaniel, S., Campbell, T., Wynne, L., & Weber, T. (1988). Family systems consultation. *Family Systems Medicine, 6,* 391–403.

McGregor, D. (1960). *The human side of enterprise.* New York: McGraw-Hill.

McGuire, W. J. (1969). The nature of attitudes and attitude change. In G. Lindzey & E. Aronson (Eds.), *The handbook of social psychology, 3.* Reading, MA: Addison-Wesley.

Medway, F. J. (1979). How effective is school consultation? A review of recent research. *Journal of School Psychology, 17,* 275–282.

Medway, F. J. (1982). School consultation research: Past trends and future directions. *Professional Psychology, 13,* 422–430.

Medway, F. J., & Updyke, J. (1985). Meta-analysis of consultation outcome studies. *American Journal of Community Psychology, 13,* 489–504.

Mehrabian, A. (1967). Orientation behaviors and nonverbal attitude communication. *Journal of Communication, 17,* 324–332.

Mehrabian, A. (1970). *Tactics of social influence.* Englewood Cliffs, NJ: Prentice-Hall.

Mehrabian, A., & Reed, H. (1969). Factors influencing judgments of psychopathology. *Psychological Reports, 24,* 323–330.

Meichenbaum, D. (1977). *Cognitive behavior modification: An integrative approach.* New York: Plenum.

Meichenbaum, D., & Turk, D.C. (1987). *Facilitating treatment adherence: A practitioner's guidebook.* New York: Plenum.

Mendel, W. M., & Solomon, P. (Eds.) (1968). *The psychiatric consultation.* New York: Grune & Stratton.

Mendoza, D. W. (1993). A review of Gerald Caplan's theory and practice of mental health consultation. *Journal of Counseling & Development, 71,* 629–635.

Menlo, A. (1982). Consultant beliefs which make a significant difference in consultation. In C. L. Warger & L. Aldinger (Eds.). *Preparing special educators for teacher consultation.* Toledo, OH: Preservice Consultation Project, College of Education and Allied Professions, University of Toledo.

Menninger, K. (1958). *Theory of psychoanalytic technique.* New York: Harper & Row.

Menzies Lyth, I. (1991). Changing organizations and individuals: Psychoanalytic insights for improving organizational health. In M. F. R. Kets de Vries & Associates (Eds.), *Organizations on the couch* (pp. 361–378). San Francisco: Jossey-Bass.

Merry, U., & Brown, G. (1987). *The neurotic behavior of organization.* New York: Gestalt Institute of Cleveland Press, Gardner Press.

Meyers, J. (1978). Resistance in teacher consultation: A relationship model. Paper presented at annual meetings of the National Association of School Psychologists, Houston, TX.

Meyers, J., Friedman, M. P., & Gaughan, E. J. (1975). The effects of consultee-centered consultation on teacher behavior. *Psychology in the Schools, 12,* 288–295.

Meyers, J., Friedman, M. P., Gaughan, E. J., & Pitt, N. (1978). An approach to investigate anxiety and hostility in consultee-centered consultation. *Psychology in the Schools, 15,* 292–296.

Meyers, J., Parsons, R. D., & Martin, R. (1979). *Mental health consultation in schools.* San Francisco: Jossey-Bass.

Michaels, M. (1989). The chaos paradigm. *Organizational Development Journal, 7(2),* 31–35.

Miller, E. J., & Rice, A. K. (1967). *Systems of organization.* London: Tavistock.

Miller, G. R. (1980). On being persuaded: Some basic distinctions. In M. E. Roloff, & G. R. Miller (Eds.), *New directions in theory and research* (pp.16–21). Beverly Hills, CA: Sage.

Miller, R. B. (1962). Analysis and specification of behavior for training. In R. Glaser (Ed.), *Training research and education: Science edition.* New York: Wiley.

Mills, E., & Brunner, J. (1988, March). Metaviews of learners: The counselor as mediator. *The School Counselor,* 284–289.

Mohrman, A. M., Jr., Mohrman, S. A., Ledford, G. E., Jr., Cummings, T., Lawler, E. E., III, & Associates. (1989). *Large-scale organizational change.* San Francisco: Jossey-Bass.

Moore, E., & Richter, D. (1981). *Personal styles analysis for educators.* Atlanta: Georgia State Department of Education, Guidance Counseling and Career Development Unit.

Moos, R. H. (1973). Conceptualization of human environments. *American Psychologists, 28,* 652–665.

Moos, R. H. (1974). *The social climate scales: An overview.* Palo Alto, CA: Consulting Psychologists Press.

Nadler, D. A. (1977). *Feedback and organization development: Using data based methods.* Reading, MA: Addison-Wesley.

Napier, R., & Gershenfeld, M. (1985). *Groups: Theory and experience* (3rd ed.). Boston, MA: Houghton Mifflin.

Napierkowski, C., & Parsons, R. (1995). Diffusion of innovation: Implementing change in school counselor roles and functions. *The School Counselor, 42,* 364–369.

Nevis, E. (1987). *Organizational consulting.* New York: Gestalt Institute of Cleveland Press, Gardner Press.

Newman, J. L. (1993). Ethical issues in consultation. *Journal of Counseling & Development, 72(2),* 148–156.

Newman, J. L., & Robinson, S. E. (1991). In the best interests of the consultee: Ethical issues in consultation. *Consulting Psychology Bulletin, 43,* 23–29.

Nezu, A., & D'Zurilla, T. J. (1981). Effects of problem definition and formulation on the generation of alternatives in social problem-solving process. *Cognitive Therapy and Research, 5,* 265–271.

Nigl, A. J. (1986). *Biofeedback and behavioral strategies in pain treatment.* New York: Pergamon Press.

Palmo, A. J., & Kuznian, J. (1972). Modification of behavior through group counseling and consultation. *Elementary School Guidance and Counseling, 6,* 258–262.

Parsons, R. (1985). The counseling relationship. In R. Wicks, R. Parsons, & D. Capps (Eds.), *Clinical handbook of pastoral counseling.* Mahwah, NJ: Paulist.

Parsons, R. (1995). *The skills of helping.* Needham Heights, MA: Allyn & Bacon.

Parsons, R. D., & Napierkowski, C. (1992). Counselor role and function. Paper presented at the annual meetings of the American Association for Counseling and Development, Baltimore, MD.

Parsons, R., & Meyers, J. (1984). *Developing consultation skills.* San Francisco: Jossey-Bass.

Parsons, R. D., & Wicks, R. J. (1983). *Passive aggression: Theory & practice.* New York: Brunner/Mazel.

Parsons, R., & Wicks, R. (1994). *Counseling strategies and intervention techniques for the human services.* Needham Heights, MA: Allyn & Bacon.

Pearl, A. (1974). The psychological consultant as a change agent. *Professional Psychology, 5,* 292–298.

Peca, K. (1992, April). Chaos theory: A scientific basis for alternative research methods in educational administration. Paper presented at the annual meeting of the American Educational Research Association, San Francisco, CA.

Pedersen, J. S. (1991). *Continuity and change: Central perspectives on organizational change and transformation in information technology firms.* (Ph.D. Series 2.91 Samfundslitteratur). Copenhagen, Denmark: Copenhagen Business School, Institute of Organization and Industrial Sociology.

Pedersen, J. S., & Sorensen, J. S. (1989). *Organizational culture in theory and practice.* Aldershot, England: Avebury & Gower.

Pelsma, D. M. (1987, January). Improving counselor effectiveness: Consulting with style. *The School Counselor,* 195–201.

Pennington, B. F. (1991). *Diagnosing learning disorders: A neuropsychological framework.* New York: Guilford Press.

Perls, F. (1969). *Gestalt therapy verbatim.* Lafayette, CA: Real People Press.

Peters, T. (1989). *Thriving on chaos.* New York: Harper Perennial.

Peters, T. J., & Waterman, R. H. (1982). *In search of excellence: Lessons from America's best-run companies.* New York: Harper & Row.

Pettigrew, A. (1979). On studying organizational cultures. *Administrative Science Quarterly, 24,* 570–581.

Pfeiffer, J. W., & Jones, J. E. (1977). Ethical considerations in consulting. In J. E. Jones & J. W. Pfeiffer (Eds.), *The 1977 annual handbook for group facilitations.* La Jolla, CA: University Associates.

Phillips, V., & McCullough, L. (1990). Consultation-based programming: Instituting the collaborative ethic in school. *Exceptional Children, 56(4),* 291–304.

Pierce, R. M., & Dragow, J. (1969). Nondirective reflection vs. conflict attention: An empirical evaluation. *Journal of Clinical Psychology, 25,* 341–342.

Piersel, W. C., & Gutkin, T. B. (1983). Resistance to school-based consultation: A behavioral analysis of the problem. *Psychology in the Schools. 20,* 311–320.

Pinto, R. F. (1981). Consultant orientations and client system perceptions: Styles of cross cultural consultation. In R. Lippett & G. Lippett (Eds.), *Systems thinking: A resource for organization diagnosis and intervention.* Washington, DC: International Consultants Foundation.

Polsgrove, L., & McNeil, M. (1989). The consultation process: Research and practice. *Remedial and Special Education, 10,* 6–13, 20.

Powell, G., & Posner, B. Z. (1978). Resistance to change reconsidered: Implications for managers. *Human Resources Management, 17,* 29–34.

Pryzwansky, W. B. (1974). Collaboration or consultation: Is there a difference? *Journal of Special Education, 11,* 179–182.

Pryzwansky, W. B. (1986). Indirect service delivery: Considerations for future research in consultation. *School Psychology Review, 15,* 479–488.

Pugach, M. C. (1988). The consulting teacher in the context of educational reform. *Exceptional Children. 55,* 273–275.

Pugach, M. C., & Johnson, J. L. (1988). Rethinking the relationship between consultation and collaborative problem solving. *Focus on Exceptional Children, 21(4),* 1–8.

Racker, H. (1968). *Transference and countertransference.* New York: Brunner-Mazel.

Raia, A. P. (1988). The consultant as conceptual therapist. *Consultation, 7,* 34–37.

Randolph, D. L. (1985). *Microconsulting: Basic psychological consultation skills for helping professionals.* Johnson City, TN: Institute of Social Sciences and Arts.

Randolph, D. L., & Graun, K. (1988). Resistance to consultation: A synthesis for counselor-consultants. *Journal of Counseling & Development, 67,* 182–184.

Rappaport, H., & Rappaport, M. (1981). The integration of scientific and traditional healing. *American Psychologist, 36(7),* 774–781.

Raven, B. H. (1965). Influence on power. In I. D. Steiner & M. Fishbein (Eds.), *Current studies in social psychology.* New York: Holt, Rinehart and Winston.

Reddin, W. J. (1984, June). *Management development in the United States: A new era in human resources development.* Paper presented at the World Congress on Management Development, London, England.

Reger, R. (1964–65). The school psychologist and the teacher: Effective professional relationships. *Journal of School Psychology, 3,* 13–18.

Reik, T. (1948). *Listening with the third ear.* New York: Grove Press.

Reimers, T., Wacker, D. P., & Koeppl, G. (1987). Acceptability of behavioral interventions: A review of the literature. *School Psychology Review, 16,* 212–227.

Remley, T. P., Jr. (1993). Consultation contracts. *Journal of Counseling & Development, 72(2),* 158–159.

Ridley, C. R., & Mendoza, D. W. (1993). Putting organizational effectiveness into practice: The preeminent consultation task. *Journal of Counseling & Development, 72(2),* 168–177.

Ritter, D. (1978). Effects of a school consultation program upon referral patterns of teachers. *Psychology in the Schools, 15,* 239–243.

Robinson, E. H., & Wilson, E. S. (1987). Counselor-led human relations training as a consultation strategy. *Elementary School Guidance and Counseling. 22,* 124–131.

Robinson, S. E., & Gross, D. R. (1985). Ethics of consultation: The Centreville ghost. *The Counseling Psychologist, 13,* 444–465.

Rockwood, G. F. (1992). Edgar Schein's process versus content consultation models. *Journal of Counseling & Development, 71,* 636–638.

Roethlisberger, F., & Dickson, W. (1939). *Management and the worker.* Cambridge, MA: Harvard University Press.

Rogawski, A. S. (Ed.). (1979). *New directions for mental health services: Mental health consultation in community settings* (No.3). San Francisco: Jossey-Bass.

Rogers, C. R. (1951). *Client-centered therapy.* Boston: Houghton Mifflin.

Rogers, C. R. (1957). The necessary and sufficient conditions of therapeutic personality change. *Journal of Consulting Psychology 21,* 95–103

Rogers, C. R. (1961). *On becoming a person.* Boston: Houghton Mifflin.

Rogers, E. M., & Shoemaker, F. F. (1971). *Communication of innovations.* New York: Free Press.

Rosenfield, S. (1987). *Instructional consultation.* Hillsdale, NJ: Erlbaum.

Rosenfield, S. (1985). Teacher acceptance of behavior principles. *Teacher Education and Special Education, 8,* 153–158.

Ross, F. J. (1993). Peter Block's flawless consulting and the homunculus theory: Within each person is a perfect consultant. *Journal of Counseling & Development, 71,* 639–641.

Ross, J., & Ross, W. (1982). *Japanese quality circles and productivity.* Reston, VA: Reston Publishing.

Russell, M. L. (1978). Behavioral consultation. *Personnel and Guidance Journal, 56(6),* 346–350.

Sandoval, J., Lambert, N., & Davis, J. M. (1977). Consultation from the consultee's perspective. *Journal of School Psychology, 15,* 334–342.

Sazaki, N., & Hutchins, D. (1984). *The Japanese approach to product quality: Its applicability to the West.* New York: Pergamon.

Schein, E. H. (1969). *Process consultation: Its role in organization development.* Reading, MA: Addison-Wesley.

Schein, E. H. (1978). The role of the consultant: Content expert or process facilitator? *Personnel and Guidance Journal, 56(6),* 346–350.

Schein, E. H. (1981). Does Japanese management style have a message for American managers? *Sloan Management Review, 23(1),* 55–68.

Schein, E. H. (1983). The role of the founder in creating organizational culture. *Organizational Dynamics, 12(1),* 13–28.

Schein, E. H. (1984). Coming to a new awareness of organizational culture. *Sloan Management Review, 25(2),* 3–16.

Schein, E. H. (1985). *Organizational culture and leadership.* San Francisco: Jossey-Bass.

Schein, E. H. (1987). *The clinical perspective in fieldwork.* Newbury Park, CA: Sage.

Schein, E. H. (1989). Process consultation as a general model of helping. *Consulting Psychology Bulletin, 41,* 3–15.

Schein, E. H. (1990). Organizational culture. *American Psychologist, 45,* 109–119.

Schein, E. H. (1991). Process consultation. *Consulting Psychology Bulletin, 43,* 16–18.

Schein, E. H. (1993). Legitimating clinical research in the study of organizational culture. *Journal of Counseling & Development, 71,* 703–708.

Schmuck, R. A. & Miles, M. B., (Eds.). (1971). *Organization development in the schools.* Palo Alto, CA: National Press Books.

Schmuck, R. A., & Runkel, P. J. (1985). *The handbook of organizational development in schools* (3rd ed.). Palo Alto, CA: Mayfield.

Schowengerdt, R. V., Fine, M. J., & Poggio, J. P. (1976). An examination of some bases of teacher satisfaction with school psychological services. *Psychology in the Schools, 13,* 269–275.

Schroeder, M. (1991). *Fractals, chaos, power laws.* New York: Freeman.

Schutz, W. (1967). *The interpersonal underworld.* New York: Science and Behavior Books.

Schutz, W. (1989). *Firo-B.* Palo Alto, CA: Consulting Psychologists Press.

Scott, J. (1990). Survey on the status of school counseling in Pennsylvania. Paper presented at Pennsylania school Counselor Association Conference, Pittsburgh, PA

Seligman, M. (1975). *Helplessness: On depression, development and death.* San Francisco: W. H. Freeman.

Senge, P. M. (1990). *The fifth discipline: The art and practice of the learning organization.* New York: Doubleday.

Shechter, R. A. (1987). Shared experthood: The working alliance in organization consultation: A psychoanalytic perspective. *Dynamic Psychotherapy, 5,* 30–46.

Shelby, A. N. (1986). Theoretical bases of persuasion. *Journal of Businesss Communication, 25,* 5–29.

Sherif, M., & Hovland, C. (1961). *Social judgment: Assimilation and contrast effects in communication and attitude change.* New Haven: Yale University Press.

Sibley, S. (1986). A meta-analysis of school consultation research. Unpublished doctoral dissertation, Texas Woman's University, Denton.

Simons, A.D., Lustman, P. J., Wetzel, R.D., & Murphy, G. E. (1985). Predicting response to cognitive therapy of depression: The role of learned resourcefulness. *Cognitive Therapy and Research, 9(10),* 79–89.

Smith, J. C. (1990). *Cognitive-behavioral relaxation training: A new system of strategies for treatment and assessment.* New York: Springer.

Snow, D. L., & Gersick, K. E. (1986). Ethical and professional issues in mental health consultation. In F. V. Mannino, E. J. Trickett, M. F. Shore, M. G. Kidder, & G. Levin (Eds.), *Handbook of mental health consultation* (pp. 393–431). Rockville, MD: NIMH.

Solomon, J., (1991, December 29). Executive blindness latest consultants focus. *Boston Globe,* pp. a23, a24.

Splete, H., & Bernstein, B. (1981). A survey of consultation training as a part of counselor education program. *The Personnel and Guidance Journal, 59,* 470–472.

Stoltenberg, D.C. (1993). Supervising consultants in training: An application of a model of supervision. *Journal of Counseling & Development, 72,* 131–143.

Stroh, P. (1987). Purposeful consulting. *Organizational Dynamics, 16,* 49–67.

Strong, S. R. (1978). Social psychological approach to psychotherapy research. In S. L. Garfield & A. E. Bergin (Eds.), *Handbook of psychotherapy and behavior change* (2nd ed.). New York: Wiley.

Sue, D. W. (1981). *Counseling the culturally different.* New York: Wiley.

Sue, D. W. (1991). A conceptual model for cultural diversity training. *Journal of Counseling & Development, 70,* 99–105.

Sue, D. W., Arredondo, P., & McDavis, R. J. (1992). Multicultural counseling competencies and standards: A call to the profession. *Journal of Counseling & Development, 70,* 477–486.

Sue, D. W., & Sue, D. (1977a). Barriers to effective cross-cultural counseling. *Journal of Counseling Psychology, 24,* 420–429.

Sue, D. W,. & Sue, D. (1977b). Barriers to effective cross-cultural counseling. *Journal of Counseling Psychology, 24,* 420–429.

Sue, D. W., & Sue, D. (1990). *Counseling the culturally different: Theory and practice.* New York: Wiley.

Suzuki, B. H. (1983). The education of Asian and Pacific Americans: An introductory overview. In D. Nakaniski & M. Hirano-Nakanishi (Eds.), *The education of Asian and Pacific Americans: Historical perspectives and prescriptions for the future.* Phoenix, AZ: Oryz Press.

Taylor, F. W. (1911). *The principles of scientific management.* New York: Harper & Row.

Terpstra, D. E. (1982). Evaluating selected organizational development interventions: The state of the art. *Group and Organization Studies, 7,* 402–417.

Tharp, R. G. (1989). Psychocultural variables and constants: Effects on teaching and learning in schools. *American Psychologist, 44,* 349–359.

Thibaut, J. W. & Kelley, H. H. (1959). *The social psychology of groups.* New York: Wiley.

Thomas, K. W., & Kilmann, R. H. (1974). *Thomas-Kilmann conflict mode instrument.* Tuxedo, NY: Xicom.

Thompson, R. (1992). *School counseling and renewal: Strategies for the twenty-first century* (pp. 123–143). Muncie, IN: Accelerated Development.

Tichy, N. M. (1983). How different types of change agents diagnose organizations. *Human Relations, 23,* 771–779.

Tindal, G., & Pendergast, S. (1989). A taxonomy for objectively analyzing the consultation process. *Remedial and Special Education, 10(2),* 6–16.

Tindall, G., Parker, R., & Hasbrouck, J. E. (1992). The construct validity of stages and activities in the consultation process. *Journal of Education and Psychological Consultation, 3(2),* 99–118.

Tingstrom, D. H., Little, S. G., & Stewart, K. J. (1990). School consultation from a social psychological perspective: A review. *Psychology in the Schools, 27,* 41–50.

Tjosvold, D. (1987). Participation: A close look at its dynamics. *Journal of Management, 13,* 739–750.

Torbert, W. (1985). On-line reframing. *Organizational Dynamics, 14(1),* 60–79.

Torrance, E. P. (1986). Teaching creative and gifted learners. In M. Wittrock (Ed.), *Handbook of research on teaching* (3rd ed.). New York: Macmillan.

Truax, C. B., & Carkhuff, R. R. (1965). The experimental manipulation of therapeutic conditions. *Journal of Consulting Psychology, 29,* 119–224.

Turner, B. A. (Ed.). (1990). *Organizational symbolism.* Berlin: Walter de Gruyter.

Van Maanen, J., & Barley, S. R. (1985). Cultural organization: Fragments of a theory. In P. Frost, L. Moore, M. Louis, C. Lundberg, & J. Martin (Eds.), *Organizational culture* (pp. 31–54). Beverly Hills, CA: Sage.

Vasquez, J. A. (1990). Teaching to the distinctive traits of minority students. *The Clearing House, 63,* 299–304.

Wachtel, P. (Ed.). (1982). *Resistance: Psychodynamic and behavioral approaches.* New York: Plenum

Warwick, D., & Kelman, H. (1973). Ethical issues in social intervention. In G. Zaltman (Ed.), *Processes and phenomena of social change* (pp. 477–417). New York: Wiley Interscience.

Waterman, R. H., Jr., Peters, T. J., & Phillips, J. R. (1980). Structure is not organization. *Business Horizon, 23,* 14–26.

Watson, G. (1971). Resistance to change. *American Behavioral Scientist, 14,* 745–766.

Watzlawick, P., Weakland, J., & Fisch, R. (1974). *Change.* New York: Norton.

Waugh, R. F., & Punch, K. F. (1987). Teacher receptivity to systemwide change in the implementation stage. *Review of Educational Research, 57,* 237–254.

Weick, K. E. (1984). Small wins. *American Psychologist, 39(1),* 40–49.

Weisbord, M. R. (1990). *Productive workplaces: Organizing and managing for dignity, meaning, and community.* San Francisco: Jossey-Bass.

Weissenburger, J. W., Fine, M. J., & Poggio, J. P. (1982). The relationship of selected consultant/ teacher characteristics to consultation outcomes. *Journal of School Psychology, 20,* 263–270.

Welzenbach, L. F. (Ed.). (1982). *College and university business administration.* Washington, DC: National Association for College and University Business Officers.

Wenger, R. D. (1979). Teacher response to collaborative consultation. *Psychology in the Schools, 16,* 127–131.

West, J. F., & Cannon, G. S. (1988). Essential collaborative consultation competencies for regular and special educators. *Journal of Learning Disabilities, 21(1),* 56–63.

West, J. F., & Idol, L. (1987). School consultation (Part I): An interdisciplinary perspective on theory, models and research. *Journal of Learning Disabilities, 20,* 388–408.

West, J. F., & Idol, L. (1990). Collaborative consultation in the education of mildly handicapped and at-risk students. *Remedial and Special Education, 11,* 22–31.

West, J. F., & Idol, L. (1993). The counselor as consultant in the collaborative school. *Journal of Counseling & Development, 71,* 678–683.

White, L. P., & Wooten, K. C. (1985). Ethical dilemmas in various stages of organizational development. *Academy of Management Review, 8,* 690–697.

White, R. K., & Lippitt, R. O. (1960). *Autocracy and demoncracy: Experiments in group leadership.* New York: Harper & Row.

Whitt, E. J. (1991). A community of women empowering women: Mount Holyoke College. In G. Kuh & J. Schuh (Eds.), *The role and contribution of student affairs at involving colleges* (pp. 120–143). Washington, DC: National Association of Student Personnel Administrators.

Whitt, E. J., & Kuh, G. D. (1991). Qualitative research in higher education: A team approach to multiple site investigation. *Review of Higher Education, 14,* 317–337.

Wilcox, M. R. (1977). Variables affecting group mental health consultation for teachers. Paper presented at 85th annual meetings of the American Psychological Association, San Francisco, CA.

Wilgus, E., & Shelley, V. (1988). The role of the elementary school counselor: Teacher perceptions, expectations and actual functions. *The School Counselor, 30,* 259–266.

Wilson, G. T., & Evans, I. M. (1977). The therapist-client relationship in behavior therapy. In A. S. Gurman & A. M. Razin (Eds.), *Effective psychotherapy: A handbook of research.* New York: Pergamon Press.

Witt, J. C. (1986). Teacher's resistance to the use of school-based interventions. *Journal of School Psychology, 24,* 37–44.

Witt, J. C. (1990). Complaining, preopernican thought and the univariate linear mind: Questions for school-based behavioral consultation research. *School Psychology Review, 19,* 367–377.

Witt, J. C., & Elliott, S. N. (1985). Acceptability of classroom intervention strategies. In T. R. Kratochwill (Ed.), *Advances in school psychology* (Vol. 4) (pp. 251–288). Hillsdale, NJ: Erlbaum.

Wolpe, J. (1958). *Psychotherapy by reciprocal inhibition.* Stanford, CA: Stanford University Press.

Wolpe, J. (1990). *The practice of behavior therapy* (4th ed.). New York: Pergamon Press.

Woolfolk, A. E. (1993). *Educational psychology* (5th ed.). Needham Heights, MA: Allyn & Bacon.

Wooten, K. C., & White, L. P. (1989). Toward a theory of change role efficacy. *Human Relations, 42,* 651–669.

Wright, R., & Harper, S. C. (1985). The consultant as anthropologist—mapping client corporate cultures. *Consultation, 5,* 173–188.

Wurtman, R. J., & Wurtman, J. J. (Eds.). (1979). *Disorders of eating and nutrients in treatment of brain disease.* New York: Raven Press.

Wynn, L. C., McDaniel, S. H., & Weber, T. T. (1986). *Systems consultation: A new perspective for family therapy.* New York: Guilford Press.

Young, E. (1989). On the naming of the rose: Interest and multiple meanings as elements of organizational culture. *Organization Studies, 10,* 187–206.

Ysseldyke, J. E., & Christenson, S. (1986). *The instructional environment scale.* Austin: PRO-ED.

Zahourek, R. P. (Ed.). (1988). *Relaxation & imagery: Tools for therapeutic communication and intervention.* Philadelphia, PA: Saunders.

Zaltman, G. (Ed.). (1973). *Processes and phenomena of social change* (pp. 477–417). New York: Wiley Interscience.

Zaltman, G., & Duncan, R. (1977). *Strategies for planned change.* New York: Wiley.

Zins, J. E. (1993). Enhancing consultee problem-solving skills in consultative interactions. *Journal of Counseling & Development, 72(2),* 185–189.

Zirges, J. D. (1981). The guidance counselor as program developer. *Elementary School Guidance and Counseling, 16,* 83–90.

Zischka, P. C., & Fox, R. (1985). Consultation as a function of school work. *Social Work in Education, 7(2),* 69–79.

Index

DATE DUE